TEX People

TeX People

Interviews from the world of TeX

Karl Berry and David Walden, editors

Portland, Oregon, USA

TEX Users Group, Publishing
P.O. Box 2311
Portland, OR 97208–2311

ISBN 978-0-9824626-0-7
First printing, 2009
For corrections, see http://tug.org/interviews.

Interviews — Chronological

Interviews — Alphabetical

Preface

Acknowledgments

First, we thank the interviewees for their time doing the interview and for sharing their experiences with the worldwide TeX community. Their interviews are current as of the dates given.

We also thank Barbara Beeton for her extraordinary effort in reviewing all of the interviews for publication in this book.

And we thank the Computer Science Department at the University of Aarhus in Denmark, which supports the main TUG server, where we post the interviews online and where we developed this book.

The motivation for this interview series

Dave had two ideas in mind when he suggested this interview series: (a) technology is created by and evolves with use by people, and the points of view and backgrounds of the people influence the technology; (b) there are lots of people (such as himself) who are relatively new to the TeX community, who therefore do not know much about the people who are already significant contributors to the community, and who may be curious to know more about past and current contributors to the TeX community. Moreover, we sense that various long-time members of the TeX community may enjoy reading the interviews and learn things they did not previously know.

Dave got the idea for an interview series from reading the books *Mathematical People* (edited by Donald J. Albers and Gerald L. Alexanderson, Birkhauser, 1985) and *More Mathematical People* (edited by Albers, Alexanderson, and Constance Reid, Harcourt, Brace, Jovanovich, 1990). The first of these outstanding collections of interviews of mathematicians includes a wonderful interview of TeX creator Donald Knuth (`http://tug.org/interviews/interview-files/birkhauser-knuth/`).

Some key members of the TeX world, notably Donald Knuth himself, Hermann Zapf, and Leslie Lamport, have previously been interviewed elsewhere. Thus, we did not seek new interviews from them. Pointers to a number of other interviews are at `http://tug.org/interviews/#others`.

How the interviews work

Interview subjects are chosen based on (a) seeking diversity in many dimensions, (b) recommendations from people about who should be interviewed, and (c) potential interview subjects being willing to be interviewed.

The interviews were all done by exchanges of emails, using plain text with a couple of exceptions which were done in LaTeX.

For the first several interviews, Dave sent a more or less complete list of questions (once the interviewee agreed to participate), on the theory that this would minimize the burden on the interviewee. However, having 10 or a dozen questions to answer at one time proved to be daunting to interviewees. Thus, Dave switched to a process wherein he sent a couple of standard initial questions (i.e., "Tell me a bit about yourself and your history outside of TeX," and "How and when did you first get involved with TeX?"). The answers to early questions guided follow-on questions.

The interviewees were encouraged to answer spontaneously and at any length they desired, both to ease the burden of answering the questions and to spur spontaneity. Once enough questions had been asked and answered, Dave converted the plain text into HTML, possibly reordered some of the questions and answers to improve the flow, did other little bits of necessary editing (all the while trying to maintain the voice of the interviewee), and submitted this near final draft to the interviewee for review and any desired changes.

Karl suggested many prospective interviewees and additional questions for each interview. He also proofread every interview before posting. Members of the TUG board often caught another typo or two immediately after publication of an interview, which were fixed and the interview reposted.

An average interview takes a few weeks of elapsed time. The shortest interview in terms of elapsed time took a few days. The longest interview took over a year. In a few cases, Dave interviewed two people at one time — people who were well known for working closely together. In one case, Dave shared the interviewing duties with another person (the interview of Frank Mittelbach, which was also published in the *Free Software Magazine*). In another case Karl shared interviewing duties with Dave Crossland — the Raph Levien interview. All the rest were one-on-one interviews.

Production

This book was typeset using LaTeX. The text typeface is Charter, designed by the great contemporary typographer Matthew Carter, and made freely available by Bitstream, Inc. We used the MathDesign version (with a few custom kerns), including math support, created by Paul Pichaureau: `http://mirror.ctan.org/fonts/mathdesign`.

The typewriter font is Inconsolata, designed by Raph Levien: `http://www.levien.com/type/myfonts/inconsolata.html`. It is also discussed in Raph's interview in this book.

The photographs were in almost all cases supplied by the interviewees. Dave did some manual processing to improve reproduction.

More details about the development of this book are given in our paper, "The TUG Interviews project" (`http://tug.org/TUGboat/Contents/contents30-2.html`).

Dan Luecking

Dan Luecking's answers on `comp.text.tex` are models of precision.

[Interview completed 8 November 2004.]

Dave Walden, interviewer: Please tell me a bit about your personal history independent of TEX.

Dan Luecking, interviewee: I was reared in a small town (pop. 350) in southern Illinois populated almost exclusively by descendants of German Catholic immigrants. I was the second of 10 children.

After three years at Quincy College in Illinois, I graduated in 1971 from Southern Illinois University at Edwardsville with a BA in math. I spent the next five years at the University of Illinois in Urbana, receiving an MS in math in 1972 and a PhD in 1976.

After college, I was an instructor at MIT for two years and an assistant professor at Michigan State for three years. I moved to the University of Arkansas as an assistant professor in 1981, was later promoted to associate professor, and am now a professor. In 1989 to 1990, I was a visiting instructor at Trinity College in Dublin.

I married my wife Jan in 1986, acquiring a beautiful stepdaughter, Lindsay. Our son, Nicholas, was born in 1987.

DW: When and how did you first get involved with TEX and its friends?

DL: It was on the sabbatical in 1989–90 at Trinity College. I was told that the fastest way to get a paper typed up was to do it myself in LATEX. I had a bit of research ready to write up and took it as an opportunity to learn by doing. I wrote the paper in about a month using LATEX.

When I returned to Arkansas, there was only one shared computer available to me. It contained a DOS version of VTEX. LATEX was an extra-cost option for VTEX at the time, so I learned plain TEX. Later I found out about emTEX and installed it on that computer. In the process, I became the Person-to-See about using TEX on a PC (the only other version of TEX around was Textures on a couple of Macs). Shortly after, that PC became my office computer. In successive computer upgrades I moved to MiKTEX in 1997 and fpTEX in 2002.

Sometime in the mid-90's I learned about mfpic and used it quite a lot to create graphs for math quizzes and tests. It was through it that I got involved with Metafont and MetaPost.

DW: Almost daily, I see your very clear, to-the-point answers to various queries on the `comp.text.tex` list. How did you come to be a contributor to the TEX community?

DL: It started with Eberhardt Mattes, the creator of emTEX. I joined an email list of emTEX users shortly after I first encountered it in 1990. I was very impressed with him.

Not only were his programs of high quality, but he monitored the emTeX mailing list and was always willing join the discussion in a friendly, open, helpful manner. That, and the fact that he provided his software without cost, impressed the heck out of me.

Then I had a disk crash and had to download and reinstall emTeX. Inspired (I think) by Mattes' example, I kept notes, intending to write and contribute a report on the experience, including the errors I made as well as the tips I discovered. I wrote this up as a sort of getting-started guide and sent it to one of the TeX archives. This turned out to be pretty popular, as emTeX was in a confusing state at the time: some of its programs were in beta and significant changes were going on. I recall having mathematicians approach me afterward to ask "Are you the Luecking that wrote Setting Up emTeX? Thank you!" Hardly anyone has ever thanked me for my math papers.

I started reading `c.t.t` around 1991 and have done so since, almost every day, and I still get a thrill when someone says "thank you" for a suggestion that helps out.

The most extensive contribution I've made (in terms of man-hours) is mfpic. I sent a few suggestions for improvements/features/bugfixes to Geoffrey Tobin and we discussed how hard it would be to make mfpic work with MetaPost. I looked into it and managed (by trial and error mostly) to get it to draw some xy-axes, except the lines produced were way too thick. I tracked down the reason for that and, before I knew it, I was hooked. Since then I have assumed the maintenance of mfpic and work in MetaPost almost as much as in TeX.

DW: The world wide TeX infrastructure is very extensive. What aspects of the infrastructure or transitional events have impressed you?

DL: I have to say that the biggest event for me was the start of CTAN. It is difficult to describe how hard it was pre-Google (pre-WWW in fact!) to track down (La)TeX material. With CTAN all that changed and I have nothing but gratitude for the volunteers who keep it going. The names I see most often in this connection are Robin Fairbairns, Jim Hefferon, Reinhard Zierke and Rainer Schöpf, but there could conceivably be others not as visible. Also George Greenwade was very much involved in the early days.

Just about as big an event was the advent of LaTeX 2$_\varepsilon$ in 1994. At the time I didn't see it as significant. LaTeX was pretty slow on my memory-limited PC and I tended to see it as bloated, but once I upgraded to a Pentium, that was no longer a significant problem and I started to see how convenient it was compared to coding in plain TeX.

Between the easy distribution of packages through CTAN and a better process in LaTeX 2$_\varepsilon$ for integrating packages, the number of packages seems to have exploded. It is also easier to find and distribute documentation, so there is a lot better process for finding out how to do things. Unfortunately, the sheer number of packages makes a second level of documentation all the more crucial: documenting what packages are available and what they do. The UK-TUG TeX FAQ maintained by Robin Fairbairns and the CTAN Catalogue (Graham Williams) are good starts (as is *The LaTeX Companion, 2nd edition*) and more is added all the time.

Finally, emTeX is not much thought about nowadays, but in its day it was probably the most-used TeX on personal computers. I think it very significant that it made a high-quality complete TeX system available for the masses even on relatively low-performance hardware.

DW: I sometimes think of my involvement with TeX as being part of a "community". Do you have any thoughts on TeX as a community?

DL: In my mind the TeX community is a vast and loosely knit group of individuals who have only their use of TeX in common. The important individuals are undoubtedly those who keep things running smoothly: the program developers, CTAN maintainers, package authors, and those who contribute help and advice either through the writing of books and documentation or through their postings to CTAN.

The strength lies in the amazing willingness of TeX users to help one another. Sure there is occasionally a bit of friction on c.t.t, but mostly it is honest advice and patient instruction, freely given. Maybe this comes from an appreciation of the example set by Knuth when he made TeX freely available.

The weakness may have a common source with the strength: many things are done by a loose association of volunteers, and things are not always done in a timely manner nor always well coordinated.

DW: Do you have an image of how TeX and the TeX world will or should evolve?

DL: I'd have to say that I don't really have any image of what will or should happen. No matter what improvements occur, there will always be more to do. There used to be endless discussion on c.t.t about how convenient it would be to have a direct tex-to-ps (later tex-to-pdf) program. Now we have it and there is the same endless discussion about some other newly perceived need.

My fascination with TeX is probably based in no small part on the TeX language itself. It may be a terrible language for coding things in, as some say, but I find learning its ins-and-outs a rewarding experience. Hiding that behind any level of user-interface has little appeal to me. But I'm probably completely atypical. If there is a successor to TeX with "better" programmability, I might be just as fascinated with it.

DW: Enough about TeX. Before I conclude this interview, please tell me a bit more about your work or activities outside the TeX world.

DL: I teach and do research in mathematics. My area of expertise is complex analysis, but I spend most of my teaching time on calculus, differential equations and discrete mathematics.

I spend my spare time mostly at folk dancing. I am one of the performers in a local folk dance group called Anoush, which rehearses one night a week. I also help run the Fayetteville Traditional Dancers, which mostly entails doing the calling at our monthly dances.

I used to enjoy playing Go, but without a ready source of opponents in this area I've not played at all in the last 15 years (Internet play doesn't appeal to me at all). I also spend a lot of time at Free Cell and Minesweeper (76 is my best score).

DW: Thank you very much, Dan, for taking the time to communicate with us. I have enjoyed our exchange and learned much from it.

Lance Carnes

Lance Carnes founded Personal TeX, Inc. (`http://www.pctex.com`), in 1985 and has been providing PCTeX ever since.

[Interview completed 13 December 2004.]

Dave Walden, interviewer: Please tell me a bit about your personal history independent of TeX.

Lance Carnes, interviewee: I was born in the San Francisco Bay Area and have lived my entire life here. After graduating from the University of California, Berkeley, I held several jobs in the computer industry, up until 1985 when I founded Personal TeX, Inc. I have three grown sons and currently live and work in San Francisco.

DW: When and how did you first get involved with TeX and its friends?

LC: In 1980 I attended a TeX conference at Stanford University (the first of its kind) while looking for a documentation system for software products. The conference organizers, mostly Stanford graduate students, provided a portable TeX system, in Pascal, on magnetic tape. Using this tape I was able to get TeX running on a small computer system. At the second annual meeting in Cincinnati I joined the board of the TeX Users Group, and served as the *TUGboat* editor for small systems.

DW: You mentioned 1980. What do you mean by "small computer system" in that era? One of those early hobbyist micro-computers, one of the early personal computers, a mini-computer?

LC: An HP 3000, which had a 16-bit word and 16-bit address space. IBM PCs, which were introduced a few years later, also had a 16-bit word but had a larger address space.

DW: What do you see as your significant contributions to the TeX community?

LC: While a lot of people in the desktop publishing industry arrived here because of an interest in publishing or journalism, I developed an interest in TeX because of computer science and Don Knuth. During the 1970s I followed the development of Structured Programming and Knuth's name came up a lot — a favorite article was his "Structured Programming with `goto` Statements". In 1980 at the first TeX Users Group conference I discovered he had developed the TeX system using many of the concepts in *The Art of Computer Programming*, and I launched into implementing it as a way of learning more about computer science.

In 1984 I moved the TeX implementation from the HP3000 to the IBM PC. In 1985 I founded Personal TeX, Inc., along with several partners and began marketing PCTeX, a

TeX implementation for IBM PCs. The product was an immediate success and remained one of the best-selling TeX products for the next several years. To answer your question, developing PCTeX and founding Personal TeX, Inc., are probably my significant TeX contributions.

DW: The first TeX system I used was PCTeX (`http://www.pctex.com`); it was recommended to me by a math guy from the Rockefeller Institute when I asked about a TeX system that would just work without me having to do lots of configuration.

I also remember seeing your name and the small systems section when I was looking at early issues of *TUGboat* on the TUG web site. How long did you serve as small systems editor, and how did that activity advance the spread of TeX?

LC: I served only two or three years as small systems editor. My future partners in Personal TeX, Inc., approached me to do an IBM PC version because of my visibility as small systems editor, so in a way that activity advanced the spread of TeX on PCs. There were numerous small system TeX versions developed and reported on in the small systems column. Most TeX users at the time were working on mainframe computers, and I always suspected they considered small computers which sat on a desktop as curious toys. There were several small systems, for example the Atari and the Amiga, which had speedy and well-designed TeX implementations — unfortunately many of these computer companies ceased making the machines after a few years. The relatively weak though plentiful IBM PC was probably the first widely-used small system.

DW: What do you see as the major eras or transitions in the evolution of TeX and its friends?

LC: Era 1 — The beginning. The development of TeX and LaTeX at Stanford from 1977 through the early 1980s. Major players included Don Knuth, Luis Trabb Pardo, David Fuchs, and Leslie Lamport.

Era 2 — TeX as a product, mid 1980s to present. Several vendors began marketing various TeX versions on different computer architectures, including Dave Kellerman and Barry Smith (Kellerman & Smith — DEC VAX), Barry Smith (Blue Sky Research — Macintosh), Dave Rodgers (ArborText — Unix and other workstations), Lance Carnes (Personal TeX, Inc. — IBM PC), and Dave Fuchs (Addison-Wesley — IBM PC).

Era 3 — TeX as a full-fledged open source system, mid-1990s to present. TeX has always been a public domain system, though its distribution was often configured by the commercial vendor or system supporter (usually a university, e.g. Berkeley Unix). Beginning in the early 1990s attempts were made to unify TeX and its thousands of files, that came to fruition by the late 1990s with the TeX Live project. Key players in this project were Karl Berry, Sebastian Rahtz, Thomas Esser, and others.

DW: What do you see as the strengths and weaknesses of TeX's version of an open source community?

LC: The major strength is the large number of dedicated people who volunteer their time to further the development of the TeX technology, through the TeX Live project, the TeX Users Group, and other national user groups. The weakness is the lack of industrial or academic support for the education and use of TeX; everyone uses it, but few put energy into promoting it or making it easier to use.

DW: Do you have an image of how TeX and the TeX world will or should evolve going forward?

LC: TeX has a solid technical base — the systems work, the fonts work, the macros work. For TeX to survive, though, users and potential users need education in the use of TeX, and there needs to be an industry which supports its continuance.

DW: What do you envision when you speak of "an industry which supports the continuance of TEX"?

LC: In the early days the American Mathematical Society and Addison-Wesley (now Pearson) were strong supporters. They provided expertise for TEX development and published books on the use of TEX, as well as using TEX in their own publishing activities. Both the AMS and AW still use TEX, as do several other publishers, but no one supports it in the same way Red Hat supports Linux, for example.

DW: Please tell me a little more bit about your other work or activities outside the TEX world.

LC: I enjoy old movies, hiking, cycling, and spending time with my grown sons.

DW: I certainly feel like I have been talking with a TEX pioneer. Thank you for taking the time for this interview and for your contributions to the TEX world.

LC: Thanks for interviewing me.

Robin Fairbairns

Robin Fairbairns maintains the TeX FAQ (`http://www.tex.ac.uk/faq`) and the UK CTAN (`ftp://cam.ctan.org`) node. He is also a member of the LaTeX Project (`http://www.latex-project.org/`) team. [Interview completed 16 February 2005.]

Dave Walden, interviewer: Please tell me a bit about your personal history independent of TeX.

Robin Fairbairns, interviewee: I came up to Cambridge University to read Natural Sciences, but changed early on to read Mathematics. I then took a graduate Diploma in Computer Science: you could only study computer science as a graduate in Cambridge in those days. I then took jobs in the Cambridge Language Research Unit; back at the Mathematical Laboratory (where I had studied for the Diploma); and then as one of the second wave of employees at a startup company which made computer graphics equipment. Seventeen years later, in 1992, I was "downsized" from the company, and once again found myself working at the Computer Laboratory (which had dropped the "Mathematical" part of its title in the 1970s).

DW: When and how did you first get involved with TeX and its friends?

RF: The company I worked for was a DEC OEM, and DEC used sometimes to send us fliers for Digital Press books. I persuaded the company to buy Knuth's first *TeX and Metafont* book (ostensibly for the software department's library). I was deeply impressed, but knew that it wasn't for us, since we had no better printer than a secretary's daisywheel used occasionally to print documentation for customers. Then things changed: I was asked to "evaluate" laser printers for the company to use, in place of those commandeered daisywheels, and spent a short happy period programming printers' PostScript engines, hacking at a freeware Digital Runoff-replacement, and so on. In the end, the company chose a DEC LN03 printer, and it wasn't long before I realised I could make TeX work on it. There was the slight embarrassment of persuading the higher management to enhance the brand-new printer to work with TeX, but apart from that, I was on my way!

DW: Practically daily I see your answers to queries on the comp.text.tex and TeXhax lists. How did you come to be a contributor to the TeX community?

RF: Once I became a TeX user, I wanted to read more about it. I found TeXhax, UK-TeX and various other online newsletters; I found the Aston archive (which I accessed via a 9600-baud X.25 network connection), and I was "on the learning curve". I read the LaTeX manual, and was impressed with Lamport's thinking (and back then, Lamport used still to post to TeXhax). Eventually, I realised I knew enough to start answering questions. So I did: it seemed the right thing to do.

I attended the inaugural meeting of the UK TeX Users' Group, and was impressed by all these people who had been running the archive and were now forming the committee of the new group. Then, when I got back to work at the University, Phil Taylor persuaded me that I should join the committee myself.

In fact, I joined the UK-TUG committee as it approached the apogee of its activity. Sebastian Rahtz edited several issues of the group's magazine *Baskerville*, and Jonathan Fine and I got it printed and distributed. The group decided to start working on a FAQ to replace the one by Bobby Bodenheimer, which had been decaying somewhat: I volunteered to produce it, and by December 1994 we had "answered" 100 questions in a special edition of *Baskerville*.

At this time, Sebastian was running the Aston archive as the UK CTAN. When Aston University's new director of computing decided he wanted to shut the archive down, the frantic search for a replacement found only one candidate host: my department. So, after not very long, I was taking over CTAN work from Sebastian, thus freeing *him* for work on TeX Live.

TeX Live was (I think) the last great effort of those glory days of UK-TUG; it was an exciting time, but I'm not sure I could keep up the pace. I served as chairman of the committee for a while, but am no longer at all active in UK-TUG. I shall, however, be forever grateful to UK-TUG for enabling me to commission a cake from a local cake shop ... with a Bibby cartoon on it: I knew it was a good cake shop, but this cake was a work of art!

DW: May we return to the FAQ for a minute? You stopped with your description of the 100 questions in a special edition of *Baskerville*, but that wasn't the end of it—you still maintain the FAQ.

RF: Actually, those first 100 questions contained a cheat, which Jonathan and I cooked up just before printing, in order to give us a nice round number (I would maintain that it didn't mislead, since it merely speculated about the future ...). As I remember, all but a couple of the answers in that first issue were written by members of the UK-TUG committee.

After we had distributed a printed copy to our members, the committee decided that we should make the FAQ available via the Web. This was a pretty radical step, at the time: the FAQ had originally been printed and distributed as a benefit of membership of UK-TUG. So Alan Jeffrey wrote a CGI script, and provided a site at the University of Sussex. Alan's script is *still* the engine through which the FAQ appears on the Web, but the site migrated to Cambridge long ago.

Other than the help from Alan, I've been mostly on my own since that first release: which is to say that I write FAQ answers, I edit things that people contribute, and I maintain Alan's script. But if people didn't "believe in" the FAQ, to the extent of making suggestions (or sending actual answers), I could never keep it up.

But I *have* kept it up: there are 375 answers in the current release, and there's also a long list of subjects for potential new answers ... just waiting for me to find some spare time!

DW: The world wide TeX infrastructure is very extensive. Please tell me your thoughts on the evolution of this community and how it does its work.

RF: I wasn't around to observe the early "glory days"—the days during which the world was starting to realise that TeX was here to stay, and worth devoting effort to.

What I most definitely recognise, in retrospect, is step changes in the development of the TeX community; and I think the birth of the newsgroup `comp.text.tex` was one of those. The newsgroup quickly took over the support rôle of TeXhax, and has attracted a group of supporters which has proved remarkably stable over the years. I suppose it's reasonable to say that much of my work has developed as a result of `comp.text.tex`.

One other, particularly valuable, change has been the recognition that TEX can provide hypertext. Hypertext was a neglected area of research until it was popularised by Berners-Lee, but now it's almost a *sine qua non* of technical document preparation.

The TEX community seems to me to function best when very small groups are doing the work. Examples would be Hàn Thế Thành (who had external advisors when working on his Ph.D., but seems to have done most of the pdfTEX work on his own), and the (almost) one-man-bands that produce distributions like Web2C, teTEX and MiKTEX.

By contrast, I have a strong suspicion that large TEX projects tend to run slowly. We may even be seeing this effect with the TEX Live team, which seems to be finding it increasingly difficult to meet deadlines for release of their excellent product. Far worse was the NTS project which, with its carefully devised committee structure and formal project reviews, delivered even its first product (ε-TEX) spectacularly late by comparison with the timetable everyone outside the project expected. The end result of such delays is that the product's impact was lessened, even though it offered things that the world actually needed.

The weakness of the community's distributed structure is its dependence on particular people. There was, for example, a real concern when Hàn Thế Thành finished his Ph.D. — who was going to continue the work? That one has turned out well (Thành himself has managed to stay active), but the potential for disruption is always present.

DW: Do you have thoughts on where the TEX community is going?

RF: I believe that the crucial next step for the TEX community should be to embrace multi-lingual typesetting. We have a limited model of multilingual work, in what `babel` (and a number of similar packages) do, but there are fundamental limitations to what we can do with that sort of approach.

The aim, in my mind, is to make the typesetting engine switch as seamlessly from one language to another, as does TEX between text and mathematics. TEX itself just *can't* hope to do this: its limitations on the size and organisation of fonts, alone, make it an undesirable engine to use, even if the character encoding issues could be resolved.

Nearly 10 years ago (I think it was), I was enthused by a presentation at CERN about Omega. Omega could in principle be a vehicle for this multilingual future (cf. Javier Bezos' experimental `mem` package). However, Omega's development base seems distinctly precarious, and no-one claims that it's currently "finished"; I really can't guess where it's likely to go from here.

DW: Your contributions to the highly technical TEX community are manifest. However, I see technological progress as being driven by people who have lives outside of technology. Will you say a few more words about your personal life?

RF: I work as a system administrator at the Cambridge University Computer Laboratory; while I do have responsibility for TEX support within the department, it's officially a minor part of my work.

I'm married (second time) to a musician; she and I are rather self-indulgent about our collection of recorded music, and I also collect old guide books (mostly to the UK and, to a lesser extent, the rest of Europe). We each have a pair of grown-up children; only one of them (my son) lives in Cambridge.

DW: Thank you for taking the time to participate in this interview. I've admired your posts to the various TEX lists and sometimes thought, "Who is this guy, and how did he get to know so much about TEX?" Now I think I have a glimmer of understanding.

Klaus Höppner

Klaus Höppner is the president of DANTE (`http://www.dante.de/`), the German TeX user group and a member of the TUG board (`tug.org/board.html`). [Interview completed 20 February 2005.]

Dave Walden, interviewer: Please tell me a little bit about yourself personally.

Klaus Höppner, interviewee: I was born in 1966 in the Ruhr area, famous for its coal mines and steel industry in former times, but heavily affected by the decline of these industries in the last decades. I studied physics at the University of Dortmund, getting my PhD in 1997. After that I had postdoctoral fellowships in Hamburg and Berlin, before I found my permanent work in Darmstadt in 2002.

Currently I live in Darmstadt, between Frankfurt (the financial center) and Heidelberg (the city all Americans know), working in the Control Systems Group of a national accelerator center.

DW: When and how did you first get involved with TeX and friends?

KH: It was in 1991, when I was in a summer student program at DESY, an accelerator center in Hamburg. I was involved in writing software for data analysis for crystallography. When I had to document the routines, I got a one hour crash course in using TeX on their VAX machines, got the German version of lshort, and had to learn it by doing. I didn't have my own PC at that time (just a typewriter), so I didn't know there were other word processors. Some time later, I tried to use WordPerfect (it was more popular than MS Word at that time), but I was disappointed by the result and writing mathematical text with it was painful. Anyway, it took me about two years to realize that I wasn't using just TeX but the macro package LaTeX and other TeX formats existed; this "small" point was missing in my crash course. When I bought my first PC, I found out that the computing center of my university distributed floppies with emTeX, so I continued to use TeX.

DW: You have become a significant contributor to the TeX community. Will you please tell me how this came about.

KH: I don't know whether I would regard myself as an important contributor to the community. I've done nothing special that couldn't be done by anyone else. My contributions started about 10 years ago when I discovered Usenet and started to write in TeX newsgroups (mainly a German one). Lots of my writing at that time was during boring night shifts doing measurements for my diploma and PhD thesis. It was also at that time that I became a DANTE member and started to go to the meetings and to meet many important contributors face to face. In time, I was asked to prepare on CD-ROM the CTAN snapshot that was distributed by DANTE in cooperation with many other user groups. I did this until 2002 when it became too time consuming — CTAN became bigger every year and it was real work to select what to include (the main reason why it's a DVD now). But I still design the covers and I don't get complaints, so they seem to be not too bad.

At the end of the 1990s, the old DANTE board resigned, so I applied for one of the open positions. I became a board member in 2000, and since 2002 I have been vice president. Most of the work is administration: talking about money, monitoring office activities, or preparing for conferences. These are all things that someone has to care about and that I like while most people regard them as boring. Unfortunately, there is no time remaining for my original TeX activity of participating in the on-line discussion groups, and not only because of board activities — life at work is much different from life as a student. The new news is that I am becoming a fresh member of the TUG board as I thought I could be helpful. The future will show whether I'm right with this opinion.

DW: What motivated you to become involved in DANTE and then to expand your involvement in the TeX world? What benefit or gratification do you get?

KH: It was a stepwise development. Sometimes I was asked whether I wanted to do something (e.g. the CTAN CD snapshot), and I didn't see a reason to say no. Finally, I ended up as a candidate for the board. Most members of the old board resigned after some disputes within DANTE. I just thought it was the right time for persons to show their willingness to take over responsibilities. I'm not sure whether I had the right expectations. It is always required that board should do "visionary work"; but, as mentioned above, my time is mainly used for administration.

I'm just happy when someone says thank you for my work, and even happier when new volunteers show up to help keep things running. I think finding them is becoming more difficult, so it's a good feeling to see the positive exceptions. An example may be Manfred Lotz who immediately volunteered after a general meeting where I said that I wanted to stop working on the CTAN snapshot. One other benefit is that I'm reimbursed for going to conferences. I was at EuroTeX in Netherlands and France, TUG 2004 in Greece, and this year I will go to PracTeX in the USA.

DW: I am sure many TUG members are like I am and don't know anything about DANTE. Can you say just a few words about the scope of its activities, how its activities are different than TUG's, and how it relates to TUG.

KH: DANTE was founded 16 years ago in Germany and currently has about 2000 members. Originally, it was a forum for German-speaking TeX users (so we feel responsible for Austria and a part of Switzerland, too). TeX was focused on American typesetting at that time (remember that it was developed by Knuth for his own needs), so some efforts had been made to meet German needs. In the first years, DANTE distributed software on floppies and sold American TeX books (when German books were rare and it was really expensive to order American books via bookstores). Also, there is the German CTAN backbone that is financed by DANTE. For activities, I would like to mention the development of NTS, an object-oriented TeX-compatible typesetter in Java, the funding for creating the Latin Modern fonts, Type 1 fonts which extend Computer Modern to all the accented characters needed in Europe, and a TeX development fund that was installed by DANTE in 2001.

I don't think DANTE's activities are too different from TUG's activities, just that DANTE is more focused on German language and Europe. The relationship to TUG is good — which doesn't mean we always share opinions. In general the cooperation of all TeX groups has improved a lot, so a lot of projects are international projects, often with shared funding.

DW: Do you have an image of how TeX and the TeX world will or should evolve going forward?

KH: There was a time years ago when I discussed with friends impressions of a recent conference and the consensus was "Nice as always, but also the same stuff as always". I don't feel the same today. Support for PDF (with pdfTeX and hyperref) has been an important step forward and, for example, ConTeXt shows the power of TeX.

What we need for the future is making TeX more user friendly. For instance, if you want to install a Perl package, you just open a shell on a CPAN mirror and type `install package-name`. We are evolving into this direction with TeX (TPM files were introduced with TeX Live, and Jim Hefferon is doing especially good work on restructuring CTAN) but there is still a lot of work remaining. Another point is the need for better documentation. So, there is still plenty of need for volunteers, even for John Average TeX user.

And finally we have to convince people that TeX is not as complicated as it looks like on first sight, especially to those without technical backgrounds.

DW: I see technological progress as being driven by people who have lives outside of technology. Will you say a few more words about your personal life?

KH: I'm a TV junkie, but no talk shows and rarely game shows. My current favorite is Monk.

DW: Thank you for your time in doing this interview. I have learned much that I did not know before.

Victor Eijkhout

Victor Eijkhout is the author of the book *TEX by Topic* (http://www.eijkhout.net/texbytopic/texbytopic.html/) and several LATEX packages, a long-time participant on comp.text.tex and various mailing lists, and was formerly associate *TUGboat* editor for macros.

[Interview completed 11 March 2005.]

Dave Walden, interviewer: Please tell me a bit about your personal history independent of TEX.

Victor Eijkhout, interviewee: I was born in the Netherlands and lived there until age 30. By then I had a Ph.D. in mathematics and decided to see more of the world. I have been living in the United States ever since. Right now, I'm in Knoxville, Tennessee, doing computer science at the University of Tennessee.

DW: When and how did you first get involved with TEX and its friends?

VE: I started using TEX somewhere in the mid-1980s when I was a graduate student in mathematics at the University of Nijmegen in the Netherlands. I was starting to write papers and had used troff/nroff for a while. Then I discovered TEX and started using that, without knowing much about the deeper aspects of it. It was mostly a matter that personal computers started to replace the mainframes and minis at that time, and there was no nroff on PCs or Apple Macs. I also found an article that compared the output of the two packages, and TEX was far superior in terms of plain typography, both in text and in mathematics. The PC that I first used TEX on was an early AT. To be able to run TEX we had to extend the memory from 512 k all the way to 640 k, at quite a cost.

Shortly after, the department bought a few Macs on which we ran Textures from Blue Sky Research, which was a very nice environment. Unfortunately, Macs were expensive in Europe, so most people used Atari 1040s, which were even faster than the Mac (8 MHz instead of 5-point-something), and they had more memory and a bigger screen.

DW: You have been a significant contributor to the TEX community. Will you please tell me how this came about (and when), why did you do it, and what you see as your significant contributions.

VE: When I started with TEX we didn't have LATEX, so everyone wrote their own macros. Doing that, with Knuth's *The TEXbook* as the only resource, was somewhat frustrating. The TEX language is and remains weird! So I started taking notes every time I finally figured out something. My notes started growing, and at 80 pages I thought they looked quite nice; I gave a copy to a TEX buddy (Nico Poppelier) when he got his Ph.D. He suggested that it might make a nice supplement for an issue of *TUGboat*, or so. The notes kept growing, and at 160 pages I decided that I should go all the way, so with 200-something pages I went to the Dutch office of Addison-Wesley. They saw that this book would be more suitable for a global market than just the Netherlands, so they sent it around, and the British office of A-W accepted it for publication. I had a limit of 320 pages; I think more than half of the chapters have their last page three quarters full. There is a lot to say about TEX.

I tried making one joke in the book, but it caused a bad page break, so I took it out. I guess I'm no Knuth....

TEX by Topic was published in 1991, sold a few thousand copies, was translated into Japanese, went out of print, and right now you can download it from my web site (`http://www.eijkhout.net/texbytopic/texbytopic.html`). PayPal contributions encouraged! The book is also in print again from Lulu.com (`http://www.lulu.com/content/2555607`).

Also in the late 1980s, the Dutch TEX Users Group (NTG) got started, and one of the issues that came up immediately was how much we disliked the LATEX styles, so I took it upon myself to write some plug-compatible replacement styles (the "ntg styles", with names `artikel1-3`, `rapport1-3`, `boek`, and `brief` — the latter is a not-compatible letter style that very faithfully implements guidelines of the Dutch bureau of norms). I believe they are part of the tetex distribution. Writing these styles was an educational experience. I learned a lot about the details of how TEX places material on the page, which was definitely good for my book. In fact, participating on the Dutch and UK TEX mailing lists taught me all sorts of obscure facts that are in the book. In retrospect it's interesting to see how I went from asking silly questions to answering silly questions.

By the way, at the time I was no LATEX user, so my only documents were tests for the styles I was writing. Since I needed only one document for three different article styles, et cetera, I was probably the only person to have written more document styles than actual documents. Since then, of course, I've been a complete convert to LATEX. The number of add-on packages is simply amazing, so even though LATEX is not a very good standard, it is good that we have this standard. I use LATEX for all my writing, and lately have started using the `beamer` package for presentations.

Oh, for my thesis I wrote my own macro package, Lollipop, with which I was going to conquer the world. Right. I believe the manual still states that a new version will come out in 1993.

Apart from a course that I taught last year, I have been mostly a LATEX user for the last couple of years. I've only written a couple of interesting macros, although one, my `comment` style, is somewhat successful. I found that it's even part of the LATEX2HTML translator.

DW: I use a little macro based on one of yours I found in `comp.text.tex` in many of my papers.

But you didn't mention that for some years you regularly wrote a section on macros in *TUGboat*. How did that come about?

VE: My involvement with *TUGboat* came about around 1990 when I was drafted by Barbara Beeton, eh, I mean: barbara beeton. We had corresponded about a conference report that I wrote with Johannes Braams and Nico Poppelier about the first Dutch TEX days. Later I met Barbara in real life, and she suggested the idea of a regular macro column to me. A number of times I wrote about macros of my own devising, and other times I explained clever macros by other people.

The column has slowed down considerably in recent years. That is partly my diminishing involvement with TeX, but also the fact that *TUGboat* is not as necessary any more as it was before the World Wide Web. Back in the days ('grandfather recalls' alert!), it was hard to find stored information. There were ftp sites, bulletin boards, archie sites, but it was hard to find out about them, so a printed resource was of great value to collect information. With CTAN, the UK-TeX FAQ, and in general good search possibilities over the web, this is no longer so much the case.

That said, information on the web is often very sketchy. "Just google for it" is an easy way of dismissing a question, but not necessarily a surefire route to an actual answer. Articles in *TUGboat* are still longer and more detailed than much of what you can find online. There is something about being in print that makes people try a bit harder to write a coherent story, so *TUGboat* is still worth having.

DW: You said that TeX is weird. Are you familiar with Knuth's informal essay on his involvement in the history of attribute grammars where he says, " . . . I haven't been able to figure out any good way to define TeX precisely, except by exhibiting its lengthy implementation in Pascal . . . surely an unsatisfying way to define semantics . . . I don't know any way to define any other language for general-purpose typesetting that would have an easily defined semantics, without making it a lot less useful than TeX. Macros are the main difficulty: As far as I know, macros are indispensable but inherently tricky to define. And when we also add a capability to change the interpretation of input characters, dynamically, we get into a realm for which clean formalisms seem impossible." What is your reaction to that?

VE: I didn't know about this article. Reading that quote, my first thought about Knuth being unable to define TeX precisely was 'Well, you brought that on yourself'. Which of course raises the question whether TeX has to be the way it is. Can something as powerful as TeX be made without having a macro expansion language—which I would agree is inherently tricky to formalize—and in particular without having the dynamic changes to the meaning of characters?

While I'm no expert on programming languages, I'm not convinced that a macro language is necessary. There are definitely some big disadvantages to the current approach: no matter how sophisticated the macros, they still fail to shield the user from TeX's lowest levels. Give a slightly wrong input, get a completely uninformative error message.

What would a non-macro version of TeX look like? I have no idea.

But consider this: most people use LaTeX, which is very simple in structure. A competent student can write the beginnings of a LaTeX parser, or a LaTeX to HTML translator, in a matter of days, a few weeks tops. In other words, what suffices for 99% of the people is actually very simple to parse. Maybe a powerful text processor should start with a simple structure that covers most bases easily, and then have a way of breaking out of that to have the infinite power of TeX with more complicated, but less used, mechanisms.

DW: That leads me to a slightly related topic. What do you see as the significant components of the TeX community? What do you see as the strengths and weaknesses of the TeX community?

VE: The greatest strength of the TeX community is also its weakness: the fact that we have this rock-solid, completely portable program to work with. Unfortunately it is that way because it is essentially frozen, with all its weaknesses. Another strength is the community of developers around LaTeX. As I already indicated, I am very impressed with the quality and the variety of packages that can be added to LaTeX for just about any functionality. That also means that people are finding ways around TeX's weaknesses.

DW: Do you have an image of how TeX and the TeX world will or should evolve going forward? Or are you thinking more about non-TeX things now?

VE: Well, I can try to see in my crystal ball, but for my opinion there are a hundred others. I'm too far out of the TeX world these days to say anything sensible about ConTeXt, Omega, NTS, and whether they can take over from TeX.

DW: From your remarks, you seem to be saying that you are not as involved with TeX as you once were. Yet you recently circulated draft notes on a course you teach on the computer science of TeX. I also think I remember some fairly recent answers by you to questions on `comp.text.tex`. What is your level of interest and involvement in TeX these days other than using LaTeX and `beamer` for papers and presentations?

VE: My involvement in `comp.text.tex` these days seems to be limited to pointing people to my book, when it's in danger of being overlooked. Really, there are many people there who very helpfully and extremely competently answer questions. I rarely have anything to add.

My TeX course, titled "The computer science of TeX and LaTeX", was an interesting project. One of the faculty members here at UT suggested that I teach such a course. The more I thought about it, the more I found that TeX can be used as an easy excuse for teaching all sorts of cool computer science and mathematical topics. Here's in a nutshell what I wound up teaching.

I gave the students an introduction in LaTeX and TeX, following that up with a segment on how compilers parse languages. They then had to use the Unix tools lex and yacc to write a simple LaTeX parser. Most people know about TeX's paragraph breaking algorithm, and that it uses dynamic programming to reduce an exponential problem ('given n words in a paragraph, which of the 2^n possible ways of breaking it into lines looks best') into something that is less than quadratic in cost. I explained dynamic programming. It is not so well known that a student of Knuth's (Michael Plass) did a thesis showing that page breaking can be NP-complete, because of the figure placement problem. I explained about NP-completeness and showed the outlines of Plass' proof, which I thought was fascinating.

Fonts, and of course Metafont, lead to splines, approximation theory, and various topics that are more usually associated with computer graphics. Certainly raster graphics is in that corner. Researching this topic I came across an interesting fact: all literature I had ever seen talks mostly about cubic splines, but one of the most common font technologies (FreeType) uses quadratic splines, which I had never seen before, and to this day haven't seen outside of the FreeType reference manual. Once I figured out the math of them, I gave this to my poor students as homework.

Character encoding, as exemplified by the `fontenc` and `inputenc` LaTeX packages, is another interesting topic, and I had fun reading up on all the intricacies of Unicode and Internet characters protocols. The one chapter I didn't finish was about TeX's macro mechanism and how it can be used to implement lambda calculus. There is an old article by Alan Jeffrey in *TUGboat* about this. I pursued this further, and got as far as implementing a prime number sieve, but didn't have time to complete the lecture notes.

Preparing for this course was a monstrous amount of work, but very fascinating. I'm going to try to turn my lecture notes into another book.

DW: I look forward to buying a copy of your book when it is available. For now, please tell me a little bit about your other work or activities outside the TeX world.

VE: In my work I'm doing numerical analysis, which I have a degree in, but gradually I'm creeping more and more into real computer science topics. I've become interested in performance optimization, and in particular automatic ways of generating optimized versions of an algorithm. Related is a recent project where I'm applying statistical decision methods to the question of picking the best numerical algorithm.

Outside work I do ballroom dancing and I make a lot of music. I play the recorder, have just bought a bass guitar, and have a number of completely electronically generated compositions online.

DW: Thank you very much, Victor, for taking the time to participate in this interview. I'll think of you more personally next time I look something up in your *TeX by Topic* book, and I greatly look forward to your future writings.

[Since this interview took place, Victor has moved to the University of Texas at Austin.]

Christina Thiele

Christina Thiele has been typesetting with TeX since 1983, especially in linguistics and other non-math/science fields. She is a past president of TUG. [Interview completed 12 July 2007.]

Dave Walden, interviewer: Please tell me a bit about your personal history independent of TeX.

Christina Thiele, interviewee: I was born in Ottawa (Canada). Other than several years studying and working abroad (France, Iran, Germany), I've lived here all my life. My husband's also a native Ottawan, a senior systems analyst at Carleton University, where I did my studies (linguistics), and where we met. We have a 5-year-old daughter, Anna.

I began using TeX in 1983, working on linguistic journals; in 1991, I started my own company and continue to use TeX to typeset linguistics and many other non-math/science materials, still concentrating on books and journals.

DW: Please tell me more about how you first became involved with TeX and its friends.

CT: In 1982, I was just starting my graduate year at Carleton University (Ottawa), with a stunning 300.00 per month grant (didn't even cover rent), so I needed a job. Fast. One of the linguistic dept. profs. was about to become editor of the *Canadian Journal of Linguistics* (CJL), and had been convinced by his co-editor (who wrote the first version of our macros, and also designed two bitmapped IPA fonts for us, called "ph10" and "ph7") to give the beta-version of this program called "TeX" a try. We could test them out on Bill's other editing/publishing project, the annual *Papers of the Algonquian Conference*, before deciding if it would also work for CJL. He needed someone to type in stuff—"et me voilà", as they say around here.

I'd never touched a computer (well, except for some non-starter hours at the Honeywell mainframe running CP-V, then CP-6) and did the roll-eyes-back-in-head thing when they said the on-switch was at the back of the box, not the front, where all self-respecting electric typewriters had 'em!

We did the keyboarding (this was in 1983—hardly anyone in linguistics had computers, and the idea of actually sending your file to someone else was simply inconceivable) on a locally manufactured Apple clone, the Peach ;-). We used a software program called "Gutenberg" (I kid you not!), designed by a linguist down in Kingston (Ont.), I think—it used explicit coding and there was no on-screen previewing.

The files were then run through a conversion program, to change Gutenberg code (?done in LISP) into plain TeX—another program with explicit in-file coding, and no on-screen previewing. The macros for the journal were based heavily on `manmac.tex`, which were used to produce *The TeXbook*. The files would then be uploaded via 300-baud modems to the mainframe, where we'd attempt to TeX the files.

My main objective was to be able to process a file through to the end. The warning and error messages spewing on the screen meant zero to me (hey, I was a linguistics grad student, not a programmer!). If I could just get the screen to read "Output written to ...", I was delighted. We'd then "proof to paper", and after paying 10 cents per sheet (!!) for using the only printer for TeX in another building, on the other side of campus, we'd fix things. Again and again. It got expensive (we also had to pay for disc space on the mainframe, so a lot of early issues were deleted as they were published!). We'd keep all the reject pages (I had a stack that eventually was as tall as the 5-drawer filing cabinet it leaned against!) and at camera copy time, we'd pore through those sheets, looking for words to cut and paste over typos, spacing errors, and so on. Which meant, of course, that there was a second (growing) pile with one or more holes in each page. Several years later, when we moved offices, I went through that pile, and created "an historical document" of our own fumblings and stumblings, complete with annotations. Bill Cowan (now deceased, but at the time, the person who showed me what a really good editor could do for an article) laughed himself red when I showed it to him—and it still makes me smile at how primitive things can get, even when you've got TeX at your fingertips. We just didn't know enough.

Eventually, we became more proficient, more knowledgeable, more "TeX-ish" in our thinking ;-) and gradually the on-screen warnings and error messages made enough sense that we could reduce the number of trees sacrificed. The mainframe eventually migrated away from the original AM fonts to the CMs; I became involved with Janene Winter's work on WSUIPA, which CJL started using in 1988. We got our own printer, so the 10-cents-a-page expense fell away.

As our experience grew, other authors and editors started to come up and ask me to typeset their projects: TeX was capable of handling the stuff they wanted to edit and publish. So, starting with a job to help pay the bills while I got a degree in linguistics, that job is now full-time: I run my own company, and typeset a lot more than just linguistics.

The CJL co-editor, Jean-Pierre Paillet, is probably the one who showed us a copy of *TUGboat* in perhaps 1985, which introduced us to TUG, which I joined in 1986. In 1987, I went to my first meeting, "sponsored" as it were by CJL, took a couple of courses, and gave a paper entitled "TeX, Linguistics, and Journal Production" for the humanities-themed meeting.

I don't seem to have strayed too far from that triad ever since ;-).

DW: Tell me about your contributions to TUG and TeX and what motivates them.

CT: After my 1987 paper, I was asked to join the TUG board in 1988 (at the Montreal meeting) and to edit the second-ever conference proceedings. The 1987 papers were the first, compiled by Dean Guenther at WSU (Washington State University, where Janene Winter worked); Dean probably figured I was so full of piss and vinegar that I should be put to more productive work ;-). In any event, I edited the proceedings (the 1988 ones were also a *TeXniques* issue; after that, they became part of *TUGboat*) for several years, worked on numerous committees on the board (including conference organising, publications, bursary, and so on), served in the executive, and finished off my board career ;-) as president (1993–95). While president I worked on getting a production team together for *TUGboat*, and continue to work (very occasionally now) on the tub-prod team.

I'm not a programmer or a developer; in fact, I'm not a terribly clever user of TEX. But I do like to organise things ;-). So perhaps my contribution to TUG has been more in the paperwork, in the structural. As a member of those many committees, I helped work on various documents and help files, which eventually ended up on CTAN in the TUG directory. I was editor of TTN (*TEX and TUG News*), our first small-scale newsletter (hardcopy was more logical at the time, just as the on-line *PracTEX Journal* is more suited to today's environment) for its four years (1991–95). TTN was a user-driven concept and publication, aimed at my level! Probably rather egocentric to say that ... but then, how many macro packages are only written because the author needed to do something for their own purposes! In our community, we seem to balance work done for personal gain by then turning around and letting everyone else in on it ;-).

I think the motivation in large part was to try and organise and present some kind of guide through the ever-expanding stream of information which was increasingly coming forth from all corners of the world. We'd moved from a user community with only one user group, TUG, to a splash of new groups in Europe (DANTE, GUTenberg, the Nordic Group, NTG, UK-TUG), which were working very hard to provide their users with user-friendly information. We all were trying to make TEX easier to understand, and to get information for users out to those very users. I think the idea of some kind of central archive was also starting to built up — again, a way of connecting macro writers with macro users. And so CTAN evolved, again in that atmosphere of trying to organise the tons of wonderful stuff for people using TEX. Wherever they were. Whatever language they spoke — or typeset in ;-).

But when my involvement in the TEX community itself became significant, hmmm ... I don't know. It's difficult to say that of oneself. I'd spent most of my time inside TUG, as it were ... I did gradually begin to realise that other people seemed to be interested in typesetting linguistics, and that what I'd been learning over many years might be useful to others. In 1993, I started up the ling-tex list (first at George Greenwade's SHSU site in Texas; then moved to Dag Langmyr's site in Norway in 1995, I think it was), and collected info on various packages available (in `lingmac.tex`). In 1992/93, TUG's Technical Council had started up several Technical Working Groups; in 1994, I was asked to chair one in linguistics. The ling-tex list still exists ... so, that means it's been around for 12 years! Wow ...!!

We've seen wonderful upgrades in fonts (TIPA, from Fukui Rei, is now almost the standard); packages seem to be very robust (I think most passed from LATEX 2.09 to LATEX 2$_\varepsilon$ — now simply called LATEX — with very little fuss); and we still see answers to questions from new users or from users new to a particular package, as well as package announcements. Most (if not all) of the package and font developers are still on the list, which really contributes to solving problems, and getting answers within a very short time. Just a great community of users. So I guess that's a significant contribution.

As for why I do it — well, it's obvious! I need all the help I can get to set linguistics with TEX! So, my own self-interest is what really fuels my contributions ;-).

But seriously ... I think it's an awareness that I earn my living using TEX, which is free. At a certain point, it seems only right and fair to give something back freely. I didn't understand every single thing that we ran in TTN — but it provided the space for those nifty little tips and tricks to become more widely known and used. I'm not the answer-person on ling-tex — but I've provided the mechanism for those answers to flow. I would like to see TEX continue being/becoming more accessible to its current and potential users. If I can aid in that effort, then that's my contribution back for being able to do what I do.

DW: What do you see as the major eras or transitions in the evolution of TeX and its friends and the driving forces?

CT: I wasn't a TUG member or even using TeX during what I've since come to view as the first phase: development. That is, people who took the TeX program, ported it to different platforms and operating systems, found and fixed bugs (not just in TeX, as I understand it, but also in compilers and other stuff), wrote drivers for printers and early previewers. All that essential groundwork which is now almost unknown to new users. You have to read through the old *TUGboat* issues to see what I mean. The site coordinator reports were in some ways the most significant and important reasons for attending the annual meetings and for reading *TUGboat.* Each issue was almost like a novel, a mystery, with "this bit solved", "that bit pending"—and, "oh my, that wasn't expected". It's compelling, in some ways. You can *see* TeX spreading, advancing, improving, and surprising people along the way. And, it seems to me, that this group of people, during this stage in TeX's evolution, are the only ones who can really tell that story. Because as TeX was evolving, operating systems and computers were changing as well. What was "fast" one year became a snail's pace the next. What was massive storage and memory at this year's meeting became limited and outdated by the next. Again, this isn't an area where I *know* the details; but I've seen enough references to this to understand that the origins of TeX were directly affected by what was available in terms of computer technology. And if we lose that information, that awareness, misconceptions about why TeX can and cannot do certain things will begin to grow. So we need to claim our history from the horses' mouths, as it were, while we still can!

I'd say the next big phase was the explosion of applications and special-purpose macros and style files (as they were then called) as exposure to TeX expanded beyond the math/science core. I've already mentioned that the 1987 TUG meeting had "TeX and the Humanities" as its theme, and there were some very interesting papers given, well removed from math ;-). Having such material come out in print probably goaded others who'd been trying to use TeX—or still considering it—for non-math/science purposes. And finding out that there might be others doing the same thing; the 1987 meeting had two different papers on typesetting Greek material ... but I don't recall whether Silvio Levy and Pierre MacKay actually knew of one another's work. And so, not only were the non-math/science applications growing but the number of people involved in each of these areas was also growing. We saw lists start up for typesetting (typo-l in 1992), setting Russian (RusTeX-L in 1989), Greek (ellhnika in 1991), and so on. Earlier general lists for help with TeX were already in place by 1987: texhax in 1986, uktex and texmag in 1987. The ling-tex list was actually rather later, in Dec. 1993. A history of lists would be an interesting side project ;-).

As for the main driving force, I'd have to say it was CTAN and its archivists! There were so many really great little (and big) packages proliferating—you'd read about them on texhax, or texmag, or just regular e-mail exchanges, or hear about them at meetings and such. I'd keep tons and tons of texhax mail, sorting it by topic, just to keep the references around in case I'd ever need 'em. By way of example (although I don't remember where the reference came from), I found some wonderfully easy to use Hebrew fonts at a site in Israel. Great stuff. A little later, some knotwork fonts from Ireland, also from a specific site. It was CTAN (in 1993) which made it possible for everyone to find everything. This made it possible not only to offer a home for all the wonderful stuff that had been created over the past many years, but it allowed both authors and users to comparison-shop, as it were ;-). In one place, you could find several options for doing the same or similar things — modifying headers/footers, or playing around with captions. Having everything in one place also probably prompted authors to write nice code ;-), improve their documentation, and address small bugs which a much-expanded user base now brought to light — not everyone does the same thing the same way or, more significantly, would think of combining this package with that one, thereby finding an incompatibility that needed fixing. In short, everything improved, from the packages themselves (we now see that almost all the newer ones in fact use the `.dtx`/`.ins` documentation approach), to the ways in which they combine and enhance other packages.

As for how CTAN came to pass, and how it has evolved since its beginnings, that's a history lesson which the archivists themselves should be coaxed to tell. I do remember sitting at an outdoor table at the 1989 TUG meeting at Stanford (California), with beers all 'round, listening to Frank Mittelbach and Chris Rowley talking about the need to "do something" about all these packages. And Sebastian Rahtz, I think, had already been trying to organise something around that time as well. It just took a while to coalesce.

The current era seems to be one of great stability: TEX and LATEX itself are now firmly settled (largely due to the efforts of the LATEX 3 team) with refinements to packages, ever-improving installation via the TEX Live CDs, better package documentation (the `.dtx`/`.ins` method of writing/documenting macros has given a tremendous boost to both the macro writer(s) and the end user, in terms of flexibility in both upgrading, and usability). We're coasting, in a sense. But that's not meant in a negative way.

We've perhaps become exhausted with the variables in installation on different platforms, and just want to use TEX, for God's sake! Keep the main TEX tool(s) running smoothly, and plugging away at improving and streamlining the components that go into a full and proper installation. It all works right now — please don't make it hard again! ;-).

And so, perhaps at present, we don't seem to have a driving force, because maybe it's not clear just where we need to go next. Of course, since I don't read texhax anymore, I may simply be loitering in an eddy on the side, unaware of the currents which are moving right over there, to the left or right of my little puddle ;-).

Which is why it's good to keep adding interviews to this collection!

DW: What do you see as the significant components of the TEX community? What do you see as the strengths and weaknesses of the TEX community?

CT: Significant components: CTAN, all the users, and the Internet to connect the two. Strengths:

- CTAN: the stats on this are probably stupendous, in comparison with other archives of computer software. I think these should be lauded more than they are — and papers given/published in computer software arenas where TEX is "just another program", to raise awareness of what's been quietly brewing all this time.
- The user community and its philosophy, if you wish, of helping out, volunteering, contributing, sharing. We see it time and again, when someone (again, either a new user, or a user new to a package or application need) posts a query, gets not only a couple of answers but probably also a pretty detailed explanation of why it's like that — all in the space of a few hours or days. Free. And it's advice that will work for any implementation. If the query's about TEX, then it's irrelevant if it's on a Linux or Unix box, PC or Mac. Of course there are system-specific issues on occasion, but if it's strictly about TEX, then it's not only an answer for that person but for every other TEX user out there. TEX is TEX, no matter what machine you're on. And that's pretty darn wonderful.

Weaknesses:

- the on-going installation hassles — until we get a product that installs like everything else on PCs and Unix and Linux and so on, we won't make inroads with TEX into the non-user community.
  Potential end users are now rarely computer-savvy enough to "roll their own"; less and less often are the end users the installers; sys-admin types (the "installers") don't want to mess with TEX because it's so idiosyncratic in installation — the fonts issue is even more sordid! Give them a TEX install routine that *mimics* what other packages need in terms of installation routines, and TEX could make significant inroads into a lot of these systems. Keep pretending that the end user and the installer are the same, and it won't get used. Keep pretending that the installer just needs to "Read The Fine ;-) Manual", and it won't get installed.
- The increasingly pervasive attitude that "beautiful documents" just don't matter — when people don't care about that, they won't give a damn about TEX. So stop preaching beauty and move on to sheer strength and power to do anything that needs "real typesetting"! In short, TEX's beauty is lost on so many people these days, so refocus the promo a bit.

DW: I don't know much about the different application areas of TEX users. Of course, I know that lots of people whose writing includes math use TEX. I myself use TEX to write about management and about technology history, but I don't know anyone else who does that, although I suppose there may be others. Are there a lot of linguistics and humanities people using TEX; do they form any sort of TEX user community?

CT: I think there are a ton of humanities applications in progress right now; probably have been all along. Dictionary projects date back already to the late 1980s! Linguistics, obviously ;-), has been around, in use by both authors and publishers. All the materials I do is in TEX, so that's a lot of books (many of them critical editions) and journals (I've been doing CJL since 1984) over the past 20 years. And all through that time, I've run into people (in person or via e-mail) who've been doing similar, very non-math/science typesetting. In some ways, we're typically humanities types: we don't group together much ;-). But we're to be found everywhere, and in the most unexpected places. Music! Now there's a great application that is pretty darn stunning. Lots of work done there by the late Daniel Taupin, who's just one of many who find this "normal". Critical editions, I've mentioned. And there are hundreds and hundreds of books out there (probably thousands or more, eh?) which have quietly been set with TEX. I do try to put a colophon into the backs of books I do, to identify them as having been done with TEX, but sometimes the page is sacrificed for economic reasons. So, in some ways, using TEX isn't the point for publishers — the point is simply to get the job done well.

And where once we perhaps loudly proclaimed that this or that project had been done with TEX, for some it's become such a given that it's not necessary to "justify" one's use of TEX — "it gets the job done, and that's all we need to know, thank you". And now that we can get `.pdf` output, there's no need to worry about not being in the MS Word world in order to participate in it. Mercifully!

DW: Do you have an image of how the TEX world needs to evolve going forward?

CT: This sort of follows from what I wrote above (in the question and answer about the 'eras' of TEX), about the present phase we're in — at least, from what I can tell.

Maybe now is the time for us to look at presenting and packaging TEX in a way that makes it more appealing to the non-user, the commercial software user.

- Will we ever get to a single installation procedure which is not rife with options (often based on available disc space, or what one *thinks* is "all" one needs)?
- Will we ever get to a simple font interface for automatic installation of all the bits in all the right places?
- Will we ever get to an installation procedure which does not require the installer (who's not the end user in most places) to know anything about TEX (or the end user to know anything about systems)? Where the installation routine is that of any other software for any given platform?

We've been serving ourselves and our own needs for a very long time—our favourite program does just about everything we'd like. So, it's pretty hard to get all worked up and excited about such seemingly mundane chores which are basically housekeeping! Putting pretty paper around the toy ;-).

Computer use is ubiquitous; however, the time needed to invest in a steep learning curve is not. And as we're the ones who know TEX, we're pretty much the only ones who'll ever be able to map its intricacies onto the non-TEX maps which the rest of the world is now quite familiar and content with. That is, instead of trying to shoe-horn non-users into "The TEX Way" ;-), maybe we should see just how cleverly we can pour TEX into other molds.

I think that is a great challenge. Make it quick and easy—and complete!—and then try to get it installed on all PCs sold by ... well, whoever you want to target! ;-).

DW: Is there anything you wish to ask me?

CT: How did you learn about TEX? What's been the hardest thing to unlearn, as it were, based on your own experiences with computers and software?

DW: Before Word, I used command-based word processing systems. A few years ago, in reaction to too many new releases of Word which changed how one used it or its file structure, I decided to try never again to write a big document using Word (although I still use Word daily for some sorts of documents). I had heard about TEX, I knew of and admired Knuth, and so I decided to write a book I had committed to write using TEX, although I soon adopted LATEX. The most bothersome thing about using LATEX has been something you emphasized—the complicated and fussy nature of installation and updates. Even though I have a software development background, when I am writing I want the system to just load and run without me having to think about configuration issues. Making up the words and trying to make them look good on the page is already more than enough work for me.

DW: Is there anything else you would like to say?

CT: Don't think so ... your questions have provoked a lot of writing ;-) and some pleasant strolls through memory lane—not to mention my old *TUGboats*, old e-mail, TUG paperwork, and so on! Thanks for the opportunity.

But one thing I'd like to ask is that any corrections to my recollections be added to the end of this interview text. And I hope that people who were involved in the early development of TEX tools can find a way to add their memories to these interviews.

DW: Thank you, Christina, for taking the time to participate in this interview and for digging into your archives. I've learned much about a part of the TEX world I knew nothing about, and it is fascinating.

George Grätzer

George Grätzer is a mathematician who has written books on TeX and LaTeX and edits a journal prepared in LaTeX.

[Interview completed 13 April 2005.]

Dave Walden, interviewer: Please tell me a bit about your personal history independent of TeX.

George Grätzer, interviewee: I am a mathematician, born and educated in Hungary. I came to North America in 1963 (first to the USA, then in 1966 to Canada). If you are interested in my mathematical papers, they are all posted on my web site (`http://www.umanitoba.ca/science/gratzer`).

You will find there a listing of my books in three categories: mathematical, LaTeX, and others. Just last week, I submitted to my publisher my latest mathematical book: *Congruence Lattices of Finite Lattices*. It should appear late fall. Do not ask me what it is about.

I also founded an international mathematical journal, *Algebra Universalis*, which can be accessed via my website.

I am a member of various academies of sciences, have lots of degrees, one honorary.

I have a wife, two children, and three grandchildren.

DW: When and how did you first get involved with TeX and its friends?

GG: In 1986, a short paper of mine, written in Word, was accepted in the Proc. Amer. Math. Soc. The letter of acceptance stated that the paper will be published in 48 weeks, however, if I submit it in AMSTeX, then they publish it in 20 weeks. I did not know what AMSTeX was, but a colleague of mine had a TeX with AMSTeX, and offered to loan it to me. Over the weekend, I rewrote the short paper in AMSTeX and submitted it. The paper was short and had simple formulas, so the transition was easy. (Unfortunately, the AMS twice misplaced the paper, and it was published much later — in 1988.) From 1986 to 1990, I wrote all my papers in AMSTeX. Sometime, this was very frustrating. For instance, my paper #146 was a survey paper containing 30 theorems and 29 problems scattered into dozens of subsections. The constant reorganization of the paper was very complicated: AMSTeX could not number! Of course, I could have switched to LaTeX, but I found LaTeX's ability to typeset math very limited compared to AMSTeX.

DW: Many people use TeX. Not so many write books and papers *on* it. How did you come to write these books for the TeX community?

GG: In 1990, at the Kyoto meeting of the International Mathematical Union, the AMS released AMS-LaTeX. It was an answer to my dearest hopes: it married the mathematical abilities of AMSTeX with the housekeeping abilities of LaTeX. There was only one problem: who could understand it?

The documentation instructed us to read a book on LaTeX, one on AMSTeX, and then the 100 pages or so of explanations that followed pointed out how AMS-LaTeX compares to

LaTeX and AMSTeX. I said to myself: there must be a better way. So I started to struggle with AMS-LaTeX and kept notes on what worked and what did not. Eventually, I decided to turn my notes into a book, so people will not have to go through the same struggle as I did.

I also had a dream: my journal will receive all the contributions in AMS-LaTeX and we will not have the huge expense of having to typeset it. Today, 15 years later, this dream has come true.

I am not a LaTeX expert, I do not understand the TeX language, I am just a user. I tried to turn this to my advantage. Since I have a difficult time (discovering and) understanding so many rules, I do two things differently. First, I write an introductory part to my book for beginners, so they do not have to go to page 240 to understand what every beginner has to know. Then in the reference part of the book I repeat what is in the introductory part, so the reader will not have to guess where to go for what information. Everything is in one place. Second, I explain all the rules with examples, lots of them; after all, most of my readers are mathematicians; they easily recognize a pattern when they see the examples. Formal rules come last.

It was very rewarding that some 50,000 people chose to learn LaTeX with the AMS packages from my books and that the Mathematics Editor of Amazon.com selected my *Math into LaTeX* as one of the ten best books of the year 2000.

DW: You mentioned your dream being achieved of not having to typeset your *AU* journal. That leads me to ask about how well you are satisfied with LaTeX and your class for the needs of your journal, or if and how you think TeX and LaTeX have to evolve to continue to be useful to mathematicians.

GG: LaTeX and the au class (which is a slightly modified amsart) does the job for the journal.

The major problem with TeX and LaTeX is that it is so badly coded. It seems to me that TeX is calling subroutines without storing the info where it is calling from; as a result, when something blows up in the subroutine, TeX does not know what went wrong, so the error messages are misleading or plain inappropriate. If you do everything right, TeX does a perfect job 99% of the time. If all users were perfect, this would be a nice work environment. But we are not. So we have to develop very defensive work habits.

Recoding TeX would be nice, but I do not see it happening. LaTeX probably will develop but not the way it would be useful for us users, but probably to better serve the needs of large organizations — the AMS, the publishers.

Now that a click or two produces pdf files from TeX, we can communicate with everybody — and electronically; this is very useful. My journal does not pay anything for postage any more, and communication is very fast.

The next big thing in mathematical publishing will be color. In a few years, color printing will be cheap. This will be a very big problem for the mathematical community. Centuries of typesetting tradition tells us how to typeset mathematics in black and white. What happens when color comes in? Shall we do theorems in blue, problems in red? Who will develop the new standards?

DW: You have contributed to the TeX community through your books that help people learn to use it. Are there parts of the world wide TeX community and infrastructure that you also draw on? Is there any sort of formal or informal community of users for specifically mathematical TeX and LaTeX users?

GG: I got very generous help from the mathematical TeX community in the form of dozens of volunteers to read and criticize my manuscripts. Members of the LaTeX 3 team and mathematicians from all over the world gave their time generously. Also, `comp.text.tex` is very useful; lots of experts give good advice.

DW: I greatly appreciate your giving your time to participate in this interview, and I am ordering a copy of your *Math into LaTeX* today.

Philip Taylor

Philip Taylor is a long time TeX user/developer who chooses to work outside of the LaTeX framework. He is also a member of the TUG board.

[Interview completed 25 May 2005.]

Dave Walden, interviewer: Please tell me a bit about your personal history independent of TeX.

Philip Taylor, interviewee: Professionally speaking, I have had a very small number of jobs, each of which has led fairly naturally to the next. I started my working life at the age of 16, as my parents were unable to afford to keep me at school any longer, and my first employer was Post Office Cable and Wireless Services, External Telecommunications Executive (http://www.spencerweb.net/telegraphs/html/electra_house_old___new.html). I started life as a (very!) humble "Youth-in-Training", and progressed via Technician IIA to Technical Officer. After seven very happy years with the G.P.O. (this would now be "British Telecomms"), I left when they wanted me to leave the duties I loved (Control Room & Electronics) and work in a Strowger telephone exchange known (not particularly affectionately) as "The Pickle Factory". I then joined Molins Ltd (a tobacco-handling machinery design company) as an Electronic Design Engineer, but left after just over two years when I realised that working for a profit-oriented organisation clashed too severely with my own work/life perspectives and ethics. From there I joined Westfield College (University of London) as a free-lance Computer Engineer, was made redundant after about three years, and moved to Bedford College (also University of London, in London's "The Regent's Park") where I had been teaching part-time, as a Computer Analyst/Programmer. I remained at Bedford College until its closure in 1985, at which time it (and I) merged with Royal Holloway to form Royal Holloway and Bedford New College (now Royal Holloway, University of London). At RHBNC I started to develop my awakening interest in computer typesetting (see next section), and when the demand for high-quality printed material began to diminish, transferred what I could of my hard-acquired skills to the world of electronic publishing, with particular reference to the World-Wide Web. I am currently Webmaster at Royal Holloway, University of London (http://www.rhul.ac.uk/).

DW: How did you first get involved with TeX and its friends?

PT: Peter Jackson, a friend from my Westfield days (affectionately known as "Pute", for reasons I have never understood) shewed me one day in (I think) 1986 some computer-typeset output produced using equipment *identical* to that which I had been using (Digital

VAX/VMS running on a VAX 780, with a Digital LN03 laser printer) but which so far surpassed the quality I had been able to achieve that I was literally gob-smacked. I asked Peter how it had been produced, took a copy of Kellerman & Smith's TEX implementation for VAX/VMS with me on 1600 bpi magnetic tape, returned to Royal Holloway and started to implement TEX on our systems. I have never looked back.

DW: You have been a long-time contributor to the TEX community. Will you please tell me how this came about and enumerate and describe your contributions?

PT: I certainly won't "enumerate and describe my contributions"! How it (or they) came about is rather easier to explain. There are some things in life to which one is inextricably (and inexplicably) drawn, rather like a moth to a candle, and I have been singularly lucky in my professional life in that I have been allowed to spend much of it exploring some of these. During the last twenty years, two such things have figured more prominently than any other: the first was VAX/VMS, and the second TEX (my *very* first love was Algol-68). In many ways they could not be more different, and Don himself must have realised this for he once said that, in his opinion, Macro-32 (the assembly language for VAX/VMS systems) was possibly the worst assembly language in the world! I was staggered by this pronouncement, since I have always thought of Macro-32 as being possibly the finest assembly language ever developed, but I just had to accept that whilst Don and I agreed about TEX, we would never agree about VMS ... I must one day ask Don his opinion of Algol-68: it would be interesting to know into which of the two categories (awful or brilliant) he would place it, since it's inconceivable (to me) that he would place it at anywhere other than one of the two extremes....

So, fairly early on in my exposure to TEX, I came to realise that it and I were "as one", as it were: I somehow *understood* the underlying philosophy of TEX, and once that is understood, understanding how to use it just seems to come naturally. The primitives that were so difficult for some to grasp (`\expandafter`, `\futurelet`, `\catcode` and so on) were for me not "difficult" *per se*, but rather were an absolutely fascinating challenge, to the bottom of which I just had to get. The more I explored, the more I learned, and the more I learned, the more I enjoyed what I was doing.

Before too long, I started to receive invitations to teach TEX, and these were, for me, my real "contribution" to the TEX world, if indeed I have ever made one. The packages that I have written are few, and of restricted interest (`cropmarks`, `letterspace` and so on) but the real joy for me was not in writing the packages (I usually did so only because I, or someone with whom I was involved, needed functionality that did not pre-exist in TEX) but in learning ever more about how TEX functioned and then passing that information on to others.

On re-reading the above, I realise that there is one contribution of which I feel sufficiently proud not to be ashamed to mention it. When I started work at Royal Holloway, one of the people with whom I most enjoyed working was Dr Malcolm Smith, then a lecturer in the Department of French (and a very keen cyclist, who would think nothing of cycling over the Alps to consult a single book in a distant French library and then cycle back again) who later became Head of Department. Malcolm founded (with financial support from the College) Runnymede Books (motto: *Scholarship made accessible*), the aim of which was to publish French texts (`http://isbndb.com/d/book/antiquitez_de_rome.html`) at a price which students could afford. I worked with Malcolm on the design and typesetting of these, and the difference in appearance between the last and the first is very noticeable indeed. My "pride" in this has nothing whatsoever to do with the quality (or otherwise) of the typesetting itself, but rather with the fact that I was able to assist

Malcolm in his self-appointed task of making scholarship truly affordable (and hence accessible). Malcolm is sadly no longer with us: he died of stomach cancer in his early forties, and is much missed. Other scholars with whom I have had the greatest pleasure in working (and continue to do so to this day) are Ian & Rosalind Gibson (the latter the author of the just-released second edition of *Principles of Nutritional Assessment* (`http://nutrition.earthlight.co.nz/`), and Julian Chrysostomides & Charalambos Dendrinos who are currently preparing the *Lexicon of Abbreviations & Ligatures in Greek Minuscule Hands* (`http://www.porphyrogenitus.org/`) [see endnote]. I was also very pleased to be able to typeset Mr K D Somadasa's *Catalogue of Sinhalese manuscripts in the Wellcome Institute for the History of Medicine* (`http://tinyurl.com/ax4nj`). There are a number of other scholars for whom I have had considerable pleasure in designing and typesetting their books, but sadly too many to list here.

DW: Please tell me about your involvement in the UK TEX Users' Group and, for anyone who doesn't know much about it, a little about the group itself. Also, please tell me something about your involvement in the NTS group and, again, a little about that group.

PT: The UK TEX Users' Group (`http://uk.tug.org/`) (or UK-TuG, as I usually abbreviate it) was—if my memory serves me accurately—the brainchild and creation of Malcolm Clark. I *think* that the pre-formation meeting took place in London (certainly I recall it being well attended) and the following year "Exeter TEX88" took place (I still have the tee-shirt, so it was easy to check the date!). My memory of the following years is pretty vague (I attended the TUG meeting at Stanford, but that has little to do with UK-TuG) and the most important thing that I can recall in the early years of UK-TuG was Peter Abbott's creation of the UK TEX Archive (the forerunner of CTAN). Peter was assisted in this by a number of people: Brian Hamilton Kelly, Neil Kempson and David Osborne amongst others. We "archive assistants" would occasionally be summoned to Aston by Peter, who invariably entertained us very well indeed, and I remember one occasion when we were dining at Aston University that it took twenty minutes to convince the servery staff that I wanted plain, ordinary, straight-out-of-the-tap Birmingham water (actually Rhayader water, from the Elan Valley, but they may not have known that), that I knew what it tasted like, that I *didn't* want bottled water, and that I would get my tap water even if it took all day! We also had some splendidly memorable meals at *The Last Days of the Raj*.

Anyhow, back to TEX. I became involved with the UK TEX Users' Group fairly early on its life, and eventually became its Chairman for a while, taking over (if I remember correctly) from Robin Fairbairns. Most, if not all, of the well-known names in UK-TuG served on the committee at some time or another: apart from those already mentioned, others who immediately spring to mind are Kaveh Bazargan, Sue Brookes, Sebastian Rahtz, Jonathan Fine, Kim Roberts, Chris Rowley, Dominik Wujastyk (these are in no particular order, and all omissions are entirely accidental), and for virtually the entire time I was associated with the Committee Peter Abbott was its Treasurer. UK-TuG was for many years a very active group, with organised meetings, tutorials and so on, but recently the level of activity has markedly declined, which *may* be an indication of a declining interest in TEX within the UK population but may equally be an indication that the Committee is in desperate need of new blood (this is in no sense intended as a criticism of the present committee, since the decline in the level of activity was already noticeable at the time that I stood down as Chairman). For several years we published a journal, *Baskerville*, but that too has now disappeared, apparently without trace.

The NTS group is another kettle of fish entirely. This group owes its existence (and the TEX world owes a very great deal) to the foresight and vision of Joachim Lammarsch, for many years the President of DANTE e.V. (`http://www.dante.de/`) During the period leading up to the Hamburg meeting of DANTE in 1992, Joachim wrote to all the TeX activists that he knew, asking if they would be interested in co-operating to design and develop a successor to TeX. I was amongst those who responded positively, and we who so did were all invited to the meeting in Hamburg at which the group was created. The group included (again, in no particular order, and with apologies for any accidental omissions) Joachim, Friedhelm Sowa, Rainer Schöpf, Peter Breitenlohner, Jiří Zlatuška, Bernd Raichle, Joachim Schrod and myself. Joachim Schrod and Rainer Schöpf left the group fairly early on in its history and the remaining members rather loosely partitioned their activities into two projects: the NTS project itself (with "NTS" standing for "New Typesetting System" and the ε-TeX project (where the "e-" can be thought of as indicating "extended" or "enhanced"). For some time the group concentrated mainly on ε-TeX, with Peter Breitenlohner taking the technical lead, and in many ways ε-TeX is also the most significant result of the group's work, since it now forms the engine on which LaTeX is based. The NTS project was put on hold until adequate funding could be secured, and once this was achieved (mainly through the generosity of DANTE e.V. and TUG, but also as a result of an incredibly generous donation by one individual who wished — and wishes — to remain anonymous), Karel Skoupý was hired as a programmer. Karel's brief was to reverse-engineer TeX, and thereby to design and implement a TeX clone which behaved *exactly* as did TeX but without re-using any of Knuth's code (and thereby avoiding coming into conflict with Knuth's express wish that he, and only he, make any changes whatsoever to TeX). Karel did this very well (albeit taking rather longer to achieve his and our goal than he had originally forecast), working mainly under the immediate direction of Jiří Zlatuška but with regular meetings with the rest of us to ensure that things were proceeding as planned. Sadly, despite the best of intentions, the NTS project started to founder for reasons which I will not go into here (this is water under the bridge, and it will serve the TeX community much better if we put past disagreements behind us and look to the future rather than the past) and the status and future of NTS are now somewhat uncertain.

One point which might not be immediately clear from the above is why the group undertook two separate projects: if it was possible to extend (or enhance) TeX simply through the medium of an additional change-file (and a concomitant change of name), why did we need to re-implement TeX as NTS? The answer is that making extensions and enhancements to TeX itself (whether through the medium of a change-file or whether using some less rigorous route such as "diff"s) is not easy: the TeX program, although incredibly well documented and despite Don's very careful adherence to the precepts of "Literate programming", remains a rather opaque piece of code with which only the most diligent can interfere without causing unexpected (and undesired) side-effects. The group was very lucky to include Peter Breitenlohner and Bernd Raichle amongst its members: Peter and Bernd are two of the *very* few people (there are probably fewer than ten in the entire world) who are sufficiently familiar with TeX-the-program that they can make changes which have *only* the desired effect. The underlying idea of NTS therefore was (and is) to re-implement TeX not only so as to avoid conflict with Knuth's wishes (this could far more easily be accomplished by the simple expedient of a change of name, *cf.* ε-TeX, pdfTeX and so on) but also to re-implement it in such a way that modifications could *easily* be made. It remains to be seen whether NTS has truly accomplished this *desideratum*. The other question which is frequently asked concerning NTS is whether the group were right to insist on Java as the language of implementation: our decision was primarily based on two key issues — (1) Java's portability (write anywhere, run anywhere) and (2) its standardisation (there *is* only one Java, since Sun owns the name). We discounted the performance penalty which the use of a semi-compiled language implicitly incurs. With hindsight, we may have overstated the importance of the former and understated the importance of the latter, yet (in my personal opinion), no other language which either existed at the time or which has come into existence since then offers any significant advantage over Java. As an aside, programming language development seems to have slowed dramatically: when I was younger, new programming languages appeared with remarkable regularity (Fortran 4, Fortran 77, Fortran 9x, Pascal, Modula, Simula, Oberon, Algol 60, Algol 68, ...) but since "C", its derivatives and its object-oriented cousins made their appearance, development seems to have slowed almost to a standstill: new interpreted languages appear from time to time (Python, for example) but compiled languages which offer genuinely new insights into programming methodology seem remarkably few and far between. I do *not* believe that this is because "C" and its derivatives are perfect: indeed, despite its almost universal adoption, I feel that "C" is in many ways fundamentally flawed, but that is rather off-topic for this interview.

DW: You have served as an officer in the UK TEX Users' Group and the TEX Users Group. You have participated on the internationally staffed NTS group, and you chaired the program committee of a TUG Annual Conference (Toruń, Poland, 1998). My point is that you have seen the TEX community from a quite international perspective and from a perhaps unusual variety of functional perspectives (research and development, education, governance, system administration, etc.). I am interested in your perspective on how the world-wide TEX community has evolved and how you think it should continue to evolve.

PT: I think that "evolution" in this context is distinctly non-linear: there was a very rapid evolutionary spurt early on, characterised by the formation of the various national groups (or "language-based" groups, as some would characterize them), a process which continues today but at a considerably slower rate, and then for a long time there was a period of stasis during which the national groups undertook the combined tasks of proselytisation, recruitment and education, tasks which are now in some cases beginning to falter.... In parallel with this, but starting somewhat later, various pan-national initiatives were launched, of which by far the two most significant are the development of CTAN (the "Comprehensive TEX Archive Network"), which started life as "The UK TEX Archive", *q.v.*, and the TEX Live series of CDs and (more recently) DVDs. Other pan-national projects which cannot pass without mention are the LATEX 3 project, which in practice is really the "LATEX 2_ε implementation and development project", and the Omega project, which might be characterised as a Unicode-based derivative of TEX.

Whilst speaking of pan-national TEX activities, one truly remarkable phenomenon is the *de facto* international status of the Polish TEX User Group's annual meeting at Bachotek (near Brodnica, Poland). This annual meeting, which takes place at the beginning of May in an idyllic forest setting by the side of a tranquil lake, was originally simply the annual meeting of GUST (`http://www.gust.org.pl/`), the "Grupa Użytkowników Systemu TEX". Very early on, however, the GUST Board and Secretariat took the remarkable step of inviting known TEX devotees from other countries (the UK, Germany, the Netherlands, Hungary, Lithuania and so on) and many of us accepted. Once there, we were completely hooked: BachoTEX (as it is now known) is a truly addictive activity, once experienced never forgotten, and what was at first simply a national annual meeting is now a regular meeting place for TEXies from around the world. Quite apart from the quality of the presented papers (which is invariably exceptionally high), BachoTEX is simply a joy to attend: there are bonfires and singing most evenings, people congregate in each other's log cabins to talk TEX, to eat and drink, or simply to socialise, the lake and its environs supports a splendid variety of wildlife (catching, photographing and releasing the many grass snakes which can be found around the lake is one of my greatest pleasures); in summary, the best word I can find to describe BachoTEX is simply "unique". If you've not yet experienced one, make it a top priority to do so: you will never regret it!

Returning to the main theme of the "evolution" of the world-wide TEX community, and considering this at a national rather than an international level, probably the most significant activity which has taken place (and continues to take place) is the "regionalisation" or "localisation" of TEX, primarily through the design and implementation of language-specific fonts. When Don designed and implemented the AM series of fonts (these were the forerunners to the more widely known CM fonts: AM is "Almost [Computer] Modern" whilst CM is "Computer Modern", both being based on the Monotype 8a design), he did so in a way which was the very model of orthogonal design: any diacritic ("accent") can be placed on any character ("glyph"), and TEX will adjust the position to suit (this is, of course, something of a simplification but it will suffice for the present discussion). A few special characters that could not easily be composed of individual elements were included (e.g., the Polish "dark L": "Ł", "ł"), which typographically is like an "L" with an oblique slash and which phonetically lies closer to the "W" sound of British Cockney than to the clear "L" of RP in words such as "roll" and "elk"), but in general the underlying idea was that accented characters would be constructed on the fly. Whilst this worked reasonably well for some western European languages (French, German, and so on; Dutch/Nederlands less so, since there is no "ij" ("IJ", "ij") ligature in CM), other languages such as Polish and Vietnamese were considerably less well served. The Poles needed an "ogonek" (think of it as a reversed cedilla: "Ą", "ą"), whilst the Vietnamese needed not just one but two diacritics on a single base glyph ("ế"), one to indicate a change of vowel sound and the other to indicate in which of the six possible tones the word is to be pronounced (Silvio Levy, amongst others, had encountered this latter problem a long time ago when designing and implementing TEX fonts for typesetting Classical (polytonic) Greek, for which one needs "breathings" as well as conventional diacritics and an iota subscript). As a response to this, the Poles, the Vietnamese, and many other nations, designed and implemented one or more TEX-compatible fonts which met *their* needs rather than being a general purpose font suitable for many languages but "ideal" only for those that eschew diacritics (English, for example!). Whilst in some cases this has been accomplished simply by re-engineering Computer Modern to include national-specific glyphs, in other cases (Polish is a good example) the designer(s) have jettisoned CM completely and derived entirely new TEX-compatible fonts based on traditional fonts from their own national typesetting tradition (Antykwa Toruńska and Antykwa Półtawskiego, for example, in the case of the Poles).

And what of the future? How should "the world-wide TEX community ... continue to evolve?" That is not for me to say! How it *should* evolve is for it to decide, not for any one individual to prescribe. All I can do is to express a wish: that TEX users world-wide continue to recognise and publicise the fact that TEX's philosophy is, and remains, at the very leading edge of typesetting technology. Whilst Franklin Mark Liang's hyphenation algorithm has now been incorporated into high-end word-processing and desktop publishing systems, TEX and its derivatives are virtually unique in terms of their programmability and scriptability. People such as Hàn Thế Thành have done more than most to ensure that TEX continues to have a rôle in the 21st century, firstly by integrating the generation of PDF (as opposed to DVI) into (pdf)TEX itself, and secondly by their research into ways in which elements of Herman Zapf's HZ algorithm (for micro-typography) can be integrated into a TeX derivative. The TeX world needs more such people, since if we are over-zealous in respecting Don's wish that TeX remain unchanged (modulo essential bug-fixes made by himself) for perpetuity, we will end up with a museum piece rather than an archetype of leading-edge technology. Yes, TeX itself must remain frozen in time, but the TeX community must adopt (and adapt) TeX derivatives with the same enthusiasm that it first adopted TeX itself.

DW: In your paper "Computer Typesetting or Electronic Publishing? New trends in scientific publication" (*TUGboat*, Vol. 17, No. 4, 1996, pp. 367–381) you give significant mention to the ARPANET RFC (Request for Comments) mechanism. As I have become acquainted with the TeX world over the past eight years, I have been disappointed that it appears that there is no TeX mechanism parallel to the RFC mechanism. It appears to me there are lots of fragmentary conversations on comp.text.tex, occasional proposals in conference proceeding, *TUGboat* or other journals, and undoubtedly lots of memos within different activity groups, but no unified mechanism for proposing a new "standard". First, am I right about my impression? If so, do you think there is any possibility of a more visible, standard mechanism for advancing the coherent development of TeX, or is the TeX world simply too fragmented?

PT: Oh, what a question! I think that we need to start by considering TeX itself, how it came into existence, and why it is what it is. I would suggest that TeX is what it is for one main reason: it is the work of one man (albeit a genius, but one man nonetheless) who was able to develop a very significant amount of time to designing and developing a program without the need to (a) justify what he was doing to anyone else, and (b) consult anyone else before making decisions. Yes, Don made great use of testers, and accepted and incorporated many of their suggestions, but the relationship was distinctly asymmetric with Don having the final say on any and every issue. It has even been suggested (but I have no evidence to support it) that TeX's somewhat arcane macro language is there *because* Don was keen to incorporate his ideas in a large and significant piece of software because the Computer Science community in general had not received these ideas with the enthusiasm which he thought they deserved. Whether this is true or not I have no way of knowing, but there can be little disagreement that TeX *is* idiosyncratic in many ways, and it is very hard to imagine that it would in any way resemble the program we know and love today if Dijkstra, Wirth, Hoare *et al.* had all had equal say in its design.

Now, it is fairly safe to assume that the majority of the audience who read this interview will agree that TeX is a *very* significant achievement, and that despite its idiosyncrasies they enjoy using it. They might be hard-pushed to identify another piece of software which attracts quite such a cult following, although Linux cannot be far behind. But the Linux kernel, too, was created in a manner not entirely dissimilar to TeX: it is the work of one man, Linus Torvalds, although in his case there was a pre-existing model (Unix) on which his work was based. Even the World-Wide Web, use of which probably occupies more computer resources than any other computer-related activity today, was "invented" by one man, Tim Berners-Lee.

Of course, in each case cited, the statement "X was invented by Y" is not meant to suggest that Y worked in total isolation, shutting himself off from all human contact until the task was complete. Of course, each project was *influenced* by what had gone before, and (certainly in the case of TeX) by what was about to come, since it is safe to assume that Knuth had more than a passing familiarity with the literature. Nonetheless, all three works listed are essentially each the work of one man.

It is therefore surely relevant to ask whether "universal consensus" is an appropriate model for further development of a TeX derivative. If we look at what is undoubtedly the most successful example of TeX-related development extant (the LaTeX 2_ε/LaTeX 3 project), then what categorises it is anything *but* universal consensus. LaTeX (originally itself the work of one man, Leslie Lamport) is today maintained and developed by a small team (I would guess about eight individuals) with strong leadership and shared precepts and principles. The LaTeX team itself decides what should be done, which areas to prioritise and so on, and then works to achieve its goals. Once stable, the results are released to the TeX world at large. What I would suggest is noteworthy about this model is (a) that it works, and (b) there is no perceivable under-current of muttering "but why didn't/don't they do X?".

Now compare and contrast this approach with a closely-related field: the development of the web-based styling language CSS. Here we have a W3C working group composed of "members of member organisations". At the last count, there were 13 distinct organisations (each of which might be represented by one or more individuals) plus "W3C Invited Experts" (see `http://www.w3.org/2004/08/invexp.html` to learn more about what one of those is!). The Working Group are answerable to no-one (save possibly the W3C itself), and it is they and they alone who decide what does, and what does not, go into CSS. Once a preliminary decision has been made, non-members are invited to comment. It is quite clear from watching the lists concerned that comments from some individuals are afforded considerably more respect than comments from others. Some comments eventually lead to change, some are simply noted, and some are virtually passed over as if never made. What *is* intriguing is to see that certain perspectives are very entrenched amongst the members of the working group, and that any suggestion which conflicts with these entrenched views is unlikely to be afforded more than cursory attention, no matter how many times the suggestion be made (and no matter by how many people). One brief example will suffice. TeX users are very familiar with TeX's macro facilities: if one wants a command (say) `\boustrophedon` and no such command already exists either as a TeX primitive or as a macro pre-defined in a standard package such as LaTeX, one is at liberty to define the command for oneself. Whether one could *usefully* define `\boustrophedon` within TeX is not the point: one can define the command and then (attempt to) implement it through the medium of pre-existing commands and parameters. Compare and contrast this with CSS. In CSS, the vocabulary and syntax are defined by the W3C working group. There are no facilities (current or planned) to allow the vocabulary or syntax to be extended by a user to meet his or her specific needs. In essence, the W3C WG says "we know best: if we don't deem it worthy of implementation, then it will not be implemented, and you will be unable to implement it for yourself because we will give you no tools within CSS so to do". No matter how many times someone points out the usefulness of such functionality, the response remains the same: "What you are trying to suggest is best tackled with an authoring tool: this tool can then allow you to define whatever additional syntactic sugar you like, and it — and only it — will then be responsible for converting your syntactic sugar to standard CSS". And no matter how many times the plaintiff points out that, in the real world, CSS is not written using "an authoring tool", but rather is laboriously hand-crafted and carefully tweaked so as to produce (approximately) the same effect in all mainstream browsers, the W3C CSS WG position remains unchanged and unchanging.

So which of these models is better? The explicit "we know best" of the LaTeX 3 team, or the covert "we know best" of the W3C? The LaTeX team do not claim to need consensus before release: they do what they think best, and the rest of us live with it. The W3C, on the other hand, claim to be open to suggestions and comment, but many who have made such suggestions and comments are unconvinced that the W3C pay little more than lip-service to the idea. For myself, I prefer the *idea* of the W3C approach but the *reality* of the LaTeX: if the W3C CSS WG were less entrenched, more open to suggestions, then who knows what the outcome would be, and whether it would be better or worse than CSS as we know it today. *Quot homines, tot sententiae* ("So many men, so many opinions") said the Roman dramatist Terence, about 2200 years ago. Had he been alive today, he might instead have said "Too many men, too many opinions".

DW: I'd like to hear a little about your personal life, if you don't mind.

PT: Not at all. I'm fifty eight, married, live in a maisonette (downstairs single-storey flat with private front and back door and gardens) overlooking allotments, have a dog "Cleo", a cat "Oscar", a pond in the garden for frogs, scythe my lawn rather than using a conventional mower, had a horse "Jingo" for eighteen years who died earlier this year at the age of 27, enjoy good food and wine (the latter is currently proscribed as my liver has issued a final public warning following anæsthesia late last year), and cycle for pleasure (lightweight, not mountain bike) when the weather is good. I spend far more of my time than I should sitting in front of a 19 inch monitor, have a steerable satellite dish (and some fixed dishes) in the back garden hooked up to both analogue and digital satellite receivers which in turn feed into my PC (used as a PVR — "Personal Video Recorder") and a television, recently invested in a hardware DVD recorder to augment my PC-based DVD burning facilities, and am currently (for this week and the next two) recording and burning to DVD the *Giro d'Italia* (a 3-week cycle race which takes place each year in Italy). My wife Lệ Khanh and I are currently trying to redecorate our home, which we took over from my father when he had to move into permanent residential care at the age of 91. The house has barely had anything done to it for the last forty years, so we have rather a lot to do, but progress is not bad and I finished laying the flooring in the hall while Khanh was away in America at a wedding (she returns this afternoon). I enjoy all forms of speed (fast horses, fast cars, fast motorcycles), drive a SAAB 9000 2.3 turbo and ride a Suzuki GSX-R1100. Khanh & I enjoy playing table-tennis when we can (we have no room for a table at home), and both of us enjoy travelling (we're off to Wales on Friday and to China in August; Khanh will later travel to her family home in Đá Nẵng (Việt Nam) in time for the lunar New year and the third anniversary of the death of her father Âu Dương Thịnh Hoài, where I may be able to join her for a part of her visit.

DW: Is there anything you think I should have asked you and did not? If so, please tell me about that.

PT: Mistakes. What mistakes have you made in your life, what mistakes do you believe others have made, and what (if anything) could now be done to redress these?

PT: And now, having asked myself the questions, I'll try to answer them ....
Yes, I've made mistakes. Thousands of them (probably more). I am (my wife's words) "confrontational, argumentative, aggressive: [you] never try to get others to agree with you, you simply state your position and thereby antagonise everybody". Fair comment. As an experiment, I asked Khanh to comment on a message I was proposing to send on a TeX-related matter: she did so, I changed the wording, and I was A M A Z E D. The first reply I received was supportive, none were abrasive, and the idea I was trying to get across was accepted without dispute (probably for the first time in my life!). So that's probably what characterises the majority of the mistakes I've made, at least in TeX-related matters. There was another one, however, the significance of which really didn't hit me until I was asked to take part in this interview. As a "TeX Implementor" (albeit minor,

unlike Messrs Kellerman & Smith, Mattes, Popineau, Esser, Carnes, etc.), I was used to defining my own TeX structure. I knew where everything fitted, and the last thing I wanted was some d@mn committee trying to foist "The TeX Directory Structure" on me: what did *they* know about how my TeX system (was/should be) organised? This remained my (entrenched, see above) position all the while I continued to use VAX/VMS as my TeX platform (which I did for as long as I possibly could). Finally I was forced to migrate to a PC. Even then I still knew best. ArborText's DVILASER/PS (as used on my VAX/VMS systems) was still the only possible way of generating PostScript from DVI (which meant I had to write my own `\PostScript` macro, to generate the right specials for DVILASER/PS) and my own PS-Fonts (since I was using ArborText's naming conventions, not Karl Berry's). I learned a greal deal by so doing (of course); I had orthogonal PostScript font selection long before PSNFSS saw the light of day, but it was of little use to anyone else since it was predicated on the use of ArborText names rather than Berry. I don't know how long it took me to finally try to install TeX Live (TeX-Live, as I insist on calling it, just to annoy Sebastian), but eventually I did. It didn't work, of course, because I took advantage of the installation option to change the default layout: Fabrice tried to help, but in the end even he had to admit that although the *option* was there, one really shouldn't try to use it, and certainly not try to use it such that one TeX-MF tree was nested under another.... (So what's *wrong* with `/TeXMF/Local/` rather than `/TeXMF-Local/`, I still want to know?!) But here I am today, using TeX Live (almost untweaked, although I still can't live with it *exactly* "out of the box"), using Karl Berry's font names (but I still don't understand them), using (G@d forgive me) pdfLaTeX when I need `hyperref` and all the other nice goodies that Sebastian *et al.* have provided for the LaTeX world but not for those of us that prefer Real-TeX [tm]. In short, I'm reformed but unrepentant. Plain TeX *is* better than LaTeX, simply because it's possible to understand every tiny detail of what is happening inside, and to change it to make it do what *you* want it to do rather than what Messrs Lamport, Mittelbach *et al.* think it *ought* to do. What else? Well, I still hate this d@mn "open source/free-means-libre" ethos. I see nothing wrong with proprietary software, use and enjoy using Windows XP, believe that an author has every right to make his software freely available *without* waiving his right to be the only person allowed to change it, and so on. Some of the packages that I've written that *might* conceivably be of use to somebody will never appear on TeX Live because I won't play the licence game. I have better things to do with my time than to waste it adding some meaningless prose to a package simply to permit it to appear on TeX Live or in the "free" (means "libre") branch of CTAN.

[Note added retrospectively when the author briefly emerged from a time-trip in 2025: "OK, I was wrong. LaTeX is the one true TeX macro package and Lamport is its prophet. All software should be open-source and freely editable and re-distributable by anyone, no matter how ill-informed or ill-intended. Licences are a Good Thing [tm] and if any of my TeX packages were likely to be of the slightest interest to anyone, I'd gladly add one and personally ask Saint Richard to approve the wording. Unfortunately they aren't of the least interest to anyone, so I won't need to...."]

And what of the other side of the question? "What mistakes do you believe others have made, and what (if anything) could now be done to redress these?". Well, if the above wasn't heretical enough to cause apoplexy in one or two readers, the next bit will be. I think Knuth made a mistake (several, in fact) in *The TeXbook*.

The mistakes I refer to are all examples, where he happily intermixes what I perceive as the three distinct rôles of TeX in a single fragment of source code. Let me try to explain. Consider the following three lines of [La]TeX. (I put the "La" in brackets because the example could just as easily be TeX as LaTeX: it is one of the Great Errors that many TeX users believe that only LaTeX can handle constructs such as \begin {whatever} ... \end {whatever}. I'll return to that point later, maybe.

```
\begin {abstract} ... \end {abstract}
\vskip \baselineskip
\def \firsttoken #1{\firstofmany #1\sentinel}
```

I will argue that each of these is *fundamentally* different from the other two.

The first is markup, pure and simple. It introduces, and then terminates, an abstract. It says nothing whatsoever about what an abstract is, or how it is to be typeset. In short, it serves only to MARK UP a stretch of text. Something else (we know not yet what) must interpret this markup and turn it into (presumably) some typeset copy, although there is absolutely no reason why it might not instead produce the text as nicely read speech, through the medium of a speech synthesiser or similar.

The second is formatting. It causes one additional unit of vertical white space to be contributed to the current page (or box). It knows nothing about what precedes it, nothing about what follows it, and nothing about how big (or how small) \baselineskip might be.

The third is (a pre-requisite to) analysis. It defines a macro, \firsttoken, that—through the medium of an adjunct macro \firstofmany—expands to yield the first token of whatever token list was passed as parameter. It knows nothing, cares nothing, about the context in which it will be used; it simply sits there, waiting to be asked to do its job.

The problem is, in many examples in *The TeXbook*, Don mixes two or even all three rôles in a single example. As a result, virtually every TeX user who first learns TeX through the medium of *The TeXbook* sees nothing wrong in interlarding his or her prose with \bigskip, \bf, or any of the other "syntactic sugar" so kindly provided by Don in the Plain format (or even with "inappropriate" TeX primitives). Once learned, habits of this sort are *very* hard to unlearn. The HTML/CSS world has already learned this lesson, and is desperately trying to remove all formatting tags from XHTML, replacing them by pure markup tags the rendering of which is left solely to the browser and/or CSS. In the TeX world, there is little evidence of a general acceptance that the problem exists (or even that it is a problem!). LaTeX *tries* to inculcate good habits, but it is still possible to write the most awful mixture of markup, formatting and analysis without ever leaving the nanny-like world that one enters by embracing LaTeX. How can this be addressed?

I believe that what is needed is a *radical* re-think of TeX-related markup and programming. No "user" should ever have to use backslashes or braces (at least, not with their conventional TeX meaning). By eliminating what are strictly "control words" from the users' vocabulary, space-gobbling will cease to be a problem. (How many books have *you* seen, typeset in LaTeX, in which one word is accidentally elided with the next because the first word occurred so frequently that the author defined it as a macro (control-word), and then forgot on at least one occasion that the macro would gobble up the following space?) If we do away with backslashes and braces, with what should they be replaced? I believe that the answer is already clear: the number of people writing web pages is probably at least 100 times as many as those writing TeX documents. Although many of those web authors will be using some sort of authoring package (Dreamweaver, or whatever) a substantial majority will—at least from time to time—be writing in "pure" HTML, in which case they are writing things such as <title>My First Web Page</title> without significant difficulty. If they can do it, so can we! In fact, "they" and "we" is a pretty big category error: there can hardly be any one of "we" who is not also a "they". Thus (almost all of us) are already familiar with an alternative markup paradigm: "all" we need to do is to make it accessible to the TeX world at large.

OK, so I believe that HTML-like markup should be adopted *as the norm* for the TeX world. I say "HTML-like" because the last thing that I want to do is to throw the baby out with the bathwater. TeX is a zillion times more powerful than HTML because *the user is not constrained as to vocabulary*. Thus if I need `\latinprose`, and you need `\greekverse`, each of us (in TeX) is free to define the command and then to implement it. Not so, in HTML, and hardly so in XHTML, despite the misleading "X" in the latter's name. Thus I argue that what we need is an *extensible* markup language, superficially similar in syntax to HTML but with the essential ability to be able to define (and implement) additional tags (`<latinverse>` & `</latinverse>`, for example). Where this gets (more than a little) complex is in determining which tag can occur in which context(s). In HTML, all is simple: the grammar is pre-defined (in a DTD) and the rules may be derived therefrom. An HTML parser can then tell straight away whether or not a document is *valid* HTML. In the system I am advocating, a user would be able to add tags to the language in an (almost) *ad hoc* manner: since writing a DTD is a distinctly non-trivial task, it is clearly *much* easier to define and implement a new tag than it is to modify the rule-set to indicate in exactly which contexts it is (or is not) permitted. More work needed here: I am floating ideas, not proposing a fully worked-through solution.

With the document marked up using HTML-like notation, we next need a means to describe how that document is to appear on the printed page (or on the screen, or through a speech synthesiser). Again, I see no reason not to learn from (and copy where appropriate) the HTML world. The appearance of HTML documents is partially implicit (rules which are assumed to exist in every browser) and partially explicit (a user may augment or modify these rules using Cascading Style Sheets — CSS). The syntax of CSS is very straight-forward, and should be easily understandable by TeXies:

```
LATINVERSE {font-style:italic; margin-left: 1em}
```

is pretty self-explanatory. I therefore believe that the *formatting* aspect should be expressed in a CSS-like syntax, but given the hard-learned lessons of TeX, that the vocabulary should be extensible rather than hard-wired (see preceding para. for caveats concerning extensibility).

Finally we need analysis, and here (of course) TeX comes into its own. Whilst more than a little idiosyncratic, TeX has proved itself capable of being used as a parser, calculator, constraint-solver, and everything else needed (including, of course, a typesetting engine *par excellence*) and thus is the perfect engine through which to process the HTML-like user markup and the CSS-like "document designer" markup.

Is this a pipe-dream, or reality? I sincerely hope that it is the latter. Backslashes and braces, space-gobbling and all the other minutiæ that characterise TeX may well have been acceptable for user documents in 1978, and even in 1982. By 1990, they were beginning to look a little passée. In 2005, they are surely *well* past their sell-by date. It is time to stand back, to take a good look at the program that we all love (and occasionally love to hate), to identify its strengths and to capitalise on them; but at the same time to identify its weaknesses, and to have the courage and the wisdom to excise them, leaving a lean, mean, typesetting system layered on which are a sane markup language and another (but clearly different) language in which formatting concepts can be clearly expressed.

DW: Wow! That gives me a lot to think about. I hope you will think it out more fully and write it up at some point.

Thank you, Phil, for taking the time to participate in this interview. The history you can recount and the perspective you bring are fascinating.

PT: Thank you!

[Endnote from Philip Taylor: It is with great sadness that I have to report that Julian Chrysostomides passed away before her *Lexicon of Abbreviations & Ligatures in Greek Minuscule Hands* could appear in print. Julian was, quite simply, unique: intensely modest, she was without doubt the most dedicated scholar and teacher with whom I have ever had the pleasure and the privilege to work. Her death leaves a great gap in the lives of her friends and family, but Charalambos and I are determined that her book will be published, albeit posthumously, and we are both working to that end as this note is being written.]

Mimi Burbank

Mimi Burbank is a member of the *TUGboat* production team and past member of the TUG board.

[Interview completed 6 September 2005.]

Dave Walden, interviewer: Please tell me a bit about your personal history independent of TEX.

Mimi Burbank, interviewee: I'm 63 years old, was born and reared in Tennessee. During my junior and senior years in high school I worked in my best friend's parents' newspaper, and got a touch of "printers ink" in my blood. I then spent the next 25 years (or so) of my "working life" in the medical field. Then I moved to Florida and began working at Florida State University, mostly doing word processing for various faculty. Having done medical research and maintained medical records, I naturally was interested in the research going on.

I will be retiring at the end of October of 2005 and will be leaving shortly thereafter to go to Uganda. I will be taking TEX with me, and I plan on using it there as well.

DW: When and how did you first get involved with TEX and its friends?

MB: Well, in December of 1985 a group of scientists at the Supercomputer Computations Research Institute (SCRI) at Florida State University were interviewing candidates for a position of "word processor" which would require learning TEX. There were some five or six physicists using it. Well, I could spell the word "computer" but had never seen one. For personal reasons, I wanted to change departments, and I refused to think there was something that I couldn't learn to do; so I said, "Sure, I can learn that." Boy, what a shock. I was hired, and they gave me a computer ("What's that?") and *The TEXbook*. I spent the first three months of my job with that book in bed with me at night, under the pillow ... it was my constant companion. Basically I spent most of my time in the index, learning the terms ... and then reading from the front of the book as I learned.

I believe that at the end of the first week, I had learned enough to operate the computer and edit my first file—which was a brief "letter" and which still resides in my personnel folder where I currently work. I was so proud.

Then came mathematical papers. One scientist, an Eastern European, handed me pages and pages of a handwritten paper. I had more difficulty translating his handwriting than I did learning TEX. After about six months, I was given some equations, and there were over 500 matching braces; perhaps it would be more accurate to say there were around 500 left braces but only 450 right braces. I then learned to indent and structure my code in such a way as to make it easy to edit later.

I attended my first annual TEX meeting in 1987, I think, and my first "Beginning TEX" course, taught by Stephan von Bechtolsheim (I eventually bought his complete set of TEX references). I met some wonderful people at the meeting — Barbara Beeton, Christina Thiele, and Blenda and Berthold Horn — and began corresponding with Christina and Barbara, and over the years have become fast friends with both.

DW: I'm interested in your experience in taking a *beginning* TEX course from a man whose book on TEX *practice* is four volumes and 1800 pages long.

MB: Stephan was (I hope, still is) an exuberant teacher of TEX. He had a great deal of experience and literally took the program apart at the seams to understand it. I still maintain that in order to understand LATEX, you need to understand the underlying "engine". My "basic" understanding came largely from his classes, and when I want to force LATEX to do something, I resort to his methods ;-). I like to know *why* something works the way it does....

DW: Tell me more about your involvement with TUG.

MB: I originally became involved in the Conference Planning Committee, along with Christina, after co-editing the Dedham conference proceedings with Hope Hamilton in 1991, along with Dian De Sha. The experience, for all of us, sparked an attempt to write up our (ofttimes hilarious) experiences in an article we called "The Tale of 4 Witties". Unfortunately, we never finished it — but the file still exists and perhaps one day we will.

I became a member of the TUG Board in 1993, serving until 1997. During this time I also served on the Publications Committee and Conference Planning Committee (until the former died a natural death somewhere around 1997). I've edited or co-edited quite a few proceedings since 1992. I also organized the 1995 meeting in St. Petersburg, Florida. In 1996, at the annual meeting in Dubna, Russia, *TUGboat* was about two years behind in production and it was becoming evident that the job was just too much for one person — however diligent she was. Computer technology was advancing rapidly and the American Mathematical Society was changing architectures and causing all sorts of "access" problems for Barbara, so I undertook to get my site (SCRI) to become the home for a team of people who would work to produce *TUGboat*. In the first year I believe we published four issues, and we caught up with production by the end of the second year.

I'd have to say also that during this time, with the most gracious and expert help of Sebastian Rahtz, all of the machines at SCRI were used for development for the early years of the TEX Live CDs — another advantage of having a very diverse set of machines to play with. We currently have pretty much the same setup we developed in 1996 — that of one central "common" TEX path for all operating systems on the floor. Originally, we had two versions of IBM-AIX, three versions of IRIX, at least two versions of Solaris, one version of Linux, Windows, and two versions of Alphas (OSF) — it has been so long I can't remember how many different operating systems we've had. There were all sorts of problems with building the binaries — Sebastian probably got a lot of grey hairs over this; he always seemed to be on the computer even though he was six hours ahead of me. (Nowadays, Karl Berry is three hours behind me, but he too, always seems to be on the computer.)

Over the past ten years, my "home" has undergone some name changes, and changes in directors, but they have consistently provided access to various team members so that we could have a production site where people would be able to work to produce the journal. I took a bit of the load off Barbara's shoulders, though. I've managed to archive all of the issues we produced and have made them available to the TUG office; and old archives reside on the TUG computer (`tug.org`) in Denmark.

Over the past ten years (or so) I've also served as one of the TUG "webmasters" — sharing the load there as well. It has always been one of the concerns of the production team to make as much information as possible about TEX available to the whole TEX community. Many people have worked on this, but I'd have to say that Sebastian deserves the lion's share of the applause ;-).

Overall, my webmaster duties take only a little time per week. My *TUGboat* duties have lessened over time as well — largely with the addition to the production team of Karl Berry, who has taught me much in the way of "makefiles" and `.cfg` files. At one point in time, I spent most of my day doing *TUGboat* editing and production; today, I primarily balance pages, fix bad breaks, overfull boxes, "eyeball" the output that goes to the printer and proof the bluelines when they return. We originally had to cut and paste some figures onto paper and mail hard copy to the printer. Today, everything is done using pdfLaTeX, ps2pdf, ConTeXt, and sometimes Acrobat Distiller — the world of publishing has certainly changed!

In general, my involvement in TUG has focused on two things: annual meetings, both organizing them, and editing and producing the proceedings, both as preprints and *TUGboat* issues; and publications: initially only editorial work on the proceedings issues of *TUGboat*, and then sliding sideways, as it were, more and more into *TUGboat* production work, to ensure that things printed correctly on paper, and then were presented correctly on-screen.

I'd have to add that one of my interests is to make publications and documentation available on the web.

DW: To what extent do you use TeX in your own work, as opposed to TUG's work?

MB: I've used LaTeX to publish several books at SCRI — always a learning experience. But I think my most memorable project was the initiation of the use of TeX for a database. In 1986–87 I was asked to provide some statistical information on publications for SCRI. It took forever to get the information, and I and my cohort, Donna Burnette, decided to write a database using TeX (after all, it was a pseudo-programming language wasn't it?) since our site would not pay to purchase a commercial database (at that time, they ran somewhere around $20,000). Well, in 1987 we began our database, and modified it over the next couple of years to produce many different types of reports — and users even used it to do their CVs for publications.... I don't believe it was until 1997–1998 that many of our users began using LaTeX. I had a difficult time making the transition myself, but once I converted, I was "hooked" ;-). One confession about the database, though — it was not Y2K compliant. In 2000, I had to completely rewrite the code ... but by then, we had changed names, and I needed to start a new database, so I heaved a sigh of relief. I hadn't written all of the original code, and it was rather cumbersome, but I managed to get it to work from 2000 to 2004 when we stopped using it altogether. The initial stages of the project were written up in the article "Using TeX for a Publications Database", *TUGboat* 13:3 (1992), pp. 362–371.

Somewhere around 1998 or so, a blind student came to work in the office with me using T.V. Raman's software, ASTER. (See T.V. Raman's article, "An Audio View of (La)TeX Documents", in *TUGboat* 13:3 (1992).) This was a young man who had been blinded as an adult in an accident while in the Navy. He was studying astrophysics, and there was no application that suited his needs with regards to mathematics, so we purchased ASTER and the necessary hardware. He left after one year, to pursue a Ph.D. program in Arizona.

Other than the above, I use LaTeX to do all of my own correspondence, and any documentation that I use. I've encouraged my children to use it (without much instruction), and I plan on taking it with me to Africa when I leave in November of this year.

DW: Let's move back to your involvement with *TUGboat* and various conference proceedings over the years. You must have worked with a lot of papers from many authors over the years. Are there some lessons learned there relevant to either the production staff or the authors?

MB: Working with authors has been a varied experience — quite! I have nightmares about some authors, and their quirks. I've never understood why an author would redefine a *TUGboat* macro to do something different than was originally intended. For several years, the biggest part of editing was going in and looking at the authors "stylistic" macros to see what conflicted.

I also have learned quite a lot from the actual production of the proceedings issues. In order to run many of these files, we actually had to *use* the software described. Often this led to conflicts with the basic *TUGboat* macros; sometimes we had to resort to chicanery in order to get something to print on paper and get it to the printer. Today, we send PDF files electronically — quite a long way from scissors and glue — but even now we sometimes have problems. Sometimes what will print on my printer will not print on the typesetter at the printing house. William Adams usually then goes in and performs some magic on the file, and we ship it off again.

DW: And what about the process of getting these documents actually printed and mailed to members? I suspect you have an interesting story or two to tell.

MB: This part of the process is actually the simplest. The procedures have been in place for a long time — when the printer is about ready to ship, the TUG office sends a file to them for the print run. Today this file is an Excel file, which is turned into a `.csv` file and mailed to the printer. We have archived this `.csv` file with each issue — for the past 10 years or so ... so that we have an accurate address for queries from members who did not receive their copy....

DW: You mentioned going to Uganda after you retire and taking TeX with you to use there: I've heard from someone who knows you well that your first trip out of the US was to a TUG meeting.

MB: Christina Thiele and I attended the Aston meeting and then we spent a week driving around the entire country of Wales — drinking sparkling ales each evening in the pub, and staying at lovely Bed and Breakfast homes. I've got some seven or eight rolls of film on that. TUG has provided a wonderful opportunity for me to travel, something I never would have been able to afford had I not been on the TUG Board of Directors and highly involved in TUG affairs. My most memorable trip was to Russia in 1996. I made a longlasting friend there.

In fact, my involvement in TUG has enabled me to make many friends around the world — and I treasure each and every one of them. I am very grateful for my involvement in TUG, and encourage more people to become involved.

DW: Thank you very much for taking the time to do this interview. I have learned a number of things I didn't know about how parts of TUG operate. (And I'm envious of your opportunity to spend time in Uganda.)

[Endnote: Mimi indeed has been living in Uganda for the last several years and reports that she loves it there. She says that she still use pdfLaTeX to do her journals, which are online on her web site (`http://www.saint-peters-archives.org/files/mamamimi/`), and keeps up with the TeX world via *TUGboat*. She says, "I miss working with the production team". Her photo on the first page of this interview is of her involved with her "favorite activity — playing with children".]

Karl Berry

Karl Berry has been a long-time board member of TUG, became TUG president in 2003, and was subsequently elected for further terms. Among other projects, he is co-administrator of the tug.org server, co-editor of TeX Live (http://tug.org/texlive), and a member of the *TUGboat* (http://tug.org/TUGboat) production team.

[Interview completed 27 September 2005.]

Dave Walden, interviewer: You and I have been working together on various TUG activities for the better part of a year, so I won't pretend I don't know a good bit about you already. In fact, I'll assume that readers of this interview are already familiar with your biographical information that is already on the web:

- a 2002 GNU Friends interview (http://tug.org/interviews/interview-files/karl-berry-gnu.html).
- your welcome essay for the 2003 TUG conference (http://tug.org/TUGboat/Articles/tb24-1/berry.pdf), which includes a description of how you became involved with TeX.
- your candidate-for-president statements (http://tug.org/election).

I'll start with a hopefully straightforward question. I presume you are not just a TeX developer and also *use* TeX or its friends from time to time. Which of TeX and its friends do you use and for what types of writing, and what distribution(s) and editing system(s) do you use and why?

Karl Berry, interviewee: I use pretty much all of the major TeX variations for one thing or another:

- For columns and other *TUGboat* material, I mostly write in LaTeX since that is the easiest to handle when I switch hats from author to editor and want to process it for publication. Almost all of the incoming material I edit for *TUGboat* is in LaTeX.
- When producing covers and other ephemera, e.g., for conference booklets, I use plain TeX because it doesn't get in the way, and because I can write it out of my head, unlike LaTeX. I even got to use Eplain (http://tug.org/eplain) again for its \doublecolumns macro for the last couple of proceedings issues, which I got a kick out of.
- My experience with ConTeXt has been fairly enjoyable, but limited to editing a couple of *TUGboat* papers, the pdfTeX manual (http://tug.org/applications/pdftex), and its amazing pdf make-up abilities, via recipes provided by Hans Hagen.
- What little technical writing I do is primarily software documentation, for which I use Texinfo (http://www.gnu.org/software/texinfo). Mostly what I write these days is email, unfortunately.

Regarding distributions, I almost always use TeX Live on GNU/Linux, sometimes even the bleeding edge development version (http://tug.org/texlive/Images/test). I occasionally use the teTEX (`http://tug.org/tetex`) that came with the operating system for testing, etc.

As for editing, I've lived in (tty-mode) GNU Emacs (`http://www.gnu.org/software/emacs`) for 20 years and don't plan to change any time soon, if ever. I started using it because (among other reasons) its incredible redisplay algorithm actually made it feasible to edit over a 110-baud modem line. It's not an editor, it's a way of life.

DW: You mentioned Eplain which you developed and Texinfo which you maintain. Can you estimate for me how many different TEX-related development and maintenance projects, large or small, you have worked on and perhaps list the three or four that you feel are most significant or you in some other way got the biggest kick out of?

KB: Counting all the projects I've worked on, not just been a principal developer of, it's probably several dozen.

The most significant ones that come to mind are developing Kpathsea (`http://tug.org/kpathsea`) (a library for path searching), and integrating it with dvips, xdvi, and dviljk, and with Web2c (`http://tug.org/web2c`) TEX (a system for converting Knuth's original sources into C for compilation). In more recent years, I've become heavily involved in TEX Live and editing *TUGboat*.

The project I enjoyed researching and developing the most was probably the GNU Font Utilities (`http://www.gnu.org/software/fontutils`), which was a tool chain to go from scanned images to outline fonts. Few fonts have ever actually been produced with it. I was amused to learn of one through a *TUGboat* paper (`http://tug.org/TUGboat/Articles/tb25-2/tb81becc.pdf`) — the authors had not contacted me while they were working on the project; I found it very impressive that they could actually get it to work. I was also happy to learn that the widely-used potrace (`http://potrace.sourceforge.net`) originated from that code. I have always had a strong interest in fonts and typeface design.

DW: Do I presume correctly that Kpathsea stands for "Karl's path searching?"

KB: Yes, I'm afraid so. I didn't want to call it anything general like just "pathsearch", and couldn't think of a better name. If I had it to do over again, I'd probably call it tpathsea (TEX Path Searching) or something else, but it's too late. Olaf Weber has done a fine job maintaining Kpathsea and Web2c for quite a few years now, so it should really be okpathsea. Which is a good description, too, come to think of it — it's not perfect, it certainly has its problems, but overall, I think it's ok.

The other circumstance in which my name sometimes appears is the "Karl Berry naming scheme" for fonts, which is those cryptic font names (`http://tug.org/fontname`) like `ptmr8r` which everyone (including me) hates. I try to just call it Fontname, but I guess that is too generic to catch on. It is strange to see my name in book indexes for this painful 8.3 naming scheme — not exactly what I would choose to be most visible for.

So it seems I'm not satisfied with either specific or generic project names. Naming is tough.

DW: What was the first TEX development project (as opposed to use) you were involved with, and what caused you to become involved?

KB: The first TEX development project I did was in 1984 or so, writing a DVI driver for a 300 dpi QMS laser printer; I started from the `.web` source for another driver (`dvi2lgp` from Lawrence Livermore, as I recall), so it was not terribly difficult. Doing this was essentially part of the very first TEX installation I did as a student at Dartmouth, since there was no other decent output device available, so it also counts as my first use. It was a lot of fun to figure out how to download fonts, etc.; this was pre-PostScript. Routinely available bitmap displays were still in the future; the standard interface to the VAXen we had was Zenith 19 terminals. I liked those terminals a lot.

At the time, all the TEX files were stored in a single directory by file type. It was a few years later, when I got (even more) interested in fonts, that I started updating the drivers I used, Dvips and Xdvi, as well as the Web2c-based TEX, to do subdirectory path searching, which eventually led to Kpathsea, the TEX Directory Structure (`http://tug.org/tds`), etc. Not sure it was the best approach to take in retrospect, but it was natural at the time.

DW: How were you drawn into involvement in the TUG board and then as president?

KB: There was no one big reason which impelled me to run initially for the TUG board in the mid-90's. I knew Sebastian Rahtz and others who were on the board at the time, which probably brought it to mind. I'd been a member of TUG for a long time already at that point, although it had always seemed a distant organization run by people I had no knowledge of, since I didn't go to conferences. So I wanted to try to contribute something organizationally, as well as technically.

About being president, I decided to volunteer for the job in 2003 because, first, no one else had expressed interest in taking it up, and second, in my personal life a little time had opened up, and I was curious to try something new. In 2005 I ran again, this time because, as you might guess, I had very much enjoyed the last two years working with the TUG board, other user group leaders (`http://tug.org/usergroups.html`), and most especially with Robin Laakso, TUG's executive director. She handles all aspects of the administrative side of TUG in most exemplary fashion, essentially single-handed.

DW: In an earlier answer you mentioned that most of your communication is by email and in your last answer you noted that you didn't go to TUG conferences. These statements bring two questions to mind. First (and this is just out of curiosity), how many people in how many countries do you communicate with in the average week or month regarding TEX and TUG? Second (a more serious question), since most TEX users probably seldom if ever communicate in person with other TEX users except at their own sites, what are your approaches as TUG president to reducing the feeling of TEX users that TUG is a distant organization run by people they have no knowledge of?

KB: Off the top of my head, I'd guess I talk TEX to maybe 50 people in an average week, in a dozen countries. I've never answered a TEX question from an Antarctica resident (though I have heard from a couple about the continent in general, as it's been another interest of mine (`http://freefriends.org/~karl/antarctica.html`)), but TEX people from all other continents have been heard from.

The "distant organization" problem is one that is in my mind in nearly everything TEXish that I do, since I felt it so strongly myself. I don't have any magic solution. I just try to write semi-regular announcements, editorials, web pages, etc., in the most direct way I can, trying to get across that TUG exists because of and for TEX users, not as some organization apart from them. Especially in these days of megacorporations who apparently control nearly all aspects of our everyday life, there's a tendency to think every company is rich, huge and either merging or getting merged. None of these are the case with TUG!

TUG has no hierarchy, no bureaucracy; everyone on the board is a volunteer, as are essentially all the developers and everyone else in our TEX world, outside of the commercial implementation. TUG per se is a framework: an office to coordinate activities, finances, and outreach, and a bit of infrastructure, like the web server this interview is posted on. It always comes down to individual(s) putting in their time to make a given project actually happen. So I try to encourage and welcome involvement at any level.

DW: As you said, TUG is a volunteer organization with few exceptions. Please tell me about any system, principles, or practices you have for getting new volunteers?

KB: I wish I had anything systematic enough to be labeled a "principle". All I really know to do is send email on whatever lists are appropriate and post notices on web pages. Mostly that reaches the same group of people (who are no doubt rather tired of my pleading by now), but occasionally someone new jumps in, which is always cause for rejoicing.

Also, especially through my editing so many articles in *TUGboat*, but also through the couple of recent TeX conferences (`http://tug.org/meetings.html`) I attended, sometimes I know an individual I can ask specifically who I think might be interested. Even if they don't have time or inclination, I've found everyone to be unfailingly gracious about these requests out of the blue. One of the things that keeps me going.

DW: In addition to your development work and your administrative work as TUG president, you also put *lots* of effort into maintaining the TUG web site and also all sorts of systems related to other aspects of TUG's activities. Yet, there are good arguments and indicators that TeX's future has passed, and clearly its time as a leading edge system is perceived by most of the world as passed, if they ever heard of it at all. What is it about TeX and TUG that keeps you working so hard on their behalf?

KB: Much of the answer lies with Don Knuth. When I first read `tex.web`, *The TeXbook*, and his other articles, programs, and books (TeX-related or otherwise), something in me was very responsive to his goal of making a beautiful program that produces beautiful output — and then giving it to the world. I never met him (until very recently), but that didn't matter. Then when I came across Richard Stallman (`http://www.stallman.org`)'s writings a couple of years later, I realized again that I felt, personally, that free software like TeX simply has an ethical basis (`http://www.gnu.org/philosophy/why-free.html`) which proprietary software does not. I also appreciate and enjoy typesetting, book design, and letterforms, so working on TeX seemed a natural place where I could contribute to the world of free software.

Although those are reasons why I started with TeX, they are also reasons why I continue with it. The computer world (and the non-computer world, for that matter) has become increasingly dominated by a very few large companies, as I mentioned. TeX resists that; it is simultaneously very idiosyncratic and very useful, and the standards mavens hate that. I love it.

As well as such philosophical reasons, TeX continues to have a large user community; interacting with users, and being one myself, are certainly big positive factors. I would be uninterested in TeX if there weren't always new problems being posed and new users, and developers, arriving.

Ultimately, typesetting combines artistry and practicality, esthetics and communication. For me, it's been a fine way to spend the last 20 years or so. Maybe it'll remain viable for 20 more.

DW: Your GNU Friends interview tells us a good bit about your personal life up to three or four years ago. Will you please give a bit of an update? Also, are there other organizations you use your technical skills on behalf of and, if so, can you give us an example or two?

KB: The other primary group I spend time volunteering for is the GNU Project. Besides maintaining GNU Texinfo, GNU Hello (`http://www.gnu.org/software/hello`), and contributing to other packages, I work a fair amount with rms, evaluating new software packages offered to GNU, keeping old projects alive when maintainers move on, administering lots of GNU mailing lists and the GNU coding standards and maintainer documents (http://www.gnu.org/prep), etc.

Locally, I do a little volunteer work for the library (http://www.cooslibraries.org), currently including hosting a tiny web page about our audio book club (http://coosbayaudiobookclub.org). (Especially as audio books, some of my favorites have been *The Memory of Running* by Ron McLarty, *Prodigal Summer* by Barbara Kingsolver, and *Hearts in Atlantis* by Stephen King, all read by the authors.) I also try to help out the great local architect and contractor who built our house, Rick Howard (http://www.howard5.net), by running a small web site for his family's business.

As for my non-technical life, the biggest change was moving to that house on the Oregon coast full time last spring — here are a sampling of recent pictures (http://freefriends.org/~mare/andkarlbythesea), mostly taken by my wife Mare. However, soon we'll be coastal part-timers again; we're making plans to spend a good chunk of time each year in Seattle, to be closer to our grandson Benjamin as he grows up.

DW: I've spent a lot of time on the Oregon coast and in Seattle — they are both beautiful, and Seattle is not exactly without coast line. In any case, thank you very much for taking the time to do this interview. You've filled in a lot I personally did not know, and I trust for other readers as well.

KB: Thanks for giving me the opportunity — and for all the work (including this interview series) you yourself do for TeX and TUG.

Barbara Beeton

Barbara Beeton has been editor of *TUGboat* for 22 years and a member of the TUG Board since it was called the steering committee. She also serves as a liaison for TEXnical issues between Donald Knuth and the TEX community.

[Interview completed 24 November 2005.]

Dave Walden, interviewer: Please tell me a bit about your personal history independent of TEX.

Barbara Beeton, interviewee: After graduating from college (applied math and German literature), I worked for a year as gofer at the Brown University Computing Lab, then found, serendipitously, a position at the American Math Society, as assistant to the assistant to the Executive Director. This position had much to recommend it — independence in carrying out varied assignments, several of them associated with experimental projects including a pioneer effort to implement computer typesetting of math. Although that project ended without producing a complete production system, many of the ideas and techniques for encoding data became key components of later projects.

In spite of interesting projects, I came to feel that my brain was beginning to rot, and returned to school (still working full time) to pursue a master's degree in structural linguistics (completed and filed under 'hobbies' in my resumé).

When it became obvious that future management of the Society's records would best be served by keeping them on a computer, I was assigned to that project, being the only person at the Society with hands-on computer experience, however lowly. The initial task was to design the system — an amazing learning experience! In these early days, the AMS approach was basically to take people who knew how things worked at the Society, and provide the means to learn the necessary computer techniques. The first applications were business oriented, but because of the particular audience — professional mathematicians — a non-business project was a pioneer SDI (selective dissemination of information) effort, the Mathematical Offprint Service (MOS). This involved the presentation, including typesetting, of bibliographic data, and the choice of computer platform (an RCA Spectra) was ultimately made based on the presence of a typesetting program, PAGE-2.

This adventure involved more than just the mainframe. Along the way, we became adept at manipulating a minicomputer (first a BIT, then a Data General Nova) to which was attached a paper tape punch; paper tape, in turn, was used to drive a Photon 713 phototypesetter (the only way to communicate with it), loaded on a reader for transmission to a remote location (mostly for business data), or sent by courier to a typesetting service bureau. This motley array of mechanical devices was great fun to work with, if on occasion frustrating when things went south under deadline pressure.

This success in handling the bibliographic data from MOS, resulting in the publication of several indexes, was noticed by the *Mathematical Reviews* staff; *MR* had been publishing reviews of the mathematical literature since 1940, the volume of material was growing steadily, as was the cost of Monotype composition. PAGE-2 could be programmed to handle indexes, but the formatting of bibliographic information interspersed with review text was too complex, and a different approach was needed.

At about this time, the developer of a new math typesetting system, Science Typographers, Inc. (STI), approached AMS. Their software was found to meet the Society's needs for setting math text, although it lacked pagination capabilities, so pages had to be cut manually from galleys, mounted on boards, and headers and footers added by hand. However, this system could be run in-house, and mag tapes sent to a service bureau with a Harris Fototronic to produce photographic galleys. My contribution to this project was development of the local user interface, training the first keyboarders, and communicating with the developers. Input media included 80-column punched cards, OCR mini-barcodes, and more paper tape; we still hadn't reached the era of direct magnetic input.

DW: How did AMS get involved with TEX, and were you part of that effort from the beginning?

bb: The STI system I mentioned served AMS well for quite a few years, but in 1978, Donald Knuth was invited to deliver the Gibbs lecture at the AMS annual meeting. The topic he chose was "Mathematical Typography" — TEX and Metafont. The then-chair of the AMS Board of Trustees, Dick Palais, listened to Don's lecture, and interpreted what he heard as meaning that TEX was ready to run, out of the box. And, unlike the STI system, which was nearly inscrutable to anyone but a highly trained keyboarder, TEX was comprehensible to an ordinary mathematician. It sounded just the thing for production of AMS books and journals.

In addition to needing new composition software, the AMS was also looking for new hardware. We had been using an IBM 360 clone, an RCA Spectra 70 (later a Univac Series 70), which still depended on punched card input, had no native upper- and lowercase distinction, and was certainly no longer "state of the art". TEX was written for a DECSystem 10 at the Stanford Artificial Intelligence Lab (SAIL) and also ran on a DECSystem 20, an interactive time-sharing system with a scrutable operating system. This looked very promising. After making sure that all the existing business applications could be converted to run on this system, the smallest machine of the line was acquired and installed in the computer room alongside the Series 70, and the programming staff was sent off for training.

Although I had become a specialist in the composition activities, the first inkling I had of how deeply I would be involved in TEX was made clear in late spring 1979, when my boss, Sam Whidden, handed me a small book with a yellow and green cover (the first TEX manual), a plane ticket, and a list of addresses. He told me to "go to Stanford, learn TEX, bring it back, and make it work."

After I finished reading the manual, I gathered samples of both typical material and some especially nasty problems encountered with earlier composition software — running heads on multi-column pages, bad breaks at ends of lines and at the bottoms of columns, uneven columns, and the like. These were mostly in administrative publications, not math journals, since that is where the need for a new composition system was greatest. I got on the plane with all of this, and during the flight, read the manual again.

A small group of TEX initiates gathered at Stanford, and settled into a rented house on the campus. The group included Dick Palais, Mike Spivak, and several others, who were to address particular tasks such as creating an AMS-specific user interface, which became AMSTEX.

I was put in the care of David Fuchs (DRF), one of Don's graduate students in the TEX project. He sat me in front of a terminal on the SAIL computer, brought up the Emacs tutorial, and told me to learn it. (I've never looked back.)

While at Stanford, I had relatively free access to Don, and with his help, addressed the problems I had brought with me. He patiently worked through them with me, occasionally stopping to make modifications to the TEX source code when something exceeded its capabilities. My little green and yellow manual has, in Don's handwriting, the first description of the `\firstmark` command, which is needed to get the proper material into the running head for the left-hand column of an index. And many of the other problems are addressed in Appendix D of *The TEXbook* (dirty tricks). (I really am quite proud of my ability to choose "good bad examples" which stretch a program and not only help in the creation of good specs, but also are useful for ongoing testing during development.)

I also became familiar with the various output devices that were available, since the whole purpose of typesetting is to generate documents that can be printed.

After the month at Stanford, I brought back a tape containing the current version of TEX, and installed it on the new DEC 20. We didn't have any output device yet, but later that summer DRF came to Providence to install a newly arrived Benson Varian 9211, an electrostatic printer which used roll paper that felt rather slimy, and liquid toner that adhered to spots energized by a comb apparatus through which the electric charge was fed selectively. Since this device had a resolution of 200 dots per inch, all output was generated at a 130% magnification, to be photographically reduced to final size for the press.

The first publication generated by TEX was the 1980–1981 edition of the Society's Combined Membership List. This was a multi-column document with data generated from a database — a perfect task for a batch system. For this first iteration, the Computer Modern fonts were used, but they proved to be too space-hungry. For the next edition, a "tphon" font was developed; this was an especially compact and narrow font based on the Computer Modern sans serif, but adding serifs to the capital I so it could be distinguished from lowercase ell and digit one. (Later, the commercial Bell Centennial fonts, designed specifically for use in directories, were obtained for this use, but that's another story.)

By the end of 1980, a slick new typesetter was installed — an Alphatype CRS, with a resolution of 5333 dpi. DRF was responsible for the driver software; this was a duplicate of the machine on which the camera copy for the five volumes of *Computers & Typesetting* series was generated. For quite a few years, we replicated the setup at Stanford to ensure that someone else would be familiar with the hardware in case something went wrong.

We didn't start to produce journals with TEX until TEX82 was stable. For much of this period, I was the principal, though no longer the sole, developer of style files.

DW: Wow! What a fascinating story.

My impression is that you have been involved with a lot of other TEX and TUG activities: *TUGboat* editor since its very early days (I'm not clear what the division of responsibility was between you and Robert Welland in the earliest issues), on the TUG board from its inception and on the steering committee before that, conduit to Donald Knuth for TEX bugs, keeping of the hyphenation exception list, at least close to the TUG office when it was at the AMS, etc. (I'm sorry if I missed a major area of TEX or TUG activity.) Can you tell us something about each of these, and any others, and how it came about?

bb: Sam Whidden, who was head of the Information Systems Development department at AMS (my boss), was concerned that, since there wasn't a commercial organization with a stake in TEX, there would come a time when Don returned to other research, and there would be no one to go to for support. Users would be essentially on their own. For this reason, it was in the users' interest to band together for the general good. An exploratory meeting was held at Stanford in February 1980, attended by about 50 people, and the framework of the TUG organization was established.

Because the AMS had such a strong interest in the success of TeX, and because TeX had been unveiled at an AMS annual meeting, the facilities of the Society were offered for the TUG headquarters and AMS staff time was allocated for production of the newsletter. Sam accepted the position of Treasurer. Since I had been involved from the start, and was volunteered to be the newsletter production crew, I was appointed to the Steering Committee.

Bob Welland, as the initial editor of *TUGboat*, collected material and shipped it to Providence for production of the newsletter. (*TUGboat* didn't graduate to being a "journal" until 1988. Even now, it's subtitled the "Communications of the TeX Users Group".) Bob didn't intend this to be a permanent position, and he "retired" after three years. In the absence of other obvious candidates, I assumed the editor's position as of the second issue of volume 4. Although the length of my tenure can be ascribed partly to inertia, and lack of planning for succession, it's been a challenging and enjoyable ride. I've learned a very great deal from this experience, and met many really wonderful people.

Probably because of my position on the TUG board and as editor of *TUGboat*, which enabled me to meet nearly all the key people in the TeX community, and because I had become a fixture at AMS, in little danger of disappearing, Don designated me to be what I like to refer to as his "TeX entomologist", i.e., bug collector. He has my address listed on his TeX web page, along with a schedule of when he will next look at accumulated reports. I collect reports as they come to me, and, after a cursory check to see if the topic has been submitted previously, farm them out to volunteers (approved by Don) who vet them. This process involves verifying that the problem is really a bug, and not a feature or user error, and the resulting report is returned to the submitter; often, when a bug really is found, the vetter provides code that might be used in repairing the relevant program. When Don is ready to look at the collection, he has his secretary request them. I organize the reports by topic, distill them to eliminate redundancy, and ship the file off by e-mail to his secretary. She, in turn, prints them out, and Don reviews and annotates the paper copy, making changes in his source code as necessary, or explaining briefly why something isn't going to be changed, and compiles a list of rewards due. He writes out whatever checks are required, and his secretary ships the annotated paper and the checks back to me for distribution. Before returning the annotated reports (and possibly checks) to the submitters, I transcribe the notes (always handwritten in pencil) into a copy of the file I sent out, so there is a history that can be passed on to the other implementors and researched when future bug reports are submitted. When I'm finished the transcription and mailing, I send the report to a list of TeX implementors for their information.

The hyphenation exception list just sort of happened. Problems encountered with books and journals set at AMS were reported to the TeXnical staff, and we started keeping a list. Since I also like to play with words, it became a bit of a game to see if I could identify similar words that had problems, and figure out why some did and some didn't. The mathematical words yielded a list that was included in the AMS-LaTeX document classes, and it seemed useful to publish the entire list in *TUGboat*. Once people saw the list, they added to it, and we've ended up with what's there today.

As for interaction with the TUG office, it started out in a corner of the AMS headquarters, and used the AMS computer hardware; avoiding contact was next to impossible. When AMS needed the space, the TUG office moved up the hill to a rehabbed fire station, where it occupied the second floor and the old hose tower. After several years in that location, and changes in personnel, there was a need for someone new in charge of the office; the office moved from Providence to be where the new manager was located. With more changes in elected TUG officers and office personnel, the physical location of the office is now in Portland, Oregon. Although I remain in Providence, I've kept in close contact with the TUG office, and still hold some of the ancient archives, both electronic and on paper. It's useful when various ideas are discussed to be able to say, well, this was tried before, and here's what happened. We can learn from history, to decide whether to repeat something in different circumstances, or go in another direction. I hope and believe that this "institutional memory" is useful.

DW: As someone who has been so broadly and deeply involved in the TEX community for so much of its history, I'm interested in what you see as the major eras of development of TEX and the TEX community.

bb: Good question. I've never actually given that much thought; I've just accepted developments as they've come along.

As for TEX itself, there are several distinct tracks. First, there are the changes made by Don himself. These seem to me to be the following:

- TEX82 — conversion from the SAIL language to Pascal;
- further conversion to the WEB language and literate programming;
- TEX 3.0, with adaptations to better handle non-English text.

Now that TEX itself is frozen, extensions to the core program may no longer be called TEX, but there are some significant ones:

- pdfTeX, which generates PDF output directly, and provides various microtypographical niceties;
- Omega, which is based on Unicode, allowing more natural processing of multilingual text.

There were great hopes for NTS (the "new typesetting system"), but it looks at the moment like a dead end.

In the complex superstructure built up around TEX, I think LATEX is the most obvious success story. Although I have some reservations about its details, the concept of logical structuring is a winner, and the fact that it's been so widely adopted means that there's a critical mass of users that makes it worthwhile for publishers to support its use and undertake further development.

Similarly, ConTEXt, although with a shorter history, has made a stunning entrance in large part based on pdfTEX.

It's perhaps obvious, but many of these developments couldn't have taken place without the arrival of some important technologies:

- functional, inexpensive laser printers and imagesetters;
- the PostScript and pdf languages.

The personal computer also made it possible for anyone, not just the well-connected or well-heeled, to have access to these tools.

The original TEX community consisted of relatively few individuals, widely scattered, mostly in academic settings. The banding together of users into many formal groups, often based on a common language, has been a major force toward ensuring the continued viability of TEX. In turn, these groups have promoted TEX's adoption in environments other than the academic one. We all know that there are still many users who don't belong to any group. Encouraging their participation and sharing of their skills and experience can only widen everyone's horizons.

DW: As we have been communicating about this interview, you mentioned your involvement in the STIX fonts project. I gather that you are doing this as part of your job at AMS. While it is not exactly part of TEX, it is still related to typesetting, and I am interesting in what dealing with Unicode has been like.

bb: I had represented AMS in an ISO working group, trying to create an international font standard, for almost ten years; this was the result of a recommendation by one of Don Knuth's colleagues at Stanford. So when the STIX project was started, I was familiar both with standards bodies and with how those bodies viewed the difference between characters (an encoding) and glyphs (in fonts).

In fact, the Unicode Technical Committee (UTC) operates in a manner very similar to an ISO working group, except that their work is able to be done without formal mail ballots by national standards groups, as there is only a single Unicode committee involved. However, since the character content of Unicode ultimately becomes the ISO encoding standard 10646, the rules for accepting and encoding new characters are just as stringent. The members of the UTC have varying backgrounds—linguistic, scientific, computing—but they are all very smart and very knowledgeable in their fields.

Although by Unicode version 3 there was a fairly large complement of characters for math and other technical areas, it didn't include all the symbols that come "standard" with TEX, much less the many additional ones included in the fonts used by the STIX organizations.

The first group of symbols submitted to the UTC was just "symbols". However, the scientists in the group realized that was only part of the problem. Letters, in different styles and alphabets, are used to represent variables, and substituting a roman letter for the "same" script letter will change the meaning of a formula quite radically. These "mathematical alphanumerics" were accepted into Unicode, but placed in plane 1, where they aren't as likely to be misused for, e.g., wedding invitations. This Unicode work has been reported at `http://www.ams.org/STIX`.

The STIX project has now progressed to the point where most of the new symbols have been created and placed in preliminary fonts for review. (I've been the person at AMS responsible for reviewing the material and providing comments when adjustments are needed.) Only a couple hundred more symbols are still awaiting delivery from the font contractor, after which a full design review will be undertaken, followed by final corrections, packaging, and creation of (LA)TEX support. This phase of the project is reported at `http://www.stixfonts.org`.

DW: Do you have thoughts you'd care to share on your view of TEX's future, both at the AMS and in general?

bb: TEX isn't about to go away. There isn't anything anywhere close to the horizon that can handle publication-quality math as well. Publishers such as the AMS will continue using TEX (or a related successor) for a long time.

TEX is also very suitable for batch processing and other applications (such as preparing custom documents from a database) where it can be used "under the covers". The latter approach is used by the German railroads to generate custom timetables, as reported in my column in *TUGboat* 24:3. It is also the basis of a new free web office suite, gOffice (`http://goffice.com`). And there have been presentations at several TUG meetings about similar uses in the insurance industry. These kinds of applications will continue to use TEX, at least in part because it's free and reliable.

Free, reliable and eminently math-aware are also the reasons that graduate students in math, the hard sciences, and linguistics will continue to use TEX to prepare their dissertations.

One ever present conundrum is, how to make these audiences more aware of the existence of TEX, and encourage them to be active in TEX organizations? I don't know the answer. But I do know that if this can be accomplished, it will help ensure that TEX remains alive for quite a long time to come.

DW: Unless you think there is a question I should have asked or that you'd like to answer that I haven't asked, I will stop asking questions and close now.

bb: I suspect that everyone who's read this far is bored to tears, so I'll mention just one that I get asked from time to time — why I usually answer e-mail in all lowercase. I've been using computers since the days of punched cards. When terminals with upper/lowercase distinction and e-mail became available, so many people were used to the single case mode that they automatically switched on the caps lock. This seemed to me too much like shouting. Although I'm a person of strong opinions, I try not to shout, so I adopted the all-lowercase mode as (over)compensation. (That doesn't mean I don't pay attention to proper spelling and grammar.) These days, it still serves a useful purpose: I will answer with my own opinions in lowercase, but for really "official" communications, when I am speaking on behalf of AMS or TUG, I will use both upper- and lowercase. Anyone who's familiar with my idiosyncrasies will therefore know when I'm making an official "pronouncement".

DW: Thank you very much for taking the time to participate in this interview, and thank you for your detailed and fascinating descriptions. I greatly admire and appreciate all that you have done for the world of TEX over so many years.

Frank Mittelbach

Frank Mittelbach has been the leader of the LaTeX Project for many years.

[Interview completed 7 February 2006.]

[Background of this unusual double interview: the *Free Software Magazine* (`http://www.freesoftwaremagazine.com`) and the TeX Users Group (TUG) both like to publish interviews. By chance, Gianluca Pignalberi of *FSM* and Dave Walden of TUG both approached Frank Mittelbach about interviewing him around the same time. Rather than doing two separate interviews, Mittelbach, Pignalberi, and Walden decided on a combined interview in keeping with the mutual interests already shared by *FSM* and TUG.]

Dave Walden, interviewer: Please start by telling us a bit about yourself and how you got involved with LaTeX.

Frank Mittelbach, interviewee: I have lived with my family in Mainz (Germany) since the early eighties, i.e., by now the larger part of my life. Besides my primary hobby (typography), which can effectively be called my second job, I enjoy playing good board games, listening to jazz music, and reading (primarily English literature). Professionally I work for Electronic Data Systems where these days I'm responsible for concepts and implementation for remote monitoring and management of distributed systems and networks.

While I was studying Mathematics and Computer Science at the Gutenberg-University Mainz, I was first introduced to TeX and later LaTeX and, eventually, this got me interested in typesetting and in particular in research on algorithms for automated high quality typesetting.

During my student days in the eighties, a friend brought back a source tape from Stanford University containing something like TeX 1.1 and fascinating news about the quality of that program (back then we did our theses using a typewriter and either hand-pasting symbols or, in case of some sophisticated IBM typewriter, changing the "ball" every couple of seconds). He tried to implement that program on the Multics system we had at the university and in fact succeeded — probably the first if not the only implementation of TeX on this operating system.

In this way I was introduced to TeX and AMSTeX and typed my first paper, achieving beautiful results. The only catch was that back then the Stanford tape only contained Almost Computer Modern fonts in 200 dpi resolution (and no METAFONT) and the only graphical printing device available to us had a resolution of 72 dpi. So the output we got was of the size of the formula in the middle of this paragraph (or bigger) — wonderful to plaster the walls, but not necessarily suitable for handing in your thesis. As a result, my friend finally had to type his diploma thesis in the traditional way, despite his efforts.

$$\sum_{i=1}^{n} x_i$$

Sometime afterwards I was asked by the department to install a commercial TeX product on our shiny new PCs and to give a series of lectures to students and professors on how to use it. And that distribution came with LaTeX 2.08 and a loose-bound copy of the manual (which later became Leslie Lamport's book on LaTeX). LaTeX compared to plain TeX looked very good to me, but alas, when trying to produce any document with it, it died while loading the "article document style" due to running out of memory on those PCs. So my introduction to LaTeX stopped after I read the manual, and I was forced to develop my own TeX macro package that implemented similar concepts while requiring less memory. A year later it became possible to actually use LaTeX at the department, and we could retire my macro package.

But this initial exercise gave me a good insight into the inner workings and concepts of a system like LaTeX and enabled me later to constructively criticize certain aspects of LaTeX—something that eventually led to Leslie passing on the development and maintenance of LaTeX to me.

Gianluca Pignalberi, interviewer: Many of our readers are familiar with LaTeX, but for those who aren't, can you introduce LaTeX to our readers?

FM: LaTeX is a batch-oriented typesetting system that uses the typesetting engine TeX or one of its variants (ε-TeX, pdfTeX, Omega).

The TeX program itself (developed by Professor Donald Knuth in the early eighties) is a programmable low-level typesetting engine whose concepts and algorithms provide micro-typographic[1] knowledge of highest quality in these days when this knowledge is slowly declining due to the fact that more and more authors are forced to become their own designer and typesetter without proper training. TeX is especially known for its excellent paragraph breaking algorithm and for its math formula typesetting capabilities, both of which are unsurpassed even though the program and its algorithms have been freely available for more than twenty years.

LaTeX is a macro package written for the TeX engine which allows the user to step back from the low-level formatting capabilities of TeX by providing higher-level interfaces that give the author the ability to mark up the text with logical markup rather than procedural markup (e.g., specifying that something is a list or a section, rather than stating that something should be set in a bold typeface with a little space above and below). The actual transformation of a LaTeX source into a typeset document is done with the help of "style sheets" and configuration adjustments that allow even radical changes to the design and layout in a consistent manner without touching or changing the source. (Well, ideally, but see below.)

Historically speaking, LaTeX was largely influenced by a system called Scribe (by Brian Reid). In turn, LaTeX's concept of logical markup was quite influential on HTML and various SGML/XML DTDs, as were its approaches for turning such logical markup into visual representation.

One of the differences between LaTeX and many other similar approaches is that the LaTeX language is in fact a community development: new packages that augment (or modify) LaTeX's markup and typesetting functionalities are constantly appearing, so that these days LaTeX offers typesetting solutions for nearly every subject domain—as diverse as game typesetting (such as chess, go, or crossword puzzles), chemical formulas, or music. Another important difference is that, although LaTeX brought the concept of logical markup to a larger audience, it also provides ways to fine-tune the results (essentially

[1]Micro-typography is concerned with the detailed aspects of type and spacing, e.g., the kerning (shortening or enlarging space) between letters, generation and placement of ligatures, line breaking, etc. In contrast, macro-typography is concerned with larger structures, such as the design of headings, lists, or pages.

providing interfaces to procedural markup), acknowledging the fact that no automated transformation of logical markup into a visual representation is able to automatically resolve all problems produced by the physical restrictions of the output format (e.g., line width or page size). While in certain applications such fine tuning adds no value (like database content publishing where full automation is required), it is crucial for typesetting high quality books and journal articles.

GP: How many people are officially part of the LaTeX Project? And how would you define the "LaTeX project"?

FM: The LaTeX Project Team is a fairly small (slowly changing) group of people who look after the LaTeX kernel and a small number of core packages that provide a stable basis for a huge number of constantly evolving packages and add-ons. Providing and guarding a stable core is (although not necessarily popular with everyone) an important part in keeping LaTeX alive as a language for document exchange. Current and past members of the team include Javier Bezos, Johannes Braams, David Carlisle, Michael Downes, Denys Duchier, Robin Fairbairns, Morten Høgholm, Alan Jeffrey, Thomas Lotze, Chris Rowley, Rainer Schöpf, and Martin Schröder with varying degrees of involvement.

Historically, the project took over maintenance and development of LaTeX 2.09 from Leslie Lamport in 1991. At one time the system was split into several incompatible variants that often prohibited successful processing by LaTeX at one site of documents created by LaTeX from a different site, even though system independence was originally one of the important goals of LaTeX as a documentation language for the scientific community. Another goal for the team was to address apparent deficiencies in the concepts of LaTeX 2.09. The project team addressed both issues in the early nineties with LaTeX 2_ε which provided a stable and consolidated platform that offered further development possibilities outside the kernel code.

Although LaTeX 2_ε already addressed most, if not all, of the deficiencies identified in the first decade of LaTeX 2.09 use, it was originally thought that LaTeX 2_ε would only be an intermediate step towards a LaTeX3 version. But over time it became clearer and clearer that the remaining open questions could not be adequately resolved within the constraints of: a) TeX as the underlying formatting engine, and b) no changes in the fundamental concepts deployed in LaTeX.

As a result, most of the efforts in the recent years by members of the LaTeX team have gone into research on features desirable for the underlying formatter engines as well as in development of experimental languages and concepts for a designer's interface to typesetting — a level of abstraction that is largely missing from today's LaTeX (which currently often requires TeX programming).

So one definition of the LaTeX project these days would be that it works on providing the foundation for the core concepts and implementation of a new typesetting system that is based upon the good aspects of LaTeX 2_ε (e.g., logical markup, extensibility), but that on the code level is not necessarily focused on providing compatibility. At the document syntax level the situation is clearly different, as reuse of older documents is certainly an important goal. But even there, the main focus will be on clean concepts and as a result compatibility may be restricted in certain cases to providing support for automated conversion.

DW: You have a long history in the world of TeX for collaborative work, e.g., famously with Rainer Schöpf in the early days of LaTeX. You must enjoy working collaboratively. Tell us a bit about your approaches to collaborative work.

FM: I do indeed like to collaborate and over the years worked successfully with many different people (on various topics and in different subject domains). For me the main value of collaboration is during the development of ideas which, in my experience, are best produced in an open exchange. My mental picture here is a table tennis or similar game which only develops if one directly reacts to whatever your counterpart thinks of and "picks up the ball as played". People who have worked with me know that I like white board drawing sessions (I do need to visualize while I play along) and brainstorming and mind mapping methods.

But I'm also a stickler for details and can spend a lot of energy and effort in actually finishing something (to my own satisfaction) when I consider it worthwhile. Collaboration on that level — after the initial concept and design development work has finished and the nitty gritty detail work starts — normally takes one of two forms: either I restrict myself largely to mentoring and let others work on actual implementations, or I put so much energy into a certain task that it outweighs other people's involvement by a large factor. My base motto here is "Es gibt nichts Gutes, außer man tut es" (free translation: Nothing good will come into existence unless you actually do it) by Erich Kästner which at least in the German language nicely rhymes.

A lot of collaboration necessarily happens via email (due to living in different countries, etc.), but I find it extremely valuable to interrupt this method of working at irregular intervals with face-to-face meetings to flesh out ideas and make them concrete enough to go ahead for a while in semi-isolation with only email and or phone calls as the means of "direct" communication. This also explains why most of the more fundamental work that is associated with Rainer Schöpf's and my names dates from the time when we both studied at the University and had a chance for a more regular exchange of ideas in front of white boards (drinking gallons of tea).

In general I think that Frederick Brooks is right when he argues in *The Mythical Man-Month* [4] that to run a successful software project you need a fairly small and structured team that is responsible for making the final design decisions. Large scale "committee" design only leads to bad results by compromising too much between different factions or by incorporating incompatible design concepts.

GP: TeX is widely considered the best typesetting system, but professional typesetters seem to prefer using commercial, visual software. Why would you advise them to use LaTeX instead of another system? Or, conversely, why not?

FM: There is no doubt that TeX has superior qualities in a number of areas compared to other typesetting systems (e.g., paragraph breaking quality, or math formula presentation, etc.). But it was designed as a batch processing program, that is, it does not allow for direct interaction with the user. In WYSIWYG typesetting systems the user can make visual corrections which are then instantaneously reflected, while with TeX (or LaTeX) you have to modify your source, and then reprocess and check that your correction produced the desired result.

Especially in the last stage of book production, TeX's tendency for making far reaching changes to achieve high quality can actually be a hindrance rather than an asset (at least if you do not account for it and adjust your working method). For example, due to global optimization in paragraph breaking, a *removal* of a single word in one paragraph will usually result in a complete reflow of the whole paragraph and might in fact make the paragraph even one line *longer* because TeX decided that a slightly looser setting of all lines produces the best possible solution. If this happens when correcting last-minute typos in an otherwise finally formatted document, it can be rather annoying.

Most graphic designers and professional typesetters are used to working visually with immediate feedback and control, so for them systems like LaTeX appear difficult to handle and they do not see any benefit in this unfamiliar working model.

Whether or not the use of LaTeX would be advisable really depends on the job at hand and cannot be answered without context. In a nutshell I would suggest using LaTeX or a similar system whenever one or more of the following factors play an important role in the job:

- User's preference is to think in logical structures
- Designs that require consistency
- Documents whose designs are not yet fully defined or that need to be presented in several layouts in parallel
- Documents that require high-quality paragraph breaking
- Documents that contain heavy mathematics
- Automatically produced content (e.g., from databases)
- Long material

On the other hand, the following factors move the balance towards using a (good quality!) visually oriented system:

- User's preference is to think in visual structures
- User not at all comfortable working with programming languages (a high-level front end for TeX, e.g., LaTeX or ConTeXt, helps here but ...)
- Designs that require a lot of visual flexibility rather than consistency (e.g., headings are designed one-off according to nearby objects)
- Designs that require text to flow around arbitrary shapes (TeX is simply not designed for this)
- Designs that change the horizontal measure from column to column
- Short material

What actually tips the balance may differ in different circumstances; for example, in *The LaTeX Companion* [9] with its nearly 1000 in-line examples, it was an enormous plus to be able to redesign example layout without touching the individual examples.

DW: Is there any relationship between TUG, DANTE, or any of the other TeX user groups and the LaTeX Project, and how might the user groups help maintain the viability of TeX and its derivatives?

FM: The relationship between the LaTeX project and TeX user groups can probably be best described as loose and informal. Several project team activities have been supported in one way or the other by a user group (e.g., by providing meeting space at a conference), but most LaTeX team activities have drawn on non-user-group resources such as support from ZDV (the computing laboratory at the Gutenberg University Mainz), royalty payments from *The LaTeX Companion*, and to a small extent from individual user contributions. The biggest joint venture with a user group was probably the development of a model for a set of extended math fonts, where the French user group financed a student for three months to work with me on this topic. The outcome of this work [13] is now finally bearing some fruits as it helped in developing the STIX fonts.

However, the user groups are extremely important to projects such as the LaTeX Project in that they provide a research framework for contacts and face-to-face discussion at conferences and journal publications. This aspect of providing a research framework cannot be underestimated; and, if the user groups would become unable to provide it, it might eventually result in the death of the community. I certainly enjoy (and I'm sure so do others) the fruitful exchange that is only possible in such a framework.

The question about what the user groups long term can do to sustain the viability of TEX and its derivatives is difficult to answer — I'm unfortunately not sure the user groups themselves will survive in the long run. The role of the user organizations has changed over the last two decades. In the beginning, just getting a TEX system installed was a major effort, and user groups were formed by interested people to help each other and exchange knowledge and ideas, and to support development effort. Back then the role of the user groups was fairly clear and the benefit for each member was immediately visible, e.g., obtaining information otherwise not available, getting help, etc.

Over time, access to a TEX installation and all its accompanying goodies (such as LATEX packages, etc.) has drastically changed — nowadays installations are prepackaged, access to all software is available in large archives, and there is much more documentation available. As a result, the typical (LA)TEX user has no need to understand the underlying mechanisms and isn't (unfortunately) any longer interested in sharing in their development — the users have largely changed from actively participating members of a group of like-minded people excited by the possibility of doing high-quality typesetting to consumers of a "finished product" who get very upset if the product does not do precisely what they want it to do. For this new kind of users, the user groups do not play an important role since, at this point in time, the user groups have no resources to actually help individuals with their problems.

This is somewhat ironic, since it was largely members of the user groups that initiated all the changes that now appear to be leading to the downfall of user groups' accepted mission and reason for existence in the eyes of the average user.

In theory, I think the best way that user groups could help these days would be in the following areas:

- Recruiting and providing the resources that keep the "product" alive and well-maintained
- Providing a suitable forum for the active development community
- Obtaining and managing research funds
- Attracting new users to broaden the base

Unfortunately none of this is easily achievable. It would need an amount of capital (and resources) noticeably beyond what is currently available to the groups, and it is not clear that this — as a charter — will attract enough new members who then could share those costs. After all, to most people the "product" and its support appear to be available free of charge, so today's consumer thinking is: "Why pay a (substantial) recurring membership fee when all that is needed is connecting to the Internet and asking a question on `comp.text.tex` or downloading some software from CTAN? — I don't go to those conferences 'they' go to, so why should I finance 'them'?" It would be necessary to break that thinking and make people understand why the user groups nevertheless are beneficial for them; but unfortunately many people take a free lunch if they can get it, without considering the consequences.

GP: Your project generated a license: the LATEX Project Public License. Thanks to the last modifications to it, LATEX can be considered a real free software. How did this fact improve the diffusion of such a tool?

FM: To be honest I always considered and still consider LATEX *real free software* regardless of the license under which it was distributed in the past or is distributed now. The term "free" has definitely different meanings for different people, and I do not necessarily agree with the understanding of some people that their freedom to be able to arbitrarily change things without any restrictions should be considered a more important good than the right of others to get what they expect when they use a certain product.

LaTeX is not just a single user product but a language being used for communication of information, and one of the important points here is that it enables processing a document at different sites with identical results, provided that the same version of LaTeX is used. This is a feature a large proportion of the community is relying on, so the original LPPL (LaTeX Project Public License) [3] in a nutshell said: do whatever you like with file X but if you change it (i.e., modify its behavior in the system) change its name to something else, so that people relying on the communication feature of LaTeX will not be affected by your modification.

Technically, this allowed for any modification and any desired change, but it gave the people using LaTeX a conscious choice to apply a changed version to their documents or not. In some cases it would have meant some extra effort for the person doing modifications but on the whole I feel it provided a nice balance between the people who think "free" means their right to change what they like and people who think they have a right to a reliable means of communicating information.

However, some developers in the free software community think that such a simple rule restricts their rights too much (not being able to change things in arbitrary ways, including ways that hide the modification to later users — even if that is not the intention), and so a discussion started about whether or not such a rule makes software non-free — the main obstacle for many being the requirement to change names if you change content. Clearly, this requirement is quite different from those posed by the majority of free software licenses, but then those licenses have been written with quite a different software model in mind (one where the focus lies on individual software components where differences at different sites do not restrict the usability of the software).[2] But since we were not interested in enforcing a name change per se (even though we still think that it mediates nicely between all different needs), I entered a longish discussion with debian-legal and, as a result, we came up with a new license which softened this requirement while still preserving the community need for stability and reliability. In essence I think the new license is better in many parts (and I'm very grateful for some folks from debian-legal helping achieve this), but it is also, perhaps unnecessarily, more complex than it could have been in other parts. In the TeX world, the original license was trying to codify what was standard and accepted behavior, i.e., when you changed or improved a package you called the result something else so that older documents would compile as expected while newer ones could make use of extended or changed features and both could co-exist.

So did the license improve the diffusion of the tools? As far as the TeX world as such is concerned, I would say "no", as even the original license was already simply codifying what most people thought to be a good model for software in the TeX domain. As to the wider world of free software in general, the modifications probably helped people to understand that LaTeX and friends are also "free" software and provided common ground for some understanding that different usage requirements may need somewhat different interpretations of "free" to be useful.

GP: Are you (or were you, or will you be) involved in other free software projects?

FM: The answer to this probably depends on the definition of the terms "project" and "involvement". Many of my interests these days are of a more theoretical nature and will

[2]For a discussion of why we think that something like the GPL is not a good licensing model for free languages, which is one aspect of LaTeX, see [2].

not necessarily directly lead to software or not to software where I will directly participate in implementations; and those projects where I most likely will participate could be labeled under the broad heading of (LA)TEX development. For example, just a couple of weeks ago Hàn Thế Thành (the main developer of pdfTEX), Morten Høgholm, and I spent a productive weekend at my home working on ideas for grid typesetting (which describes designs that are based on an invisible underlying grid restricting the placement (and size) of objects); so, even if I most likely will not participate in actual implementations, there is and will be involvement in projects outside of LATEX. And who knows, as I'm doing completely different work in my professional life, perhaps that too one day will lead to one or another free software package in that area.

DW: You, among others, have written about the need to move beyond the limitations of TEX and suggested improved approaches. In your biography in *The LATEX Companion* [9] you say you want to work at bringing extensions such as Omega and ε-TEX together as a base for an actual LATEX 3. Obviously, you have a track record for accomplishing big, complex, TEXy projects. Do you envision getting involved with something like the $\varepsilon_{\mathcal{X}}$TEX project or starting your own low-level implementation project for an enhanced TEX?

FM: When I wrote "E-TEX: Guidelines for future TEX extensions" [7] in 1990, the time was not yet ripe for improving TEX, and many people actually considered it an affront to Don that I suggested there could be something worth improving in his product (I remember, for example, public musing about strange theories from unknown and obscure German typographers — well, those "strange theories" had been suggested to me by none other than Hermann Zapf, who, though German, may not be precisely called unknown let alone obscure). But be that as it may, what I was challenging in that paper was the typesetting quality at the micro-typography level; but, as TEX was technically so much better than anything else at that time, my challenge was probably premature, and it took nearly a decade until the first real experiments were conducted on that level and moved things ahead in that domain (largely with the development of experimental versions of pdfTEX but also experimental code by others, e.g., Matthias Clasen).

When discussing improvements to TEX one needs to distinguish three largely disjunct areas. First is the area of the programming language and the fact that this language is incomplete and for certain tasks difficult to use (or, as some people state, "a mess"). On that level (without diverting from the fundamental paradigms of TEX), extensions like ε-TEX and to some extent Omega tried to ease the programming task by providing missing primitives that bridge the obvious gaps in the base language. But since such additional functionality was only easing the programmer's life without actually improving the typeset results and the function of (nearly) all the new primitives could be achieved with some extra effort in the base language, we decided to stay away from them in the LATEX development as their use would have resulted in a LATEX version that would then only run on a small fraction of the installations without any practical gain for the user. The LATEX Project together with people from ConTEXt and ε-TEX actually made some effort to produce an enriched syntax definition for ε-TEX [5] that we thought would provide enough benefits to switch to a TEX successor implementing this extended set. Sadly, shortly after this proposal, work on ε-TEX effectively came to a standstill, and so none of this was ever implemented. Nevertheless, something has changed since then: the installed base of ε-TEX-enabled installations did grow beyond critical mass (largely because of pdfTEX which included the ε-TEX extensions), so that some time ago the LATEX Project officially announced that it will base future LATEX versions on this extended set of primitives — and recently started to actually produce code that made use of these extended features (although so far only outside the kernel code). In essence we never wanted to go away from being able to have LaTeX run "out of the box" on a large base of installed interpreter programs and valued this higher than a potentially easier or better adjusted programming language that nearly nobody could use.[3] So instead of only trying to influence the TeX language by extending it, I and some others in the LaTeX Project also worked from the inside by developing the "Experimental LaTeX programming language" [6]. This was done over several prototypes, the first already done in 1993 or so; and the current version is something we think can be successfully used and we have started to provide the first public packages in this language [1].

The second area is the one dealing with micro-typography issues, e.g., those that I was mainly concerned with when discussing shortcomings of TeX in [7]. In this area my involvement was largely confined to initiating work by others.

The third area is the one that concerns itself with the generally open and unsolved questions of computer typography, e.g., models for representation of logical [8] and visual content material [12]; transformation between logical and visual representation using automated methods that nevertheless provide highest quality according to a defined metric [10] to give some examples. Part of that research is to understand and codify typography rules and to develop concepts and algorithms that can be driven by parameterized rules, e.g., to produce high-quality float placement.

Do I envision starting my own low-level implementation project to improve on TeX? Most certainly not, but I do envision getting (re)involved with the developments currently happening and hope to bring some of those developments together. Whether this will be in a project like $\varepsilon_{\mathcal{X}}$TeX or pdfTeX is largely irrelevant. At this point in time there are still many unresolved questions, and it is still the time for experiments (which may happen in different projects in parallel), but one important goal would be to bring the various developers together to talk to each other about their ideas and the concepts behind the ideas.

GP: You mentioned two operating systems LaTeX was ported to, and we know it runs on several free and non-free (whether commercial or not) OSes. Which kind of OSes and programs do you mainly use? And why?

FM: To be precise, LaTeX is interpreted so it is not software that needs porting to any OS; LaTeX runs everywhere where TeX has been ported to — and TeX to my knowledge has been ported to more or less every operating system ever in existence (with the exception of something like the Palm OS), e.g., I have used it on mainframes, VMS, Unix, Multics, and Windows.

I use both free and commercial operating systems; it largely depends on the environment and the task at hand. At home I run mainly Linux with VMware to access certain programs only available on Windows. On my laptop the situation is reversed: here I run XP native and use Cygwin for a decent command line environment with all the benefits of a good Unix system. My favorite editor is Emacs which I use on nearly every platform. I like to structure things using mind maps and here the only really good program I found is commercial and works only on Windows — it is one of the reasons that these days I use Windows fairly regularly.

In the professional world, where I earn my living, the predominant OS on the desktop

[3] I learned that this is a critical factor when we tried to introduce LaTeX 2_ε in 1994 which required the installation of T1 encoded fonts (i.e., fonts containing characters with diacritics). The switch to the new system nearly collapsed because users in the US saw absolutely no benefit in a system that contained all these useless characters only needed by Europeans. Fortunately enough, LaTeX 2_ε had other benefits that eventually won over nearly all LaTeX users, but it was a close shave.

is Windows; and in the server world you'll find commercial Unix variants but also a growing number of Linux servers.

What I use depends largely on the task at hand: for some, e.g., project management, the Windows world simply offers the better tools; in others free software (running on commercial or free OSes) provides better quality or features otherwise not available. Examples would be Perl, Apache, CVS, Subversion, and others.

DW: I remember Knuth saying that writing *The TEXbook* led to hundreds of changes in TEX, because he was forced to explain things to the reader, and when he couldn't, he changed the program. You have written a number of books as well as been a major developer. Did your work as an author influence your work as a developer, or vice versa?

FM: I think Don is absolutely right in making such a statement: I think it is extremely valuable to combine the development of software (actually anything) with the task of writing about it in some way. Trying to explain to others the functions and concepts behind a creation helps a lot in finding out whether or not something is going to work in practice. If you can't explain it or if the explanation turns out to be horribly complicated, then there is something fundamentally wrong with your creation and you should return to the drawing board.

Very important here is that one does not stop at simply documenting functions or menu items (though that is a start) but effectively tries to document the usage flow and the reasons why one would do things in one way or the other. Often enough (with free software as well as commercial software) you find only rudimentary documentation that tells you that such and such feature exists but never explains why one would want to use the feature in the first place. That type of documentation, while necessary, will not help in improving your tool (and often enough it turns out that such features only got implemented because they were easy to add without providing any real benefit).

So yes, documenting ideas and work flows has always been an integral part for me of developing and/or improving software, both my own as well as software from others. In *The LATEX Companion* [9], for example, a good proportion of what I describe is software developed by others, and the process of trying to explain how to use this software and finding good usage examples led in many cases to improvements in syntax or features after some discussions with the authors.

Therefore my advice to developers is to always try their hands at documenting their own creations or at least find somebody who does it for them (starting from the initial development!) — and carefully evaluate the findings from this process: it will result in noticeable improvements in the product.

DW: Thank you very much, Frank, for taking the time to do this interview with us. Your insights about TEX, LATEX, and the development and diffusion of complicated systems in a distributed development environment are fascinating.

And thank you, Gianluca, for agreeing to let me share this interview with you. It has been a pleasure to work with you.

GP: Thank you, Frank, for giving the *Free Software Magazine* readers a very well explained essay about an important piece of free software. Moreover, your LPPL explanation clarified some obscure points in a previous article [11]. And thank you, Dave, for giving me the possibility to do a combined interview, which is much more interesting than a "normal" interview.

FM: Thanks Dave and Gianluca for conducting this interview in the way it was done. I enjoyed seeing it unfold, question after question — despite the time it took (my fault) and the fact that we lived far apart it felt like doing a live interview face to face, which, I think, is the way it should be.

[1] LaTeX3 Project Team. The LaTeX Project CVS Repository. http://www.latex-project.org/cgi-bin/cvsweb/.

[2] LaTeX3 Project Team. Modifying LaTeX. Available with all LaTeX distributions, file modguide, December 1995.

[3] LaTeX3 Project Team. The LaTeX Project Public License (Version 1.3). http://www.latex-project.org/lppl/, December 2003.

[4] Frederick P. Brooks, Jr. *The Mythical Man-Month; Essays on Software Engineering.* Addison-Wesley, Boston, Massachusetts, 2nd edition, 1995.

[5] David Carlisle. Notes on the Oldenburg ε-TeX/LaTeX3/ConTeXt meeting. http://www.latex-project.org/papers/etex-meeting-notes.pdf, 1998.

[6] David Carlisle, Chris Rowley, and Frank Mittelbach. The LaTeX3 Programming Language—a proposed system for TeX macro programming. *TUGboat*, 18(4):303–308, December 1997. http://tug.org/TUGboat/Articles/tb18-4/tb57rowl.pdf.

[7] Frank Mittelbach. E-TeX: Guidelines for Future TeX Extensions. *TUGboat*, 11(3):337–345, September 1990. http://tug.org/TUGboat/Articles/tb11-3/tb29mitt.pdf.

[8] Frank Mittelbach. Language Information in Structured Documents: Markup and rendering—Concepts and problems. In *International Symposium on Multilingual Information Processing*, pages 93–104, Tsukuba, Japan, March 1997. Invited paper. Republished in *TUGboat* 18(3):199–205, 1997. http://tug.org/TUGboat/Articles/tb18-3/tb56lang.pdf.

[9] Frank Mittelbach and Michel Goossens. *The LaTeX Companion*. Tools and Techniques for Computer Typesetting. Addison-Wesley, Boston, Massachusetts, 2nd edition, 2004. With Johannes Braams, David Carlisle, and Chris Rowley.

[10] Frank Mittelbach and Chris Rowley. The pursuit of quality: How can automated typesetting achieve the highest standards of craft typography? In C. Vanoirbeek and G. Coray, editors, *EP92—Proceedings of Electronic Publishing '92, International Conference on Electronic Publishing, Document Manipulation, and Typography, Swiss Federal Institute of Technology, Lausanne, Switzerland, April 7–10, 1992*, pages 261–273, New York, 1992. Cambridge University Press.

[11] Gianluca Pignalberi. The LaTeX Project Public License. *Free Software Magazine*, (7):52–54, 2005. http://www.freesoftwaremagazine.com/articles/tex_license/.

[12] Chris A. Rowley and Frank Mittelbach. Application-independent representation of multilingual text. In Unicode Consortium, editor, *Europe, Software + the Internet: Going Global with Unicode: Tenth International Unicode Conference, March 10–12, 1997, Mainz, Germany*, San Jose, CA, 1997. The Unicode Consortium. http://www.latex-project.org/papers/unicode5.pdf.

[13] Justin Ziegler. Technical report on math font encoding (version 2). Technical report, LaTeX3 project, June 1994. http://mirror.ctan.org/info/ltx3pub/l3d007.*.

Steve Peter

Steve Peter is a publisher and linguist, does freelance book design and typesetting, and uses TEX daily. He is also a member of the TUG board.

[Interview completed 7 February 2006.]

Dave Walden, interviewer: Please tell me a bit about your personal history and life independent of TEX.

Steve Peter, interviewee: I was born and raised in Quincy, Illinois (where, coincidentally, Dan Luecking went to college). Early on, I wanted to be an astronomer, but discovered that physics and I did not mix. I slid one section over in the Dewey decimal system and landed on foreign languages, and found I had talent there.

After high school, I spent a year as an exchange student in Bremen, (then West) Germany. I returned to Illinois, attending the University of Illinois at Urbana-Champaign, where I majored in linguistics and Germanic languages. I did my graduate work at Harvard, working on historical Indo-European grammar.

While I was at Harvard, I met my future wife Susan, who had come for a summer program in Ukrainian. She was a graduate student at the U of I, so I moved back to Urbana to be with her. We were married in 1997, and spent a year in Vladimir, Russia, for her to research her doctoral dissertation.

DW: When and how did you first get involved with TEX?

SP: After I moved back to Urbana, I needed to find work. I answered an ad in the local paper, and found myself as a technical translator at Wolfram Research, the makers of Mathematica. One of my co-workers, Bill White, had two great passions: Emacs and TEX, and he introduced me to both. The company library had past issues of *TUGboat* and numerous TEX books, so I plunged in.

DW: I know you now live in New Jersey, and I know you are now deeply involved with TEX; how did these transitions come about?

SP: My wife teaches at the City University of New York on Staten Island. We had been in New Jersey the year before she got that job, while she was a fellow at Rutgers. Since we knew the area somewhat, we stayed.

After I worked for Wolfram Research, I worked for a database company here in Edison. (Our upstairs neighbors were this little company doing VOIP nobody had heard about at the time — Vonage.) After a while there, I decided to do publishing full time.

I have to take a step back to explain. Already back in graduate school, I had decided to start my own publishing company with a couple of friends. We had been complaining of the high cost of our academic books, and when we saw two books in particular, we decided we could do better. (One of the books was put out by a major university press, but was mysteriously set entirely in Courier, causing massive [literal] headaches if you read more than a page or two. The other was a book that had a cover set in yellow type against a white background! I will omit the names to protect the guilty.)

One of my jobs at Harvard was as typist to my advisor, Calvert Watkins, who was working on a book (published as *How to Kill a Dragon: Aspects of Indo-European Poetics*). He went to meet with the press, and they asked him if he could provide camera-ready copy. Assuming I was handy with a computer, he told them it was no problem. Then he told me. So my introduction to book typesetting was an accident.

I must admit that we used PageMaker for the book, since I had used it a bit in college for one of the independent student newspapers. Nevertheless, I found that I enjoyed typesetting and typography. After that I set several more books for Harvard colleagues.

As I said, I used PageMaker, QuarkXPress and InDesign in those early years. I dabbled with TeX, but hadn't felt confident enough to use it for real work. Then one day I got frustrated trying something in InDesign and decided to try the same thing in TeX. (I don't recall exactly what it was.) It worked, and the solution was simpler. I transitioned away from InDesign, and now only use it when a client makes me. (Ditto for QuarkXPress.)

I got involved with TUG after Karl Berry put out a request for someone to translate an article for *TUGboat*. The more I got involved, the more fun I had, so I've kept at it.

DW: Did you, in fact, start a publishing company, or is your business more book design and typesetting, or both?

SP: I did start a publishing company (together with Ben Fortson), but I continue to do a separate business as a freelance book designer, typesetter, and TeX consultant.

DW: Please tell me about the spectrum of your use of TeX and friends today and the hardware and software configurations you use to support this use.

SP: At heart, I guess I'm a fan of multiple ways of approaching a problem. For example, I've studied dozens of languages. When I got in touch with my inner geek, I started to collect operating systems, so I had machines running NeXTStep, BeOS, OS/2, Mac OS, GNU/Linux, QNX, Windows, etc. Today, I'm down to just Mac, Windows, and Linux, but I have TeX installed on all of my machines. My iBook tends to be my production machine, so I keep the software (Gerben Wierda's distribution) fairly static, updating only between projects. My older Windows/Linux machine I use as a sandbox, installing and uninstalling far too often :-).

I apply the same approach to TeX formats as well. I learned LaTeX first (in the most painful way, using a LaTeX 2_ε system and a LaTeX 2.09 book). Then I learned Plain TeX and Eplain, and discovered ConTeXt. I use all three formats on a daily basis. In addition, I like to play around with other formats like Texinfo and MusixTeX. I should probably do more real work, but that's life.

DW: A while back you recommended to some of us that we buy and read Bringhurst's book, *The Elements of Typographic Style*, to get some general understanding of what typography is all about. I bought the book and on a recent pair of cross-country plane flights, I dipped into the book in many places. I'd like to ask you some questions about how what Bringhurst says relates to TeX use. For instance, he discusses kerning. I found his basic explanation quite helpful — that kerning is about how tight pairs of letters fit together, such as the letter "a" being tighter against the bottom of the letter "V" in the sequence "Va" to the point where "a" overlaps "V", but that "o" cannot overlap "A" in the sequence "Ao". He then discusses "kerning tables" that are part of some typesetting software that he has in mind. He describes these kerning tables as including all pairs of sequences of two letters with information about how tightly the letters in a pair should be packed together. He also notes that the person doing a quality typesetting job may want to make manual adjustments to what the software did based on the kerning tables. For me this discussion immediately raised the question, “Does TEX have something equivalent to such kerning tables, or what ‘automatic’ support does TEX have for kerning?” Also, “To the extent that manual kerning adjustments are needed when using TEX, how do you handle them with TEX?”

SP: Kerning tables are actually part of fonts, and when you install fonts for use with TEX, you install the kerning information (in the form of TFMs). So, TEX has and uses kerning table information.

Not all fonts have good kerning information. Sometimes, just a few pairs are missing. For example, I find that many otherwise well-kerned fonts lack kerning pairs for en-dashes and numerals; thus, in a page range like 1–6, the en-dash will appear to be too far from the 1 and/or too close to the 6. Other fonts (usually the cheap ones) are a complete mess, providing only the most basic kerning information.

How to approach this depends on how often you hit the pair, what license the font has, and how devoted you are to hacking a good solution. For something that comes up infrequently, you can use TEX’s `\kern` primitive (e.g. `1--\kern.01em6`). You can also edit the TFMs, either via the virtual properties or via font software like FontForge or FontLab.

But the most exciting thing in TEX is what Hàn Thế Thành added to pdfTEX in terms of microtypographic extensions and the hz algorithm. These allow for very subtle variations in the width of characters and protrusion of punctuation to achieve a better paragraph.

DW: Well, that brings up the obvious questions, “What are microtypographic extensions?” and “What is the hz algorithm?”

SP: The answer to that requires a book-length treatment, or at least a thesis-length one. Fortunately, Thành wrote that thesis, called *Microtypographic extensions to the TEX typesetting system*, which is available online (`http://tug.org/TUGboat/Contents/contents21-4.html`).

One of the easiest extensions to grasp is hanging punctuation. If you look at a page of text typeset in the ordinary manner, with the right edge of all the character bounding boxes lined up to form the right margin, it won’t look perfectly straight if there are lots of sentences that end with periods on the margin, or lots of hyphens. So, to produce the *effect* of a straight edge, it is necessary to allow those visually smaller characters to protrude a bit. This is described in Thành’s article from the 2004 Practical TEX Conference `http://tug.org/TUGboat/Articles/tb25-1/thanh.pdf`.

Hermann Zapf, to my mind the greatest living type designer, created the hz algorithm in work done with URW. You might want to look at Frank Mittelbach’s laudatio for Zapf, which was reprinted in *TUGboat*: `http://tug.org/TUGboat/Articles/tb22-1-2/tb70laud-revised.pdf`.

DW: Is there any general advice you can give on how a naive user can find a “good font” rather than one that is “a mess”, or does each person have to figure this out for himself?

SP: Alas, there is none. The main advice is to avoid any of those “10 gazillion fonts on CD for $4.99”, since they will likely be bad. Most good foundries and font vendors like Adobe, Linotype, Terminal Design, Munchfonts, OurType, etc., offer PDF samples so you can see. Any good vendor will also answer questions, and the smaller foundries are generally very friendly. On the free side, the Polish TEX Users Group has released some excellent types.

More important to me when I shop for fonts is the glyph coverage. To do proper book typography, in my opinion you must have several things. For example, true small caps.

If you mechanically fake small caps by scaling down regular caps, the resulting small caps are too anemic. (If the font family has a very large range of weights, you can get away with mechanical scaling by selecting a reasonable heavier weight—but most font families don't have the required range to do that.) Also, for non-technical texts, I find hanging numerals to be necessary. I avoid the term "old-style numerals", as if good quality typography were somehow old fashioned and quaint. Finally, the typeface must have a full range of ff ligatures (or its design must be such that it does not require them).

DW: Bringhurst's book has about 75 pages (pp. 213–287 in my edition of the book—version 3.1 published by Hartley & Marks) of brief descriptions of fonts and suggestions of when they might be used. I was excited to contemplate the use of some of these fonts, but then the questions arises of which of these are easily usable with TEX. Can you say something about this?

SP: All of them are easily usable with TEX, once you get past the initial hump of learning how to install fonts for TEX (or use a system like XƎTEX). I highly recommend Philipp Lehman's excellent Font Installation Guide (on CTAN—`http://mirror.ctan.org/info/Type1fonts/fontinstallationguide/`). A word of warning though: don't expect to read it through once and understand everything fully.

Hans Hagen also has a nice tool for font installation called TeXfont, which is included in the ConTEXt distribution (for the manual, see `http://www.pragma-ade.com`).

DW: Another question from Bringhurst's book: he describes random variation on pages 188–190. Is this another microtypographic extension such as we were discussing earlier, or is this another category of fine typesetting? Does TEX have any capability for this?

SP: It's not really an extension of the kind we discussed above, and I don't think TEX has any special capacity for it, at least none that I have ever used.

Metafont, however, is an excellent tool for type designers to experiment with random variation as Bringhurst discusses. It's a shame Metafont isn't more widely used among type designers.

DW: Tell me about your process for selecting a set of fonts for a book you are designing. Do you think in terms of anything like Bringhurst's chart on page 55?

SP: Most books on typography will have some trite recommendation like, "If you're setting a 19th-century romance novel, use a 19th-century font." Well, fine, that's easy, but what about a textbook on Etruscan? Or what's a good typeface for a book about TEX?

To be honest, the first thing I do is see if one of the fonts I already have is suitable for the project. Since most of the books I do are designed for continuous reading, I favor a good serif. As I said above, I usually require that the font have hanging numerals, ff ligatures, true small caps, etc.

An issue I face often in typesetting linguistics is matching different writing systems. This has two facets. First, I often need to have a roman typeface that includes a matching set of IPA (International Phonetic Alphabet) symbols. Not all that many typefaces do, so I sometimes need to mix and match. Second, there are times I have to come up with a roman typeface that looks good with a completely different writing system, like Hebrew, Arabic, Cherokee or Etruscan. In those cases, I simply try out as many typefaces as I can, looking over specimen books, etc. By now, I've trained my eye to spot good combinations.

DW: I am not a professional in any aspect of the publishing world. I just want documents I write to look pretty good. What basic set or two of fonts (roman, sans serif, typewriter, etc.) would you recommend to me, and where might I get quality versions of these for free or, if I have to pay, where should I buy them and how much should I pay?

SP: I think a good collection of fonts will have one or two good typefaces from the major categories. You might try hanging around the Typophile web site for interesting discussion (http://typophile.com/forums).

For what it's worth, our last book was set in Adobe Caslon Pro, our current book is being set in Carter and Cone Galliard, and our next is being set in Terminal Design Rawlinson. If you have the chance, buy directly from the type designer.

Once you get away from the more conservative tastes of book typography to display fonts (among which I generally include sans), fashion takes over, and what is a great choice this year will look dated next.

DW: You said you have "studied dozens of languages". Does this mean you know enough about the alphabet, punctuation, etc., to be able to typeset a language, or do you actually speak or read many of these?

SP: Many of the languages were ones I studied when I was a graduate student in linguistics, which means lots of dead languages. However, I do speak and read a number of modern languages, and can (and generally love to) typeset them all.

DW: As a professional book publisher, book designer, and typesetter, what can you say about your future use of TeX? Do you foresee using it into the indefinite future? Are you under pressure to use something else? What do you think the TeX vendor and development communities need to provide to keep TeX viable for you?

SP: For my own work and for clients who don't require me to use a specific program, I will continue to use TeX until it isn't available for current processors (which is to say, forever). I rarely feel pressure to use anything else, although I do try to keep up basic skills on both InDesign and Quark, since there are a few of my clients who require them.

The main challenge I see for the present involves TeX being able to take advantage of OpenType and all the features that are being thrown together in that format.

One thing that would make my life easier would be to have an option to suppress hyphenation from recto to verso (i.e., over a page turn), but allow it from verso to recto (i.e., across a spread). I don't know of any typesetting system that can do that automatically, but I'd love to learn if anybody has hacked it.

DW: I think I have about exhausted my technical questions for now, but please tell me a little bit more about your personal life — what you do when you are not working in the world of publishing.

SP: Outside the world of TeX, but still broadly in the world of publishing, I'm quite interested in font design, and I'm working on a couple of designs right now. From time to time, I try my hand at programming, too, but I'm still very much a beginner.

I'm an avid reader. Aside from the technical stuff, I enjoy science fiction and travel books. I like to cook, adapting all kinds of recipes to make them vegetarian.

Most of all I enjoy spending time with my wife hiking, traveling, exploring new restaurants, and going to concerts.

DW: Thank you for taking the time to do this interview. It's very interesting to learn how you — a publisher and designer — use TeX.

Hans Hagen

Hans Hagen is the principal author and developer of ConTEXt (`http://www.pragma-ade.com`), past president of NTG (`http://www.ntg.nl`), and active in many other areas of the TEX community.

[Interview completed 2 March 2006.]

Dave Walden, interviewer: Please tell me a bit about your personal history independent of TEX.

Hans Hagen, interviewee: I live in Hasselt in a house situated in the middle of the town, on a kind of dike, looking out over the Zwarte Water (Black Water). It's a rather large building (former bank, 52.35.20 N 6.05.30 E) of which Pragma uses a few rooms, including the former safe rooms which we use for the server farm. I did a lot of rebuilding myself (a hobby) and made sure that the infrastructure was right (and that I had enough room to store my collection of books — another hobby).

My educational background is: gymnasium with a science focus followed by a few years physics and finally educational technology (at that time a nice mixture of exact and social sciences). Being among the first group of students doing this new direction, I had access to rather modern VAX/VMS computer equipment but TEX was not part of the game. We had to write many papers and used simple ASCII editors for that; the output was printed by high speed Daisywheel printers. I had a number of part time jobs in the academic department which gave me the opportunity to explore my programming skills (data analysis and such). Since we didn't have formatters, I wrote a pagination program (in Pascal) that acted on ASCII input. The program was used by other students as well.

After graduation in 1986, three other people from the same year and I started Pragma which focused on consultancy and development of learning materials, mostly for companies. At that moment we used personal computers in combination with our own editor and pagination software (faster and more efficient than what was available on the market ... it was the MS-DOS era, before Word Perfect and Word showed up).

DW: How did you get involved in TEX and come to develop what is now called ConTEXt?

HH: At that time I knew TEX only from *The TEXbook*, which I had bought because it looked intriguing. At a certain moment we ran into a project where complex math was used, and I decided to give TEX a try. We bought MicroTEX and started playing with LATEX. We had to hack our way around in order to get rid of the funny chapter openings and such. Fortunately the US hyphenation patterns gave acceptable results for Dutch. Typesetting was slow and printing even slower, so it gave us an excuse to get a bigger PC and to buy a high-end printer (one of the first fast duplex laser printers). Configurability of LaTeX was zero which was rather frustrating. After a few chapters we had managed to upset the customer, and the project was canceled; they were kind of offended that we had redone the typesetting which they had (proudly) done with a multi-head typewriter.

We kept using TeX, but with a low profile. We moved on to PCTeX and spent some money on buying updates for LaTeX, Dutch hyphenation patterns, manuals, etc. After the first update of LaTeX, I found out that I had to redefine the structuring commands again (to get rid of English labels), and so we started wondering about a more configurable setup. I started looking into other systems (Arbortext, 3b2, Berthold, Interleaf and the like), but in the end I decided to stick to TeX. I ordered LAMSTeX and INRSTeX, TaBlE and PiCTeX, and for a while we used those (I've never understood why LAMSTeX didn't replace the LaTeX of those times). I found out that I could configure INRSTeX quite well (it had better hooks than LaTeX for customization without digging deeply into the `.sty` file itself). I started writing wrappers around the code; by "wrappers" I mean macros that provide particular functions while hiding the code that implements those functions. Actually, we already used wrappers around LaTeX code, most noticeably to provide higher levels of abstraction for itemization, for example:

```
\startitemize[n] : numbered
\startitemize[a] : characters
\startitemize[1] : symbol '1' (bullet)
```

The more I understood TeX, the more pieces of INRSTeX we replaced, and after a while we realized that we had a kind of new macro package.

Also, if I hadn't been able to implement proper graphic support by then (none of the TeX packages we'd run into provided what we needed), we'd probably have abandoned TeX. We needed all kinds of graphic formats, scaling, and more placement options; normally graphic inclusion is controlled by specials. Such things are very driver dependent, so a `\special` driver system was one of the first things that we made; nowadays there are all kind of packages for that but not when we were beginning. Also, we were not "on the net" and didn't have email (both were rather academic at that time), so we were on our own. I had to (re)invent wheels. -)

What evolved was a system that, like LaTeX, provided a set of macros for coding a document; both structuring and layout definitions were part of it.

DW: When did you begin to call it ConTeXt, and why did you choose that name?

HH: Somewhere around 1996, I think. It was pragmatex before that. Context = con tex t — "text with tex".

DW: Please continue your description of its evolution.

HH: Right from the start it was keyword driven which in the end made us run into TeX's memory limitations. We got around that, and as a side effect we were able to provide a multi-lingual user interface. (Originally, ConTeXt had a Dutch user interface.) Implementation of a multi-lingual user interface was triggered by the fact that there was demand for our TeX macros by LaTeX users of an English version of a chemical typesetting package that we had written. All our development is rather user driven (by my own needs, my colleagues' needs and, in the last couple of years, users' needs). Fortunately the design of the system makes extending it easy. The time involved in writing macros mostly goes into figuring out how best to interface that feature, how to let TeX deal with it (TeX has its limitations), and how to make sure that it does not interfere with existing code.

The development was purely driven by demand and configurability, and this meant that we could optimize most workflows that involved text editing. I wrote a more integrated editing environment (in Modula 2) which enabled us to structure projects in such a way that we could produce multiple outputs from one source. This is where some of the reusability features come from. Writing the macros took time, but we could update documents and (progress) reports so quickly that it paid off. We could offer authors high quality output immediately. Another driving force was the lack of communication: we were not aware of the user groups, and we were isolated from the net (not being involved at a university). By the time that we started visiting meetings and getting TeX CDs, ConTeXt was well on its way.

The tools that we used grew with the macros — faster machines, bigger TeX's (most noticeably emTeX). We bought a high end, high resolution, and high speed Océ laser printer which was probably the only printer put in the market as a DVI printer; but, at the time we got it, it only understood PostScript. The only way to achieve the quality we wanted was to use dvipsone and outline fonts. Years later, by the time we moved to pdfTeX, we had traded the machine for an even better one. The reason that I mention this is that, with the improving quality of the printers, we also set higher standards: there is a big difference between the 300 dpi bitmaps (a rather bold look and feel) and high res outlines. It's the high quality that got us hooked to TeX. Nowadays I cannot imagine using TeX on a low resolution screen either, especially since we started using MetaPost graphics.

Around 1996 ConTeXt started being used outside Pragma. The first users were Taco Hoekwater, Berend de Boer, and Gilbert van den Dobbelsteen; the first international user was Tobias Burnus who did a lot of testing. Around that time the company started shifting its focus to more advanced typesetting jobs (complex manuals, interactive documents). We wrote specialized environments, for instance for cross-linked dictionaries that we needed in projects. Currently we mostly work for educational publishers (PDF-to-PDF and XML-to-PDF workflows) and we make specialized styles for companies who use ConTeXt for typesetting purposes.

DW: I gather that in addition to the basic pdfTeX engine, you also use MetaPost. What other major subsystems like this do you use in your collection of tools, and can you say a few words about how you integrate their use?

HH: For a long time now, MetaPost support has been tightly integrated in ConTeXt which means that one can make graphics that adapt to specific situations (layouts, structure, etc.).

Because TeX lacks a command line interface, the preferred way to run ConTeXt is to use `texexec`. Originally this was a Modula program, later it became a portable Perl script, and nowadays it's a Ruby script. Because TeX jobs normally involve multiple runs, `texexec` can keep track of how many runs are needed; there is one utility file where all cross references, indexes (there can be multiple), lists (there can be many), and other information goes; index sorting is done by `texutil`, which is now integrated into the Ruby version of `texexec`.

The `texexec` program can take care of making formats, running jobs, efficiently running subjobs (like MetaPost) when needed, etc.; there are also provisions for runtime graphic conversions and the like.

ConTeXt comes with many additional tools, most notably `texmfstart`, which can be used to launch programs in the `texmf` tree; most of those tools have names like `textools`, `pdftools`, `tmftools`, `ctxtools`, `rlxtools`, etc.

Contrary to plain TeX and LaTeX, ConTeXt comes with its macros preloaded and there is no distinction between backends, so there is no "pdfConTeXt" or the like. There are different versions of ConTEXt, but only with respect to the user interfaces (so in a French user interface, one uses French commands and keywords).

Sometimes there is a tendency in the TEX community to "put things in corners" (as we say in Dutch — "pigeonhole" in American English): if I show examples of using ConTEXt for educational documents, then people think ConTEXt is meant for educational stuff; or, for some time, I was always one of the first to show advanced interactive trickery and, thus, ConTEXt specialized in interactive documents. When I was sitting in on one of the excellent ConTEXt tutorials by Günter Partosch, he once remarked that "it took him a while to realize that ConTEXt was a complete system". So, even if you do presentations, write articles, etc., it takes a while for people to see the whole picture. I found that quite interesting to observe. Less fun are remarks such as "why do you use TEX if you don't need math?", but nowadays I seldom hear that.

DW: How big is Pragma now?

HH: Two of the other three original founders later dropped out, another got associated, and so now we're two in Pragma-ADE (www.pragma-ade.com) and three in Pragma-POD (www.pragma-pod.com).

DW: Do you have designers on staff, or do you mostly implement what your customers want?

HH: We don't have designers. I design the documents that we make here. For publishers, in most cases we get a design made in a DTP program and then turn that into a style. The biggest problem there is that such designs are seldom fully consistent (which may make mapping messy), there is no real systematic font and color usage (so one cannot make a nice systematic set of definitions), and the tests are done with unrealistic samples (so that one ends up with patch upon patch). Where possible we try to use ConTEXt core functionality. When implementing a style, most effort goes into the many kinds of graphic placements and in layout-dependent graphics. Also, grid-based designs can have their own dark corners. I'm pretty sure that most users don't run into those things and therefore may wonder why some features are supported in ConTEXt.

By the way, a good example of a design that could be implemented quite well is the journal of the Dutch math society, NAW magazine (http://www.math.leidenuniv.nl/~naw/serie5/index.php), but there the designer knew that a systematic design was needed which resulted in a very diverse and interesting design (many sub-layouts).

DW: You mentioned supporting ConTEXt users. Is there a distinct ConTEXt discussion list?

HH: There is a quite active ConTEXt user mailing list: http://www.ntg.nl/mailman/listinfo/ntg-context. There is also a development list, a bug/feature tracker, and a very actively maintained wiki called the ConTEXt Garden (http://contextgarden.net). The wiki project is led by Patrick Gundlach and sponsored by DANTE.

DW: To what extent are you involved in TUG, the Dutch TEX users group, or other TEX user groups or other more or less formal TEX "institutional" activities?

HH: I'm just an ordinary member of TUG, go to conferences, occasionally provide an article, and participate in program committees when asked. I'm currently the president of NTG, the Dutch-speaking user group. We have some 300+ members, two meetings per year, and a magazine. We are financially healthy which means that we can participate in projects that need funding. Regarding other user groups, I try to attend GUST (Poland) and DANTE (Germany) meetings since they are, apart from being TEX meetings, also meetings of TEX friends. I have been to other user group meetings as well.

There is considerable informal contact between the presidents of TUG (Karl Berry), DANTE (Volker Schaa), GUST (Jerzy Ludwichowski) and NTG (me). All of us are involved in projects that involve multiple local user groups, and we try to keep each other informed about projects, conference schedules, and issues that concern the TeX community.

DW: There is frequently talk in the TeX world about the limitations of LaTeX, the need for improvements to TeX, and sometimes about what a "mess" the underlying TeX engine is (both fundamentally and with the enormous patch files that are used to modify and extend the basic TeX engine). You have taken matters into your own hands regarding making TeX work for you (and other users who see benefit in the things you have implemented). What do you anticipate as the future of your development efforts: more incremental developments and additions to your existing set of tools as new problems need to be addressed, or something dramatically new? And why?

HH: I wonder if I should comment on the limitations of LaTeX, because I don't use LaTeX. Users should use what they like best. What I do remember is that writing styles and extensions involved hacking around in the kernel. I believe that extensibility has never been part of the concept and that shows. I also know from talking to the core LaTeX people that it's very hard to improve things once users start doing that kind of hacking. Also, the output needs to be "as it was before", a restriction that I didn't put upon myself with ConTeXt. When solving a bug gives better output, so be it; patterns change, fonts change, and on the average no user will notice differences. In practice ConTeXt output is rather stable and does not change, unless you change your settings.

Anyhow, the LaTeX people are forced to operate within far more strict boundary conditions than the ConTeXt people. Also, I found ConTeXt users to be very demanding but realistic: if they want some feature, they send examples and are willing to test. ConTeXt users have no problem with updating frequently because some new feature will suit their needs. Because the documentation lags behind, users go into the source code (where they often can find examples), and so far this has not led to users hacking around and making kernel-dependent extensions. There are well defined hooks for that, and users know when to ask for a new hook.

Regarding the basic TeX engine, I agree that things could be improved. TeX is written for a "write a style per book or series" kind of workflow. Because not everyone is willing to program, macro packages fill in a gap. One can reuse code, more easily configure the output, etc. When writing more complex macro packages, one longs for a language that has a bit more of the features found in modern scripting languages, like Ruby. (By the way, a future version of pdfTeX will have an embedded scripting engine, Lua, but that's another story.) It takes a while to get a grip on the TeX language and more time to get a feeling of what TeX is doing. Because most TeX code that is written (especially when computers were more limited) is quite unreadable, I never spend much time on looking into other macro writers' code (apart from INRSTeX). I learned it the hard way and at a certain moment entered a stage where one could "think in TeX". Every now and then I spend some time cleaning up the code. We have more memory now, so we can write more verbose code. Sometimes I keep old code around, just to show the stepwise improvements.

Should TeX be extended, and in what way? I often wish that TeX could give me more information about the state it's in. We can use a few more features as well, but not all wishes fit well into the way TeX operates. For instance, writing a decent multi-column routine (with advanced float support) is non-trivial. If one does not want users to clutter up their document source too much (one of the ConTeXt principles is that users should never have skips in their documents), one for instance needs the ability to set the height and depths of top and bottom lines in boxes (now a pdfTeX feature). One needs proper list processing (non-interfering whatsit nodes), more control over inserts, etc. However, whenever I look into this, I realize that Don Knuth stopped putting more features in TEX at the moment when the solution space became too fuzzy. Take for instance grid snapping (our customers demand that). In desktop publishing one can manually arrange things on the grid but what to do in a automated system: does a graphic's caption need to be snapped on the grid; with multi-line captions in a smaller font, is the first line snapped or the last line; what if there are several graphics stacked; what is the expected size of a graphic and what does the top of a photo align with? No specs, no solutions. ConTEXt can handle these things quite well; but, apart from some support from the TEX engine, I cannot imagine a generic model that will fit all macro packages equally well. This means that one will find alternatives in ConTEXt: multiple table mechanisms, more than one multi-column routine, and (more hidden) knobs to change the heuristics.

A good example of extensibility is ε-TEX. It provides a `\protected` definition prefix. Both ConTEXt and LATEX can use that, but if you look at the low-level already existing `\protect` macros, you will notice that they are needed in completely different situations. ConTEXt needs protection in its key value parser while, if I remember right, LATEX needs protection when one writes to the table of contents and such. Another example is `\dimexpr`. Instead of a clean expression engine, we have something that is modeled after a macro package (I'm told) which makes it less useful than had it been very generic. Or take `\scantokens`, which has some limitations built in that make it difficult to use in the situations where ConTEXt could benefit from it. So, each macro package has its needs, and it's hard to satisfy all. It's also hard to convince implementors that you need a feature that they themselves see no need for. Now that ConTEXt has become more widely known and accepted, things get easier. Also, pdfTEX now has become a place to add new features which happens on a regular basis.

The future is hard to predict. We're lucky that we didn't announce ConTEXt 3. I think that we can safely say that we now have the ConTEXt 2 code base, not that users will notice. The major change in the last couple of years was the (mostly automated) conversion from low-level Dutch to low-level English, so that more developers can participate. The formal user interface has always had a formal definition (nowadays in XML) so as long as this file is in sync with the code base, manuals that use the automated syntax charts will be adapted automatically. Not dramatically, but also not without impact, has been the integration of MetaPost. I think that it resulted in more MetaPost users and more interesting documents. Things like the evolution of color support (more color spaces, separation, etc.) are not that much of interest to users (apart from those active in high-end publishing).

For practical reasons we will skip version 3 of ConTEXt, and move on to version 4. That version will use the Lua scripting engine for certain tasks but it's hard to foresee to what extent. Who could have foreseen that adding MetaPost support would have resulted in arbitrary (nested) backgrounds behind the text flow? We will keep cleaning up the code, provide more support for Aleph-related features (bi-directionality), support OpenType, and keep exploring PDF features. So far I have always able to do whatever I wanted with TEX and ConTEXt, but that may change when we really hit the limits. In that respect it's interesting that most of our projects demand rather advanced styles, but seldom high quality typesetting (no hyphenations, ragged right, inconsistent font and color usage). One of our current projects involves manipulating PDF files (we split files, reassemble them, parse code and renumber chapters, sections, graphics and whatever, add fonts and other resources) while it would be more trivial to generate the files directly from (for instance) XML sources. Here ConTEXt is just an advanced reassembling tool that, in the process, adds some pages. So, who knows what version 4 will bring. I'm pretty sure that there is already much more in ConTEXt than the average user realizes.

When we talk about ConTEXt, we are also talking about the scripts. These are becoming more and more advanced, a process which is driven by the ways we use ConTEXt in more complex workflows.

One area where ConTEXt will expand is fonts: we now have two complementary font mechanisms; and, as soon as some restrictions from TEX are removed, I expect more advanced (OpenType) features to become available through the user interface. Another thought that I'm playing with is the ability to make spin-off macro packages: smaller, less and/or more directed features, for special purpose usage.

DW: Major advances in the world of TEX often seem to be the work of a key person who is largely self-directed and perhaps a few helpers (e.g., TEX originally, LATEX with Lamport originally and Mittelbach later, you with ConTEXt, Hàn Thế Thành with pdfTEX, etc.). The user groups don't seem to have the financial resources to undertake major advances, and them commissioning people to do such work doesn't seem to work so well anyway. What do you think the few best things are that the user groups can do to have significant impact on the future viability of TEX?

HH: Financing is not really needed for TEX to get developed, unless you know what you're spending the money on. Good examples are the font projects: there is a clear goal, we know that the people involved can do it, and the budgets can be kind of fixed. For example, recently the user groups decided to fund the integration of the free fonts that come with TEX and to make OpenType versions; such a project will cost between 30000 and 50000 euro (especially if we also deal with math). I'm one of the initiators, so in a sense responsible for spending quite a bit of user group money; but knowing the people involved, I trust that the work will get done (as long as we don't discuss the project to death). One reason to fund this project is to allow the people who are involved to spend substantial time in a small time-span; also, the project needs to be done fast, because we need (free) OpenType fonts in order to be able to let pdfTEX go OpenType. No OpenType support means the end-of-TEX, just as no PDF output would have meant the end-of-TEX some time ago. If TEX cannot be used in high-end publishing environments, it will end up in the margin.

Apart from small scale funding, I think that putting money into TEX development (a replacement) is not needed and counterproductive. There has been an attempt (the NTS project), but this also demonstrated that something really new is also politically tricky. It divides the TEX community; one ends up in discussions about programming languages, what's best and who better and.... Don Knuth once said that the developer, first user, and writer of the first manual should be one person, and I think that he's right. If I wasn't using ConTEXt (in all its aspects) myself, it would not be as it is now. As an example, look at XƎTEX, an extended Mac version of TEX. It's done by someone who works in an environment where it's used. It evolves in an environment of demanding users. Being a Mac thing, it is no surprise that the focus is on fonts.

When there are talks about a radically new implementation, my first thought is always "nice, but the problems don't change". The problems that we're faced with that are hard to solve in TEX do not necessarily have a well defined solution space. This is why many efforts end up in interesting (in themselves) discussions, but no solutions. Also, I'm pretty sure that the solutions that I'd like are not the same as those that others want or need.

pdfTEX is a nice example: Thành just did it, used it himself, and now we have something that simply works. Of course, there are now more people involved in the development, but it's Thành who got it rolling. Some people joined in, used it, and gave feedback, but I'm pretty sure that a "program by committee" would have led to nothing.

One of my favourite examples is positional information. With TeX there has always been a lot of talk about not knowing the position of something (for example, a bit of text) on a page. It does not really fit in a system where the flow drives the makeup (breaking paragraphs and pages) more than manual positioning. Discussions quickly lead to "it cannot be done" and "if we should do it, where and what and how to do this and that". So, at a certain point I asked Thành for a way to tag positions and write out those positions after a page was done, and within a day I got an experimental feature. It was after a while that I realized that this feature had been available in TeX right from the beginning: use specials, postprocess the DVI file, and use the relevant information in the next run. As a result I could convince the dvipdfmx author to provide this positional capability, too. For twenty years this solution had been sitting there and kind of went unseen because discussions made it too complicated.

Another example is line numbering, which would be a piece of cake if we had an `\everyline` feature. If we simply accept that the line-based content is not part of the paragraph but is added after the lines are broken, I can imagine a solution (it's a bit similar to the output routine). On the other hand, if we keep thinking of a feature that interacts with the paragraph, no solution is visible. TeX implements generic mechanisms, but sometimes a less complete solution is okay for what we want to achieve. For instance, think about multi-directional typesetting — not all directions have the same demands; or compare languages — Chinese line breaks are based on the surroundings of a character, and so we can make do with a more limited paragraph builder but with different characteristics. This is why an incredibly simple positional system can be so powerful: macros can do the rest and the author knows what he's doing and what cannot be done.

The best things the user groups can do is to organize meetings and collect people. DANTE and GUST are great examples of that. DANTE has spent much money getting people together to discuss distributions. User groups can also sponsor (small scale) meetings of developers. When I run into someone who I think should attend a user group meeting, I try to get him or her there; money on that is well spent, because once such a person knows the crowd, he or she may continue to participate. Diversity in spending money is better than focussing on a few projects. Therefore, the user groups can best spend their money on making conferences cheap and collecting people. That will keep the candle burning.

One thing that's also needed on the long run is a solid TeX code base. It is sad to see that the Unix and Windows development trees are not in sync (combined). When Fabrice Popineau (who had to merge his changes into a copy of the code base each time an update was made) decided to quit participating in TeX Live (and maintain an independent tree, just as the MiKTeX people do), I wonder how many people realized that the TeX development community had failed badly. We see big and complex programs being made available on the major platforms, but somehow the TeX world does not manage to get that done in an easy way. We cannot afford to lose people like Fabrice that way.

DW: A final question: what are your ambitions for your company and ConTeXt going forward?

HH: The future of Pragma is hard to predict. I hope that we can keep making a living the way we do now. I also realize that a small company like ours has limited possibilities, and supporting ConTeXt (reading mailing lists, fulfilling user requests, attending meetings, participating in user groups) takes quite some time. One problem our company faces it that we always get the kind of tricky projects (time consuming, imperfect resources, etc.), while you sometimes need a few easy going ones, simply because we then can have some return on investment on the tools we made. TEX-based solutions scale incredibly well, and it would be nice to have more projects that scale to the extreme. There are numerous possibilities for applying TEX, and I wish we had a few projects that we could "do on our spine" as we say here. Unfortunately TEX is not always seen as part of a solution. Anyway, we have been around for a long time, and we will not go away easily.

As for ConTEXt, the user base is growing, and I see users doing very interesting things. TEX still draws new (and young) users and that is good. As long as I have needs, and when users have requests, ConTEXt will be extended. Of course I have some ideas about new directions, but I don't want to make false promises. Lately, users have started making their own modules, writing their own manuals (either using or not using the ConTEXt "MyWay magazine" style). And what is important for me is that there is a growing group of users who know the source code and can contribute. The time when ConTEXt was a mostly one-person job is behind us. For instance, Taco Hoekwater is now the driving force behind releases and the subversion repository (dating back to 1996). He's the best TEX-analyst (program and macro code) I know, and without him ConTEXt would not be where it is now. We have users like Adam Lindsay and Henning Hraban Ramm who are very active with fonts, and by now Mojca Miklavec is a real encoding guru. I could mention more names, but I'd say, take a look at the wiki and see who contributes. Take some time to look at the wiki anyway, and you'll see what wonders Patrick Gundlach did with the source browser and quick references browser. Long ago, a user told me that one of the charms of ConTEXt is that there is a short distance between the users and the core developers, and I hope that we can keep it that way.

DW: Thank you, Hans, for taking the time to participate in this interview. I find your ideas to be highly insightful and stimulating. I will have to give ConTEXt a try with the book I will start work on in the near future. I also hope I meet you in person at a future TEX conference.

Christian Schenk

Christian Schenk is the author and principal developer of the popular MiKTeX distribution of TeX. [Interview completed 15 April 2006.]

Dave Walden, interviewer: Please tell me a bit about your personal history independent of the TeX world.

Christian Schenk, interviewee: My life began 1962 in the western part of Berlin. I studied computer science at the TU (Technische Universität) Berlin where I got my Diploma in 1988. Now I am working as a software engineer (still in Berlin). I am a very enthusiastic road bike rider. For relaxation I enjoy playing guitar.

DW: Was your degree in computer science or some other field?

CS: Computer science.

DW: What kind of software engineering project do you work on at your place of employment?

CS: My company develops platforms for convergent information and telecommunication technologies. I am a member of a team which develops software tools for the maintenance of large PBX systems.

DW: Do you compete on the bike?

CS: I am not a racing cyclist. Nevertheless I do participate in mass sport events. The next event is the Vaütternrundan, a 300 km ride around Lake Vaüttern in Sweden.

DW: Do you play the guitar in any sort of groups or just for yourself?

CS: I took classical guitar lessons when I was a teenager. But my "career" came to an end in the early 80's when I began to develop other interests. Now I am playing just for myself.

DW: Please tell me about how you first became involved with TeX?

CS: I wrote my dissertation in LaTeX. On a Atari ST, IIRC.

DW: Was that required or did you choose LaTeX over other alternatives and why?

CS: The faculty's official typesetting system was Waterloo Script, which ran on an IBM mainframe. But luckily it wasn't a requirement to use it. I chose LaTeX because it was (almost) gratis and because I did like the idea to "program" my writings.

DW: Do you still personally use (LA)TEX?

CS: Yes, mainly for correspondence. In my job I use Word or XEmacs/DocBook to write documentation.

DW: You are well known in the TEX world for MiKTEX. Please tell me why you got involved in developing and maintaining a TEX distribution.

CS: MiKTeX started as a fun project when I owned my first PC in the early 90s. Today it is a hobby.

DW: What is your distinction between a "fun project" and a "hobby"?

CS: A fun project is something you start spontaneously out of a mood. It is usually a short-lived business.

DW: Developing a complete TEX distribution on multiple releases of PC operating systems is a pretty big "fun project". What was your motivation for taking on such a big project?

CS: It evolved. Implementing a pure TEX system isn't hard. But there is always one thing you can improve, so you sit down and hack. I know people who solve puzzles. MiKTEX is my crossword puzzle. And the work on MiKTEX has a nice side effect: I have learned a lot of new programming techniques by studying the open source programs around TEX and friends. This kind of training is very valuable.

DW: What did you start from — Knuth's release, Unix change files, ...?

CS: I began studying Web2C. But it seemed impossible to transfer it to DOS — too many shell scripts and calls to Unix system functions. There were other PC TEX implementations. But these were written in Pascal and after all I wanted my own TEX. So I began from scratch. The main task was to write C4P, MiKTeX's Pascal-to-C translator. Then I downloaded Knuth's files from the Stanford FTP server and wrote the change files. The file searching routines were inspired by Karl Berry's kpathsea library.

DW: I assume you started developing MiKTEX alone. How have things evolved over time? How was/is MiKTEX developed (editor, compiler, installer, etc.)? Do you work alone or is there a MiKTEX team; if the latter, how do you divide up the work? What is your release process — how often, how tested, how distributed, etc.?

CS: The core MiKTEX development was and still is a one man show. The actual code base is relatively small. The main components are:

- the MiKTEX kernel which implements (among other things) the file system interface
- the package manager
- Yap (the previewer)
- the setup program (hand written)

I do most of my code editing with XEmacs. The code is compiled with Microsoft Visual C++.

The MiKTEX release process follows the usual pattern: first a series of beta releases, then the general availability release. MiKTeX 2.4 was released in 2003. MiKTEX 2.5 will be released this year. I think three years is not such a long period of time for a one-man project.

Packages are updated regularly but untested. Each package update has the potential to break the whole system. Luckily, Windows users are very bold persons.

DW: How do you see MiKTEX in comparison to other distributions of TEX — special features, limitations, ...?

CS: MiKTeX's main strength is its integrated package management system. Its main weakness is that the distribution isn't always in a stable state — due to frequent package updates (see above).

DW: What are your plans for the future, both for MiKTEX itself and for your involvement with it?

CS: In the near future I am planning to make a new release: MiKTEX 2.5. Then I have to think of a way how I can open the MiKTEX package repository for submissions because I want to concentrate on programming. MiKTEX 3.0 shall be runnable on Unix platforms. But that's all still up in the air.

DW: More generally, please share any opinions you have on the future of TEX and friends in the world increasingly dominated by Word, Quark, XML, etc.

CS: It's very hard to make a prediction about the future of TEX. I fear that TEX is a phase-out model. But there's life in the old dog yet. And then there is a chance that we will see a successor in the not so distant future.

DW: I personally use MiKTEX these days via the ProTEXt distribution. Are you actively involved in creating that or does your participation stop at agreeing ProTEXt can include MiKTEX?

CS: ProTEXt wasn't my idea and I was not involved in its creation. For newcomers it offers a nice entry into the world of TEX. In that respect it is a real improvement compared to the bare MiKTEX setup wizard.

DW: Do you have significant involvement with any other parts of the TEX world, e.g., user groups such as DANTE, the LATEX team, etc.?

CS: No.

DW: Looking at your birth date, I calculate you were about 27 when the Berlin Wall came down. Going to university, was there interchange with the students in the east. Did the unification of Germany make any significant difference in the world of computing that you saw, in the spread of TEX, etc.?

CS: Well, growing up and studying in West Berlin wasn't exceptionally good or bad. We had no official contacts with students in East Germany. That was unthinkable.

It is certainly true that the unification increased the TEX user base significantly: there were many computer enthusiasts in the Eastern bloc (not only East Germany) and they were greedy for Western technology.

DW: Thank you very much for taking the time to participate in this interview. It is wonderful to know a bit more about the TEX distribution I use and its developer.

Werner Lemberg

Werner Lemberg developed the CJK (Chinese, Japanese, Korean) package for LaTeX and has been involved in a number of other computer-based typesetting projects.

[Interview completed 28 April 2006.]

Dave Walden, interviewer: Please tell me about your personal history independent of your involvement with computer based typesetting, etc.

Werner Lemberg, interviewee: I'm Viennese. I went to school in Vienna and studied music at the Hochschule für Musik (now Vienna University for Music) — I finished with five diplomas (composition, conducting, master class for piano, chorus conducting, and singers' coaching). At the same time I started studying mathematics and Chinese, both of which I had to abandon two years later because of lack of time. Since both my parents and brothers are musicians it was quite natural for me to do the same, and I started at my parents' working place, the Vienna State Opera. My parents are now retired, but my brother still works there, being a member of the Vienna Philharmonic Orchestra.

In the following years I worked at various theatres in Austria and Germany; since five years ago I have been engaged at the Municipal Theatre in Koblenz, Germany — the town where the Mosel flows into the Rhine — as a conductor head of the music department (the exact term is "Studienleiter").

DW: How and when did you first get involved in computer-based typesetting?

WL: Well, around 1989 I wanted to write a "Diplomarbeit" (a thesis) about the Chinese mouth organ, the shēng (笙), and I also wanted to have Chinese characters in the German text written by the computer and not inserted by hand. At that time there were just a few, quite expensive programs for MS-DOS which could do that. And there was TeX: A good guy from DANTE told me that LaTeX could do what I wanted using Thomas Ridgeway's "poor man's Chinese" (pmC) package. This was the start of everything. By the way, this master's thesis was never written, while the CJK package for LaTeX actually came into existence....

DW: You said you studied Chinese for a couple of years. Was that enough for you speak or write Chinese?

WL: Not really :-). I now have an idea of the language and the script, and my colloquial Chinese is sufficient for daily life, but anything more specialized makes me desperate. My written Chinese is not sufficient for any purpose.

DW: Can you say a bit about the difficulty of developing these fonts; did you design the characters from scratch, using some kind of software?

WL: I didn't develop any font! My package just provides the necessary infrastructure to use the CJK fonts with LaTeX.

DW: What is the current status of the CJK package and your involvement with it?

WL: Basically, it is stable. I plan a new version in the near future that will extend the Unicode support beyond the BMP (Basic Multilingual Plane, covering the character range U+0000 to U+FFFF) — the stuff is already in the development repository.

DW: So your first experience in computer-based typesetting was with LaTeX, but today you are a lead contributor to Groff. How did that come about?

WL: This happened by pure coincidence. If I remember correctly, I reported a Groff problem, and Ted Harding and I got into some public discussion, and finally we were asked whether if we were interested in further maintaining Groff because it was orphaned. Today I'm still doing this.... It's quite fun to compare the different paradigms of Groff and TeX: Some problems are much easier to handle with the one program and vice versa.

DW: By easier to "handle problems", I assume you mean as a user rather than developer, correct? Will you please give me examples of the type of thing that is easier to handle in Groff and in TeX?

WL: Groff has the concept of "traps" to catch vertical events. For example, it's rather simple to make the first line of a paragraph be printed in small caps, something which is quite difficult in TeX, as far as I know. Another advantage of Groff is its capability to move easily to absolute positions on a page.

The perhaps biggest disadvantage of Groff is the lack of shrinkable space, both vertically and horizontally (vertically stretchable space is also missing). Thus formatting of columns with a small line width works far better in TeX. Groff's algorithm to format a paragraph is also much less sophisticated.

DW: I presume you use both LaTeX and Groff: which do you use for what and why?

WL: For me it is a must to have good man pages! And this is what I am using Groff for. For longer documents I use LaTeX.

DW: What makes Groff better for good man pages?

WL: For me a good man page displays well on various output formats, at least as plain text, PostScript, and HTML. Groff works fine for all those formats (HTML output is still somewhat experimental, though), while support for (formatted) plain text output is completely missing from TeX.

DW: At the (`troff.org`) web site, it said you did the style files for ESSCIRC and ESSDERC, which have to do with solid-state electronics. Do you work with solid-state electronics, too, as well as with music and computer-based typesetting?

WL: No, not at all. Developing those two style files was a paid job.

DW: You've also written `c2cweb`. What is the purpose and reason for that?

WL: This program is a kind of preprocessor to `cweb`. It takes C source and header files and pretty-prints them, together with handy variable and function indices. Unfortunately, I don't have time to maintain and improve it, and it seems that other, similar programs do a better job.

For perfect C (and C++) source code formatting a complete language parser and preprocessor is needed, I think. I can imagine that someone adds a special output mode to `gcc` which doesn't emit compiled code but language tokens (comments, identifiers, operators, etc.) which can then be printed out.

DW: Is it correct to assume that you yourself sometimes use computers to typeset music? What program(s) do you use? Also, please tell me your view of the current state and future of music typesetting in comparison with the state of typesetting other things that can be done, for instance, with LaTeX.

WL: Indeed, I not only use GNU LilyPond for typesetting my music, I also actively participate in its development. It works very similarly to LaTeX; that is, you write a text file which is then compiled to get a PostScript (and consequently a PDF) document. Personally, I like this most since I try to avoid the mouse as much as possible. Up to now I know only a single program, Score (and its recent descendants), which produces output comparable to manually engraved documents. There are still a lot of things to do in LilyPond (volunteers welcome), but the future looks quite promising.

DW: Can you show me an example of LilyPond input markup, e.g., for a measure or two of a tune?

WL: Here it is. The following input

```
\relative c' { g'4 e e2 | f4 d d2 | c4 d e f | g g g2 }
```

gives the following output which I believe is almost self-explanatory:

DW: You are a pianist, so I might assume there is a problem with keyboard input as at least the preliminary input to a music typesetting program. Will you please sketch the set of issues that leads you to do input via a text file rather than either a mouse or from a musical instrument with digital output?

WL: I don't object to inputting data with the mouse or with a musical instrument—the latter is definitely the natural input method for most of Western music. The Score program offers both, and I've indeed used those methods (you can do that with LilyPond too, using a front-end, but I've never tried it). Interestingly, my experience has shown that neither mouse nor musical instrument input is actually faster than input with a computer keyboard if you need more than the most basic music data. The movement forth and back between the computer keyboard and the mouse or the musical instrument outweighs any time savings you would have by using the "natural" input method. Of course, this holds for a trained user only.

My particular reason for using a keyboard-only solution is that I do most of my work on a laptop sitting in a train, and using the laptop mousepad for serious mouse-based input is perverse in my mind. While I use GNU/Linux exclusively, I'm quite happy that Microsoft has forced the hardware manufacturers to add the Windows and Menu keys to the keyboard. This gives me free Super and Hyper modifiers in addition to Shift, Alt, and Control which I use for switching windows and virtual screens :-).

DW: You mentioned the Score program. What is different about the Score approach from that of LilyPond that allows Score to produce better output?

WL: Score is an old MS-DOS based program which was written by Leland Smith, then a professor at Stanford (my memory is very vague about this; it might be a different university). It is quite expensive (about $1000 and more, I think), but it produces marvelous output. This is old information since I haven't used it for years, and I haven't seen the port of this program to Windows. Big music publishing houses like Schott (Mainz,

Germany) and Universal Edition (Vienna) use or have used it, and the results are quite convincing if you look at scores from contemporary composers.

LilyPond is still under development, and it can actually produce even better output than Score. It tries to mimic manually engraved music (based on German tradition) as closely as possible. The amazing thing about LilyPond is that the number of tweaks necessary to get good looking output is very small under normal circumstances, far less than are necessary for Score — it can deal with most of the object collisions. Similar to TEX, LilyPond's default formatting capabilities are excellent.

DW: What is an object collision?

WL: When two musical objects like a note head and the "f" sign (which indicates "forte") overlap or nearly overlap.

DW: LilyPond used to use TEX, but doesn't any more. Why did the project switch away from TEX?

WL: There were several reasons:

1. LilyPond needs much control over the layout process; especially, it needs to know the font metrics. The development process has revealed that delaying text layout to TEX causes more problems than it solves. (There still exists a TEX back end which provides a two-step implementation: LilyPond first emits a file containing all the strings TEX should render. Then you have to run TEX to create a log file which holds the strings' dimensions (width, height, and depth). A second run of LilyPond reads in this log file and does the final typesetting. However, this might not work currently because there isn't much interest in maintaining it.)
2. A logical consequence of point 1 is to directly access a rendering engine (Pango). This decision gave us three additional benefits: (a) support for complex scripts, (b) support for complex fonts, and (c) native UTF-8 input encoding.
3. LilyPond's music fonts can now hold any number of glyphs since the limitation of 255 glyphs per font is gone.
4. Depending on a TEX distribution was a pain, especially since LilyPond runs on both Windows and Macs. LilyPond itself is already a big package; not relying on TEX both removes a package dependency and reduces the necessary downloads for potential Windows and Mac users — most Windows and Mac boxes don't have a pre-installed TEX system.

DW: It sounds like you are pretty deeply into computer programming and you said you were two years into a math program before you had to give it up for lack of time. Having a person from arts and music be deeply interested in computers and math seems sort of surprising at first blush. On the other hand, in my professional world of computers and math, many people are amateur musicians. Is the reverse true? Do you find many people in your world of professional music who are amateur computer and math people, or do you see yourself as an exception?

WL: Honestly, I don't know. The famous example is William Herschel, discoverer of Uranus, who was both a composer and astronomer. The fact is that I don't think that any of my colleagues here in the theatre do something similar to me. But there are a lot of computer freaks actively participating on the LilyPond mailing list who are professional musicians and composers — since LilyPond uses Scheme as its extension language a certain computer background doesn't hurt....

DW: Thank you, Werner, for taking the time to participate in this interview. I found it fascinating.

Duane Bibby

Cartoonist Duane Bibby is well known for the lion illustrations used in numerous TEX books, starting with *The TEXbook*, and by TEX user groups.

[Interview completed 19 May 2006.]

Dave Walden, interviewer: I believe your first contact with the world of TEX was with Donald Knuth himself. How did you two come in contact with each other?

Duane Bibby, interviewee: My first contact with Don came about because of a chance conversation an editor I was working for, Bonnie Bernstein at Fearon Publications, had at a Stanford function. At the time I was jumping around freelancing in the San Francisco Bay Area and had done a couple of book illustration jobs for them. I think Don mentioned he was looking for an artist for his book and my name came up. The call came just as we were packing up to move north, literally into the woods along the California coast near Eureka. We met, I showed some samples, and we almost immediately set to work.

DW: How did the lion motif come about?

DB: During that first meeting, Don showed me some writing he had done that had been published in Mad magazine. That not only greatly impressed me, because I had a fair stack of rejection slips from them, but helped in thinking about perhaps using a character to bind things together — somewhat similar to a job I'd just completed with Eleanor Mennick, the design director at Fearon. Don liked the idea, but we didn't have a clear vision at that time of exactly what sort of character. The obvious was, we thought, a kind of computer guy, of which I did some exploratory sketching around. But, as my wife Jeanette Ahlgren noted as I doodled in our cabin in the trees, also kind of boring. I'd also had a chance to read the manuscript and found the tone light and engaging even though I knew nothing of computer software. I think that influenced the approach too.

Various animals came to mind and pad, but a classic lion finally began to pop to life. A possible source of the lion idea was a very large Maine Coon cat — a rather large breed of house cat — that was wandering around. It had been abandoned, was looking for a new home, and was giving us new arrivals the look over, trying to decide if he would adopt us. He later did. We still have cats around; the photo shows Jeanette's current guys, Cisco and Swank.

I tried the lion sketches on Don, which he liked right off, and we then began working out each chapter idea which further defined the character. Later when it came to Metafont, Don felt the lion needed a mate and so that made it easy.

DW: Do you view yourself as an illustrator or a cartoonist or an artist more generally?

DB: All of those and less. Seems I've not totally committed to one area over the years, being more what was once called a commercial artist. Lately the nature of artist/designer/illustrator/cartoonist is being further blurred, or maybe transformed, by computers and cyberspace — like everything else. I've always been fine with bouncing from one interesting area to the next, but lately I have been concentrating with some personal projects around the possibilities of the long format of Manga. I have a 200 page sort of auto-related anthology work nearly done and have equally long spin offs from that well under way, all in a silent, almost no words vein. And I'd like to finally get together a book on the TEX drawings over the years, development, etc. So I'd have to say I view myself as trying to move toward being that new thing artists will have to be in the computer connected world.

DW: In the previous answer, I don't know what "long format" means with regard to Manga, which I believe is a Japanese name for a sort of book length comic. Also, by "auto-related anthology" do you mean a collection of your drawings relating to autos or do you mean something else?

DB: Some Manga stories commonly have a thousand page arc and more. That and the graphic novel, both of which naturally have to be approached differently than, say, a standard 32-page super hero comic or 2-page gag panel, appeal to me as a way to stretch out as a cartoonist and designer, and of course, really test one's ability to engage and hold the reader. The anthology is a collection of short and shorter pieces, none much more than 30 pages, which are sort of a tying off of the work I once did for the likes of *DRAGcartoons, Cycletoons, Cycle* magazine, and *Hot Rod* magazine, and bringing it forward, hopefully with appeal to more than the motor minded. More hopefully, some of those shorter pieces are now springboards for longer things that won't be characterized as automotive. The plan is to make them available directly on the Internet at some point.

DW: Did you study your art formally?

DB: The best formal training came my way up to the 5th grade at Tulelake Elementary. Not sure there is even a school there anymore, in the new corporate farming world, but at that time there were many small homesteads in the area just south of Klamath Falls along the Oregon–California border. Every day the teachers would devote at least an hour, and many times half the day, to art projects. I did a mural of ducks on the lake with help of a blow-machine in the 3rd grade. We had a kiln in the room in the 5th grade and the ceiling was covered with model airplanes. We could hardly wait to get to the 8th grade where the room was nearly impassable because of art and science projects. But when we homesteaded again in southern Arizona there were zero art classes. So volunteering to do posters for school functions and the like was my art training thereafter until graduation from high school. I did collect rejection slips from *Mad*, as mentioned, and also from *Cartoons*, a hot rod humor magazine. Maybe building a couple frame-up hot rods at that time was also good design training. I think the local teachers had me tagged as an engineer when I went off to Arizona State, but I surprised them by signing up as an art major. I barely lasted the year, being fresh off the farm, and ended up in a three-year Army hitch. I did finally crack *Cartoons* during that time and continued to draw like crazy even after returning to Arizona State as an electrical engineer major. But that didn't take and within a year I switched back to art for the next year. Then off to Art Center College of Design in Los Angeles for three semesters, which was invaluable, before leaving for the enticing world of freelancing.

DW: Do you do your work out of your home or have a separate studio?

DB: To turn it around, as a smarty cartoonist, I'd have to say we have a home in our studio. It's efficient and convenient but one has to be alert to wandering distractions and tangents.

DW: Googling for background information for this interview, I found an article on your wife's "bead-loomed structures" (*Bead&Button*, February 2006, pp. 100–104). Is there any cross-pollination from having two artists in the family (beyond her getting inspiration from your taking her Porsche apart, as reported in the *Bead&Button* article)?

DB: Quite a bit, since we did meet at Art Center and she has two more semesters than I there, I'd have to say I steal more from her than she borrows from me. She had classic oil painting training from early on growing up in Palo Alto and was an art major at Stanford and San Francisco State before Art Center. Her color sense and practical ability to effortlessly mix the exact right color the very first time is amazing. I try to pay attention to her adventures in color and design, which is always instructional. Currently Jeanette is working full-time, as fast and furious as tiny beads allow, for her next show at Fuller Craft Museum, opening nearly now and one later at Mobilia in Cambridge, Massachusetts, this coming October.

DW: You have done the illustrations for several computer-related books in addition to those by Knuth. The connection to Lamport's LaTeX book seems obviously to have happened because of your work on Knuth's book. Did the others (for example, the books by Friedman and Felleisen on programming languages) result because they saw your work in Knuth's books?

DB: I assume that is the case because, rather than me approaching publishers to do further software books, I began getting contacted by art directors who had writers requesting my illustrations. Most involved the creation of a mascot to represent software which I greatly enjoy. Don had given me the stamp of approval, I suppose, and other sorts of smaller jobs also materialized. MIT Press used me for a catalog cover at one point, and over the last few years I've been pleasantly surprised by TEX user groups around the globe commissioning drawings used for posters, t-shirts, coffee cups, and whatever else they might imagine.

DW: Do you ever get tired of drawing the TEX lions?

DB: No, not yet and I don't expect I will. Seems each assignment has a unique situation which, if I can, I try to bend or expand the lion character to react or at least seem to fit well in whatever new world or garb comes along. Quite often there's some research involved with getting props and the background right especially if it's for an exotic location and I get jogged awake learning something new.

DW: For what other types of books or documents have you typically done illustrations?

DB: Looking back, I'd guess the bulk of my work has been doing kids' books for the educational system. Teacher's aids, workbooks, posters, some textbooks, and even coloring books. Almost equal to that is technical illustration for manuals and teaching materials in the work place. During one year, along with doing *Hot Rod Cartoon* stories through the mail and occasional Bay Area illustration jobs, I spent some of most every week in the air, flying to jobs drawing training materials for one of the world's largest business consulting firms. I was their west coast artist and drew mainly factory machines, scenes, and the processes to make things. Those illustrations had to be done quickly, in color markers, and at a borrowed desk; so they were nothing like TEX drawings. In another vein, not long ago I did a group of vector tech drawings totally in Adobe Illustrator on how to fix or hot rod your PC. At the other end of the spectrum, I'm currently doing color covers and interior watercolor and pencil drawings in a very soft style for *Herb Quarterly*.

DW: I'm curious how the illustration business works. Do you typically sell a drawing and all rights for its reuse as part of your fee, or do you license it for limited use (e.g., in one of Knuth's books) and retain the reproduction rights?

DB: Mostly it's a "work-for-hire" situation or I assign all rights of individual drawings. Actually, everything is negotiable, depending on all the typical business criteria and is a tricky part of the art of the business of art.

DW: There is a note posted from you and your wife at `http://www.912registry.org/racing/rcommnts.htm` that suggests a hot rod or classic car connection, you have already mentioned doing illustrations for car magazines, and there is that note in the article on her beadwork about you taking her Porsche apart. Is auto-related stuff a big hobby of yours?

DB: Yes, as a typical teen kid of the sixties, I was nutty about cars, not so much to race, but how they look and act. At the time there were plenty of abandoned junk cars laying around in the desert, so putting together a mode of personal expression or death trap was fairly easy. I went through the standard string of dubious dune bugs, manic motorcycles, and rambling street rods, but lately have mainly restoring some perky Porsches. Jeanette is also an enthusiast, so that helps — or we're both hopelessly lost, depending on perspective.

Lately, I think we've stopped looking for the next project, and are more concentrated on trying to keep what we have working—which makes so much sense, better not hold us to it.

DW: Let's finish with one more question about TEX. Have you ever used TEX, LATEX, or any of the other TEX-derived systems yourself? More generally, you mentioned using Adobe Illustrator. Do computers play a significant role in the way you do your art?

DB: So far, I've not had the "need to know" and haven't dug in yet. My thought was, a while back, when I did some work toward getting together a book on the early TEX drawings, that it should be set in TEX, natch. At that time, I probably didn't try hard enough to find a version I could run on my ancient Mac, and then, in other scattered ways, got bogged down. Still think it's a good idea. Meanwhile, the computer, besides being essential just to connect to the world, has greatly speeded up the give and take of rough drawing development, since a file can travel to many parties quickly, relieving a lot of the stress in moving a job along. Its ability to scan and manipulate is nearly magical. But it seems for me, everything still always starts with a pencil sketch.

DW: Thank you very much, Duane, for taking the time to participate in this interview. I am sure I am far from alone in the TEX community in being very glad to know more about the man who draws the ubiquitous TEX lions.

Thomas Esser

Thomas Esser created and maintained the popular teTeX distribution of TeX.

[Interview completed 5 June 2006.]

Dave Walden, interviewer: Please tell me a bit about yourself independent of the world of TeX.

Thomas Esser, interviewee: I studied mathematics and computer science at the University of Hannover. After achieving a diploma in mathematics, I worked for five years at the databases and information systems group as a research assistant.

I am now working as a system programmer in a company that provides services for banks. In my job, I am responsible for the configuration of our Unix servers and the middleware software running on them. Being part of the "development" department, I am not responsible for keeping the production systems alive; but our group is responsible for providing a configuration that is feasible to manage and that works gracefully in all kinds of situations (i.e., even under heavy load).

My family, i.e., my wife, my five-year-old son and I, have just recently moved into a new house in which we now live.

DW: Please tell me about how you first became involved with the world of TeX.

TE: As a student, I had a side job in the databases and information systems group (the same group where I had my primary job after my diploma). In that job, I had to do Unix system administration and to write documentation using LaTeX. The exciting thing for me was that I had never had done anything before with Unix, C and TeX. The good thing about the side job was that the research assistants helped me a lot and I somehow got into it.

DW: You are well known for the teTeX (`http://tug.org/teTeX/`) distribution of TeX. I suppose the letters "te" in teTeX are your initials; is that correct?

TE: Yes. At the time that teTeX was born, a lot of students used emTeX by Eberhard Mattes. So, basically, the idea to use the initials as part of the name of the distribution comes from emTeX.

DW: Do you yourself use TeX substantially? In this interview series, I have been surprised to discover that some of the most advanced TeXnicians don't actually use TeX very much — perhaps their full time jobs mostly force them to work with things other than TeX — and it is people who have major writing projects that are the biggest users of TeX and beneficiaries of the efforts of developers like you.

TE: During my time in the University, I used LaTeX regularly and almost exclusively for all my writings. Since then, I hardly write any documents at all.

DW: Not very many people undertake to create and maintain a complete distribution. How did your life with TeX evolve such that you decided to create teTeX?

TE: As part of my side job, I had to maintain the workstations of the department. This included a TeX installation which at some time, I have updated. It used to be a hard job to find and install all the necessary pieces (Web2c, LaTeX, CM fonts, LaTeX fonts, SunView previewer, X11 previewer, various printer drivers, etc.) and to use the directory structure that I wanted.

At some later point, I found that a Linux distribution (SLS or slackware) had a slightly newer TeX than I had. I contacted the maintainer (unfortunately, I don't remember his name) and he told me where to find the absolute latest `tex.web` (namely, Knuth's ftp server at Stanford) and how to patch Web2c.

The TeX installation in our workstation pool was used by a lot of students who wanted to have a similar system for their Linux boxes at home (so that they could use the same style files, etc.). I started to create floppy sets for these students and this was the beginning of teTeX.

While I was enhancing my TeX system (still only used by the local department and some students), I saw that the standard TeX distribution for Linux (NTeX at that time) was inferior in many ways. My first attempt was to try to help to improve NTeX, but somehow that failed (I can't really remember, but I think that bugs that I had reported still appeared in the next release, etc.). I felt that I could make a better distribution.... The first release of teTeX was Linux only, but uploaded to the large Linux sites (tsx and sunsite).

DW: Not being a Linux user myself, I don't know what tsx and sunsite are. Will you please explain? I also am not a teTeX user, so I don't know if you were implying above that teTeX is now available for non-Linux systems.

TE: `tsx-11.mit.edu` and `sunsite.unc.edu` are two of the bigger and more well known ftp sites which carry Linux software. They both have plenty of mirrors, so one can easily spread some piece of software all around the world by uploading to these sites.

Very soon after the initial release of teTeX, which was teTeX-0.2.1 in 1994, I started to make it more portable so that it could be compiled on other Unix systems, too. I think that after a year or so, teTeX was already portable to most Unix systems. Today it should run on nearly any Unix system and some people even use teTeX on Windows by using the Cygwin build environment or the mingw compiler (a gcc variant that creates Windows binaries).

DW: Karl Berry remembers that he first saw your work with teTeX about the time he was developing Kpathsea and Web2c. Was there cross-pollination between what you and he were doing? If so, how did your projects affect each other?

TE: All teTeX versions are based on Web2c/Kpathsea. It is true that Karl was the maintainer at the time that teTeX started. I had my own ideas about performance and a few internals and teTeX started using features of Kpathsea in a way that Karl did not predict. So, in fact, some tweaking of Web2c/Kpathsea was needed. My way of doing that was to arrange with Karl about changing things upstream (i.e., in Karl's code). I have never kept my changes private. teTeX would not have existed without Web2c/Kpathsea, so Karl's work was essential for me. About Karl's view about teTeX: my guess is that he was glad that he did not need to care about the things that teTeX has in addition to the "core" of Web2c/Kpathsea.

DW: Karl once told me that the changes went both ways and used words very similar to your presumption of how he viewed things.

My understanding is that teTeX is more than a collection of TeX packages and fonts— that it also includes a number of helper scripts such as `fmtutil`, updmap, etc., that are now viewed as fundamental parts of the system. Tell me about your ambitions or philosophy that guided your evolution of the teTeX system, or did the evolution just track user requests or your own needs?

TE: I have always seen teTeX from the administrator's view. My goal was always to create something that is simple to install, to use and to maintain. Let us take the example of font handling. All the drivers have their own rules (different set of "built in" fonts, their own map file syntax, etc.). I could have tried to rewrite these programs, but my way of doing the integration was to write a few scripts which provide one interface for all drivers. So, now, you make a map file known with updmap and all drivers can use the fonts. The scripts that I have provided thus hide details which most users don't want to care about.

A lot of scripting has been done by me — even existing scripts for automatic font generation have been rewritten more or less from scratch (which Karl has adopted later with slight modifications). But, some scripts have been contributed by other people. I can remember two: `texdoctk` and `texdoc`.

DW: By virtue of teTeX being including with Linux, it may have become the most used of any of the TeX distributions. How did this make you feel? Did it cause problems for you?

TE: I am glad that teTeX has been useful to a lot of people. I had used GNU software on SunOS and Linux almost from the beginning and teTeX was my way to give some work back to the free software community. By means of Red Hat Linux, teTeX has even reached the computer where Don Knuth maintains the master sources of TeX. Knuth has written a few emails to me and I know that he was pleased to see teTeX has provided an "intelligent" installation of TeX. Well, definitely, that filled me with pride.

It never was a problem that teTeX has had many users. In the early days, I had the time to dig into every problem a user reported. Of course, I can't provide this service any more. But, generally, people understand that I can't solve all of their problems and they are usually grateful if I can provide them with pointers to documentation or other resources (e.g., mailing lists).

The distribution grew, because people asked for things to be added like `dvipng` (a DVI to PNG translator), Xy-pic, PSTricks, the `memoir` package, etc.

teTeX started as a reasonably small thing, but it ended up as something which was too large for me to handle with a reasonable amount of time.

DW: Do I gather correctly from this that you did teTeX pretty much alone, or did you have other people helping you with various things?

TE: The job of putting individual parts together was done by me alone. On the other hand, I could make use of the work of many people who wrote the software that teTeX is made from. As far as documentation (`http://tug.org/teTeX/tetex-texmfdist/doc/`) is concerned, there was some help by various people: Dirk Hillbrecht wrote the first version of the teTeX manual, Claire Connelly and Frank Küster have contributed several manual pages and Keith Refson wrote the teTeX documentation guide which was later maintained by Joao Palhoto Matos. Several teTeX releases have included binaries — most of them have been compiled and contributed by other people.

DW: Please describe some of your relationships with other parts of the worldwide TeX community — user groups, conferences, projects such as TeX Live as it has evolved over time, other developers, etc. Have they played a useful role in your work? Is there some better coordination or support that could be provided?

TE: The development of Web2c, teTEX and TEX Live have always been very close to each other, i.e., all developers have always been in contact with each other. Web2c/Kpathsea was the core of teTEX, and teTEX was the core of TEX Live.

It was always a great pleasure for me to join conferences and meet all those people who I formerly had only known by mail. I am very grateful for all invitations to TEX conferences that I have received.

Regarding coordination: I think that the TEX community lacks some level of coordination. Just two examples: (a) There is no naming convention for hyphenation pattern files nor is there a standard about what exactly is allowed in such files or which catcodes can be assumed. This is a problem for packages such as ConTEXt (which target more than one TEX distribution). (b) There is no common standard about the internal structure of a package uploaded to CTAN. It would be great if either there would be a uniform structure or if each package would be accompanied with metadata which provides the necessary information about how a package should be transferred, unpacked and installed.

DW: I recently interviewed Christian Schenk who developed the MiKTEX distribution. Do you know him?

TE: I met him once in Bremen at a meeting of CTAN maintainers and people making "big" free TEX distributions (sponsored by DANTE e.V.). I know that Christian has taken over files from me (via TEX Live, I think) and that he also has his own replacements for scripts that I have invented.

We have not talked a lot to each other, but I remember well what he has said at this meeting. It was about enhancing the CTAN infrastructure to allow accessing the files on CTAN as packages which can be installed/updated as units (possibly over the Internet). Christian told us his ideas about what would be needed (e.g., package metadata, some web services and things like that). The point is that nothing has happened about package-based access to CTAN and MiKTEX's repository (which is essentially a repacked subset of CTAN) is still the only thing which offers this service. [Editor's note: since this interview was completed, TEX Live also now offers updates and installation over the Internet.]

DW: You have recently announced that you will no longer be supporting teTEX. Was there a specific change in your life and interests that led to this decision, or was it a more long term and general evolution of priorities and interests?

TE: This is a decision that evolved over time. Each release took me a longer to prepare than the release before. During the preparation of teTEX-3.0, I felt that I was already stealing too much time from my family. But, I did not want to announce the end of teTEX immediately after that release. First, I wanted to make sure that there are no severe bugs that need immediate fixing.

DW: Looking back on your experience developing and maintaining teTEX, how do you feel about it the effort you put into it and the results?

TE: First and most important: it was fun and I have learned a lot.

I am happy that teTEX has been useful to many users (and system administrators) and that the distribution itself has a good reputation. I think that it would have been better to be more restrictive about adding packages to the `texmf` tree or to increase the level of automation in maintaining that `texmf` tree. My dream is to see an infrastructure that allows TEX users to update their distribution directly with packages that authors upload to CTAN (without repackaging by anybody else).

DW: Is there a plan for someone to continue maintaining teTEX, or do you hope someone will take over its support?

TE: My hope is that someone or a group of people make up a good successor. I have no worries about the source tree which is still maintained as part of TEX Live. In my dreams, the texmf tree maintenance is replaced by an infrastructure to install/update CTAN packages. For "offline" purposes, someone would just need to download a list of packages from CTAN and make them available as a release.

DW: Do you have plans for the time that will be freed up by no longer maintaining teTEX — a new "hobby" perhaps?

TE: I will still spend time on TEX related matters: answering mail and maintaining a few things in the TEX Live repository. Without the need to make a big release, I will no longer have to steal time that I should be spending with my family.

DW: Thank you very much for taking the time to participate in this interview. I am sure that many TEX users will be interested to learn something about the man whose TEX distribution is so important to them.

Aleksander Simonic and Adriana McCrea

Aleksander Simonic and Adriana McCrea are the "WinEdt team" that develops and supports the WinEdt editor popular with many MS Windows users of TeX.

[Interview completed 28 June 2006.]

Dave Walden, interviewer: I am going to assume that readers have already read the partial history of WinEdt at `http://www.winedt.com/story.html`. Therefore, let's start with some background information. My memory from sending you a check for my copy of WinEdt is that you are in Halifax, Nova Scotia. The couple of times I've visited Halifax, I've loved it. Are you both from the Halifax area, or did you come there from elsewhere for school?

Aleksander Simonic, interviewee: I personally don't know any true Canadians: we all came from somewhere else....

Adriana McCrea, interviewee: Awh, c'm on; the answer does not reflect the question: us in Halifax. I came here by a roundabout route. But too true; Halifax is small but beautiful....

AS: Right: I came from Slovenia as a PhD student in 1990. I wanted to work with Heydar Radjavi (my advisor), whom I'd previously met in Ljubljana. I wasn't sure (didn't think to check) which coast Halifax belonged to (had a vague idea it was on the west, and hearing something about a big explosion (`http://www.cbc.ca/halifaxexplosion`) having taken place there, assumed it was near Pearl Harbor [wrong war/wrong coast]). Anyway, it was a career decision which I don't regret, despite some nasty winters....

DW: And so, Adriana, from your last name I presume that you had ancestors that were part of the great Scots migration to Canada (although I guess there may also be McCreas from Ireland)?

AM: I'm a (more) recent emigré, Dave, having come from Belfast to Canada in 1977. Still have a bit of an accent....

DW: Alex, I see from the Mathematics Genealogy Project database (`http://genealogy.math.ndsu.nodak.edu`) that your mathematical ancestors include Leibniz, two Bernoullis, Euler, Lagrange, Poisson, etc. — pretty impressive. Please elaborate on your motivations for developing your own editor rather than just using an existing editor? Presumably you were already using some version of TeX to write mathematics, right?

AS: The names you mention are indeed impressive; I don't quite consider myself in their league! As for the second part of the question: that's easy. As your PhD studies are stretching into their 3rd year and your supervisor is gently reminding you that PhD studies are not exactly a full-time career, you tend to discover that you have talents unrelated to your studies.

In my case creating a personalized computer environment to typeset the research results (when I'd have them) looked like a reasonable way to spend the evenings.

It is true that I was considered a TeX guru on Unix as I had used TeX since the 1980s (on VAX at that time). At the Math department at Dalhousie I used Emacs as an editor, but when I got my own PC with Windows (3.1) I wanted some sort of GUI for TeXing. That was 1993. It was surprisingly easy to make an application do exactly what I personally wanted it to do.

AM: The hard part came later when Alex had to make WinEdt do what other people wanted it to do. For example, there was practically no Help or guidance in the early days (I'm talking about 1997, now, when I was on board) as Alex's idea of guidance was "if you don't know what this is for, it's not for you".

DW: What was the reaction in your math department to your work on a new editor? Did you get your colleagues there to use early versions of it?

AS: I kept this for myself as my supervisor made me repeat an oath I made that I was serious about completing a PhD in Math.

AM: In the 1980s, in Slovenia, Alex had a tendency to drop out of school for a couple of months while working on some pretty lucrative computer/software projects. His supervisor at the Math department at Dal knew this and had asked him to be sure that he wanted to come to pursue a Math PhD.

AS: A few friends at the department (Dal) had suggested I should install one of the early versions of Linux and X Windows and use the same software as we did in the math department. I was inclined to do so, but my computer had only 8mb of memory while 16 was required for such installation. With memory at $100 per MB, that was not an option....

AM: In 1995 Alex announced the availability of WinEdt on the TeX newsgroup. So the very first users of all the early versions came from the TeX community, mostly in Germany. We have very fond memories of many of these early users: as we dropped out of our respective academic fields and lost touch with our peers, they became our friends and colleagues (erstwhile, alas, as many of them have since gone on to other things, leaving WinEdt behind). Truth be told, we lead a very isolated life and have done so for about 10 years now....

DW: The photo of the two of you and caption about half way down the page at `http://www.winedt.com/about.html` (and reproduced at the beginning of this interview) suggests the WinEdt team is just the two of you. Do you have other people working for you or is WinEdt in fact just the two of you?

AS: It's just the two of us. Programming is done by me and Adriana is for the human touch :-).

DW: I've seen lots of math people drift into the world of computers — I myself did so. But how do you feel, Adriana, about finding yourself helping support a computer program rather than doing whatever you took the trouble to train to do?

AM: Well, five shortlistings and several squandered opportunities for tenure track positions in History departments across Canada later, as well as a strange career choice (at the end of my post-doc I took a contractual university administration position) have steered my boat into this harbour. My admin and people experience have, I think, served WinEdt well. Mind you, my typing still sucks and an ambition to actually learn TEX is still on my to-do list....

DW: The title for the unwritten part of your history at `http://www.winedt.com/story.html` suggests the path to WinEdt32 was not easy, and now you have WinEdt 5. Can you give me a few of the highlights and "lowlights" of those stories?

AS: I'll let Adriana answer this one as I tend to focus on "lowlights". Just how many times can you answer a problem report that the "LATEX button in WinEdt does not work" before you lose it?

AM: "All work and no play"; Alex often feels rather burned out and suffers many lows.... Another role I try to fill in WinEdt is to keep things in perspective; sometimes successfully, others not. But back to the question at hand: One of the biggest highlights has been getting the Mailing List as a forum for discussion and exchange. That was in 1997 and it is still going strong. The greatest lowlights, for me at least, have been fraudulent license orders and the knowledge of the prevalence of crack codes in the Internet. I suppose the latter might be considered proof of the popularity of the program. Interestingly though: after 9/11 (September 11, 2001) we had several people contact us to register, mentioning that they had come to consider software piracy a type of terrorism (and regretting they had been using a crack)....

DW: What is your feeling about the effort it takes to keep up with operating system releases as opposed to effort put into adding capability features to WinEdt?

AS: I don't try to program for tomorrow's operating systems or ever faster computers. I try to keep WinEdt suitable for the average computer of today, but eventually tomorrow comes and I have to rewrite big chunks of code and recompile them with newer and better tools — with their own set of inherited problems which have to be discovered and fixed. Always, the two issues require a compromise, and adding a new feature does not please everyone. There is always a wish list for new features (see `http://www.winedt.org`), and I keep a to-do list. I try to give priority to features that are reasonably feasible and would benefit the largest number of users. There are editors more powerful (others more easy to use) than WinEdt: for better or worse the program has evolved a certain way....

AM: I have to say that Alex gets numerous feature requests and he is often caught up in deciding what *not* to do (or implement yet)....

AS: New operating systems are, nevertheless, a reality and cannot be ignored if you want to keep a desktop application alive. Thankfully, there is usually a grace period of six months to a year in which I am able to catch up. Regarding XP for instance, functionality has been important, but the look counts as well: for example, people might assume that an application that does not support XP themes, is obsolete and unsupported.

DW: How about keeping up with the TEX distributions? Do you make any special efforts to keep up with MiKTEX and TEX Live? Do you have a lot of WinEdt users working with particular commercial distributions you have to keep up with?

AS: I always check new or upcoming versions of MiKTEX and make sure that WinEdt's default settings work with it. If there is any incompatibility I am usually alerted in advance by the keen users that are participating in beta testing. As far as WinEdt is concerned, there isn't much difference between MiKTEX and TEX Live as long as the TEX binary folder is included in the Windows PATH thus making launching executables easy regardless of where TEX is installed. Relatively few WinEdt users work with other TEX distributions. Y&Y TEX comes to mind but since it is no longer being developed there is no need to maintain WinEdt's configuration for it; it can stay the same....

DW: You have a significant user community (the `http://www.winedt.org` site mentioned earlier). You mentioned above that you monitor the WinEdt wish list. In what other ways do you coordinate with that community, reacting to user needs, deciding what you do and what community members do, etc.?

AS: In the late 1990s Adriana noticed that several users had set up web sites in which they offered useful advice and instructions on how to solve some language or task specific issue in WinEdt. Contributions were announced on the Mailing List but were hosted on web pages of the contributors. Many of these were students and their web pages disappeared after a while; also, some information becoming obsolete, we thought to set up a WinEdt.org site. This decision was really prompted by a nice collection of contributions by Robert Schlicht, who agreed to manage the domain; he is the author of many useful contributions and co-ordinates the activities there.

AM: Alex does not coordinate or decide what happens at WinEdt.org. However, he is a subscriber to the Mailing List and participates in discussions. . . .

DW: By the way, thank you, Alex, for showing me (in a set of messages parallel to this interview) how to set up some macros in WinEdt to allow me to copy text from the clipboard into different text buffers and then copy those text buffers back to the clipboard in a different order — I used this capability for alternately pasting `AM` and `AS` as I converted this interview into HTML. Is this the sort of thing you yourself might help with on the WinEdt discussion list if someone else doesn't answer first?

AS: Yes. If a WinEdt-related question on the Mailing List isn't answered in a timely fashion I usually post a reply. Sometimes it is just a pointer in the right direction and sometimes it contains more detailed instructions (especially if the documentation is not clear on the subject). Occasionally, the question exposes a bug or a lack of functionality in WinEdt and such problems are fixed, or, when feasible, the functionality is improved for the next version. The Mailing List gives me a chance to explain or justify certain behavior and it also provides valuable feedback on which many development-related decisions are based.

DW: I recently interviewed Christian Schenk, the creator of MiKTeX. Many users of WinEdt also appear to use the MiKTeX distribution. Was there any coordination between you and him that led to the joint popularity of your two systems?

AS: MiKTeX has been (and continues to be) a godsend to anyone wanting to TeX on their PC running Windows.

AM: Without any personal co-ordination, WinEdt and MiKTeX have been growing up together. As far as we know Christian does not use WinEdt and it has been many years since Alex has actually used TeX: these days it is only to ensure that WinEdt's default settings are properly configured to invoke MiKTeX and related TeX accessories.

AS: Although WinEdt is mostly used for TeXing it is designed as a reasonably powerful all-purpose ASCII editor.

AM: Yes: it was really cool using the HTML configuration in preparing the new HELP . . . .

DW: As an old computer programmer, I have sometimes thought that it might be nice to have a little piece of software that I could develop and support, be my own boss, and make enough money selling it to support me. Of course, I haven't actually done that because (a) I'm afraid I might have to spend more time dealing with operating system and compiler issues than dealing the actual application I am interested in, (b) I don't have a good idea for something a lot of people might like to buy, and (c) even if I had a good idea and started selling some copies, I fear I'd have no protective barrier from a large vendor subsuming my system's capability in some system the large vendor offers. You are apparently living this dream that I and probably others have had. How do you feel about the course your life has taken with WinEdt?

AS: I did not have much control over the sequence of events that led me into developing WinEdt and trying to make a living as a shareware author. It's been an interesting 10 years and I've learned a lot. I am almost ready to write a book on how to really write an editor :-). As for my living the dream, it is the occasional nightmare as well....

AM: Our way of life demands (or at least we think so and give it) almost 24/7 attention, although we do take time off to sleep and eat. The effort has been rewarding: we now have a nice roof over our heads and Alex has a fine garden in which to replenish his soul. And he is well respected for his work.

AS: To treat each of the points you bring up:

(a) At first you can focus on features and ideas but after your application reaches a certain amount of users, operating system and even hardware specific problems take more and more of your time leaving you less to focus on new or missing features. If there is any chance of a conflict with another application or a process, it will eventually happen to someone. The idea is to correctly diagnose the problem (often with the help of the first victim who encountered it) and then find the way around. It is a non-rewarding and time-consuming job but essential for the application's survival....

(b) Nor did I. Developing a tool that you (the author) would like to have for yourself is a good starting point. Thinking about marketability of the application comes later when the product is ready to meet the world. At that point you can put some kind of a reasonable price and conditions on the application's use, depending on how much effort and time you've spent developing it and how far you are willing to go in supporting and maintaining it. And don't expect any miracles: it takes time to build a reputation. And unless you came up with the idea for a "killer" application (the first word processor or Internet browser comes to mind) there are always alternatives; some of them likely well-established with a solid user-base — yet another reason to focus on quality and ease of use of your application.

(c) This may indeed be an issue with some "hot" applications. However, these days it is not very likely that a desktop application (like a TEX-oriented editor) will get the attention of "the big guys". The more work and experience you put in your application the less likely it is that somebody will succeed in trying to get you out of business.

AM: I seem to recall that we'd dream of Bill Gates contacting us, offering 10 million dollars to take over WinEdt. Then we saw the Simpsons episode when Homer attracts BG's attention and it does not turn out at all well for him.....

DW: If you are willing to answer, based on your experience with WinEdt and its interactions with the world of TEX, how do you see the prospects for TEX? Do you have a growing number of TEX users, or do you find yourself having to push those parts of WinEdt that make it suitable for improving its utility in other domains?

AS: TEX will not go away any time soon. The interfaces to it may evolve (perhaps into something more WYSIWYG) but TEX's ability to properly typeset mathematics equations will continue to be a challenge to alternative typesetting systems and word processors. I find that new users realize, after a while, that having to typeset their work with a markup language has its advantages even if it is not completely straightforward and it requires some learning. An editor can help by highlighting environments, matching delimiters, etc.... I always try to make such functionality in WinEdt customizable and thus suitable for most markup languages rather than hard-coding TEX-specific rules. However, TEX users remain the majority of WinEdt's clientele and I don't expect this to change just yet.

It is important that TEX systems support conversion of currently popular document formats. Currently this is PDF, while PostScript and DVI are no longer the preferred final format for compiled documents. DVI is still suitable for a working format especially because of source specials linking the source files with the compiled file in a DVI viewer (e.g., MiKTEX's YAP) that supports such functionality. I suspect that TEX would lose some popularity if it was not possible to compile it into PDF. But that's obviously not a problem as there are many ways to achieve the task with accessories that come with today's TEX systems.

DW: Have you learned about the business side of software development in the "school of hard knocks" or have you been able to find some sort of education or mentoring that helped you? Is there any sort of industry association for independent software developers such as yourselves that lets you share experiences and address common business problems?

AS: It was all from school of hard knocks. Lots of mistakes, thanks to my ignorance and lack of experience, were made in the early years. I had to learn my lessons fast and when Adriana took over the business side of the project I was relieved to be able once again to devote my time and energy to programming.

The last 10 years have been an interesting time. A lot has changed when it comes to the culture of downloading and installing software — gone from Kermitting files and ftp to instant broadband access and speedy installation. It's been interesting to have been here all along and live the changes as they have been occurring.

AM: There is a Shareware Software Association, but we've done things alone and learned by trial and error.

DW: Is there some obvious question you anticipated I would ask but haven't? If so, please give me the question and answer.

AM: I was wowed that you wanted to include us in this corner of the TEX site. I guess I live in fear that the fact that we want money in exchange for WinEdt will in the end leave us with no new registered users. We occasionally get the equivalent of hate mail for not being freeware.

DW: Thank you for taking the time to participate in this interview. I've enjoyed talking to you, and it's great to have a little more insight about the couple who provide the editor that I use for many hours every day.

AM: It's been fun. Maybe this will be the spur for me to bring our story up to date on `winedt.com`. We have enjoyed remembering this road less travelled, and have been reminded to be grateful for our talents....

David Kastrup

David Kastrup is a frequent contributor to `comp.text.tex` and manifestly a TeXnician (see the answer to Exercise 1.1 in *The TeXbook*).
[Interview completed 21 August 2006.]

Dave Walden, interviewer: Please tell me a bit about yourself personally, outside the world of TeX.

David Kastrup, interviewee: Well, I am afraid I'll have to use the T-word when talking about jobs: for the last few years I tried working on TeX-related tasks, self-employed, but this will have to change soon since it does not pay the bills — partly because of the expectation of people that free software should be written for free, partly because of my preference to focus primarily on things deemed impossible. Unfortunately, there are few tasks not involving clearly possible parts.

I started fiddling with computers at about 13, first working with an Olivetti minicomputer, then later switching to the Cyber 175 in the university computing center. So I actually worked with punch cards as main storage and input media for some time. My own first computer was a Nascom II (Z80-based) which I soldered together myself. I also eventually wrote a CP/M BIOS for it (which became somewhat ubiquitous) and designed, wired and soldered most of its extensions.

For the largest part of my life, I lived in Aachen, Germany, where I eventually got my diploma in electrical engineering. I went to Bochum for a doctorate, but it remains pending completion. For quite some time I have been living on my own with no family to support.

Apart from various computing diversions, my main hobbies are rock climbing and music, with a focus on the Baroque. As part of that I am currently singing alto in some choirs, and I am working on a scheme for employing this voice type in non-classical settings. In the process, I recently added the accordion to my bag of instruments (already containing violin and guitar) to deliver Yiddish, Irish, Russian and German stuff mostly of a folk character.

As a curiosity for your American readers, I never owned a car and do almost all of my transportation by bike (the kind with human propulsion) within a compass of 15 miles.

DW: How and when did you first become involved with TeX and its friends?

DK: I actually don't remember too well. There was some project where porting TeX to some embedded system was considered, but it never got off the ground. That was the time when I got *TEX: The Program*, in hardcover. Of course, this was still TEX 2.0. LATEX came into play at some later time. I also had to write my own printer driver when the HP Deskjet+ came out (which cost about US$1000 at that time): it was the first "affordable" printer capable of printing graphics as fast as text. I adopted a driver from Nelson Beebe but had to significantly change it to make it work on a computer with 640kB of RAM (with 300 dpi output) *and* keep the printer busy in spite of a rather slow computer. Nowadays I am probably mostly known as the maintainer of AUCTEX, a job I took over from Per Abrahamsen.

DW: Can you tell me and other readers who are not familiar with AUCTEX (`http://www.gnu.org/software/auctex/`) something more about it.

DK: AUCTEX is a TEX/LATEX/ConTEXt/Texinfo editing support package under Emacs (probably the world's greatest editor prototyping platform). AUCTEX is a combination of editing functionality (summarized under a menu called `LaTeX` or similar) and job control (summarized under `Command`). It can run the various TEX processors and utilities and jump to the location of prospective errors in the source. Per was the second maintainer of AUCTEX and got tired of it. Development was pretty much stalling, and so I finally took up his offer of taking over maintenance. AUCTEX's job control is more sophisticated than that of the default modes: it can seamlessly switch between producing PDF and/or DVI files, it deals well with multiple-file documents, it can make use of forward and backward search for DVI (using source specials) and even use pdfsync for PDF. Its text formatting and indentation is pretty "natural", it can understand the outcommented document structures in a `.dtx` file and appropriately format them, too.

It also offers folding away of syntactic structures (like footnotes) in order to better focus on the important parts of the document. And, of course, it can replace math and similar constructs in the source buffer by WYSIWYG renditions of them, by using the magic of preview-latex (a combination of `preview.sty` for extracting images and glue code in Emacs for running LATEX, dvipng, Ghostscript and other utilities and placing the resulting output in the buffer).

DW: I see *many* contributions from you on the `comp.text.tex` discussion group. What are your motivations for participating so much for so long?

DK: Showing off, I guess. TEX is so contorted and idiosyncratic that it gives ample opportunity for impossible things. Apart from that, it annoys me if stuff gets done in unnecessarily complicated or inelegant ways, even if the elegance comes at a price.

DW: Will you please elaborate on your view of TEX, the language.

DK: Let's be blunt: TEX is not a language for quick-and-dirty solutions. There are those things it has been specifically created for, and those tend to be quick-and-easy. That set is limited. Anything else is more in the slow-and-painful department. And sometimes there are shortcuts through the pain. It is like ripping a band-aid off instead of slowly pulling it. Here is an example:

```
\def\sorttext#1{\setbox0\vbox{{\language255\hsize=0pt\hfuzz\maxdimen
   \parfillskip0pt\noindent#1\par}\sortvlist\unpack}\unvbox0 }
\def\sortvlist{{\unskip\unpenalty \setbox0\lastbox
  \ifvoid0\noindent\else\setbox0\hbox{\unhbox0\ }\sortvlist\sortin\fi}}
\def\sortin{\setbox2\lastbox\ifdim\wd2>\wd0{\sortin}\fi\box2\box0}
\def\unpack{{\setbox0\lastbox\ifvoid0\indent\else\unpack\unhbox0\fi}}

\sorttext{%
```

```
The fall (bababadalgharaghtakamminarronnkonnbronntonner%
ronntuonnthunntrovarrhounawnskawntoohoohoordenenthur%
nuk!) of a once wallstrait oldparr is retaled early in bed and later
on life down through all christian minstrelsy. The great fall of the
offwall entailed at such short notice the pftjschute of Finnegan,
erse solid man, that the humptyhillhead of humself prumptly sends
an unquiring one well to the west in quest of his tumptytumtoes:
and their upturnpikepointandplace is at the knock out in the park
where oranges have been laid to rust upon the green since dev%
linsfirst loved livvy.
}
```

[Editor's note: you can see the output of the above `\sorttext` definition at `http://tug.org/interviews/interview-files/david-kastrup-example.pdf`.]

Now the above code is dense. Every token has a definite purpose and could not be replaced by something shorter. It is the essence of elegance in TeX programming, and yet it is a total incomprehensible mess, even though it is supposed to solve a simple programming task.

There is an annual obfuscated C programming contest. The same would be rather pointless for TeX: every nontrivial task has only obfuscated solutions, anyway.

TeX is suitable for typesetting *The Art of Computer Programming*. That's about it. Its natural extension language is Pascal, but hardly anybody uses that: I can't think of anybody who has ever invented new whatsits, one of the basic extension mechanisms in TeX.

Instead, macros are used as a substitute for programming. TeX's macro expansion language is the only way to implement conditionals and loops, but the corresponding control variables can't be influenced by macro expansion (TeX's "mouth" in Knuth's terminology). Instead assignments must be executed by the back end (TeX's "stomach"). Stomach and mouth execute at different times and independently from one another. But it is not possible to solve nontrivial programming tasks with either: only the unholy chimera made from both can solve serious problems. ε-TeX gives the mouth a few more teeth and changes some of that, but the changes are not really fundamental: expansion still makes no assignments.

DW: My understanding is that you have been a participant in the $\varepsilon_{\mathcal{X}}$TeX project (`http://www.extex.org`). What is your role in that, can you tell me something about where it stands, and more generally what are your thoughts on a successor to TeX?

DK: I am not at the current point of time involved in $\varepsilon_{\mathcal{X}}$TeX. They did consult me while in the initial planning phase as an expert on TeX's internals, in order to derive a good understanding of TeX's existing architecture, and a good understanding how to best modularize it in a manner useful for extensions. We also tried fleshing out what kind of extensions would be desirable, and how to accommodate them. I have not, however, followed the project's progress afterwards.

I have my own ideas about how to make work on a successor to TeX not drown in complexity, and that includes an implementation language which can express the kind of optimization TeX indulges in in a natural manner. Like Emacs Lisp, an implementation language that has evolved with Emacs itself, I think that such a language should coevolve with a typesetting system. In a way, the traveling junkyard of editing solutions that is Emacs has been able to grow much beyond the initial single-person project because of Emacs Lisp and resulted in a decrease in complexity for an average programmer.

TEX, written in a procedural language, is as complex as a single person of extraordinary capabilities is able to manage. Better modularization, as done in the $\varepsilon_{\mathcal{X}}$TEX project, can only somewhat reduce the complexity any single extension project will have to deal with.

DW: I presume that the implementation language ideas you just mentioned are the same as those reported in the recently published EuroTEX proceedings. I'll go read that article again.

Since this interview is for the TEX Users Group, it occurs to me to ask if TUG or any of the other TEX user groups have relevance to your work and if you see relevance for them regarding the future of TEX?

DK: For me, naturally the most relevant local TEX user group is DANTE in Germany, of which I am also a member. The relevance of this group and others for TEX development is mixed: even though DANTE is the best funded LUG as far as I know, its means are not sufficient for funding long-scale full-time work being done in Germany. DANTE is quite important for organizing conferences and enabling developers to attend them, also for keeping server structures going and so on: in short, they do a lot to maintain a space where hobbyist work will reach its audience and communication is possible. The project funds also are helping to keep work focused (like that of the Latin Modern fonts) and developers willing to finish what it takes to deliver value to the users.

However, the limitations of budgets require working with an efficiency that is not viable in commercial programming projects: with customary project management, programmers are to some degree replaceable, and a project's goals can be finished even with some fluctuation in the personnel. This does not really work for projects funded by the TEX groups: basically, they can only fund persons, not projects, and which projects happen to be funded depend strictly on what people want to do and can be expected to do. If people leave a project, it is usually not viable to replace them.

So in a lot of ways, the user groups do the best they can to increase and support the existing impetus of TEX development, but can't really do much in the way of steering it.

DW: My previous interview was of Alex Simonic and Adriana McCrea who develop and support WinEdt. It sounds like they are at least eking out a living with their shareware package. You indicated in your first answer that making a living in the world of TEX is tenuous. Do you think there is something wrong with the "open source" or "free software" model under which much of the TEX and TEX-related work seems to be done?

DK: Please note that shareware is not free software. The principal problem with free software as a business model is that there really is little in the way of bootstrapping it. Programmers tend to be "mad scientists" to some degree or other, and TEX programming mostly has attraction for the worst of those. This means that you often have people with a bad judgment concerning business requirements and project management and time planning and customer interaction. For proprietary software, this is less of a problem: if you are the only supplier for a marketable product, poor market interaction does not kill your business prospects. In a free software market, however, being the developer of a product gives you just a headstart for marketing your own product, but it does not put anybody else out of the race.

And that makes the transfer of a project into a self-sustaining business with a working marketing department and project management quite a bit harder to do with free software. There are companies like Red Hat and a lot of other solution providers who managed that transition, but it is by no means easy. You need to keep an innovative edge over your competition throughout, and that is not easy.

On the other hand, making actual progress instead of reinventing the wheel can't be expected to be easy, and the current market dynamics focused on proprietary software waste a lot of energy on duplicate efforts.

DW: Thank you very much for taking the time to participate in this interview. I hope we will have an opportunity to meet in person at some point.

DK: You are welcome.

Peter Flynn

Peter has worked on TeX interfaces at many levels for many years, including SGML, XML, dual web and print presentations, within the context of excellent typography. He is also a past board member of TUG.

[Interview completed 19 September 2006.]

Dave Walden, interviewer: Please tell me a bit about your personal history independent of TeX.

Peter Flynn, interviewee: My infancy and early childhood was spent moving, although I remember little detail. At that time, if your company said 'move', you moved, and my father's job took him all over southern England. In 1961 the pace slowed down and we moved from rural eastern England to the Midlands for five years. Then my father was moved again, this time 'home' to Ireland (although I'd been born in England, we still had strong family ties to Cork) but rather than disrupt my schooling I stayed on as a boarder, returning home in the vacations.

The school was to have a major effect on my life, as it was there I discovered the big box of little bits of metal with letters on the ends: the remnants of the school printing press, which nearly got me expelled for printing a scurrilous leaflet about an unpopular teacher! Nevertheless, I eventually left school for Exeter University to read languages, and filled in as a reporter on the student newspaper. But I discovered that 'languages' in a British university meant 99 percent literature and 1 percent language. I loved the reading, but I wasn't a lit. critter, and I only stuck it for a year.

The next year was spent earning a living back home, first selling paint, and then delivering laundry, until those little letters called me, and I ended up doing a business degree at the London College of Printing. 1976 was not a good year to graduate: Maggie Thatcher was crushing the print unions, and Fleet Street was decamping *en masse* to the docklands. I was given the chance to do a taught MA in computerised planning at what was then the Central London Poly, and I emerged in 1978 working for the Printing and Publishing Industry Training Board, trying to browbeat a reluctant industry into training people in the 'new technology'.

When Mrs Thatcher summarily wound up all the ITBs and put us onto the street, I fled printing for a few years to sell dialup computing services to an equally reluctant financial clientele who spent most of their time in City wine bars. I had got married in the meantime, and for some years had been quietly looking for a job in Ireland. The university in Cork was expanding its computing support, and I joined them in 1984. Everyone said I was mad to work in a state with over 50 percent income tax, but what clinched it was that instead of a 2-hour commute which left me not seeing my baby daughter from Sunday night until the following Saturday morning, I was into work in seven minutes. It's been an uneven ride: I thought I might get a few years off in the groves of academe, but the pressure in a university can actually be far worse than in business. However, it has given me the chance to work at the edge of some new technologies, and to pass that knowledge on to another generation, which is always rewarding.

DW: When and how did you first get involved with TeX and friends?

PF: In the early 80s, when I was still at the PPITB, we were doing a major survey of the effect of new technologies on employment levels. We all knew the depressing news: that direct-entry systems would eventually bypass the hot-metal compositor, but the unions weren't having any of that alarmist rubbish (what was good enough for Gutenberg was good enough for them), and all the systems available required specialist dedicated computers.

A colleague came back from a visit to Stanford with news of a professor who had written a typesetting program that would run on a normal computer. We laughed. But as it happened, we had one: a DEC 20/20 leased from ADP, and with a little goodwill and some transatlantic calls we got a tape. A friend who knew more Pascal than I did spent some frustrating nights getting it to work, sitting in my loft at a TI-700 running up a huge dialup phone bill. We finally showed it to a meeting of print technologists from PIRA and the NGA. The union guys freaked: "You can't let people see that", was a typical comment.

When I moved to United Information Services (part of United Telecom of Kansas, "the second-largest non-Bell telephone company", as they liked to style themselves) my life went crazy. I was supporting a remote database from London to the money-makers, statistics processing from a basement of DEC-10s in Pittsburgh to drug companies, and stress-analysis packages from a Cray in Kansas to engineers. I tried to interest my employer in desktop typesetting, but the unions wouldn't let any printing company print stuff that didn't have an NGA sticker on it to prove it had been typeset by their members. The only cute jobs were reprogramming a daisy-wheel printer to form real typeface letters by steering the period character to print high-density dots, and the discovery that a little work on the manual for P-Stat, which we got as a Fortran print-file on tape, would make it print near book quality on the new-fangled laser-beam printer in the Xerox office down the street.

Oddly, it wasn't me that introduced TeX to UCC. We had a VAX, but no graphical displays or printers, and I was tied up with debugging the crystallographers' Fortran. The credit goes to a colleague, the late and much-missed Mike Gordon, who bought some copies of PCTeX for an admin application. In 1986 I was in hospital for a thyroid operation, and Mike smuggled in my IBM twin-floppy luggable with a modem card and cable so that I could get my email, chat on RELAY, and possibly even do some work. He dumped the TeX disks on my bed and said "you're the printer, see if you can make sense of this." I spent the next few days playing with macros and writing a short story which proved beyond doubt that I can't write fiction to save my life.

It wasn't until 1988 that we had enough users to justify me going to a TUG meeting to find out what was going on. Exeter had changed a lot since I had been there in 1973, but LaTeX was a revelation to a dyed-in-the-wool plain TeX hacker. It took me another year to make the connection with SGML, which I had to support for an EEC-funded project, for which we got a converter to LaTeX called Daphne. This came from the DFN in Berlin[1], and it sticks in my mind because I signed the agreement while I was there at a RARE WG3[2]

[1]Deutsches Forschungsnetz — Germany's National Research and Education Network.

[2]RARE was the Réseaux Associés pour la Recherche Européenne, the Association of European Research Networks, who were contracted to DGXIII (Directorate-General 13: Information Technology) of the European Commission to report on the future direction of networking in Europe. Working Group] 3 (Directories and Information Services), of which I was Secretary towards the end of its life, produced the blueprint for what would have become an X.500 directory service and a network of information servers. But working for a bureaucracy that size meant technology overtook us before they could react, and those of us who preferred the TCP/IP path to the OSI path voted with our feet.

meeting the day the Wall came down, and we suspended discussions to go and hack off a chunk to keep.

I then missed the 10th anniversary meeting in Stanford, but I had offered Cork as the location for a combined TUG and EuroTeX meeting in 1990, which turned out to be fairly pivotal, not just for the organisation of the font files, but for the organisation of TUG, and for the use of TeX in the university. This too has been a rocky road, and the effects on TeX of the use and abuse of synchronous typographic interfaces is something I'm still exploring in my own research.

DW: No doubt many long-time TeX people know about the impact of the Cork 1990 meeting, but having come to TeX more recently, I don't. Please fill me in on what happened at Cork that addressed font files and affected TUG and your university.

PF: I wasn't directly involved, as I wasn't on the Font Committee, and of course I had my hands full organising the meeting, but the major change was the agreement on a 256-character font file layout. Before this, TeX fonts had a 128-character font file, and diacritics were all composed from floating accents. The 'Cork encoding', which includes essentially all the letters needed to typeset in Western European languages, allowed TeX fonts to have a direct representation of the characters in what is now the ISO-8859-1 character repertoire, where the diacritics are precomposed, and many additional characters included. Computer Modern is represented in this format by the EC fonts which we now use for the T1 encoding. The move brought TeX into line with what is now conventional practice, and started to pave the way for the full use of Unicode which we now see in XeTeX. The TUG organisational issue was separate, and reflected a growing dissatisfaction among non-US members at the perceived US-centric approach. Just holding the first TUG meeting outside North America was a major step, and it also had the effect of boosting the profile of TeX within my university.

DW: You said, "It took me another year to make the connection with SGML"; please elaborate on what you mean by that.

PF: I'd been familiar with markup for a long time, back as far as RUNOFF (an early text processor), so when I encountered TeX, it was that much easier to assimilate. When some of my users asked me to help them with SGML for project reports, I could see how it worked, and the concept of a file format that could be independently verified was attractive, but I couldn't see how to get it converted to TeX for printing. It was at the meeting in Berlin that Gerti Foest, the DFN member of RARE WG3, told me they had a program that did exactly that — and it suddenly dawned on me that other people had had this requirement and had solved it. That meant it was possible to store information in a format that didn't predicate its appearance (and could therefore be maintained by the author without damage), but which could be converted to a typesettable format as and when required. I haven't authored anything major directly in LaTeX ever since: it was all in SGML, converted to LaTeX for printing (and now XML, converted to both LaTeX and HTML).

DW: That approach sounds interesting. Will you give me a few more details of how you compose in XML (e.g., do you use an XML editor), what programs you use for the conversions to LaTeX or HTML, and how you control the chapter, page, etc., design of the LaTeX document (if XML allows these things to be specified)?

PF: I use Emacs because I'm used to it and it does most of what I want. I can't imagine trying to write XML without an XML editor: a bit like trying to compose a piano sonata without a piano. I've used dozens of SGML and XML editors, especially since I started research in that field, but although it might be aesthetically more satisfactory to use a synchronous typographical editor, the current interfaces just get in the way. They're not designed for authoring, and require far too much foreknowledge of the technology to be useful for the non-expert.

It's interesting that OpenOffice, AbiWord, WordPerfect, and Word can all save their own files in XML, but pretty much all they do is save an XML description of the visual arrangement of your document: this offers no advantage over a proprietary binary format except that it can (with difficulty) be post-processed into something more meaningful. So long as their interface makes no attempt silently to capture meaning from the author, meaningful, re-usable XML will remain out of our grasp.

To convert to LaTeX I used to use Omnimark, which was available free for a while in the SGML days; but once XML got off the ground I started using XSLT with Mike Kay's Saxon processor for standalone work, and Apache's Cocoon for interactive online documents. XML documents traditionally hold no information about format or layout, only structure and meaning: appearance is the responsibility of the stylesheet (an XSLT program); and of course once it's converted to LaTeX, you have the full range of styling and formatting available.

Put simply, it means that

```
<chapter id="intro"><title>Introduction</title>
```

can trivially be output both as

```
\chapter{Introduction}\label{intro}
```

and as

```
<h2><a name="intro">Introduction</a></h2>
```

so you get the best of both worlds: proper control over document structure while editing, and proper control over formatting when you want output.

DW: I see from the TUG web site (`http://tug.org/board.html`) that you were on the TUG board from 1992–1996 and editor of TTN. Please tell give me your perspective on TUG and its place in the TeX world then versus now. Also, I don't know what TTN was: please fill me in on what it was and what happened to it.

PF: By 1992 it was clear that TUG was not the only TeX user group, and that the falling membership was not just due to local user groups: the increasing spread of the Internet meant that individuals and organisations were questioning their need to remain members; and the lack of coordination between the TUG office and the activists and users was making TeX look less relevant. I wanted to try and improve things, and I guess I also felt that I had got a lot from TeX and wanted to put something back. There was a certain amount of political infighting, as always in volunteer organisations, but a huge amount of goodwill and effort went into redirecting TUG into becoming more responsive and more attuned to the changing needs of the users. TUG meetings used to be held in big, expensive hotels, with strong participation from well-funded companies and universities. As this all fell away, the organisation needed to change tack, and at the same time cope with technological change and competition from synchronous typographical editing software. Sadly, a new regime in my own institution didn't see my participation in TUG as useful, so I had to resign at short notice when the funding rug was pulled from under my feet. I think TUG is in much better shape now, organisationally, but it did take over a decade to get there.

TTN was "TeX and TUG News", a news-sheet separate from *TUGboat* which Christina Thiele capably edited for a long time. I offered to take over from her when she became President, but I was unable to give it the attention it deserved, and it was subsumed into *TUGboat*.

DW: What do you think about the roles TUG and the various local user groups play today and what they should being doing if they are to be useful in the future?

PF: I've been out of the inter-group politics for a long while now, so I'm not up to speed on their interrelationships. TUG clearly has a custodial role as the progenitor of TeX user groups, as well as the one representing the interests of North American users and those users who either don't have a local user group or who just prefer to join TUG. But TeX is so widespread that TUG can't possibly service the huge diversity of interests in other cultures alone, so the local user groups are the primary focal points for TeX in their domain. LUGs can do things like organise local meetings, write culture-specific documentation, and represent the views of their members to TUG more effectively than individuals could do alone. Some of the LUGs are so active that they can take on major roles in driving the technology of TeX forward.

For the future, I think the existing cooperation is an excellent model, but we do still need to publicise TeX more widely, and crush some of the myths that have grown up around it. The hegemony of the word processor has meant that even the original core of TeX—universities, industrial research, and the computer industry—is now largely unaware of TeX (or only marginally aware), and computer users outside the core are wholly unaware of it.

These Unawares are prey to the FUD that surrounds the word processor, which is supported by millions of dollars of marketing. We can't compete with that level of effort, so the only way we can ensure TeX's survival is by making sure that *when* new users encounter TeX, they get the very best and most accurate information possible. The `comp.text.tex` newsgroup, TUG's web site, *TUGboat*, CTAN, the FAQ, the LUG web sites and their journals, and all the documentation (paper and web) need to find a way to ensure that the user can get useful and usable information. Right now, the new user is often presented with too many apparently conflicting options and unnecessary detail. We *need* that Marketing team with the tin of polish and the soft cloth to stop the 'basement enthusiast' image putting new users off (while keeping the basement enthusiasts, of course, including me!).

DW: When I surf around on the web looking for your name, I find many interesting places, for example:

- `http://silmaril.ie/`
- `http://xml.coverpages.org/faqs.html`
- `http://tug.org/tug99/program/node20.html`
- `http://www.ctan.org/tex-archive/info/beginlatex/html/`
- a number of instances of your Typographers' Inn column in *TUGboat*, *e.g.*, `http://tug.org/TUGboat/Articles/tb25-2/tb81inn.pdf`
- etc.

You are a very active fellow. Is there an overarching goal or theme or your activities—is there some model you are trying advance in the world? Or are you just interested in helping people in a variety of areas that you find interesting?

PF: Some of it is just stuff I got involved in which happens to have left a trace. One of the members of that RARE Working Group was Tim Berners-Lee, who demonstrated his new hypertext project to us in Zürich in 1990. In Cork we were just starting a major new project to publish transcriptions of Irish historical and literary documents, which would all be in SGML, and this seemed like an obvious way to put them on the Internet. I downloaded Tim's *httpd* software, and UCC became the ninth web server in the world. In fact the server you mention (`imbolc.ucc.ie`) is that very machine, now the world's longest-serving web server still in use. It's a Sun Sparc IPX running SunOS 4.1.3, and in over 15 years it has never crashed once, and only been offline four times (three times for an office move and once to add more memory).

The effect of all this was that I unwittingly became Ireland's first webmaster, and also the first person on the web to break a link (I renamed a file without thinking of the fact that it was linked from Tim's machine at CERN, and I suddenly started getting email asking what I'd done to it). The historical and literary project also got me far deeper into specialist markup than I had expected, and that brought me into the design of HTML and eventually of XML. The consultancy, Silmaril, had been a loose association of myself and some colleagues, but by this time the others had moved away or changed business, so now it concentrates on XML and LaTeX.

So there isn't any overall game plan, but there are lots of areas I am interested in, like typography (which reminds me I owe *TUGboat* another column), and I guess some of it is for helping people. I can remember being a clueless newbie myself (and most of my meanderings are probably still sitting on some server somewhere), and being deeply grateful to the people who gave their time and expertise to show me what I had done wrong so that I would learn to do it right. It's probably not entirely altruistic: the better we can document TeX, the less time we have to spend constantly explaining simple things, so the more time we can spend explaining more difficult things, or finding out how to do things better.

This has culminated in the research I'm doing for a late-life PhD. Not to put too fine a point upon it, the editors which newcomers use for XML and LaTeX — both plaintext and typographical — suck lumps of lead. I'm not talking about experienced users (Emacs does me just fine) but about the next generation. There are dozens of unnecessary interface barriers to the editing of structured documents, and they are all usability errors which are forcing people back to using word processors and deterring the rest even from trying LaTeX or XML. I presented a good chunk of my argument at the Extreme Markup conference in Montréal this summer (`http://epu.ucc.ie/articles/extreme06`) and I've been delighted with the support I have had from users. Oddly, the manufacturers and vendors don't seem interested (with one exception).

DW: How do you think that TeX has to continue to evolve to remain relevant in a world increasingly focused on XML, MS Word, and big vendor driven standards for fonts (or what should TeX's place be in the larger world)? Which of things like the Web2C version of the basic TeX typesetting engine, pdfTeX, XeTeX, ConTeXt, and hoped-for developments such as LaTeX 3 and the often desired redo of TeX's capabilities integrated with a non-macro-based programming language seem most relevant to you for TeX's continued usefulness, or do you believe other changes or expansions of TeX are more important for the future?

PF: The fact that TeX is still here after nearly 30 years is proof enough of its usefulness and reliability, but what I said earlier about fighting the FUD continues to be true. We simply don't shout loud enough about what we've got.

XML is no threat: on the contrary it's a whole new field of opportunity, especially while the XML-to-PDF language (XSL, as distinct from the XML-to-anything-else language, XSLT) continues to be expensive and time-consuming. There was an article a long time ago called something like 'PostScript versus TeX' as if PostScript were some kind of threat!

Big vendor software like Microsoft Word, and its competitors both commercial and free, online and offline, will always look more superficially attractive because they work on the basis that making it look pretty means that it's correct. Microsoft in particular is very good at selling this line, so much so that I suspect the majority of the population now believe it to be true. There is no point in trying to peddle to the general population the benefits of open source software, data preservability, the reusability of information, and the accessibility of document structure, because they simply aren't relevant to the kinds of documents they write. There is equally no point in trying to sell these aspects of TEX systems to business, because most businesses aren't looking that far ahead, and it's cheaper to pay the Microsoft licenses than to re-train everyone to use LATEX.

Individual divisions *within* businesses, however, sometimes *do* have people looking more than two quarters ahead, and they are part of our market, as are people sick and tired of losing time and data trying to make a word processor do stuff it wasn't intended to do. And we still operate a *laissez-faire* attitude to universities, our biggest training-ground by far, where we should be in there handing out TEX Live CDs and leaflets describing how LATEX can improve output and save time. We need to tackle this one at the roots or we'll lose the upcoming generation for ever.

By the same token we can't compete with the big boys in funding TEX people to sit on international committees for fonts or anything else. It costs $6,350 for a non-profit based in the USA to join the W3C, for example, before getting onto a committee and before paying the travel to get to the meetings. But the various TEX user groups worldwide include among their members from time to time a number of the very experts whose opinion might be consulted by these committees. What we *could* do is offer these individuals some kind of incentive — it may not even have to be financial — to ensure that TEX's voice gets heard. In fact this probably happens anyway if the relevant gureaux[3] are TEX users, but it would be nice to *know*.

This has a corollary: we have to listen to them even if the direction things are going in isn't palatable. If the world takes on a new technology that obsoletes something TEX does, we need to change. We did this with PostScript; we did it again with PDF; we're doing it with Unicode. We'll have to do it with fonts, too.

What we do with our engines is a slightly different matter. My guess is that most people are still using the 'standard' TEX binaries to produce DVI, even if they end up converting it to PostScript or PDF; and that relatively few so far are using pdfε-TEX as their engine. I may be wrong: we need to start collecting some of this information, and I hope the proposed TEX Counter will help here. Other developments, including ConTEXt and XƎTEX are going to be just as important, and at this stage it's difficult to pin down one way of doing things and say 'that's the only route for us', except that producing PDF seems to me to be the right direction, and coping silently and sensibly with multiple font formats and arbitrary Unicode input is going to be a huge advance (but we're going to need an editor to go with it all!).

TEX in its original form is architecturally incapable of being integrated into the synchronous typographic interface. Various reimplementations of it have nevertheless made it possible: for example Textures, LyX, Scientific Word, and the reuse of large chunks of the TEX engine in assorted word processors and DTP systems as well as in 'native' systems like Instant Preview and preview-latex. Whether or not we reimplement TEX in a Next Generation version, we have to understand that the world is moving towards digital seamlessness, and that in a few years, a majority of people will expect everything to 'just work' — and if it doesn't, to drop it on the floor. Right now, a majority of people are still accustomed to incompetently-written operating systems and applications software failing too frequently, but the expectations are rising, and we're going to have to rise with them. There will always be a need for TEX Wizards who can work behind the control surface,

[3]A colleague of mine recently came up with this plural of 'guru'.

but up to now, the TeX community has tended to concentrate on them to the exclusion of everything else (and done a damn fine job in the process, too, of course, but things change). If we want the use of TeX systems to expand, we're going to have to crack the interface problem: it's not going to go away. Alternatively, we return TeX to the computer scientists with grateful thanks for all the fish, and look for something else.

DW: Thank you, Peter, for participating in this interview. It was wonderful to hear about your background and current projects.

Dave Walden

Dave Walden coordinates the TUG Interview Corner. This interview of him is intended to provide an answer to the question some readers may have: "Who is this guy and why is he interviewing TeX luminaries?"

[Interview completed 30 September 2006.]

Karl Berry, interviewer: Please tell me a bit about your personal history independent of TeX.

Dave Walden, interviewee: I grew up on the edge of the San Joaquin River Delta in California. I had some trouble finding a college major I was both interested in and good at; I went to three schools and had four majors before I graduated from San Francisco State College with a degree in math but a weak understanding of the subject. Fortunately, I had found the campus IBM 1620 computer center in my junior year at San Francisco State and quickly became captivated by computer programming. One of the students working in the computer center (Stan Mazor, who later was co-inventor of Intel's first 4-bit micro-computer) helped me learn to program and recommended me for a part-time job in the computer center during my senior year. I spent so many hours playing with the computer (to the further detriment of my math studies) that I kept a sleeping bag in the computer center for when I was there too late to bother going back to my apartment for the remainder of the night.

As my senior year was ending, I applied for jobs as a computer programmer, was hired by MIT Lincoln Laboratory, and moved to Cambridge, Massachusetts. At Lincoln Laboratory I was assigned to help a brilliant computer programmer (Will Crowther) with the major real-time system implementation he was leading. I shared an office with Will, and he gave me (initially small) assignments of my own to work on. I stayed at Will's side as he integrated the various software components from several programmers into a working system. Will was always available to help me when I was struggling with an algorithm or the programming of the algorithm, and over the next couple of years I became a pretty experienced programmer with good insight into overall design, implementation, and debugging of substantial real-time systems.

After three years at Lincoln Laboratory, I followed my group leader, Frank Heart, to Bolt Beranek and Newman Inc. (BBN) in Cambridge. In those long-ago days, a computer programmer was a lower rank employee at Lincoln Laboratory than the engineering and physics graduates who held the first class rank. When I eventually complained about this to my new group leader (after Frank left), he told me that I could get to be a first class staff member after I finished the Masters degree in computer science I was working on at MIT. This was unsatisfying to me, so I visited Frank at BBN and asked if he had a job for me. (In the end I didn't turn in the Masters thesis and received no degree from MIT, but I greatly enjoyed taking all those computer science courses.)

Will Crowther joined us at BBN about 18 months later after I got there. In 1968 Frank, Will, and I and a handful of other engineers and scientists wrote a competitive proposal to U.S. Advanced Research Projects Agency (ARPA) to participate in the ARPANET development. Our proposal won the competition and BBN was awarded the contract to develop the packet switches for the ARPANET, the first operational packet switching network and the precursor of the Internet ("The Interface Message Processor for the ARPA Computer Network", F.E. Heart, R.E. Kahn, S.M. Ornstein, W.R. Crowther, and D.C. Walden, *AFIPS Conference Proceedings* 36, June 1970, pp. 551–567). Will, Bernie Cosell, and I wrote the software as part of a seven-person team led by Frank (Bob Kahn, Severo Ornstein, and Ben Barker were the other initial team members). I feel very fortunate to have been at the right place at the right time.

KB: Very neat, to be in at the beginnings of the Internet. Did you have a sense you were participating in something that would grow to be as ubiquitous as it has, or was it just another development project?

DW: I don't know what other members of our initial team, or people at other institutions who participated in the initial development of the Internet, would say. For my part, it was initially an interesting development project for which I was invited to help write the proposal. As I learned about what the government was asking for, I began to believe we were working on something very important — a big change from circuit switching and message switching, the technologies then in use for data communications, and particularly a change from time-and-distance charging for service. The more I heard the phone companies talk dismissively about the ARPANET, even after we had demonstrated it actually working, the more important our effort seemed. (A good rule of thumb may be that the more current entrenched interests denigrate something as impractical the more important it probably is. Of course, now, 35 years later, the phone companies have themselves acquired much of the packet switching infrastructure.)

But honestly, I had little idea in 1969 how pervasive our technology would become. However, in 1971 when another BBNer, Ray Tomlinson, demonstrated networked email, and its use immediately "took off", I then began to imagine a world where every toaster and doorknob contained a miniature packet switch (or router) and every domain of life worldwide was connected. My big surprise was that the explosive Internet popularity we saw with the spread of the World Wide Web in the mid-1990s did not happen 15 years earlier. Networked email, ethernet, routers, FTP, TCP/IP, etc., had all been around for years. I guess the average person needed to wait for availability of the point-and-click GUI interface, HTML formatting (versus plain text email), and HTTP and URLs which could access individual files in a remote computer system without explicit use of FTP. Of course also by that time, the computer vendors' efforts to ignore the Internet and promote their own proprietary networking protocols were increasingly being rejected by the big companies buying computer networks who were insisting on capabilities to interconnect with the Internet. In any case, some kind of "tipping point" (as Malcolm Gladwell calls it in his book of that name) happened in the mid-1990s, and it hadn't happened back in 1980 when I thought it would happen.

KB: I heard you had something to do with inventing Telnet. Could you briefly tell us the story?

DW: I became involved with Telnet a couple of years later. But first, after the ARPANET was up and running for about nine months, I spent a year (1970–1971) working for Norsk Data Elektronikk in Oslo where I influenced the development of the second packet switching network; see "Remembering the LFK Network", Nils J. Liaaen and David C. Walden, *IEEE Annals of Computing*, Vol. 24, No. 3, July–September 2002, pp. 79–81 — a preprint is online (`http://www.walden-family.com/dave/archive/net-history/lfk.pdf`). In

1971 I returned to BBN and rejoined the ARPANET team there. By this time the focus of effort of the fledgling ARPANET community had moved from the basic connection of computers at user sites to the backbone network of packet switches to communication among the user computers across the backbone network. This meant work on Telnet, FTP, email, etc. In no way did I invent Telnet: it had been conceived by some Network Working Group participants from 1969 or so as a way for dissimilar physical and virtual terminals to connect to the variety of operating systems running on the various user computers. However, as different options had to be handled (e.g., line-at-a-time terminals versus character-at-a-time terminals, and local echoing of characters versus remote echoing of characters, etc.), a method was needed to find a common set of capabilities between a (virtual) terminal and the host operating system to which the terminal was communicating at that moment. Bernie Cosell invented Telnet's `will/won't/do/don't` negotiated options scheme. I helped by listening to his ideas and asking "but what about this?" and "what about that?"; the initial design session was done on cocktail napkins on an airplane flying from Boston and to an ARPANET meeting in Los Angeles. In Los Angeles, Bernie presented the scheme, people liked it, and I promised we would write it up and circulate the appropriate RFC, which ended up as number 435 (`http://www.faqs.org/rfc/rfc435.txt`). Later I drafted the modification to the Telnet spec to include this capability.

I've had a lot of good fortune in my life. In addition to being at the right place at the right time at the beginning of the Internet and working on a variety of early Internet technologies — for example, the first distributed dynamic routing implementation (`http://www.walden-family.com/public/bf-history.pdf`). I was also fortunate to work beside several programmers with skills far greater than mine. I already mentioned Will Crowther. Bernie Cosell was another. Of course, I wrote a lot of code too and had a number of good ideas of my own, but often part of my contribution was being aggressive about documenting (`http://www.walden-family.com/public/whole-paper.pdf`) what we had done or were about to do.

KB: Will Crowther was one of the very first names I came across after encountering computers (long before I'd heard of Knuth). You can probably guess why — because of Adventure, well, Advent, since names were limited to 6 characters on the Dartmouth mainframe I had access to. I spent many hours exploring Colossal Cave. Did you work on Adventure?

DW: At BBN Will and I had adjacent offices, and he, Bernie, and I and several others played in a weekly Dungeons and Dragons game that often took place on the living room floor of my home. After playing in this D&D game for a long time, Will wrote Adventure. I had nothing to do with it except to have it demonstrated to me, but I like to tell people that I was there while Will Crowther was creating the first computer adventure game.

KB: From what you've said, and from some of the articles you've given me, it seems BBN was one of the major contractors in what used to be called the "military-industrial complex". Did the fact that so much funding for cutting-edge research and development came from the military ever seem odd to you, or be of concern?

DW: Having graduated from college in 1964, working on Department of Defense contracts, first at MIT Lincoln Laboratory and later at BBN, provided me with a deferment from being drafted for the Viet Nam War. So there was some hypocrisy on my part in being against the war and avoiding it by working on DoD contracts; on the other hand, I believe a strong *defense* is essential for national security. Also, much of the work we did for ARPA was not inherently military. In some sense, ARPA at the time was like a ministry of industry in the computer area (even though the United States has no such institution as an explicit part of the government). ARPA was funding research in time-sharing systems, programming languages, artificial intelligence, speech recognition, natural language understanding, networked data communications, computer user interfaces, database management systems, and so forth. With J.C.R. Licklider as the first director of the ARPA Information Processing Techniques Office (IPTO), ARPA was funding Lick's famous vision of "Man-Computer Symbiosis" based on the paper of that name (`http://memex.org/licklider.pdf`) he wrote while at BBN before founding ARPA IPTO. Of course, all of these technologies have military uses, but the impact on the larger world has been much greater than any military use. Still, there was a certain ambivalence around BBN about working on defense contracts. I remember one time BBN was scheduled to be picketed by some anti-establishment group, and a dozen or so BBN employees marched out the front door of BBN to join the picketers. (Then one of the BBN vice presidents invited all the picketers to move onto BBN's front lawn — private property rather than the public street — the police didn't have to arrest anyone, and the demonstration did not become a cause celebre.)

Returning to your original question about my personal history, after returning to BBN from Norway I was at BBN for another 24 years in a series of technical, technical management, and general management positions.

When I retired from BBN in 1995, I spent several years working part time for a non-profit industry consortium (mostly developing and teaching management courses) and part time for the MIT Sloan School of Management (teaching a business improvement course I helped develop). About 2000 I retired completely from paid work.

Over the roughly four decades since I first got involved in computers, I have spent roughly a quarter of the years on each of computer programming, technical management, general management, and teaching and writing.

I have been married for over 40 years, and we have one child, and his wife and he gave us a granddaughter in 2007. We live primarily on Cape Cod but spend a good bit of time in Boston which is only an hour away.

KB: When and how did you first get involved with TeX and its friends?

DW: Even before I wrote my first published book (in the early 1990s), I had always written a lot — technical papers and documents both for publication and for internal use. I had also helped my wife self-publish an oral history of my mother (I did the typesetting, such as it was, with MS Word). By the late 1990s I had become fed up with MS Word, its data incompatibilities and major changes of the user interface from version to version, its hidden, proprietary and undocumented markup, its weak editor, the inconsistency between WYSIWYG editing and what gets printed, and Microsoft's apparent strategy for forcing users to buy an upgrade every few years. I made a vow that from then on I would write significant documents using a powerful editor working on plain text files. I had long known of the existence of TeX and I admired Knuth from my years in the computer world, so I decided to try TeX. I had previously used RUNOFF, MRUNOFF, nroff/troff, and WordStar, so command-based "word processing" versus WYSIWYG was no worry for me.

I found a version of TeX somewhere on the Internet and bought a copy of *The TeXbook*. As I almost always do when I try to learn something new, I looked around for "the organization", found TUG, joined, and began looking at the issues of *TUGboat*. I quickly became aware of LaTeX, bought some more books, switched to learning LaTeX, began to watch `comp.text.tex`, and began to develop a major revision and expansion of my first book in LaTeX. The book was eventually retypeset using QuarkXPress by the publisher's compositor, but I was pleased with the process and experience of writing a book using

LaTeX and was glad to have the LaTeX-based manuscript in hand.

KB: I remember your paper based on that experience which Barbara and I edited for *TUGboat*.

DW: I like to summarize a major development experience in writing to consolidate my thinking about what actually happened and to help me think about how to do it better next time. Coming from a technical world where there is personal and business benefit for publishing, my natural inclination was to submit my draft for possible publication somewhere; aiming for publication also improves my motivation to actually do the write-up I know I should do and want to do. I found an invitation from *TUGboat* editor Barbara Beeton in the *TUGboat* area of the TUG web site inviting papers from non-expert TeX users; so I submitted my write-up, and it was accepted (and I learned some new things about LaTeX from the editing changes Barbara and you made to my source file).

KB: My memory is that you then asked if TUG could use some low-level volunteer labor.

DW: Yes, my thought was that by getting more involved with TUG I could perhaps connect up with people who really knew TeX and LaTeX which could result in me learning more and in time perhaps actually become a useful resource. *The PracTeX Journal* (TPJ) on-line journal was just being formulated at the time (August 2004), and you and the editorial board invited me to participate in that, perhaps contributing content on basic, nitty-gritty use of LaTeX such as I had described in my *TUGboat* paper. I had been the editor of an on-line journal (*Center for Quality of Management Journal*), and had lots of ideas about how an on-line journal might be better "published" than the approach we used with the CQM journal. In particular, I had ideas about writing a program to generate the web site for an on-line journal that the TPJ editorial board eventually embraced, which led me to volunteer to write such a program. I previously had written some little Perl programs (my professional programming days were over by the time I began hacking with Perl); and when I learned that you knew a lot about Perl, I became excited about writing a more substantial Perl program with someone knowledgeable around from whom I could learn.

My general view of learning any new subject is that the more I put into it the more I will learn. For me volunteer work is not so altruistic; I don't volunteer for things unless I really want to know more (or I already know a lot and can help without much work). If I feel the need to contribute to an area I am not interested in learning, I give money rather than time.

In any case, we wrote the TPJ web site generation program over the course of a couple of months although the job was much more substantial than I anticipated because you kept suggesting things the program should do (such as creating author and title indexes) that I hadn't imagined being part of the job when I volunteered.

KB: I had a great time working with you on that project, and am very glad you had enough desire to know more about TeX that you joined TUG and pitched in to help in various ways. Are there particular areas of TeX that you are interested in delving into more? Do you think your next book will have much different needs than its predecessors, or have you reached a sort of steady state by now?

DW: Today I use LaTeX and pdfTeX from the proTeXt distribution, WinEdt, and various packages, macros, and techniques I have found useful — described in *The PracTeX Journal* 2006-2 (`http://tug.org/pracjourn/2006-2/walden`) and 2006-3 (`http://tug.org/pracjourn/2006-3/walden/`). Probably I will use more or less what I know now for my next book as I want to get it done relatively quickly. However, I am sure I will slowly keep expanding my TeX capabilities. I will probably try ConTeXt for the book after that, and relatively immediately now I may try doing my own indexing for the first time, perhaps using an Eplain-based technique for creating a non-embedded index that John Culleton described to me in the Yahoo self-publishing discussion group.

KB: One TEX/TUG project you initiated and have been steadily involved with is this interview series. Have you done anything similar before? What impelled you to start the project? Have you gotten what you hoped for out of it?

DW: As I suggested earlier, I like projects where I also can benefit from what I am doing. I also prefer projects that can be done incrementally so I am not under too much pressure to finish too much too soon; one of my rules of thumb is to avoid trying things that are so hard or have such near term deadlines that it becomes stressful or an unpleasant burden to work on them. Thus, this Interview Corner project was a natural for me: I get to learn about various well known TEX people and gain perspective on how the various parts of the TEX world fit together and why, I only have to finish an interview every month or so to feel I am making good progress, and — with good input from the interviewees — organizing and formatting the interviews is a very achievable job.

Wanting to know more about various TEX people (and suspecting that others might also want to know more), I remembered the *Mathematical People* and *More Mathematical People* books edited by Donald Albers, Gerald Alexanderson, and Constance Reid (the second book only) based on a series in the *College Mathematics Journal* of interviews of well known mathematicians. The best extant interview of Knuth, in my view, is in the first of these volumes. Thus, I thought, why not have a similar interview series for TEX people? I have done lots of interviewing of customers that resulted in detailed write-ups of what they said; as a journal editor I have done some interviews for publication (one example is at `http://www.walden-family.com/public/cqm-journal/rp07900.pdf`); and I have interviewed authors in order to help them create first drafts of papers they later took command of and made their own.

I'm very pleased with how the interview series is turning out, and hope someone is reading them besides me.

In general I try to twist jobs I volunteer for so they are not so hard to do that I soon will stop wanting to do them. This is the main reason my "Travels in TEX Land" column for *The PracTEX Journal* mostly describes something I did rather than claiming to be a tutorial on a subject that I would then have to really become expert about. It would be hard to become an expert, but it's relatively easy to describe what I did. (By the way, the title of my column is a paraphrase of the title — *Narrow Roads of Gene Land* — of the three books of the collected papers of William Hamilton, the amazing evolutionary biologist. I was deeply moved by his introductions to the papers when I read volume 1.)

KB: By the end of your tenure at BBN, I gather you were ultimately responsible for major budgets and a whole division of workers. Despite TUG being perhaps the direct antithesis of a large corporation, do you have any thoughts on or improvements for TUG as an organization, pro or con, from your experience and study of management?

DW: At various times at BBN I was responsible for a division or a subsidiary. The largest was a contract research and development organization with approaching 1,000 people. One was a start-up that failed (we created the first multi-platform networked email system, InfoMail, much before there was a market for it), one was a turn-around, and one involved shutting down a "mature" product line. All were quite small activities in Fortune 500 terms (total annual revenue of all divisions and subsidiaries only reached about 300 million in circa 1990 dollars while I was with the company).

I think there are more similarities between a modest sized for-profit corporation like

BBN and a modest sized non-profit organization like TUG than there are differences. Both have to serve some sort of "customer" or there is no reason for existing. Both have to adapt to a changing competitive environment and changing customer desires. Both have to have good financial controls and remain solvent. Both need to develop new products or services from time to time, produce and deliver existing products and services reliably and efficiently, and communicate with existing and potential customers. Of course, an obvious difference is that an organization like TUG depends primarily on volunteer labor, but I'm not sure this needs to make as much practical difference as most people assume it does; there are also resource conflicts in for-profit organizations and the same principles for creating viable business processes apply to both types of organizations. (My co-author Shoji Shiba and I talk about this in our book *Four Practical Revolutions in Management* (`http://www.walden-family.com/4prim/`).

KB: Although you are something of a relative newcomer in the TeX world, do you have any opinions about how it should be moving?

DW: I think TUG and the other user groups should continually work to make sure potential new users are aware of the availability of TeX but should not waste much time worrying about why people like "inferior Word" better than "superior TeX". Concentrate on making TeX better, more available, and easier to use for the people who are already inclined to its use; help them learn to use TeX and then help them stay users. One thing I wish I'd had when I was starting out with LaTeX was documentation that assumed and described the beginning use of LaTeX in the context of a whole environment (operating system, TeX distribution, editor, major format/package, etc.) and was prescriptive ("this is how you should do *whatever*") rather than a reference work ("here are some capabilities that will let you construct *whatever*, depending on which OS, editor, TeX engine you are using)". ProTeXt with its WinEdt option and installation script seems like one good base for such documentation for Windows users. Also, the more documentation that is written in terms of programming-by-example the better, I think — more documentation like chapter 3 of *TeX for the Impatient* (`http://mirror.ctan.org/info/impatient/`).

KB: It's been a pleasure to get to know and work with you over the last several years, Dave. Thanks for making this interview series happen, and all your other work for TeX and TUG.

[Endnote: After this interview was completed, a follow-up interview for *MAPS* (`http://www.ntg.nl/maps/34/16.pdf`) was conducted by Frans Goddijn.]

Kaveh Bazargan and CV Radhakrishnan

Kaveh Bazargan (left photo) and CV Radhakrishnan (right) use TeX extensively in their typesetting business.

[Interview completed 20 September 2006.]

Dave Walden, interviewer: Please tell me a bit about your histories and lives outside the world of TeX and your company River Valley.

Kaveh Bazargan, interviewee: I travelled as a child of 11 with my family from a small town in Iran (Bojnord), near the Afghan border, directly to London. Needless to say it was a culture shock, but as a child I quickly blended in.

I got a Bachelors degree in Physics at Imperial College, London University, and then a Masters degree in Optics, which was a field that fascinated me from childhood. During this course I got interested in the emerging field of display holography. I went on to do a PhD at the same department, entitled "Techniques in Display Holography". For those who are interested, a scan of my thesis is online: `http://www.focalimage.com/public/kaveh-PhD.pdf`.

My main contributions were developments in color holography (using three lasers) and the invention of a compact display system, still marketed in the US as the VoxBox:
`http://www.apple.com/science/profiles/voxel/`
`http://www.holorad.com/products.htm`

CV Radhakrishnan, interviewee: I live in Trivandrum which is the capital of the southern Indian state of Kerala. Kerala is the first state in the world to have a communist government through elections! We are leftists, but at the same time addicted to democracy. It is the most literate state in India (100 percent literacy), with empowered and educated women folk unlike other parts of India where gender discrimination is still common, lowest infant mortality rate (comparable to that of the first world), fair income distribution among the population, and above all the most green state in India. We recently banned production and sale of Coca-Cola in this state. Now, I hope, you have a fair idea of where I live.

I am a chemistry graduate and dropped out of University during my post-graduate studies. I worked in the shipping ministry of the Indian federal government for several years after my studies.

DW: Mr. Radhakrishnan, please help me and readers who are not familiar with Indian names understand about them. How does naming formality and informality work in (your part of) India and how should I address you?

CVR: In the first place, you should call me Radhakrishnan which is my given name or CVR for short which is much more palatable to the western tongue.

Nomenclature in south Indian states has a bizarre style which might elude the comprehension of people of other countries. In this matter, our brethren in north India are truly international. They have first, middle and surname in their names, e.g., Mohandas Karamchand Gandhi, Indira Priyadarshini Nehru, Rabindranath Tagore, etc. It is predictable and you will be correct in most situations.

But in southern India, we have names with multiple components where the last part will be the first name or given name and the first one or more parts will be father's name with or without family name. My full name is 'Chandroth Vasudevan Radhakrishnan' where Chandroth is my family name, Vasudevan is my father's name and Radhakrishnan my given name. The first two components are invariably compressed and denoted as initials. Hence, I become C.V. Radhakrishnan which is again shortened as CVR (it is my userid in the Linux world at work and hence forms part of my email too). But with the advent of western education, so-called modern naming practices are followed here too — Rajiv Menon, Nisha Nair, Aneeta Rajendran, Uday Shankar and similar ones can be found abundantly nowadays here in Kerala. My own peasant parents were not 'civilized' enough to adopt unambiguous naming for their offspring, nor am I ashamed of my name though it may represent an old and discarded system.

DW: How did each of you first get involved with TEX?

KB: I have always been obsessed with presentation of information, so I was determined to write my thesis in the best way technologically available. Having started to write the thesis in 1983, before laser printers, PostScript, PCs, etc, I used troff on a mainframe with the output on a phototypesetter. It looked good for all but equations. At that point I discovered that the computer center had a prerelease of something called TEX, which I was told was "mathematically intelligent". This was enough to draw me to it. I found *TEX and MetaFont* in the bookshop and I was hooked from that day on. With great difficulty and persistence I managed to finish my thesis. Of course all the diagrams had to be done using a Fortran program I wrote myself, delivered on microfilm, and printed in the photographic lab. All this meant my thesis was delivered in 1986!

During the time I was writing my thesis I started a company with a colleague with the aim of marketing display holograms, and my invention. It grew fast, too fast, and it went under three years later.

Around 1986 I got interested in the Macintosh, so much so that I spent all my time on desktop publishing. So in 1988 I decided to leave holography and set up a company (Focal Image Ltd, now trading as River Valley Technologies). I started by offering a graphics service to publishers using Illustrator version 1.1. At the same time I let it be known I was also familiar with a system called TEX. The IOP (Institute of Physics of UK) showed an interest, and soon I was typesetting papers for them. After a few years, competition in illustration meant I concentrated on typesetting, and I took on a few people to help me. Since then typesetting books and journals has been my occupation.

In recent years, I have been spending a lot of time trying to revitalise display holography, and I intend to continue to do that, now that my business gives me free time. Setting up `http://www.holographer.org/` has been quite successful.

CVR: I switched to computers and then to TEX as an escape from my motor neuron disease. As I told before, I joined the shipping ministry in Delhi as a junior staff member, whose sole job was to examine shipping contracts and report the defects to the shipping companies and ask them to submit revised ones. During the end of fifth year of my service or so, one day I suffered a kind of buckling in my legs and I went for a checkup in the hospital. The doctors told me that I have a serious neurological disorder namely, perennial muscular dystrophy (the kind of disease which made Stephen Hawking immobile). They said that muscle mass in my body would slowly waste away starting with the lower limbs, I would be bed-ridden eventually and within a period of five years or so I would pass away. The doctors warned that my terminal days would be with an alert mind and a dumb body, so I should be prepared for this predicament.

Needless to say, this was shocking and agonizing news, but eventually I decided not to give up without a decent fight with my destiny although I knew well that I was waging a losing war. I resigned the job in the ministry and returned home to live the rest of my life with parents. The thought of solitary terminal days began to haunt me. I had a feeling that none of my people will have the patience even to sit beside me and they are quite legitimately right in that matter. So, I began to find ways of keeping the last days busy. Suddenly, it appeared that computers could be one of the best possible solutions; after all, it is a piece of equipment that can communicate. Since it is inanimate, it won't get bored.

But I didn't have any formal education in computers nor any training. It was a time when PCs were slowly making their appearance in the market. I bought an XT machine (present day toys are much more powerful than an XT) and slowly started learning the disk operating system (DOS), Wordstar, Lotus123, etc., since I had copious amounts of time. After a year of this self learning where I made substantial progress, I could buy a PC/AT with 2 MB RAM and a 20 MB hard disk which were considered to be luxuriously resourceful in those days.

It was around this time that Prof. Nambooripad of the math department of Kerala University suggested that I learn TeX since it would best fit my scheme of things. TeX itself is a complex language which would take a good amount of time to master, which fortunately I had in abundance. Indeed, it was true and it took around four years for me to write reasonably good macros or packages in (LA)TeX. TeX proved to be a good pastime on one hand and on the other hand it began to fetch money when I did typesetting work for researchers in the University for submission to various journals around the world. By this time, I was entrusted with the typesetting work of *Entomon* (an entomology journal of the University of Kerala Department of Zoology, indexed in Current Contents) which I still do as a matter of gratitude to its editors. In short, TeX became the sole basis of my existence and saved me from unimaginable levels of mental agony and frustration.

Twenty-five years have passed since I was afflicted with the motor neuron disease. I still survive, although with a weakened physical state (I can barely walk now and soon will be dependent on a wheelchair). I owe considerably to TeX and its originator, Don Knuth, for my current state of well-being. I enjoy each and every moment of my life since it is a bonus to me and I consider myself as one of the most happy persons in the world! — because I have nothing to lose and anything, no matter how small or big, is an achievement for me.

DW: Kaveh, please tell me how you came to get together.

KB: Around 1995 I started hearing for the first time about publishers sending some typesetting work to India. I also started getting contacted by Indian companies telling me I could subcontract work to them and they could do it economically. In 1996 I decided I should pay a visit to India to see what was going on, thinking that things might be about to change. This was probably the best decision I ever made in my entire life!

So while other much larger typesetting companies in the west didn't take the challenge from India seriously, I spent a week in Chennai visiting several suppliers there, some with literally thousands of employees. I didn't find any of them inspiring. After that week I decided to take a week's vacation in Kerala, on the southern tip of India. I had heard about River Valley Technologies there, a group that was setting up TUGIndia. It was run by Radhakrishnan and his brothers, with some 10 employees. I paid a visit to them. I asked what software they used to typeset pages, and they said TeX was their only tool.

This was the reply I wanted!

For a year we subcontracted work to them, and all went smoothly. In 1997 we decided to join forces and merge into one company. My company had been called "Focal Image Ltd" since its inception. They agreed to change the name to this. A couple of years ago we decided that "River Valley Technologies" felt better and described us better. You can ask CVR about the origin of the name if you wish....

Things have gone really well in the 10 years we have worked together. There is never a dispute, and we see eye to eye on almost all issues.

DW: Radhakrishnan, what is the origin of the name "River Valley Technologies"?

CVR: I was born in a village 40 km south of Trivandrum. Fifty years ago, it would have been like a habitable forest; the main occupation of the people was farming. This agriculturally based society lived at a very slow pace and depended on nature for everything. Rice, bananas and vegetables were the main farm products. Kerala has such a large number of rivers and backwaters, no matter where you live, you need to cross a river before you reach your destination. Often, it adds scenic beauty to your habitat, but it is not without its own miseries. During monsoons, floods are quite common, devastating huge farm lands and crops. Floods also caused displacement of human settlement at least once in a decade. During my school days, we needed to cross at least one river whichever way you chose to reach the school. We, all the children in the neighbourhood, always walked to the school which was roughly three kilometres away. During monsoons, as you can imagine, the rivers will be flooded. We used to remove our trousers and shirts, bundle them along with our textbooks and swim across the river by holding the bundle high above the water level. Upon reaching the other shore, we wore the clothes and ran to the school. The affluent amongst us, particularly girls, had the privilege of their parents accompanying them with country boats and rowing them across the flooded river. These girls while sitting in the comfort of their boats and security of their elderly people used to howl at us for swimming nude, but we were hardly bothered.

Anyway, rivers had a big impact on our lives, whether it be floods, rice production, human displacement, scenic beauty of our surroundings, drinking water, rowing and boat races, etc. They are an inseparable element in our lives and hence I chose a romantic name which imbibes the spirit. Also, I hated to think of having any name with words like info, infotech, sys, etc., which most of the software or related companies have.

DW: Radhakrishnan, had your work with TeX already expanded and turned into a business before you met Kaveh?

CVR: Yes and no is the answer. I had a large quantum of text processing work from the University which I couldn't do single handed. On the other hand, I was not organised enough to run a full fledged company on a commercial scale. So, when the pressure of work and demand for services escalated, I decided to open up a company along with my two younger brothers (Rajendran and Rajagopal). Thus River Valley Technologies came into existence in the premises of the Software Technology Park (STP) in Trivandrum. We here in India have several STPs sprinkled all over the country as a support mechanism to help incubate entrepreneurs like me who want to do business in software or IT-enabled services. STPs provide one-stop shopping for all government clearances, infrastructure like communication, uninterrupted electric power, floor space, broadband connectivity, etc., at a subsidised cost so that newcomers like me who are not resourceful enough can suddenly afford and make use of the above services. Apart from this, any registered company in the STP need not pay taxes or duties of any kind (like customs) for the first eight years of its registration. This way, start-up problems of a new company can be minimised so that more and more people will be attracted towards the software business. On a reciprocal basis, companies have to export software or allied services to other countries which is obligatory on each and every company registered in the STP system.

River Valley had an export target of one million dollars to be achieved during the first five years of its operation (STP would decide our fate for the next four years once this was achieved). Since I didn't have any contacts anywhere outside India, doing an export business was a very distant dream for me. At the same time, I needed to do it, otherwise I would face stiff penalties from the government. Naturally, I forgot all the strains and hardships which my physical body was facing due to the disorders; that was one of the advantages of this business endeavour.

I was also passionately working on a not-so-unrelated area called free software (not open source software — they have subtle political differences), the Linux operating system and its propagation, and also organising TeX users in the country. During this period, I came in contact with Sebastian Rahtz who was working for Elsevier at that time. He was also a member of the UK TUG Board. Indeed, he prompted me to organise a TeX user group in India so that he could come and help inaugurate it if we were to have any kind of a formal ceremony. So we formed a user group at a meeting of like-minded TeXies held on 16 December 1996 (this day is very important in my business life). Prof. Nambooripad was the first president, and I became the first secretary. The evening of the same day, I sent mail to all the TeX user groups around the world announcing the formation of the Indian TeX Users Group (aka TUGIndia), its mailing address and a who's who of TUGIndia.

The mail went to all user groups around the world. It reached UK-TUG when its board meeting was taking place, where Kaveh was also present as a board member at that time, along with Sebastian and Dominik Wujastyk. Kaveh was intending to visit India within a week or so, so he told the board that he would meet the guys when he visited India. The UK-TUG Board decided to send Sebastian to India to inaugurate TUGIndia formally and paid the flight charges from its funds.

Sebastian and Kaveh were present in the inaugural ceremony. It was a huge success; nearly eighty people from different parts of India attended and signed in on the first day.

In the meantime, Kaveh and I had enough discussions about our business plans as Kaveh already mentioned. Returning to the day of the formation of TUGIndia, it reminds me of what Paulo Coelho wrote in *The Alchemist* — that Nature often conspires to help us achieve our goals, keeping dropping omens and hints for us to latch on to. Although we would be, particularly our rational mind would be, more than happy to reject such Vedic thoughts, often I am tempted to see an element of truth in it. There we were! Kaveh actively searching for a business partner in India and I looking for someone in the West. So we joined hands without any hesitation.

DW: Kaveh or Radhakrishnan, how do you divide up the business activities between Kaveh's branch of your company in London and Radhakrishnan's branch in India, and has your partnership allowed you to obtain different kinds of business or just to expand your original businesses? Also, my understanding is that mostly only electronic files go between your two branches, and River Valley doesn't get involved in actual printing and the physical aspects of publishing; is this correct?

KB: I feel I have the best deal, as Radhakrishnan takes care of all operations in India, including production and all the R&D. I see myself as the client interface and also a strategist. Thankfully I still have enough knowledge of each part of our technology and I often come up with new ideas of combining the technologies (i.e. software), making things more efficient, going into new areas, etc. An example might be our current foray into multimedia. I feel that publishing should be in any medium, and not purely text.

The plentiful supply of talent in India means that it is possible to follow up some of the wild ideas that I have, so it has given me more freedom than I had before.

It is correct that there are virtually no physical items passing between us and all is electronic. The final product of our company is PDF files and other electronic deliverables. The publisher then arranges printing.

DW: Radhakrishnan, at the recent PracTeX'06 conference in New Jersey, Kaveh's presentation on River Valley's approach to managing vertical stretch in TeX was the most relevant presentation to my needs as I had just finished typesetting a book in LaTeX and the major issue was balancing the text bodies on a two page spread. Kaveh indicated that you did the coding of this technique. Please tell me a bit about the business problem you were solving and hint at the method of the solution (no need to repeat what will be in Kaveh's paper from the conference).

CVR: Nature Publishing Group (NPG) is our newest client. We typeset a few of their journals which are predominantly mathematical. Also they wanted to accept author submissions for their journals in TeX format, which would attract authors who prefer to use TeX as their document preparation medium, authors who would have otherwise been turned away owing to the requirement of submissions in a word processor format. I feel this was more of a decision based on business directions on the part of NPG rather than the typographical elegance that TeX can bring to their journals or any love for TeX. The design of NPG journals is not conducive to the typesetting process of the TeX engine. It is more of a glossy magazine type with several fancy fonts in a multitude of shapes and weights than that of the simple but elegant publications that we usually find in academia.

As you can imagine, we faced several technical problems of typesetting their journals in LaTeX. Many people are not aware of the limitations of using multiple fonts for math in TeX. You run the risk of a 'too many math fonts' error very soon. There were no math symbol fonts available in either the free or proprietary worlds that could go with Minion (light, medium, demibold, bold) or Helvetica Neue (light, medium, condensed, bold condensed, bold, extrabold), the text fonts used as serif and sans-serif families respectively, So, we had to generate several virtual math fonts that drew symbols and extension characters from mathtime, STIX fonts and a variety of free fonts in CTAN and math characters from Minion italic (light, regular and bold) and Helvetica Neue italic (light, regular, condensed, bold, extrabold). This process ended in defining several math versions like normal, bold, sans, sans condensed, bold sans condensed, etc. Every time we typeset a document, we are at the verge of reaching the font limits of TeX!

The woes didn't stop there. All NPG journals are in two column format. And in the normal traditions of two column typography NPG wanted grid snapping which evoked a terrible problem in LaTeX. ConTeXt has a grid snapping facility, but LaTeX sadly lacked this feature. LaTeX always uses several glues which are often uncontrollable too. Unfortunately math characters with varying heights need this feature to adjust various boxes to get a reasonably acceptable page. Luckily, however, the design of NPG journals helped us in solving this problem. Their scriptsize and scriptscriptsize were so small that math notations with two levels of sub/superscripts won't touch the adjacent lines, meaning we did not need to worry about surprises in interline skips between columns in a page. If we used the standard math sizes (for a 10 pt base font, scriptsize is 8 pt and scriptscriptsize is 7 pt while that of NPG happened to be 6 pt and 5 pt respectively), our grid snapping mechanism would obviously fail.

So, the next culprit that can upset the grid snapping is the floats and float separators.

We simply rounded off the float height to the nearest baseline and the grid snapping problem was solved. We did a similar thing with various heading levels too.

This way, we began to deliver PDFs to NPG that conform to their precise specifications. Had it not been done, it would have always been a black mark on us and our competitor companies can snatch away the journals from us for this reason.

DW: Please tell me a little about how your typesetting process works?

CVR: Authors generally provide TeX sources, but authors of some journals prefer to submit MS Word sources. Our journal publisher clients generally upload author sources in their ftp site and send notifications to us. We grab the archives and book the items into our tracking system. Elsevier has a more advanced system; they copy author sources to an electronic warehouse along with a purchase order in XML format. Our tracking system communicates with this warehouse at fixed intervals, grabs the documents and automatically books the jobs into our tracking system based on the XML order. Then someone will print the author PDFs and add the document sources to a CVS server. Once the job is booked into our tracking system, it will be listed in the TODO list of all our staffers who have privileges to do it. Sorting of items is done on the basis of return date.

Structuring and enrichment of author sources is done in a semi-automated way, then structured LaTeX → XML → LaTeX → PDF conversions are done completely automatically, the result is proof-read, bugs are fixed, a dataset is made, and the tracking system will upload to electronic warehouse automatically with an XML ready signal message.

Our workflow is completely automated, except the first stage of structuring and enrichment of author sources which is done semi-automatically.

DW: What sort of workers do the actual typesetting?

CVR: If you mean their qualifications, they are all science graduates.

DW: What set of TeX components, formats, and classes do you use in your business, and whose distribution?

CVR: ε-TeX and pdfε-TeX, LaTeX, and custom classes.

DW: What TeX distribution do you use?

CVR: TeX Live, and we keep our configuration in the local TeX tree.

DW: What editor or editors do you use within your business?

CVR: Vim and FTE (Folding Text Editor), although I personally use Emacs.

DW: Are you able to stay in the world of TeX and free/open source software or do you also use commercial products as well?

CVR: We do use Photoshop and Illustrator to process figures, because there are no free equivalents available that can create production quality graphics. All the rest of operations are in free/open source software, including our stable operating system, Linux. Ours is a Microsoft-free zone.

DW: I am fascinated by the statement at your web site (`http://www.river-valley.com`) under the heading 'Culture of Innovation' that "We always work at around 60 percent capacity, using the remaining time to explore new avenues. The whole team is encouraged to innovate, and the sharing of resources is pivotal to our success, not only between staff, but also with our clients." Please tell me about how you came to have these goals and how they work out in practice; in particularly, how are you able to resist the temptation so many businesses have to schedule everyone at 100 percent of capacity and work them at over 100 percent when unexpected things come up?

KB: Our staff are our greatest asset, and we think that looking after them is more important than looking after our clients. Quite literally. If we work them into the ground, they'll leave eventually and all will suffer, including the client. In fact we have literally thought of having as our motto: "River Valley: Where the Customer Comes Second!".

Neither Radhakrishnan nor myself are money oriented. Making money is one of the goals of the company, but only after doing the right thing, and in the right way.

On the practical side, I believe that our extremely high level of automation, and our reliance almost exclusively on free software, has allowed us to minimize costs, therefore there is less pressure on us to bring money in. And we really enjoy the relaxed atmosphere in the office. In the long term we are convinced this is the way to do business. So far it has worked very well.

DW: Was the 60 percent number chosen on theoretical grounds — because that is where the knee of queuing curves frequently begin to turn toward infinity?

KB: Radhakrishnan can give a better answer to your question than myself. For my part, I just go forward intuitively, making sure no one is actually wasting time. So if 60 percent of their time is taken up by production, then 40 percent should be spent on trying out ideas, general R&D, etc. If people just sat around doing nothing I would be worried.

CVR: I think what you're saying is from a management expert's perspective. I am not a management expert nor have I studied management at any level during my studies. Everything I did and do now originates from experiences of day to day life. Before getting into the current business, I too happened to work in organizations that were busy, schedule driven and where several management experts interacted for extracting maximum output from the staff members. Needless to say, most of them failed to deliver the desired results, the main factor, I think, being the negligence of human factor in their planning. So I contemplated on many occasions that I would have an entirely different approach to people if I happened to head a business in the future. I will summarise my wishful thinking in the following manner:

- Clear vision of how the organization should be a decade, say, in the future and what its short and long term objectives should be. None of the staffers, no matter how low or high their position in the hierarchy, should be marginalized in the matter of awareness of these factors.
- I should be meticulously honest and transparent so that I can request/expect these virtues from others in the organization too.
- Avoidance of unending meetings of executive members which starts early in the morning, go on and on, and when one ends another starts with people having to rush to the next meeting.
- Avoidance of imposition of schedules on staffers which I clearly know are humanly impossible to achieve. Managers usually impose impractical schedules to extract more work from employees.
- Lastly, due consideration of the 'Indian factor' which is special to India alone.

In India, unlike other parts of the world, an individual doesn't live for himself; instead he lives for his family. Whether it is good or not, his individual life is mostly dominated by the interests of his family, (s)he will sacrifice anything for the sake of the well being of the family. The interests of the family is the most dominant factor in one's life. So, when you have seventy staff members in your organization, you are not interacting with seventy individuals; instead you are talking to seventy families which makes things much more complex than expected. Motivating such an work force is very difficult unless you take into consideration the hardships brought about by the family factor on each individual's life.

I have deeply analyzed this problem at length, because I was irreverent about this family factor in my life. I was a radical from the very beginning, challenging every rule imposed on me by my family establishment and eventually liberating myself from its irrational clutches, for which I had to pay a big price in terms of emotional tranquility. The five thousand year old history of Indian civilization is nothing but a history of obedience. In the beginning, at the macro level, it was the subjugation by cruel monarchs for several millennia, then that of the colonial masters for a few centuries till the middle of the last century. At the micro level, the ruling of masters of the families who might be grandparents or parents or teachers, or elders or husbands, etc., controlled the individual lives. The concept of freedom and free will were brought about by the colonial masters through English education (indeed that is the greatest contribution of our British colonialists), but the execution of freedom and free will was reserved for British masters, while natives were deprived of these. Our democracy is only sixty years old which is unlikely to be a sufficient time span for making the individual psyche mature enough to perceive the world as our counterparts in other civilizations do.

As such, when you have seventy staffers with you, on the one hand they wait for your orders since they are trained to obey only but on the other hand, they are at the mercy of the dictates of their family establishment which may at times conflict with that of their work establishment. An average Indian is always in the middle of this internal conflict of interests, and at least one third of his mental resources would commonly be preoccupied with the polemics brought out by the family. Productivity of an average Indian is very low when compared to his counterparts in other Asian countries.

Since one cannot find enough brave individuals who feel unconstrained by the challenges of family establishment, one is left with the scenario of finding the best people one can from the population to organize a workforce and allowing them to be as effective as they can be. So, I decided to use only 60 percent of the capacity of each individual with a tolerant attitude so that he would be motivated to bring out the best out of him—which is always over 60 percent in my experience.

Our company is very small and I can manage my workforce very easily without any rumblings or hatred since I know each and every individual at a personal level too. I still do not know how this factor can be effectively handled if the workforce numbers in the thousands.

DW: I know Kaveh is involved in TEX user group activities; I recently met him in person at PracTEX'06, and he is on the editorial board of *The PracTEX Journal*. And Kaveh mentioned Radhakrishnan's company was involved in setting up an Indian TUG when the two of you met. Please give me your views of the value of TEX user groups (areas where they can help and areas where they can't help much), and tell me a little bit more about your personal involvement in them.

KB: I used to be active in the UK TEX users' group, until it effectively disbanded some years ago (although there has been a recent and welcome revival). The major advantage of TUG for me is the TUG conferences which I try to go to.

CVR: I was involved with the formation of TUGIndia as we described before. Usage of TEX in India is mainly confined to various text processing companies and as such not much development effort is directed towards adding new features or writing more useful packages. If there is any development at all, it is confined within the business houses and in essence they are unknown to the world at large. Although India has a huge establishment of higher education, usage of TeX, unlike in other parts of the world, has traditionally been confined to a very few academic institutions of higher learning such as the Indian Institute of Technology, spread across ten different centers, and Indian Institute of Science, India's premier scientific research institution. So TUGIndia decided to propagate TeX among academia. With novice users in mind, we wrote a tutorial spanning seventeen chapters, generated attractive screen and print versions which were disseminated through our web site `http://www.tug.org.in/tutorials.html`, along with sources and supporting packages so that people can play with them if they want to compile the documents by themselves. We released a notification to the academia about this venture. The effect was dramatic, there was a quick surge of registration of subscribers for the mailing list and the membership soared to more than 600 immediately. Suddenly the TUGIndia mailing list became very active and attracted subscribers from other countries as well.

We arrived at a logical conclusion that key factors for promotion of TeX are good documentation and quick technical support for the needy. We then started writing another tutorial for TeX graphics, the first part of which is still going on with ten chapters completed and released so far. The total download of graphics tutorial is a whopping number of 162,408, and that of our LaTeX primer is 26,579 as of September 19, 2006, from `sarovar.org`, the free software portal where tutorial projects are hosted.

TUGIndia is not positioned as a forum to support the business houses; instead it is aimed at helping any TeX user when his problem surpasses the limits of his expertise. However, I find a great potential role for the TeX user groups to act as a prime technical support base for the text processing industry. Since TeX is free software, no commercial outfit is available for technical support when companies in the industry look for paid support. I would love to assume a kind of role for the TeX user groups which is akin to what Red Hat provides to the promotion and support of Linux — a mutually complementary and beneficial relationship. This would dispel the anxieties of the text processing industry when they decide to deploy TeX systems for their daily operations. During private talks with executives of several other companies, I got the impression that they would love to deploy TeX systems having seen our silent and peaceful operation, but they were scared of the scant technical support on commercial terms.

It is worth mentioning a recent development in the text processing world. As you may be aware, most of the text processing companies use 3B2 for academic journal typesetting. Arbortext recently acquired Advent (which owned 3B2); people were a bit scared, but Arbortext came for their rescue saying that they would support and continue 3B2. But within six months, Arbortext was acquired by another CAD/CAM company (I forget the name). The new owners were silent about the continuance of 3B2 system. People are really scared now, and the belief that proprietary systems are more reliable than free/open work has vaporised. Some companies have already started development centers for TeX in India which is good news for TeXies. I have had a few requests for consulting too, but declined owing to my own neck-to-neck routines.

At this point, one could logically conclude that a Red Hat-like company for TeX would be relevant. But realities are different. TeX programmers, like any other free software gurus, are an eccentric lot. They still have a method in their madness, but it is more fit for fixing an algorithmic imbroglio in software than salvaging an enterprise which is drowning in upset schedules. Red Hat is a great success: they could somehow go beyond the threshold which delineates the insane and sane judgements. But similar experiments elsewhere failed miserably. You might have heard about FreeDevelopers.net (FD) with headquarters in Washington, a global company of free software developers (of which I had a reasonable role among TeXies — Ross Moore was at the top of the ladder) which tried to evolve a free software business model. Richard Stallman was also part of FD. Looking back, the achievement of FD was nothing but megabytes of mail archives which discussed at length about business, software freedom and ethical values. So we concluded that free software has no business model and FD disintegrated.

However, I find something relevant to this discussion is taking place in the TeX world — the release of TeX Live every year (almost) without fail and the maintenance of the CTAN repository. Often I have admired at the veracity of all developers involved in TeX Live releases. It is here that I would ponder about the possibility of offering TeX Live systems just like Red Hat offers Linux in two versions — one for enterprises on a payment basis for support and another for the community for free. If TUG comes out to organize a set of willing developers into a support group on a payment basis, they can sell this service to the industry for a price, it would be beneficial to both the parties.

DW: How do you see TeX and your use of TeX evolving going forward?

CVR: This is a big issue and what I am talking about is the usage and longevity of the TeX system in the text processing industry. Several factors go against the TeX system:

- conflicts among paradigms of modern and traditional typography
- problems brought out by the proliferation of electronic media
- the apparent user friendliness of WYSIWYG typesetting systems
- structural unification of document sources into XML and apparent disabilities of the TeX system in processing XML as dictated by the XSL-FO specifications of W3C
- conflicts of interests within the TeX community that hamper promotion and usage of TeX as a preferred typesetting engine
- the fear/psychosis of successors of Knuth in the matter of redesign of the TeX compiler

Advent of digitized typesetting has its own ill effects on typography. I have a Calculus book published by Cambridge University Press in 1963 typeset in the traditional way, manually composing the pages using metal typefaces. It is far superior in typographical elegance to any mathematics book which I have seen typeset digitally. Knuth has made a remarkable effort to bring about this quality in digitized typesetting when he developed TeX and he realized a good degree of success. However, publishers are not interested in perpetuating the typographical traditions and finesse attained over decades or centuries of typographical innovations. Often publishers are driven by convenience and cost reduction and typographical excellence becomes a last priority item.

When math structuring was unified by W3C with the emergence of MathML, the typographic finesse attained by TeX gave way to structuring priorities. For instance, we have several kinds of multiline constructs like matrices, arrays, cases, aligned equations, centered multilined equations, etc. MathML considers all these as math tables. But in TeX these are different constructs (although the base building block is a math array) with ultimate control over both horizontal and vertical spacing between math elements. Hence, even if you use TeX engine to process MathML-coded XML, all these constructs have the same kind of spacing. Since it preserves the semantics, publishers are more in favour of it than doing things in TeX's native way. So, systems like 3B2, which does exactly what publishers want, are promoted by the text processing companies which erodes typography further.

When we started our business, the deliverables required by the clients were confined to printable output (mostly a PostScript or PDF file). But with the advent of the web as the medium of dissemination, the number of deliverables has increased, including a print version PDF, screen version PDF with low resolution figures and hyperlinks, gif images of all math inline and displayed formulae for delivery of a document in HTML format on the web, full length XML of the document, header XML, and bibliography XML. TEX systems became sidelined owing to technical difficulties although TEX can very well generate all the above as we do in our company.

The main problem described against the TEX system to generate these various deliverables is its batchmode processing properties. Since, people are wary of command-line mode and they love WYSIWYG typesetting systems which are available in various incarnations like InDesign, 3B2, etc., TEX systems gave way to them. But the fact is that TEX systems are much faster, highly programmable and provide the desired output flawlessly within no time so that a high level of automation is possible. To give a specific instance: generation of 3,000 serially numbered gif images of inline and displayed math formulae in an article conforming to the specification of a client would take hardly 40 seconds using TEX, while using the procedures in many of our competitor companies entails hours of work. One of the suppliers of Elsevier Science who recently visited our company to see our workflow told me about their long backlogs of gif generation. However, they feel taking this trouble is a lesser evil when compared to taming the horrendous macro language of TEX.

XML is now the definitive document source format which is a great achievement of mankind. Not only humans but also machines can communicate each other by interchanging XML data and initiate processes, the best example being our tracking system and the electronic warehouse of Elsevier Science. Since it has become the definitive source, efforts are needed to translate each and every author submission into XML format and derive the final deliverables from the XML source for safeguarding the accuracy and fidelity of source and output. W3C has come up with a specification on a style sheet language called XSL and a formatting objects specification, XSL-FO, which are very useful in determining how to process the XML data. There are many formatting object processors (FOP) around, in both the commercial and free worlds. RenderX is a leading processing engine in commercial world while Apache FOP is a leader in the free world. But none of the processors so far are as intelligent as TEX in math awareness and the best option would be to process XML documents with math content with the TEX engine. Unfortunately, TEX doesn't have the capability to process XML documents directly, forcing one to translate the XML back to TEX again with an XSL style sheet and then generate PDF as we do in our company. I do not forget the features available in ConTEXt, but I am sure, it will raise myriad issues to generate the desired output from XML.

However, there has been intense work going on in the Apache FOP project to integrate math processing capabilities into their engine. Once, this is accomplished, I feel the relevance of TEX as a preferred typesetting system will find greater challenges than it has ever faced and its usage will dramatically decline. Some of the inherent weaknesses of TEX like processing multiple columns, wrapping text around floats, grid locking of lines across columns, placing floats across two spreads, etc., are part of the XSL-FO specs and accomplished by some of the existing FO processors, and push against the propagation of TEX in an XML-dominated world.

To make matters still worse, there are several schools of TEX usage in the world like plain, LATEX, ConTEXt, AMSTEX, Eplain, etc. All these macro systems provide several features which the others do not have. However, when one tries to do a job, all the features needed to process that job may not be available in a single system. For instance, I was trying to shift our typesetting part from LATEX to ConTEXt owing to its better column handling, graphics, MetaPost integration, etc., but postponed that effort since it sadly lacked features like line numbering in column mode, advanced math processing, bibliography citation handling, etc., which are still not production ready. Such problems would incline a production house to go away from TeX unless one has an infatuation with it. Personally, I have been advocating for integration of differing macro package systems into a common kernel with a facility for modular loading as and when the user needs it. This happened once in the TeX world when AMSTeX and LaTeX married each other which provided all the advanced math features of AMSTeX and sectional units, tabular, lists, bib citation, cross-referencing, floats, etc., of LaTeX in a single kernel. The user has the freedom to load the required modules. Similarly, if LaTeX is conceived as a module of ConTeXt or vice-versa, it would have been a great achievement towards unification of divergently capable systems in a single one. But I do not think, LaTeX and ConTeXt purists would agree to this; people would still re-invent wheels and users would continue to learn different commands to create similar looking output using different macro packages.

And finally, there is an apparent fear among the successors of Knuth in redesigning TeX to suit the present day XML world. I am not fully qualified to understand the innards of TeX the program, but when I talked to subsequent compiler designers who did much work on pdfTeX, NTS, etc., they all shared the same view that TeX is a composite program which resists all forms of redesigning while keeping the backward compatibility with addition of new features. Either you rewrite a newer one or keep the current one as such. Rewriting a newer one is a daunting task which should accomplish what TeX has already done plus the extra features needed. The brave efforts to create LuaTeX which is an integration of pdfε-TeX, Lua, MetaPost and Aleph into one engine, may be a worthy answer and raises hope for the future.

Having said the above, TeX is not without its positive points for survival. It is a superb authoring tool that can defeat all other systems, the main advantage being the separation of format from content which provides enough momentum to one's train of thought to avoid falling victim to formatting nuances while authoring. And since it is free software and academia is not endowed with equivalent proprietary text formatting systems, authors will prefer to use TeX. Certain math constructs like proof trees composed of deductive logic steps can be typeset only in TeX; I can't imagine any other easier methods than what is provided by TeX in this matter. Shading of proteins in a DNA molecule as done by the `texshade` package is yet another example of how horrendous tasks can be easily done in TeX which saves a lot of headaches for researchers in protein chemistry. Multiple accented characters, composite glyphs, footnotes inside footnotes, different kinds of footnotes in same page are some items useful to researchers other than those in scientific disciplines. Therefore, it is hard to find such a suitable authoring tool for several years to come unless someone comes up with an alternate system.

TeX is one of the best tools for database publishing. The phone directory comprising 400,000 subscribers of Trivandrum Telephones was made using TeX. That story can be found at `http://www.tug.org.in/bsnl.html`.

A print-on-demand system can be designed based on this capability of database publishing. Suppose a tour operator wants to provide information based on the custom requirement of a customer; he can surely make use of TeX. He can keep information about several tourist destinations of different kinds with different price lines in XML format with a properly designed XML DTD. He would provide a web page where people can login and submit several scope conditions such as, I want information about destinations which fall under such and such price line, with a homestay-like accommodation, away in the hills, tropical countries, etc. An XSL style sheet will search the XML data and create a

TeX input file based on the conditions provided by the user. pdfTeX can be called in the background, and a beautifully typeset PDF with all gizmos can be sent to the user and he will be very happy. I have heard about several print-on-demand servers functioning around the world providing formatted educational material as per the custom requests of users. One system in Germany provides bus/tram timings and fare rates between two destinations; the underlying engine is TeX.

Several corporations use TeX in different forms. Trivandrum Telephones makes use of pdfTeX to dynamically generate and provide telephone bills when the user submits an online request. The PDF is tamper proof, has a dynamically generated barcode and is exactly like the regular printed bill. This has been working for several years now successfully. I know one telephone company in US employs pdfTeX to create telephone bills of their clients because it is the most viable system for them since each client bill is around twenty thousand pages! No other system can generate the bills so fast in batchmode from a database.

The most exciting work which we did during the past was the report generation of a World Bank study of school dropouts in Kerala. The database comprised 1.6 million records each with 174 fields. Complex statistics were applied to this data and a report generated in the form of a TeX input file which when typeset yielded 748 tables of 64 columns and 32 rows each. All pages were complete in all respects: page numbers, headers, footers, heading/subheadings and captions for tables. This saved us from the horrendous task re-keying the statistical results in a word processor or whatever, printing and proof-reading the output. Needless to say that the World Bank was immensely happy.

So I believe that although several factors apparently seem to go against the interests of TeX in general, it is still usable in many areas of human activity and as such the disappearance of TeX is very remote, at least in my lifetime.

DW: Thank you, gentlemen, for a fascinating interview. Your story makes me want to find a partner in India and start a business, except I suspect the synergy of your relationship may be impossible to reproduce.

Taco Hoekwater

Taco Hoekwater is heavily involved in implementing many significant upgrades and improvements to various TeX-based systems.

[Interview completed 13 October 2006.]

Dave Walden, interviewer: Please tell me a bit about your personal history independent of TeX.

Taco Hoekwater, interviewee: I grew up in a small town in the Netherlands, and after some moving around, I now live in the nearby city of Dordrecht. My wife and I live in a small house that stands on the side of a dike. We have been married since 1993, and we have three cats and two dogs.

Ever since I was a small kid, I have had an interest in history, and especially the history of the applied arts. I read lots of fantasy and SF novels (that is a very nice way to spend the many rainy nights we have here in Holland).

I have started studies in art history and philosophy, but never finished those because I got side-tracked when I was drafted for the army in 1992 and came in touch with computers & TeX.

DW: When and how did you first get involved with TeX and its friends?

TH: In the military, I was trained as a system administrator for a communications minicomputer that ran Unix System V. Because the actual machine was not a very suitable teaching environment we were encouraged to install Linux on the PS workstations that came with it.

The distribution was one of the earlier Slackwares that came on a few dozen floppy disks, with a sub-1.0 linux kernel, and a bunch of the floppy disks were labelled "nTeX". I was immediately hooked, mostly because of the 'arts and crafts' feel of TeX compared to the 'industrialized' approach of line-printers and telexes that were prevalent.

When I was released from the army, I discovered that thanks to changed laws, I could not financially afford to finish my studies, so I searched for a job, and soon found one as a (LA)TeX expert for Kluwer Academic Publishers.

DW: How "expert" were you with computers and TeX by the time you got out of the army and went to work for Kluwer?

TH: The nice thing about being drafted for the Dutch army at that time was that there wasn't much work to do, leaving lots of time for study. After two years of doing that, I was pretty good with PCs (MS-DOS) as well as Unix systems.

However, my knowledge of TeX and friends was basically limited to the plain and manmac macros. The first document I have ever compiled was Michael Doob's 'A Gentle introduction to TeX'. I was definitely not a 'TeX wizard' when I started working for Kluwer, just a more or less competent 'TeXnician'.

DW: Do you still work for Kluwer, and what did you or do you do at Kluwer — are you still a "(LA)TEX expert" or do you do something else for work now?

TH: Working at the prepress department of a large publisher proved to be a very fast way to improve my TEX knowledge. In my first year at Kluwer, I wore out one copy of *The TEXbook* and one copy of Lamport's book completely. The job was two-sided: provide support for the TEX-based authors, and help the internal LATEX typesetters with the fine details of typesetting documents according to the typesetters' instructions.

This meant creating a modularized LATEX 2$_\varepsilon$ class file to replace the two dozen or so separate 2.09 styles, and the compilation, distribution and maintenance of an internal TEX distribution based on emTEX so that all typesetters were guaranteed to use the same TEX macro and font files.

Later on, Kluwer's interest shifted away from TEX and toward SGML documents and workflows. I worked roughly two years on the development of the SGML article DTD and a backend system that could typeset those SGML documents — using TEX, of course. These SGML-related activities took up almost all of my office hours, but my TEX support work continued on a freelance basis. I had a private company for that: it was called Bittext and it did typesetting, macro programming, and Metafont developments.

In 2000, I left Kluwer and abandoned Bittext to join a three-person company that my brother-in-law had started. The company is called 'Elvenkind', and I still work there today. We focus mostly on database text format conversions and creating web applications to access that data, but we also still do a small amount of style file (I should say class file) design and even a some actual typesetting. Currently, I am working nearly full-time on the successor of pdfTEX, thanks to a grant from Colorado State University.

DW: I saw your name listed on the announcement of the upcoming ConTEXt users meeting; please tell me how you became involved and about your involvement with ConTEXt and, I assume, Hans Hagen.

TH: I ran into ConTEXt first when I was working on that SGML backend system for Kluwer, around 1996. For that, I needed a macro toolkit that was more reliable and predictable than LATEX could offer at that time. As it happens, Hans Hagen had just given some lectures about ConTEXt during one of the Dutch Language TEX User Group (NTG) meetings.

ConTEXt was still commercial software then, so we invited Hans over to the Kluwer office for talks about licensing and eventually reached an agreement. So, Kluwer ended up being one of the very first users of ConTEXt, and I have been in touch with Hans ever since.

DW: But that doesn't describe your current involvement with the world of ConTEXt.

TH: I have to go back in history a bit first. In the beginning, ConTEXt was lacking in a few areas that were a must-have for academic publishing. Most notable of those were mathematics and bibliographic referencing, so I wrote the initial support for that. Also, Kluwer needed an SGML parser on top of the core macros, so I developed one. (That SGML parser is not the one used in ConTEXt right now, by the way; the current code is an independent development by Hans himself.)

All of that increased my knowledge of low-level ConTEXt enormously, and being one of the first users of ConTEXt outside of Hans's company Pragma ADE quickly turned me into a 'resident TEXnician' on the ConTEXt mailing list. I've been answering quite a lot of questions there over the past years.

Right now, I manage a few of the details related to releasing new versions: I compose the release notes for every official released version of ConTEXt, I run a mirror of Pragma

ADE's web site (`http://context.aanhet.net`), I take care of uploading the distribution to CTAN, and I am the maintainer of the 'museum', a repository of more than a hundred old versions dating back almost a decade: `http://foundry.supelec.fr/projects/contextrev`.

DW: Please tell me how you became involved and about your involvement with MetaPost and your ambitions for that project.

TH: You may be aware that ConTEXt uses MetaPost as an in-line drawing engine for TEX. Hans being Hans, he always has feature requests for every tool he uses, and MetaPost was no exception. Bogusław Jackowski, also a heavy MetaPost user, also had some wishes. Somehow they got together, and because Hans knew I had some experience in WEB programming, he dragged me into it, mostly to verify the feasibility of some of their requests.

As it turned out, John Hobby himself was no longer interested in doing development on MetaPost, and he generously agreed with a group from the TEX user groups taking over. Hans and Bogusław do quality assurance and testing, Karl Berry takes care of the web site, Troy Henderson has just volunteered to keep the manual up-to-date (he takes over from Karl), there is a mailing list with people contributing requests and patches, and I do actual web coding, release new versions, and travel around giving talks and gathering bugs and feature requests.

I do not have much of a mathematical background, so my personal goals for MetaPost are mostly related to software engineering. Like, I want to make it possible that MetaPost be built as a library that can easily be embedded within pdfTEX. And we have a pending patch from Giuseppe Bilotta that increases the precision of MetaPost's internal calculations quite a lot, but it needs quite some extra web source code that is not written yet. It would also be nice if one day MetaPost could output OpenType fonts directly.

All of these are fairly modest goals; larger projects will have to wait until later. Hopefully, a steady stream of news will convince some people to give MetaPost a try, and then perhaps the core group will grow enough so that we can tackle larger tasks like three-dimensional drawing or real world modelling.

DW: You mentioned earlier that you are now working on a successor to pdfTEX. Scouting around a bit, I find that you are (also?) involved in supporting OpenType fonts in pdfTEX, providing better support for Arabic typesetting in TEX, and with LuaTEX. Are these different projects really one and the same or, if not, how do these various projects (and any others that may be related) fit together? Also, does this mean you are working closely with people like Hàn Thế Thành and Martin Schröder? I guess my meta question is, "Are you in fact working (with others?) on a plan to create a consolidated successor to several separate projects that have existed in the past and thus, to some extent, provide the long awaited production-quality successor to TEX?"

TH: All those TEX-related projects are facets of a single big project: making a worthy successor for pdfTEX. pdfTEX is lacking in some areas; for instance, it does not have the multi-lingual functionality of Aleph or XeTEX, it does not handle OpenType fonts well, is hard to extend, and it still has many hard-coded limits. This is a team effort, with everybody from the core pdfTEX team contributing. The big difference between me and the rest of the team is that I am now working on it almost full-time.

Thanks to a grant from Colorado State University I can spend a large amount of my office hours working on improving the Arabic typesetting capabilities of pdfTEX, adding Unicode and OpenType font support and assimilating bits of Aleph into pdfTEX — or rather, into LuaTEX.

The LuaTEX project was started a while back as a means to extend pdfTEX in an extensible way, by adding the Lua script interpreter to the executable and giving Lua scripts access to the internals of the typesetting engine. Also, there are plans to add MetaPost to the executable as an embedded library.

Eventually, all of this work will result in a completely new program called MetaTEX. This will be the successor of the current pdfTEX (and probably Aleph), and the final non-MetaTEX pdfTEX will become frozen and only updated for bug maintenance, for people that do not want to move forward with us. We hope to have this all done by the summer of next year.

DW: At the recent PracTEX Conference in New Jersey, I saw Jonathan Kew demonstrate using the existing fonts within his operating system with XƎTEX—no big process of converting to the TEX internal formats for font descriptions. Is what you are doing with pdfTEX going to result in a system that will make working with fonts that easy, or will it still require the conversion to the traditional TEX formats for fonts? Also, is there communication between what you are doing with pdfTEX and Jonathan's work on XƎTEX? Is some further consolidation there likely or possible?

TH: The goal is that for simple use of a font, like in XƎTEX, OpenType fonts can be used as they are, without any conversion. For harder stuff, like hanging punctuation, pseudo-hz font expansion, and top-quality Arabic typesetting, extra information is needed that is normally not included in the font. Font loading and instantiation will be under the complete control of the Lua script language, so it will be possible to add that extra information using augmentation files instead of actual font conversion.

There is some communication between us and XƎTEX, but the two projects have very different approaches to the problems of typesetting engines, so neither of us is working towards a merge right now.

pdfTEX aims for the absolute best quality and as much configurability as possible. Therefore, it does all typesetting tasks, everything itself, often at the expense of more source code and therefore longer development cycles. XƎTEX aims for the highest ease of use for users and economy of implementation. Therefore, it uses external libraries for some of its tasks. The result is that XƎTEX is not able to do micro-typography like pdfTEX, and pdfTEX is way behind XƎTEX when it comes to Oriental script support.

Perhaps the projects will grow closer together in the future, but I am not aware of any plans in that direction that are active right now.

DW: Scouting around, I also find your work on the koeieletters and koeielogos fonts and your conversion of the Metafont logo font and a couple of the other miscellaneous original TEX system fonts into Type 1. Can you say a word about the motivations for these?

TH: The older fonts I needed for internal use at Kluwer. They were converted using Richard Kinch's `metafog`. In fact, I was also commissioned to created an extended math font set for Kluwer, using the same production process. That font set never got to production quality, but I still have a thousand plus Metafont glyphs in an archive somewhere.

I feel fonts are a very interesting subject, so I've been playing with them now and again for quite some time. The koeieletters font is the most fun (and funniest) thing I've worked on in years. Because of their graphical nature, fonts are closer to art than to programming, and I would love to earn my money creating fonts. Sadly, that does not seem feasible, so I am stuck with TEX and web application programming for now.

DW: Your original interest in art history and philosophy seems pretty distant from the set of skills you need for the work you are doing today with TeX: Pascal, WEB, C, TeX, typesetting, programming languages, PDF, etc. Or is there some connection with your earlier interests or some different history and philosophy with which you are now enthralled?

TH: Programming itself is quite distant. It turned out I am halfway decent in it, and it pays the bills. Luckily, working on and with TeX and MetaPost is closer to the arts than most other IT jobs. After all, the goal is to create something that is as beautiful as possible. When I see a medieval illuminated manuscript, I am always wondering how nice it would be if we could make TeX produce documents that are just as pretty.

DW: This has been fascinating, Taco. Let me ask you a couple of somewhat philosophical questions and then we will be done. First, a question I ask of most of my interviewees: What is your view of TUG and the other user groups and how they can best, and practically, continue to support TeX and TeX users and perhaps push the world of TeX ahead?

TH: The way I see it, the most important task of the user groups today is facilitating developments that are taking place, stimulating projects where needed. TeX is free software and the active user base is fairly small, and as result there is not much of an external drive for new developments. Forward movement has to come from within our own community, and the user groups have a very important role in that community. Since this is pretty much what the user groups are already doing, I can only say: you are doing a fine job, keep at it!

DW: How does open-source/"free" software fit into your view of the world? You are developing a lot of software and you say it is "paying the bills", but....

TH: This is a tricky question. It is very easy to slip into a very long monologue about the pros and cons of communism versus capitalism, and I really do not want to do that. I prefer to think of programming as providing a service, as opposed to the production of goods. Let's leave it at that.

DW: Thank you very much for taking the time to participate in this interview. Hearing about all the work you are doing has been inspiring to me.

Peter Wilson

Peter Wilson is the author of the well-known memoir class, has been involved with the development of several other classes, and has worked extensively with fonts. In the photo he is operating a Chandler & Price 1910 old style hand press and is in the process of inserting a sheet of paper to print on the second side.

[Interview completed 8 November 2006.]

Dave Walden, interviewer: Please tell me a bit about yourself personally, outside the world of TEX.

Peter Wilson, interviewee: I was born in Cambridge, England, due to that being where my mother was at the critical moment. After the war my family moved to Kenilworth (which was on the losing side in the Civil War) and went to school in Warwick (which was on the winning side); one has a magnificent castle while the other has child-friendly castle ruins. The school claimed to be the third oldest in England with a purported founding date of 914 AD. I later found out that that was the date of the first mention of the town, and the school boosters made the heroic assumption that if there was a town there must have been a school.

I read Mechanical Sciences at Trinity College, Cambridge, and began employment with British Thomson Houston, the then leading electrical engineering company in the UK, working on developing planar transistors (this was in the days well before microchips), firstly at Rugby then in Lincoln where my two children were born. Later I moved to the Lucas Research Centre in Birmingham and during this time I obtained a PhD in Semiconductor Physics from Nottingham University.

I was one of the few at the Research Centre using the computer as I needed to do a lot of numerical calculations. The powers that be decided that if you could do one thing on a computer you could do anything so I was ordered to start working on Finite Element Stress Analysis and, by the way, "You'll be teaching a course on it in a week's time to 25 engineers!" Misquoting Groucho Marx, "The secret is real knowledge. If you can fake that, you've got it made." It appeared that I could fake it well enough to survive the week. Later I ran a group developing solid modeling CAD systems and in spite of my best endeavors was elected to be European Chairman of the CAM-I Geometric Modeling Project, CAM-I being an international consortium of major industrial companies supporting relevant R&D projects. One of the many good things about CAM-I was that it rotated its meetings around Europe and the United States so I got to visit a lot of interesting places. On the personal side I married for the second time in the middle of this.

One thing led to another and I was headhunted by GE in Schenectady NY to manage the solid modeling group at their R&D Center. At this point I got involved in a national project developing a data interchange standard called PDES for CAD/CAM/CAE systems. This later became an international effort to develop an ISO standard called STEP for the same purpose. There were some major concerns by the non-US countries that they were just going to be asked to rubber stamp the PDES specification, and likewise some US representatives were suspicious of the others' motives. This was resolved by changing the underlying words of the PDES and STEP acronyms to "Product Data Exchange using STEP" and "STandard for data Exchange using PDES".

Headhunters tend to hang heads out to dry and I became a Visiting Research Professor working on information modeling techniques at Rensselaer Polytechnic Institute, the "oldest continuously operating technical university in the United States". I was invited to join the Editorial Board of the IEEE Computer Society "Computer Graphics" magazine and shortly after I accepted was asked if I would be willing to be put on the short list of 3 or 4 for the forthcoming election of a new Editor-in-Chief. Naively I agreed and at that point the short list was closed as they had managed to get a name to go on it. I held the position for 4 years, serving the maximum of two 2-year terms.

While at RPI I was part of the founding team of a small company called "STEPtools" started by Prof. Martin Hardwick of the Computer Science Faculty. The business plan was to commercialise results coming from the STEP endeavour and provide EXPRESS-based tools to support the ongoing development of the standard. Unlike many small companies it is still in business after 15 years (`http://www.steptools.com`) even though it has been many years since I was involved in it.

Circumstances changed at RPI and I spent some 3 years in the Washington DC area with joint appointments as a Research Professor at the Catholic University of America and Visiting Researcher at the National Institute of Standards and Technology in Gaithersburg, still working in the information modeling area.

I am now living in Seattle having retired after some years with the Boeing Company where I remained involved in developing the STEP standard, in particular extending it to cater for fluid dynamics analysis systems and wind tunnel experimental data.

I'm interested in the development of languages and writing systems but find that there isn't as much time for those as I thought there would be, as my wife and I are doing as much traveling as we can before moving back to England in a couple of years' time. We have no family in the US but there are two children and five grandchildren in the UK. This year the major trips have been to New Zealand and South America — both easier to get to from Seattle than from the UK.

DW: How and when did you first become involved with TeX and its friends?

PW: During my CAM-I days my group at Lucas had a contract to develop and demonstrate a data exchange system between solid modeling systems. We had to provide reports on the work and also user-level and programmer-level code (FORTRAN at that time, 1979) manuals. We were using a PR1ME computer and they had a simple but effective program to neatly print tagged text, which was my first exposure to "typesetting" and the joys of not having to involve a typist and typewriter. I think that the program was called RUNOFF.

At the time work on the STEP standard started ISO wanted typescripts which they would then rekey into a form suitable for their publishing system. We knew that STEP would be large by ISO terms (it now involves several thousands of pages crammed with technical information) and we wanted to try and supply camera-ready copy which would eliminate the rekeying and typo-adding aspects of ISO's traditional process. My major technical contribution to STEP was the development of the EXPRESS family of information modeling languages (ISO 10303-11:2004 Product data representation and exchange: description methods: The EXPRESS Language reference Manual; ISO/TR 10303-12:1997 Product data representation and exchange: description methods: The EXPRESS-I language reference manual; and ISO 10303-14:2005 Product data representation and exchange: description methods: the EXPRESS-X language reference manual.) As a sideline I agreed to become co-editor and integrator of the various aspects of the standard. LaTeX had just appeared and we decided to try it. It met all our needs, after we had learned how to write macros, and at the peak we produced a 1500-page document encompassing the standard. Since then it has been split into many individually published parts, although some of these are around the 1000 page mark. I developed a LaTeX class specifically for ISO standards and a corresponding package for the STEP series of standards in particular. These have proven very effective as ISO kept changing their minds about the layout of their standards. For example by changing the margins and text area, changing font size specification for figure/table captions, numbering notes continuously to numbering per clause (chapter), and so on. A few updates to the class and all were catered for.

The initial developer of EXPRESS, Doug Schenck, and I felt that the language needed more explication on usage than was allowed by ISO rules which limited the standard document to specification only. Consequently we wrote a book on it (Douglas A Schenck and Peter R Wilson, *Information Modeling the EXPRESS Way*, Oxford University Press, 1994), using LaTeX to prepare the camera-ready copy for the publisher. Again it was easy to make any global layout changes that they requested, like lengthening each page by two lines, or using a different font and position for chapter headings.

DW: How did you go about learning TeX and LaTeX enough to use it for a large document and to be able to write your own classes, e.g., what learning resources did you draw on or did you mostly learn by trial and error?

PW: I got Lamport's book which I understood, but I found that *The TeXbook* was too confusing, so learning during the early years was mainly through trial and error. In 1989 I learned about TUG and became a member; *TUGboat* was a great source of ideas and code. Sometime later I signed onto the email-based precursor to the `comp.text.tex` newsgroup which was another good resource. When it came out, the documented source code for LaTeX 2_ε was, and still is, an enormous help. My progress is still basically one of trials, tribulations and errors.

DW: What are the names of the two LaTeX classes you developed for ISO and STEP standards?

PW: The general class for ISO standards is `isoe.cls` and the package is `stepe.sty`. Both are on CTAN: `http://mirror.ctan.org/macros/latex/contrib/isostds`. The distributions also include configuration files for TeX4ht to enable conversion to HTML. It is four years or so since I looked at all this, so my recollection has faded somewhat.

DW: Until now you have been best known to me for the memoir class. Please tell me about your effort to develop that, and to what extent is it related to the above mentioned two classes?

PW: ISO, and also the STEP management kept altering the typographical requirements and it occurred to me that a class providing easy methods for a document designer to adjust things would be very useful. I started on that in the early 1990s but never got very far. However over the years I did produce a bunch of packages that treated different aspects of document layout. Eventually I resurrected my "design" class ideas. The end result was the memoir class which started out as a bundling of many of my packages. It has now taken on a life of its own and provides the functionalities of over 30 packages. At the moment I don't think that there is a need to add any further major extensions and there appears to be nobody clamouring for more.

The STEP standards principally specify the information represented within CAD systems and standard means of representing data corresponding to this information. The EXPRESS language, which has a mix of data specification, constraint specification, and regular procedural code programming languages, is used to formally define the information. A

STEP standard document typically includes both text and EXPRESS code. The LaTeX sources were organised so that the whole document could be typeset and it could also be fed to an EXPRESS compiler — the verbatim environment was used for the EXPRESS code and the other parts of a document were in the form of EXPRESS comments. I found this so useful that I started to document my normal C code in the same manner — I was aware of the various systems like web and noweb for literate programming but they seemed overkill for what I wanted to do. There is a graphical form of EXPRESS called EXPRESS-G which is a member of what a colleague used to call the BLA class — Boxes, Lines and Annotations. This was also used in STEP to provide a graphical view of the information structures. I wrote a MetaPost package, called `expressg` (available from CTAN), to provide a basis for drawing pretty much any kind of BLA diagram. I had used Frank Mittelbach's `dtx/ins` system for documenting LaTeX packages, found it very useful, and wanted to use it similarly for MetaPost. To this end I wrote a package called `docmfp` that provided extensions to the doc system to documenting languages other than LaTeX (`docmfp` roughly stands for DOCument MetaFont and MetaPost). From that time on I used it for documenting all my other code, like Java. One source document provided the commented code for typesetting and the code itself could be extracted for compiling.

I think another major contribution has been the `ledmac` bundle of packages for critical editions which has been used by the humanities community. I did this mainly as an intellectual exercise, having no interest in nitpicking the wording of old manuscripts. If someone would like to take it over I'll gladly hand over the glory and responsibility.

DW: Your answer leads me to follow-up questions in both areas you mentioned. First, the memoir class includes, as I remember, a big manual on good book design as well as instructions for using the class. Please tell me a bit more about your interests and motivations that led you to carry through with such a complete class development effort.

PW: There were LaTeX books and manuals that effectively said "If you want the output to look like that, then do this", but there was rarely, if ever, any mention of why or why not it was a good idea for the output to look like "that". My ISO/STEP experiences showed how awful some design decisions could look so I started to read up about typography and book design; Robert Bringhurst's *The Elements of Typographic Style* (Hartley & Marks, 2nd ed. 1999) is an excellent and elegant exposition. I felt that providing some background on book design would help users to, in Knuth's words, "... create masterpieces of the publishing art". However, in spite of this I don't think that the memoir manual falls into that category.

DW: Second, I am unfamiliar with the `ledmac` bundle. Will you please tell me a bit more about it. Is this related to your paper on early scripts and fonts at `http://tug.org/TUGboat/Articles/tb26-3/tb84wilson.pdf`?

PW: `ledmac` and friends have nothing to do with my work on scripts and fonts.

In 1990 John Lavagnino and Dominik Wujastyk created the edmac set of macros for TeX (`http://mirror.ctan.org/macros/plain/contrib/edmac`) designed for authors of "critical editions". A critical edition appears to be one where various versions of a manuscript are compared to try and come to a definitive version of the work. This involves lots of footnotes describing variant readings, explaining allusions that a modern reader might not follow, and so on. The main requirements seem to be that every line is numbered, and can be referred to by its number, and at least four different series of footnotes with differing layouts (for example in double or triple columns, or run together as a single paragraph).

Around 2003 I happened to notice that someone on `comp.text.tex` was asking for a version of edmac that would work well with LaTeX and thought that it would be interesting to try and do that. My first ledmac version was a fairly simple conversion of edmac from TeX-ese to LaTeX-ese. Then came requests for it to be able to handle verse and tabular material and I converted TeX code from Wayne Sullivan and Herbert Berger to do this. Later there were requests for a means of putting two different texts in parallel on facing pages together with separate sets of line numbers, footnotes, etc. I eventually managed to produce the ledpar package as an add-on to the ledmac package to enable this. The bundle now includes ledarab for critical editions that include Arabic texts which involve a mixture of left-to-right and right-to-left typesetting. ledmac is intrinsically complicated as it has to typeset everything twice for the line numbering mechanism. I must admit that I don't really understand exactly how it works; I have never even read a critical edition, and know nothing about Arabic.

In answer to a next-to-be-asked question: Reading books on typography one keeps on coming across different fonts and I got to wondering where the letter shapes originally came from and this got me interested in the origins of the alphabet and writing. There was nothing complicated about the shapes of the early letter forms and I got the idea to create Metafont versions of them, which was relatively straightforward. One thing leads to another and there was a gap in my understanding of the development of the letter shapes from monumental forms to printed forms, so that led me to looking at (reproductions of) manuscripts and calligraphy. I produced a Metafont series of fonts representing several of the main kinds of writing (called bookhands) used for formal purposes between roughly 1 AD and 1500 AD when printed books started to appear, thus completing the main thread of the Latin alphabet letter shape development from 1200 BC to the present day. I have converted the archaic scripts from Metafont to PostScript Type 1 format (http://mirror.ctan.org/fonts/archaic) and am in the slow process of extending the bookhands (http://mirror.ctan.org/fonts/bookhands) and converting them to PostScript Type 1 form.

DW: You have written a regular column for *TUGboat* for a number of years, called "Glisterings". The first installment was apparently in 2001 (http://tug.org/TUGboat/Articles/tb22-4/tb72wilson.pdf). Please tell me what "glisterings" means and what was your motivation and intention with this column.

PW: For some years Jeremy Gibbons wrote a column for *TUGboat* called "Hey—it works!" This contained small pieces of (LA)TeX code solving some particular problems. When Jeremy wanted to stop writing his column I, for some reason, was asked to take it over. I agreed to do so but I wasn't too confident that all the code I got or wrote would work properly, so I wanted to change the column's title, and also so Jeremy could not be blamed for any of my wrongdoings. I eventually came up with "Glisterings" based on the phrase "All that glisters is not gold" (Shakespeare, Merchant of Venice, II, 7) to indicate that there might be some doubt about the quality of the contents. So far, though, there has been no fool's gold that I am aware of. The Editorial Board agreed to the title even though it is a word of my own invention. What I have tried to do with the column is to pick some frequently asked question from comp.text.tex and provide some kind of answer, usually based on one or several that have appeared on comp.text.tex; sometimes, though, I reluctantly have to create my own solution.

DW: You mentioned Bringhurst's book and there is of course your on manual on document "styling". Do you have any other recommended books in this area?

PW: The UK FAQ has a section on books on typography. I think that if you only read one then it should be Bringhurst's (it is probably also the easiest to find in your local good bookshop). Others, saying nothing about their respective merits, in author order are:

- Ruari McLean, *The Thames and Hudson Manual of Typography*, Thames & Hudson, 1980
- Jan Tschichold, *The Form of the Book*, Lund Humphries, 1991
- Adrian Wilson (no relation), *The Design of Books*, Chronicle Books, 1993

DW: Now that you are retired, do you plan to remain active with TEX et al., e.g., after you have finished converting the bookhands to Type 1?

PW: I'll remain active — I need some intellectual challenges and TEX can be uniquely challenging. However as I have plans to do quite a bit of travelling away from computer resources my response time to any questions or requests will get longer and longer. Early in my career I found that the method of "masterly inaction" in response to others' problems to be extremely useful. Given enough time, and urgency, the problem could usually be solved by the originator. (Rereading this, I must have started to become generally realistic, also known as cynical, at an earlier age than I thought).

DW: I'd appreciate hearing any thoughts you have on the future of TEX et al. and of how TUG and the other user groups can best help support TEX and TEX users.

PW: (LA)TEX wouldn't be where it is today without the TUGs. Fortunately there are several, as on occasions one or other of them flag somewhat. TEX Live and friends are a tremendous help in actually getting and installing a TEX system. I am disappointed that the *TUGboat* publishing schedule seems to be in a permanent state of slippage but the online *PracTEX Journal* magazine goes a way towards filling the gap. [Editor's note: since this interview was completed, the *TUGboat* publication schedule has caught up.]

(LA)TEX still provides the best non-professional typesetting system for non-ephemeral works but (a) it is not well known (it doesn't come on your MS laptop), (b) it requires some willingness to learn (it's not iconified WYSIWYG), and (c) there is still the "LATEX look" about too many documents. In my last company there were very few LATEX users basically because everyone, and especially management, used MS and couldn't cope with anything outside that narrow window onto the computing world. Generating PDF is a great boon as everyone can at least read and print a PDF document. Perhaps with OpenOffice and ODF it will be easier to make bridges into the "regular" world. More examples of fine non-LATEX-looking typesetting would help, together with how they were done. I don't think that LATEX will ever conquer the world as too many are satisfied with "good enough" instead of "as good as possible".

Font installation is exceedingly hard anywhere except, I gather, on a Mac. It would be a great boost to be able to push a button/type a single command and everything then happens automatically. New fonts are not just nice but if you are typesetting using a non-Latin alphabet or script they are essential. [Editor's note: since this interview was completed, XƎTEX and LuaTEX have been released, offering access to native fonts on all platforms; see the interviews with Jonathan Kew and Taco Hoekwater.]

DW: More generally, you have spent a lot of time studying, thinking about, and working with aspects of printing, fonts, and related crafts. Do you have any general thoughts on the continuing development of these fields.

PW: I'm glad you said "crafts" as typography is a craft, not a science. You have to have an eye for what is appropriate and what is not and often the distinction is subtle. I freely admit that I don't have such an eye. I look at typography magazines and they are full of attention grabbing stuff, which is fine if you are trying to compete with the adjacent advertisement but not useful otherwise. You can find a lot of fonts on the web but there are exceedingly few that you would be comfortable reading more than one line. Creating a new font seems a fun thing to do, especially if you are using a graphical program. Perhaps folk will, in time, learn to be more constrained.

It is good that increasingly people can, and do, design and create their own document styles. Some will undoubtedly become craftsmen.

DW: Thank you for your participation in this interview. I knew your name before, and I'm glad to now have much more understanding of your long term work with TeX.

[Update from Peter Wilson: Over the past couple of years I have been fortunate enough to have been invited to spend a day or two each week at a local printshop where I have produced a few small books and ephemera using the traditional methods of handsetting lead type and printing on a hand press. This has brought home to me more forcefully than before that typography and typesetting are skilled crafts and I am filled with admiration, and even awe, for those who worked before the advent of Linotype or Monotype typecasters and especially before LaTeX, Adobe products, and offset lithography.

Regarding the photo at the beginning of interview: The press is motor driven with a cycle time of about 15 seconds and if your fingers get caught then no fingers. In the foreground is a Heidelberg press, sometimes referred to as the "windmill", that we use for foiling. There is a lot more to it than is in the photo. The Chandler & Price can do nasty things to fingers but the Heidelberg with its rotating arm feeding mechanism can do horrible things to anything above the waist. You can tell it's old because the only safety guard is a small piece of sheet metal at head height. I haven't learnt how to use it; I only do small print runs and use a hand foiler instead.]

Gerben Wierda

Gerben Wierda is well known for his tools for installing TeX and other capabilities on Mac OS X systems.

[Interview completed 28 November 2006.]

Dave Walden, interviewer: Please tell me a bit about your personal history independent of TeX.

Gerben Wierda, interviewee: I live together with my wife (Renée) and two kids: Renske, a 6 year old girl, and Mark Douwe, a 3 year old boy. I have had many various jobs; my day job currently is that I am the IT Lead Architect of the Judiciary in The Netherlands, that is all the courts in The Netherlands, roughly 10,000 employees. My wife, by the way, is service level manager for an IT service organisation of the Dutch Ministry of Justice. Both our careers originally started in the private sector.

I hold an M.Sc. in Physics from Groningen University (`http://www.rug.nl/`) and I hold an MBA from RSM Erasmus Rotterdam (`http://www.rsm.nl/`). Renée also holds an M.Sc. in Physics from Groningen University.

With two careers, two kids, and two Physics majors, you can understand that our kids do not have it easy ;-).

DW: When and how did you first get involved with TeX and friends?

GW: Before using TeX I have used amongst other things typewriters and for instance the IBM Visitext when I was editor of the University magazine for math/CS/physics/astrophysics departments and WordMarc at the university. I wrote my Master's dissertation ("A search for resonant Bhabha-scattering in the MeV-region") with TeX. I got hooked because of the nice math, nice typesetting and I think above all because of the logical way of writing with LaTeX. TeX was available for my Atari 1040ST, my first personal computer. Since that time, I have written my letters with LaTeX and some other things. I did typeset a political party local election program with plain TeX once, on the basis of a design by an artist. That was done on a NeXT Cube. That was the first time I had to compile and install TeX myself. The TeX environment on the NeXT was unsurpassed at the time, mostly thanks to Tom Rokicki's TeXView.app.

DW: Please tell me a little more about TeXView.app and what made it useful or unique for its time.

GW: In a time of PK fonts, it presented a very nice integrated handling of screen and print output and it had very good custom anti-aliasing, so it also looked gorgeous on screen. And it used the signalling function of TeX to display the first page of a multi-paged document immediately after it had been produced, long before the DVI file was complete. This made it almost lightning quick in your experience on hardware that did not have a fraction of today's processing power. I understand that this kind of a linear setup is hard to do with PDF.

DW: You are well known for enabling TeX's installation on the Mac; what did you actually create — a distribution or a way to install an existing distribution?

GW: This one is difficult to answer in black and white. It all started with a shell script that installed teTeX for you. The shell script came with patches for the code to make it compile and run. This script was also the input for the first fink teTeX redistribution. But such a system required installing the Developer Environment and running shell commands, something pretty alien to most Mac users.

Soon thereafter I produced a very simple GUI front end application that installed (or uninstalled) TeX and Ghostscript and let you set the paper size. I think it was at that time I started to extend the teTeX distribution with stuff I thought could be part of it. This resulted in a second `texmf` tree with my personal additions to teTeX, mostly based on user requests for missing stuff. One could say that at that point it became a separate distribution of sorts. The tree with my additions is called `texmf.gwtex` and the gwTeX name was later proposed by people as a name for my (re)distribution.

A while after that I switched to TeX Live for the binaries and programs and used teTeX for the main `texmf` tree and it has been like that until I recently moved from teTeX to a subset of TeX Live because of the demise of teTeX. There is still some stuff in `texmf.gwtex` that is not available in TeX Live, but it is not much. So, slowly, it has become more a redistribution again.

Apart from *what* is installed there also is *how* it is installed. There, I have done the most work, but also there, it has been a lot of interfacing with standard tools in TeX, like fmtutil and updmap. The interfacing in itself is complex and extended. Keeping all of this operation on my own (and supporting users via email) in my spare time has required very strict philosophies on how to maintain redistributions.

DW: Can you give an example of a "strict philosophy"?

GW: I almost never patch anything myself. If something is broken, I spend my time in trying to get the original authors to repair or extend something. That takes more time initially, but it prevents an explosion of work later. If I patch something and a new release arrives, you can probably imagine the number of combinatorial problems you can run into. I only patch stuff that is not maintained anymore by someone else.

It is also a matter of discipline. Investing time in as painless as possible (for the user, that is) scripts, pays itself in fewer calls for help later. The quick solution is seldom the best solution in terms of time needed.

DW: You mentioned that you started with teTeX; do you know Thomas Esser well (he was interviewed earlier this year as part of this series)?

GW: I may have seen him once. We had e-mail contact at a semi-regular basis during the early years. He was very helpful in adapting his scripts and configuration files so they were usable by my scripts. Because he was willing to extend his scripts and change layout of his configuration files, I was able to present the user with a GUI for some TeX settings. Without his changes, it would have been possible, but it would have been very difficult. His work eased my work enormously.

DW: I used a Mac for eight years before I switched to MS Windows (a conscious decision to be in the mainstream of computer use even if such use wasn't as much fun). One of my fondest memories of the Mac in comparison to Windows was that I could do installations on the Mac by dragged the program to a directory, while Windows required "installation": can you tell me a little more about why "installation" is now necessary on a Mac?

GW: For one, because Mac OS X is in fact a Unix system, which to the administrator looks a lot like BSD Unix. Installing for multiple users requires writing in system-wide areas, areas which are generally protected.

But even then, drag-and-drop installs are still preferred. This is even true for software that has to install stuff in system locations. It is possible to make a drag-and-drop install (say for the TeXShop application) and let it come with its own internal TeX setup. It is also possible to let that application notice at first startup that some stuff has to be installed, give the user an authentication panel and then run some specific install script with administrator rights. This solution is however not generic, but specific. If you want to be able to install all kinds of software, not just TeX as part of your particular front end, but TeX, Ghostscript, ImageMagick, etc. as back end to be used for many front ends (TeXShop, iTeXMac, etc.), system-wide installs are the norm and drag-and-drop is too specific and a lot of work for those Unix-type tools.

TeX itself does not need administrator rights and can be installed anywhere. But other tools like ImageMagick for image format conversion or Ghostscript do, mainly because they often require very fixed locations for supporting libraries and data. On a multi-user system like Mac OS X, this means a system-wide protected area. Enabling TeX use on the command line for all users also requires sysadmin access.

DW: What was your motivation or goal that "dragged" you into doing so much detailed development work on TeX?

GW: I want to use TeX. This means I want it available on the systems I use. That meant that when I got an Apple PowerBook with Rhapsody (Mac OS X precursor), I wanted to install and run TeX on it. I moved to Apple when they released Mac OS X, as for me, Mac OS X is the logical next step after NeXTStep. I do have a project to write a book and it is written with TeX. But as others have found before me, TeX itself is able to distract you from the contents of your work.

What dragged me into all the support work is the simple fact that people asked me for help, and I tend to help people if I am asked. E.g., after I had publicized my script and patches to install teTeX on Mac OS X, people asked me (I think it was Dick Koch, a mathematician at the University of Oregon and author of the popular TeXShop front end) if I could not create a binary installation without the need for users to install the Developer environment and use the command line. That was TeXGSInstaller.app.

It was also a matter of available expertise. I have been involved in porting a lot in the past, e.g., you may find my name in the Squid annals as contact person for running Squid on NeXTStep. Together with a friend (and technically these projects were mostly his work) I was active in getting to run stuff like CNews, Taylor UUCP and Perl on NeXTStep. For me, this has also been a way to keep involved in the technical side of IT as I moved more into management. With skills, it is "use it or lose it". And I believe firmly that you need to have feeling for the things you manage if you want to manage it well. You need to be *able* to connect to the content of the people you manage even if you should not do their content in their place. It also helps to have such skills if you want to select the right people for the job. There are also downsides to this philosophy. Anyway, I do need to do some technical things as a hobby to be able to do my less technical job well. As I recently have moved back more to technical content in my work as I have changed focus from strategy and policy to architecture, it becomes less imperative to keep on doing these technical hobbies privately. And there is still enough left besides TeX and friends.

DW: What are the "downsides to this philosophy"?

GW: I think the downsides are outside the scope of this interview, but let me give you one: if you manage professionals you are in a position of power over them. For a professional, this power by the manager can be balanced by the fact that the professional has skills and knowledge the manager does not have. This balance makes many professionals feel better (and less uncertain). Having a manager who also can be considered a (near) technical equal may make some employees uncertain and afraid, not states of mind that are good for the organisation or anyone involved.

DW: Let me get all these names and functions straight in my own mind. Your program TeXGSInstaller.app can help install gwTEX on a Mac, but that is somehow different than your i-Installer? (Described in "i-Installer: The evolution of a TEX install on Mac OS X" (http://tug.org/TUGboat/Contents/contents26-3.html), *TUGboat* volume 26, number 3.) And where does TeXShop, which you apparently did with Dick Koch and Dirk Olmes (http://cc.uoregon.edu/cnews/summer2002/koch.html), fit into this set of tools?

GW: TeXGSInstaller.app was a simple front end for a script that could install and uninstall TEX and Ghostscript. i-Installer is a generic software installer, like Apple's own Installer.app.

TeXShop is a front end, in fact it is at first a text editor where you edit your TEX source. When the TEX source needs to be compiled into PDF, it runs pdfTEX in the background and when the result is ready, it displays this. So, TeXShop is an editor/runner/viewer, but leaves the TEX compilation job to a command line tool at the Unix level. You still need a TEX to do the work. i-Installer is an application that can install software on a Mac and one of the i-Packages available for it has a TEX.

I did almost nothing on TeXShop, by the way. It was all the other guys.

Someone trying to understand the details of these distinctions could read the *TUGboat* article you mentioned or maybe visit http://www.rna.nl/tex.html, although that will not be maintained in the future.

DW: At the end of the presentation of your paper ("TEX Live — Life with TEX", co-authored with Renée M. E. van Roode) at TUG 2006 in Marrakesh, you announced you were going to stop public support and maintenance of all this installation support software. Why are you stopping, is there any connection to Thomas Esser stopping his efforts with teTEX, and how do you see things going forward without you? Also, what about your on-going support for the other tools we have mentioned?

GW: It is partly a direct consequence of Thomas Esser stopping. For the rest, I also need to write this up in detail for the article that comes with the talk and that is to appear in *TUGboat* later: in general it has to do with the way TEX Live is maintained. I expect an increase in the support work because it is larger and less strictly edited than teTEX was. For examples, if the file rohyph.tex is renamed to rohyphen.tex (which happened recently), the existing user language.dat files in TEXMFLOCAL or TEXMFHOME are suddenly broken because they have a wrong file name. Imagine the surprise of a user who selects Romanian in the TEX i-Package configuration phase and time and again he ends up with a TEX format without Romanian. Either my scripting would have to become even more extended, or my direct user support would increase manyfold with changes like these.

Note that I have not announced the complete end of maintenance. What I have announced is that I will not support the users anymore and only do maintenance if I need it myself. So, it is a slower death.

I have no idea on going forward, but if someone or a group with the right skills steps up, I will gladly help in an advisory role during a transition period. I intend to leave everything in a state which has enough documentation, etc. However, that is uncertain as the deadline of January 1 is fixed and there are limits on what I can do.

DW: I presume your co-author Renée M. E. van Roode is the same person as your wife Renée, an IT person herself. Is she also a TEX user, and has how has she been involved with your various TEX and Mac support projects?

GW: She has been instrumental in the availability of my work, but not technically. We had a deal: she supported my putting money and time into this; I bored her to sleep with technical stories.

DW: I remember your paper "Mac OS X Fonts in pdfTEX" (`http://tug.org/pracjourn/2006-1/wierda/`), TPJ 2006-1, with Thomas A. Schmitz and Adam T. Lindsay. Is there any connection between your work with font installation (or any of your other work) and XeTEX?

GW: Thomas and Adam were the TEX and font gurus and I am the packager. I know relatively little of TEX ;-). The paper is theirs almost entirely; they forced me to be the co-author. XeTEX is a great development, but there is no connection.

DW: I believe some of your work was supported by the TEX Development Fund. Which work was that and was the support enough to matter?

GW: A few years ago, before I could get DSL in my neighbourhood, I was doing the uploads and stuff on an ISDN line. At one point, I got bills of $400 a month for communication. 99% of that was TEX support. I needed to buy hardware, of course, and software. I can afford all of this, but I felt that it was crazy to spend all this time *and* all the money. If I would not have had financial support, I would not have been in financial trouble, but it would have been hard to convince myself to go on with something that in fact was me paying a considerable amount of money so I could spend too much time on helping others. Without the support and donations, I would probably have quit years ago. The donations and support were never enough to balance the cost, though, but enough to minimize it somewhat. The largest donation I ever got was from Dick Koch, who graciously split the winnings from the Apple Design Award he won with TeXShop.

DW: Do you typically work in "Unix mode" on the Mac or do your work via a GUI IDE; in other words, does Mac OS X being based on Unix made a difference to you? Also, do you have any strong biases on the question of free software tools versus Apple-provided tools and other commercial tools?

GW: The i-Package maintenance, building TEX and trees and such is mostly Unix command line work. Make, shell and Perl are the most important tools. The README is RTF done in a GUI text editor. i-Installer itself is developed in Cocoa, and I develop using the nice Apple XCode IDE which comes with the Developer environment. Typically I work in mail, anyway ;-).

If Mac OS X had not been based on Unix, I would never have used a Mac. When I bought my first NeXT Cube, I was looking for a good Unix with a GUI. Believe it or not, the NeXT was by far the cheapest option in a time as I recall you had to pay $250 for TCP/IP, $250 for NFS, $250 for X11, $500 for Motif, etc. when you were trying to build an SCO Unix system on x86 hardware. It was even cheaper for me because I bought mine second hand (but never used) from some US university when the dollar was at a historical low. I also have been a proponent of object-oriented design, and NeXTStep had all of this. The NeXT was so well engineered in many ways, that I have been using it as my main machine for almost 10 years and only at the end some things became a bit slow. I plan to de-mothball my NeXT later and maybe try to compile TEX Live on it ;-).

I have no bias for either royalty-free or commercial software. My own stuff is free (BSD license) and available from SourceForge.

DW: The biographical note on your fonts paper with Thomas A. Schmitz and Adam Lindsay says, "Gerben Wierda has been working on a book since 1995 but has been sidetracked by typesetting ... Having used mainly LATEX since 1986, he recently switched his book project to ConTEXt." Given your extensive history of succumbing to user's cries for help with complex systems, are you taking any precautions to avoid being "dragged into" the very active world of ConTEXt support?

GW: I switched to ConTEXt because I dislike the typical "LATEX style". I liked memoir, but at first glance, ConTEXt looked better organised and set up. I have mixed feelings about ConTEXt. Especially, it is less conceptual writing than LATEX. ConTEXt itself is visually oriented more than logically oriented. I understand that the conceptual orientation is more a task for XML and other stuff where ConTEXt is only a typesetter. I can understand that, but I'm certainly not going to write XML instead of TEX. As support for ConTEXt goes, I will be a user, nothing else. I have pretty poor TEX skills.

DW: Thank you very much for participating in this interview. As someone who previously did not know anything about the world of TEX on the Mac, I found our conversation very educational and I can see why the Mac TEX world holds you in such high regard and is working hard to find ways to replace the support you have provided.

John Culleton

John Culleton uses TEX in his indexing and typesetting business. He also participates in various Internet-based discussion groups related to printing and publishing where he is vocal about using TEX for typesetting.

[Interview completed 2 December 2006.]

Dave Walden, interviewer: Please tell me a bit about yourself and your life before you got involved in publishing and with TEX.

John Culleton, interviewee: Well, it has been a long life! I worked for 23 years for the Social Security Administration in Baltimore, in two stretches. During the first stretch, when I was in Financial Management, I asked for a nine month summary of certain financial numbers. The programmer told me he couldn't do it, then I asked for quarterly summaries. Same answer. I asked why. He told me I wouldn't understand. So I decided to become a computer programmer.

After almost three years in the private sector as a programmer, system analyst and manager of programmers I returned to SSA. In the course of those remaining years I dealt with some small systems and became acquainted with Unix. After retiring from paid employment I fiddled with some Linux systems. When I took over the publication of a Breeder Directory for the local kennel club my typesetting choices were Groff and LATEX. I chose LATEX. I put the breeders in a DBMS and generated the LATEX code through some little Perl programs.

DW: It is not clear to me from your Wexford Press (`http://wexfordpress.com`) web site if you got involved with publishing at the same time as you got involved with TEX or earlier. Please tell me about the sequence of events of your getting involved with publishing and with TEX.

JC: First came TEX—LATEX and later plain TEX with the Breeder Directory. Then, looking around for a lucrative hobby I began indexing for money. My method of indexing was and perhaps still is unique. I convert a PDF file to plain text, saving the page breaks, then insert Eplain syle indexing tags, and then run the file through plain TEX. I keep the generated index and discard the rest. This gives me the advantage of embedded indexing (no page number errors) without the tears of, e.g., MS Word. The transition to typesetting for fun and profit (small amount of each) was a natural progression.

Like everyone I dreamt of publishing a book someday, which led me to Pub-forum and later `self-publishing@yahoogroups.com`.

DW: While I first came across your name in one of the TEX discussion groups, I really became aware of you when I joined the Yahoo-based Self-Publishing discussion group of which you are one of the three owners and moderators and a frequent contributor yourself. Please tell me about your involvement in this discussion group and your motivations related to and for it.

JC: As indicated before, the sequence was Linux, Breeder Directory, TEX, indexing, the publishing mailing lists, including `self-publishing@yahoogroups.com`. When the self-publishing list lost their moderator suddenly, I volunteered to take it on. I recruited some assistants, who after a while fell by the wayside. Then I had the great good fortune to recruit J.C. Simonds (http://www.beaglebay.com/) and Marion Gropen (http://www.gropenassoc.com/) as assistants. I decided that to keep these bright and energetic people on board I had to treat them as equals and not assistants. They are great friends and neat associates. I met them in person just once, when BEA (Book Expo of America) came to Washington, DC.

I also ran a book review for a couple of years which gave me review copies of books on self-publishing. I bought some more, plus books on typesetting and so on. I now have about 30 such books within arms' reach of my computer workstation. By reading books and also reading posts I became a kind of curb-side expert on self-publishing.

Technically we don't *own* self-publishing@yahoogroups.com. It is owned by SPAN, Small Publishing Association of North America. SPAN was founded by self-publishing authors Tom and Marilyn Ross and the administration later passed to Scott Floria. He seldom injects himself in the management of the list. Now and then we call on him to decide a difficult case.

Because of my tireless championing of TeX on the mailing lists I have become known as a TeX "guru" on those lists, which will no doubt be the cause of great hilarity on, e.g., comp.text.tex, among the real experts. I am of course a perpetual amateur, but that is not a bad thing. When I say something foolish I can look forward to a savage correction by some of the experts, but in the process I learn something. As a married man I have been yelled at by an expert. I can take the comp.text.tex critiques in stride.

DW: As you champion TeX, what arguments do you give them for using TeX, and what do you recommend to people who are interested in trying TeX about how to best get up to speed with it?

JC: First I suggest that they read "A Gentle Introduction to TeX" by Michael Doob. Although this was written before we had PDF output it gives the essentials in user-friendly form. For those interested in highly formatted books such as textbooks I recommend "TeX, an Excursion" by Hans Hagen et al. I am writing my own e-book on the use of TeX for novels but I never seem to find time to finish it. I should add that I do not use or recommend LaTeX. Its verbosity and multiple sources for commands turns me off, and may turn off others.

DW: How about the first part of my question: What arguments do you give for using TeX, or do you not argue for it but just emphasize from time to time that you use TeX rather than InDesign, QuarkXPress, etc., which other self-publishers are always talking about.

JC: I do a little of both. I mention TeX as a quality typesetting engine. I mention that the H&J routines of InDesign are taken from TeX. I note that "TeX is free, which is too expensive for many." I mention the online support from various mailing lists which often involves the author of the macro in question, not some underpaid telephone answerer with a copy of a manual. I mention that upgrades are free. I mention that the document source format is plain text with embedded tags. I mention that very old files are still processable in TeX. I mention that TeX cannot destroy your source file, even if you kick the plug out of the wall in mid-process. I mention that an editor plus TeX plus a PDF viewer is the truest form of WYSIWYG.

I do not try to sugar coat the learning curve with TeX. But all new software has a learning curve.

DW: How about the reverse? What would you say to people already interested in TeX about the advantages and disadvantages of self-publishing, how to best go about it, and how it compares with the TeX-rejection reactions one often gets when trying to get something TeX-based published by traditional publishers?

JC: Most printers accept a PDF file for the book interior. Since TeX prepares well-formed PDF files with fonts embedded, etc., there is no problem with the submission to the printer or publisher. In self-publishing getting published is the easy part. Selling the book in an era when over 100,000 titles are added each year is the hard part. I also push for people to do their homework by reading some books. I have an annotated book list, almost a set of mini-reviews, at `http://wexfordpress.com/tex/shortlist.pdf`.

I also warn people away from subsidy publishers such as iUniverse, Authorhouse, Infinity and so on. There are new ones popping up every day. They make it easy to publish but almost impossible to sell books. I do suggest as a more sensible alternative the use of a good book coach or consultant. My list of these is at `http://wexfordpress.com/tex/packagers.pdf`.

DW: What is your TeX setup — distribution, editor, formats you typically use, major packages, etc. Would this change if you were writing a book yourself rather than typesetting someone else's book? If someone hires you to typeset a book written in MS Word or InDesign, how do you proceed, and what sort of electronic files do you return to the author?

JC: I have a Slackware Linux system. I use Gvim exclusively as my text editor. I have a few shortcuts that I have assigned to F keys. I simplify matters by putting each book in its own subdirectory. The master file is always called `book.tex`. It is my main file which calls subfiles, such as `macros.tex`, `half.tex`, `title.tex`, `copy.tex`, `ack.tex`, `body.tex` and so on for the different pieces of the book. Often I just copy the `.tex` files from an earlier project and then insert new material. Each project is unique but the unique material is inserted into a common base structure. With the use of F keys I can compile and/or display the book from the Gvim window. By displaying the PDF file using xpdf I can update that window with a single keystroke `r`. This gives me a semi-WYSIWYG approach.

My customers almost always submit work in MS Word `.doc` format. Often I convert the `.doc` file to rtf in OpenOffice, then run rtf2latex2e, then edit out or replace the LaTeX tags with mass changes in Gvim. I only use pdfε-TeX or ConTeXt.

Another technique where italics are not frequent is to just save the file as plain text. It becomes my `body.tex` file.

In plain TeX and indexing I use `eplain.tex`. I use the table building routines from TeXsys for things like invoices. Interested parties can obtain sample code by writing me at `type@wexfordpress.com`.

My typesetting customers get a PDF file of the interior. My indexing customers get an ASCII file derived from my `.ind`. No printer has had trouble with any of my PDF files.

DW: How do you see TeX faring in the continuing increase in the popularity and dominance of systems such as Word, InDesign, etc.?

JC: TeX enjoyed a heyday of sorts with the academic presses. That is fading as more alternatives are brought forward. But newer versions of TeX, such as pdfε-TeX and ConTeXt, offer clear advantages over word processors. With respect to preparing PDF files, Word is playing catchup. And Word, InDesign and their ilk remind me of the poem: When they are good they are very very good and when they are bad they are horrid. It is hard for one person to debug remotely another's problem with a WYSIWYG product, but it is easy for one person to view a code snippet and perceive the hidden flaw. I get help all the time on `comp.text.tex` and the ConTEXt mailing list.

Indirectly the growing acceptance of open source software such as Linux, Apache and so on has paved the way for TEX as an open source publishing program.

DW: What do you think the user groups, e.g., TUG, should be doing to better promote people's (particularly self-publishing people's) use of TEX? Could there be some more explicit effort, e.g., a TEX introduction or course at a self-publishing conference? You became involved in TEX because you had a publishing project in what I presume was a hobby area having to do with your local kennel club; I am also reminded of Joe Hogg's work with TEX (`http://tug.org/pracjourn/2006-3/hogg/`) in the area of his hobby as a docent at the Los Angeles Zoo and Botanical Garden. I wonder if perhaps TUG should be volunteering to offer introductions or courses at many different kinds of hobby organizations — many will have some need to typeset and publish something.

JC: That might be useful, though it is probably more of a one-on-one thing. I never tried to proselytize the doggie people in TEX. For a club newsletter, MS Word is fine. My approach to the breeder directory, using an RDBMS to store the date and a Perl program to format the output for TEX, was perhaps a bit idiosyncratic. I was after all in my salad days as a programmer. Most doggie people aren't or else have a different programming background than mine.

I suggest an adult education non-credit course in "TEX without tears" could show self-publishers, for example, the way to prepare their novel, etc., in first rate form without expense. It might be worth proposing to the local community college.

DW: Or perhaps to an adult education program of the sort where someone can take a course in contract bridge, Chinese cooking, or scrapbooking. And maybe the TEX approach could be a major component in a course on self publishing. Neat idea, John.

With that, I'll say thank you for participating in this interview, and I hope we can meet in person at some point.

JC: It would be my pleasure!

Pierre MacKay

Pierre MacKay is a classics professor who was a TUG board member from 1983–1991, TUG president from 1983–1985, and Unix site coordinator from 1983–1992. He was with TUG from the start.

Unfortunately, long term commitments prevented him from completing this interview.

[Interview done in early 2007.]

Dave Walden, interviewer: Please tell me about yourself independent of the world of TeX.

Pierre MacKay, interviewee: My training and my official teaching career is as a humanist, but I had become intrigued by the notion of the computer even before I joined the faculty of the University of Washington to teach Classical Greek, Arabic and Ottoman Turkish. In those days (1966) the only thing ever suggested to a humanist with an interest in computing was a KWIC concordance, and I was led to consider such a project, but in Arabic, not in English. I learned a little Snobol, in hopes that a string-based language might offer better capabilities than assembler or Fortran, but I had not proceeded very far when I realized that there was no available form of output that would be intelligible to the kind of scholar who might find a concordance of Hariri useful. The programming consultants for the CDC 6400 which was then used as the general purpose academic research machine assured me that its six-bit character set would never be able to handle Arabic and, by good fortune, I listened to them.

On the advice of a student, I stepped across the hall to the newly established Computer Science laboratory with its brand new Sigma tie()5 machine — an entire 16,000 32-bit words to play with; I remember the excitement when memory was increased to 24,000 words. Over the course of about six years, I put together two major programs, learning each technique directly from the the graduate students I would sometimes have to evict from the Sigma 5 because I needed almost the entire memory, in addition to overlays called in from one of the earliest disk storage systems. One program (HATTAT) described font characters in the format used by the VideoComp phototypesetter, an American version of the Hell Digiset made by RCA and later taken over by Information International Inc. (III).

It was clear after the very first experiments that the context-sensitive fluidity of Arabic character shapes could best be provided for by making up a limited number of stroke components and assembling them into fully-formed characters on the fly. This approach has been adopted by many later systems, and was also used in the 1960s by the Caldwell Sinotype for Chinese Ideographs.

Since it was obvious in 1967 that no existing composition system could possibly manage the task of assembling the stroke components into letters, I developed a second program (KATIB) to take in a stream of quasi-alphabetic character codes (including many digraphs to extend the Latin letter punch card alphabet) and to replace them with strings of font glyphs and command sequences for positioning adjustment. In the most extreme instances it proved necessary to remember as many as eight preceding input characters and to look three characters forward in order to shape the desired Arabic character correctly. This led me to write what I have since characterized as an ad-hoc, poorly structured, kindergarten version of TEX. It even had a macro interpreter.

This program, which, so far as I have been able to determine, was the first fully automated digital composition system for Arabic script, succeeded in the production of a single book, Diocles, *On Burning Mirrors*, but it had necessarily been written very close to the architecture of the Sigma 5, and when that machine was decommissioned, so was my program.

DW: How did you first become involved with TEX?

PM: After the disappearance of the Sigma tie()5, I spent some years of ineffectual floundering (including a foredoomed attempt to return to the CDC 6400) until I learned from Rick Furuta about TEX. (I was flattered to discover, when I wrote to Don Knuth, that he knew about HATTAT and KATIB.) It was obvious at once that TEX and METAFONT were the well-designed replacements for my haphazard programs, and Rick and I set to work on introducing TEX to the University of Washington. We worked first on the VAX version, and also on the original SAIL version of METAFONT, which we ultimately used to drive one of the three (or was it four?) Alphatype phototypesetters that ever produced TEX output. We watched, although we never participated in, the brief development of the XDS printing system, and we wrote drivers for a wet toner 200 dpi device. (I still use surplus rolls of the paper from this device as a very superior shelf paper.) I was out of the loop in Greece for the academic year 1978–79, but when I returned, I enthusiastically rejoined the TEX community.

DW: Did you start using TEX78 and then phase over to use of the "final" version? If so, can you tell me a bit about this transition in the TEX community or at least at the University of Washington.

PM: When Rick Furuta and I began our association with TEX, TEX78 was the only working program available. We were fortunate enough to have access to a good-sized DEC-20, so we were able to import a SAIL compiler, and to run both TEX and METAFONT. The only alternative I can remember was PascalTEX, which was a moderately successful attempt to translate TEX78 to a more accessible platform. In addition to the DEC-20, we had access to several different sizes of VAXen, which were being earned by the Computer Science department through a commitment to develop a Pascal compiler for VMS.

TEX78 did not make many converts at the University of Washington, owing less to the characteristics of the program itself than to the lack of acceptable output devices. These were the days of strict vertical integration in the printing industry. At the low end there were impact printers with more or less proprietary print-balls and print-wheels, and at the high end the digital expression of font characters was still in its infancy. The main University printing department was still using photo-plates, which cost horrendous amounts for any new character set and were neither accessible nor of interest to an academic research department. Research papers were produced with Scribe and similar formatters on various impact printers, and refinements such as variable-width characters were generally regarded as frivolous extravagance. High resolution digital output was available only on colossal image-setters whose font format was a precious trade secret. There do not seem to have been many of these in Seattle anyway until well into the 1980s, and they would not have been made accessible to a program like TEX which made a speciality of providing "non-standard" characters. To give an idea of the climate of the time, consider that the VideoComp font formats had somehow slipped into the public domain, but neither RCA nor III could ever resign themselves to it. At one time I tried to work on a METAFONT to VideoFont converter, and would send down occasional tapes to III in Los Angeles. I got reasonably good images back, but the company invariably erased all traces of the font I had created from my tapes.

Image-setter companies such as Compugraphic claimed, truthfully, I am sure, that they regularly sold their machines at a loss so as to create an appetite for fonts. If one happened to need a character not in the existing repertory, they could consider producing it, but no one in the academic world could possibly afford it. Movable lead type had been rather a democratic technology, if you could afford the labor and the lead. For about five decades, as lead was disappearing, typesetting moved backward into a feudal world.

The development of PostScript as a machine-independent way of managing both fonts and layout re-democratized the industry, especially after Adobe somewhat unwillingly released PostScript specifications to the public. The first 300 dpi LaserWriter (Apple's largest computer at the time) changed many minds about the possibilities of TEX, and the discovery that the Canon print engine in the LaserWriter was actually a 600 dpi machine made it possible to produce near book-quality output. I used to produce 600 dpi output with TEX at `\magstep1` which could then be photoreduced to an effective 720 dpi, which was a resolution used by at least one low-end digital image-setter.

None of this development was obvious in 1979, and we certainly had no notion how fast it would come about, so the potentials of TEX were poorly understood. Knuth managed to talk Alphatype Corporation into allowing him a restrictive license to code directly for the Alphatype, and he once said that writing Alphatype programming was the worst task he ever undertook. Unlike other image-setters, this Rube Goldberg device traced a single, notionally 5500 dpi character at a time on a small television screen and moved lenses, mirrors, and the photosensitive medium itself back and forth and up and down, by means of a complex assortment of worm gears that whined rhythmically, playing what David Fuchs called the [Alphatype] beguine. You had to perforate each tabloid-sized sheet, fasten it accurately onto a pin register, and wait around in the darkroom, while the characters of one page, or anything up to 16 pages, were individually flashed onto the paper, then pull it out and shove it into the developer tank at once. The small television screen was unable to image a single character much larger than 16 pt. For larger characters Knuth devised a way of slicing them into quadrants to be reassembled precisely by the machine. When I finally got to run one of the four or five Alphatypes that ever produced TEX output, I was unaware that if I used this feature for titles, I had to turn it off explicitly, so I ended up setting an entire book in broken 11 pt type. This was interesting, but not beautiful, and it increased the length of each "beguine" by a factor that felt like 10. I think only one person other than myself ever used the Alphatype.

Rick and I wrote one of the low end output drivers for the 200 dpi liquid toner Versatec, and we won a few converts to typesetting with that device, but it was the LaserWriter that changed most attitudes to TEX. By the time it was available, the translation to TEX82 and METAFONT84 was complete.

Will Robertson

Like many graduate students, Will Robertson has gotten involved with TeX; he is also representative of a minority of such TeX-using graduate students who take the next step of contributing significantly to the TeX community.

[Interview completed 25 March 2007.]

Dave Walden, interviewer: Please tell me a bit about your personal history independent of TeX.

Will Robertson, interviewee: Turning 26 this year, I'm not old enough yet to have a personal history. I can tell you who I am, however. I am currently in the second phase of my PhD in Mechanical/Mechatronic Engineering, for which I'm (approximately) trying to build a table that floats on magnets. My current plans are to finish up in about a year, but we'll see how that goes.

I'm living and have always lived (but most probably won't *always* live) in Adelaide, in South Australia. We have apparently the greatest number of serial killers (or is it murders?) per capita in the world. We have the second largest Fringe Festival (arts, theatre, dance, and so on) in the world, a statistic I can't really comprehend given our size. It certainly transforms the city for almost a month of every year, which is just starting up as we speak. Outside the city, we've got a fantastic wine industry. Hopefully it remains sustainable while we run out of water.

I also work at a Chocolate Cafe, which keeps me busy when I'm not researching. While it helps pay the bills, I mostly do it for the side benefits: access to lots of great chocolate and people. Although I'm biased, we serve the best hot chocolate I've ever had: we use actual melted Belgian chocolate, instead of chocolate powder or syrup, frothed up with steamed milk. And we can also make it with soy milk, to cater for the vegans. Real chocolate doesn't have dairy in it, you see.

DW: How did you first get involved with TeX?

WR: My friend introduced me to TeX at the end of my third year of uni (Mechatronic Engineering), which was around the end of 2001, I suppose. I started out using LyX, and relatively quickly migrated to LaTeX proper. LyX is mostly fine if you don't know LaTeX and can live within its restrictions. Knowing LaTeX, I now find LyX rather clumsy when I'm forced to help people in the department customise their documents. Some of its features are quite convenient, though.

At first I was using LaTeX for technical purposes: reports and so on. It was the little things that we liked about it — ligatures, automatic numbering, sensible float and referencing behaviour, and so on. All this (except the better output quality) we could do with Word at the time (provided you were very finicky when writing the document: "styles" provided the content/formatting separation we laud in LaTeX) but it was less effort in LaTeX. I don't know if that is still the case, but I'm very glad that Word is getting a proper maths renderer in Office 2007 (we'll probably return to this point later in the interview). At last, mathematical documents produced in Word will be readable!

Anyway, after I started my PhD, I begun exploring the LaTeX world in depth. Contrary to all of the recommendations, I actually found that I didn't need a book to learn anything. Long hours exploring packages and reading mailing lists sufficed. It took me a couple of years, I guess, before starting to program with it proper, and now I can't really give it up. I no longer take my laptop to uni, in order to concentrate more on my work, so I don't have the opportunity to spend more than a few hours a week on LaTeX at the moment. That's good, else I'd never get anything done.

DW: You mention helping people in your department. Please tell me a little more about this; for example, is there "official" support for TeX in your university?

WR: As for the usage of TeX that I see, I can only speak for what I know in my department, specifically, but I suspect it's probably a similar situation for many other universities. In general, it seems that many people aren't very computer literate. This is a broad problem; people will do data analysis in Excel rather that a decent program like Matlab; mathematics is still done by hand on paper rather than with Mathematica (well, I guess this is more understandable; I think you need to "click" with Mathematica before it's very useful); Word is used instead of LaTeX.

However, not everyone uses Word. My PhD supervisor used LyX for his thesis, and he recommends it to all of the new PhD students. Anyone I can influence uses LaTeX, because I tell them I can't (or won't) help them much if they use LyX. This is kind of true: some things I simply don't think are possible within the LyX environment; my main excuse is generally that it's a pain to debug LyX when things go wrong from a LaTeX point of view.

Michael Murray, who is (or has been, when I was) active on the Mac OS X TeX mailing list, is actually the Head of the maths department of our university. Over there, LaTeX is just what everyone uses. When you're writing maths day-in, day-out, I guess it only makes sense. Mechanical Engineering doesn't follow their lead, but maybe Electrical Engineering does.

As far as TeX support goes, as might be obvious to an observer, there is none. The university runs training courses in various Microsoft products, but that's as far as it goes. We have a very strong "pick it up as you go" culture in the software world (as I see things generally), which means that software needs to be designed with this in mind — able to be grasped non-committedly and coaxed to produce something without too much effort. Bearing this in mind, LaTeX can be a little difficult to approach (to say the least) for the casual user.

Furthermore, where would TeX support come from? It would be unfeasible to suggest that TUG could provide any, and there aren't any Australian "LaTeX User Groups", as far as I know. So people rely on the local expert, which is me — and eventually I teach them how to use Google Groups to answer their questions, as they are usually trivial to solve.

DW: Do you have any contact with or awareness of TeX users in other universities such as Baden Hughes in Melbourne (who was a founding member of the TPJ editorial board) or Ross Moore in Sydney (who is a member of the TUG board)?

WR: Like I said above, there is no Australian TeX user group that I know of, and so communication between "well-known" Australian TeX celebrities only happens through happenstance. I didn't know that Baden Hughes was from Melbourne, but Ross Moore and I have been working on some XeTeX things together for a little while now (not that we've met — we're 1400 km apart). We started collaborating through XeTeX connections, however, so it's just coincidence that we're compatriots.

DW: You and I first became acquainted through working on *The PracTeX Journal* (TPJ). How did that come about and what is your motivation for putting effort into this TUG activity?

WR: That's right. To be honest, I can't remember how I got roped into all that! The email conversation that initiated it seems to be temporarily lost in time (I'm sure it's somewhere in my mail), but I vaguely remember offering a bunch of suggestions early on, and presumably Lance Carnes (Editor) thought that my opinions were along lines that weren't well-represented with their then-members of the board. (That is, if I was just re-iterating opinions of the board, my help would have been less valuable.) Somehow he also recognised the opportunity to share some of the production burden, and I started "production editing" a couple of papers per issue almost immediately.

These days, we've got more helpers, and I've been less able to spend as much time. To be honest, I see the production work I do (sending off articles for review, reviewing articles myself, and copy-editing others) as an enjoyable chore with the side-benefit of learning a good amount about how (online, at least) journals work from the inside. As a hobby, there are much worse ways I could spend some of my time.

DW: Also, I see from the author index that you have written three articles for TPJ.

WR: I'm much happier *writing* the articles, but that takes a lot more time. Like you say, I've written a few now, on a somewhat diverse range of topics. My motivation for them comes from a few sources. Firstly, I need to practise writing. I wouldn't say that I love writing, nor that I am "a writer" (although I wouldn't mind trying it one day), but when I write well I enjoy it, and I can only write better with practise. (Whether I write "well" ever, anyway, is certainly up for debate.) Most important, probably, is the aspect of sharing knowledge around. The things I write about for *The PracTeX Journal* aren't new or novel, they're just reporting facts and opinions — the journalism side of technical writing, I guess you could say. When I spend time looking into, to use an example, the features of the Latin Modern fonts, and many people still seem to be ignorant of them, it only makes sense to write about it and make the time I originally put in better spent. The LaTeX world is a bit of mess due to its age: there's a lot of useless stuff lying around in CTAN that should be retired but can't be for backwards compatibility. Trying to teach people to use the current "best practise" seems a worthy cause to me. That's the type of thing I can't really quantify, though. Lastly, to be egotistical, it's nice to see your name in print.

DW: My memory is that in addition to serving as a production editor, you took over maintenance of the LaTeX class for TPJ.

WR: The pracjourn class was the first document class that I published for people to actually use, I think, and really got the ball rolling for me in terms of getting used to the issues involved with that. Formatting the frontmatter (name, affiliation, email address, etc.) was an interesting typesetting job, and I (still) think the design I settled on works quite well. At least, I haven't tired of it yet. I've never actually heard feedback from anyone whether they like or even notice it, though.

DW: I think it functions well for its purpose.

WR: I've gone on to write fairly basic classes for a few conferences that I (or colleagues) have attended. I've been quite disappointed with the quality of some of the ones I've come across that I haven't written; in some cases, the conference organisers have just coerced a poor graduate student who might know how to write a LaTeX document into writing the class. The results aren't pretty; the last one I saw had instructions to write sections something like

```
\section*{\centerline{1.1 THIS IS A SUBSECTION}}
```

That's right. Manual section numbering. Manual formatting. Not exactly what we're used to.

Going a little off-topic, I think organising some sort of TUG-organised, community-driven service for conference organisers to create one-off classes for conferences would be a decent thing to have to ensure that this sort of thing doesn't happen in the future. After all, once you've written one conference class, there's not too much that needs changing to adapt it for new typesetting guidelines.

DW: Since you reached the point where you could "program with it proper", you have obviously gone a lot deeper into it than many TeX users with only a few years experience. Can you give me a brief sketch of the purpose or function of fontspec, and how your development of it came about? I noticed you wrote an article for *TUGboat* about it: "Advanced font features with XeTeX — the fontspec package" (`http://tug.org/TUGboat/Articles/tb26-3/tb84robertson.pdf`).

WR: This answer needs a little bit of background. Bear with me while I try to be brief. As we probably all know, TeX was invented before computers were powerful and even before the notion of a "computer font" was well established or at least standardised. So its methods for dealing with fonts have been very quaint for some time now.

In order to overcome the many limitations that TeX imposes on the fonts it can use (as well as the input of multilingual text), Jonathan Kew wrote the XeTeX program, an extension of TeX that accepts Unicode input and supports OpenType fonts. Unicode input is important to be able to *write* in any desired language, and OpenType fonts are important to be able to *typeset* them.

To cut a long story short, the way XeTeX interfaces with OpenType fonts is rather low-level. Font features such as using lowercase numbers instead of uppercase numbers are activated with hard to remember strings such as `+onum`. The fontspec package provides a more readable (and hopefully memorable) interface to such things with keyval-type options such as `Numbers=Lowercase`.

Secondly, LaTeX itself wasn't designed to accommodate the idea of "font features", whereby a broad range of minor typographical details could be varied between instances of any one font. (Only "macroscopic" variations, such as boldness or shape, are directly provided for.) The fontspec package allows users to select fonts with any combination of font features, and to change the font features mid-document.

But most importantly, fontspec simply allows users to select fonts *easily*. No need to mess around with extra files that need to be written, or swathes of font definition code. In its simplest form, `\setmainfont{Baskerville}` is all that is required to select Baskerville as the main document font.

DW: Do you have prior background/interest with fonts, typography, etc., or did your interest develop in parallel with your experience with TeX?

WR: I'd always been finicky about layouts and fonts, but it was TeX that really brought out my major interest. Before XeTeX, I experimented with various fonts that could be installed in TeX, and before that I was experimenting with GUI fonts to a small degree. Mac OS X is bundled with a nice selection of interesting fonts, and I was fascinated with two in particular: Frere-Jones' Hoefler Text, with its wide range of font features such as swash caps, engraved caps, dedicated subscript/superscript characters, and so on (and so on!) — all within a single font — epitomised the abilities of modern fonts to provide for every last detail (in the limiting sense). Secondly, Hermann Zapf's Zapfino was the first script font that I'd used with a large number of contextual ligatures and alternate characters. XeTeX allowed us access to these fonts within a LaTeX environment, the best of both worlds.

DW: How did you get connected with the XeTeX system? Is your fontspec work coordinated with a larger group of people working on expanding the capabilities of XeTeX?

WR: The Mac OS X TeX mailing list is certainly what got me started in my TeX hobby. It was there I began asking my naive beginners questions, and slowly learned enough to start answering others'. So for a couple of years, I was quite active there. But I realised eventually that I wasn't gaining anything by spending so much time reading and replying there, and chose to leave. Only so much time in the day, and all that. But these days I browse the `comp.text.tex` newsgroup, which takes a similar amount of time. There's no escape, it seems.

Via the Mac OS X TeX mailing list, we learnt about this new XeTeX project in April 2004. I started using it a few months after that, but not for any serious work. Even back then, my knowledge of TeX and LaTeX was that of a user; I didn't have any knowledge, less experience, of any actual programming in TeX. Over time, it became obvious to me that something needed to be done to make fonts easy to set up in XeLaTeX (that is, LaTeX when using the XeTeX engine). Bruno Voisin had a template for setting up NFSS families in LaTeX with XeTeX-native fonts, but that method was a little inaccessible.

I played around for a while with various interfaces before creating fontspec. You only learn from doing, and this was my first TeX programming project. At first, fontspec simply let you select a font to use immediately. Then to select the font for the whole document. And then to select font features as well. My old versions are lost in time (I didn't know version control back then; I've only started learning it within the last year!) but I remember the slow understanding of how TeX programming worked. Now, I'm a little more confident of my ability to put a package together, and I'm working on a new package for dealing with Unicode maths. Jonathan has been putting in features to follow Microsoft Word 2007's lead in OpenType maths font features, and I've taken up the project to provide the user interface for it all, much in the same way as fontspec is a user interface for XeTeX's font access in general. (It's a little bit embarrassing that the TeX community has to follow the lead of Microsoft Word, of all programs, but oh well.)

Chris Rowley and Ross Moore are helping me out with various parts of this "Unicode maths" project, but there isn't a group of us working together to improve XeTeX in general. Jonathan works on whatever he feels motivated by, which rather recently has been to improve the maths support of XeTeX after Microsoft gave him a model to follow. Similarly, I do what I can with fontspec and a couple of minor packages, and Ross has a "Unicode text" package that's been essential for new users of XeTeX to have compatibility with their old LaTeX documents. But we've never met, and we communicate mainly via the XeTeX mailing list.

It seems to work best this way, in the open source software world — too many people working together gets everyone bogged down trying to work collaboratively, rather than just heading off in their own directions and seeing what happens.

DW: I assume you will use TeX to write your thesis. Do you think you will stay with TeX after you graduate or drop it as so many other graduate students do after having used it for the few years needed to write a thesis?

WR: I am quite surprised by this question. Of course I will stay with TeX! My interests have extended far beyond what I need to typeset my thesis. I'm reasonably confident, however, that my office mates will have a hard time sticking with LaTeX, even though they like it, because they only have me to ask when they run into problems. They don't know where else to look.

This leads me into a few words about where I think the big problems of LaTeX lie. Because it's obvious that it is much harder to learn than it could be. And the crux of the problem, the long and the short of it, is that the LaTeX kernel has been intentionally restricted to the functionality originally designed for it. Now, this is a good thing, by and large. Standards need to be frozen in order for them to be adhered to. But it's past time to move on and create a new standard. There are fast approaching competitors that will eventually overtake LaTeX if we continue to stagnate. (Not to mention ConTeXt, which has surpassed LaTeX in essentially every area. Maybe the solution is just for everyone to switch to that.)

As far as a document preparation system goes, LaTeX has a lot of work to catch up to what's happened over the last five years in HTML. Introductions to LaTeX often laud the separation of form and content in the LaTeX syntax, but the implementation is only skin deep in comparison with the things that HTML+CSS can do.

Most of LaTeX's shortcomings are solved with various packages, and many of those packages are so widespread now that their use is essentially mandatory. The memoir class attempts to unify many aspects of document preparation, but even that noble effort cannot hope to accommodate everything.

The LaTeX 3 project is supposed to be working to update LaTeX. But they face another problem: they've invented a wonderful extension to the LaTeX programming language in order to do all of their coding. But now they're stuck with a system that no-one knows how to use, and no-one will learn it to write their packages because no-one's using LaTeX 3 yet. On top of all that, LuaTeX is set to be released in a year or so, perhaps obviating all their hard work on the low-level design.

If I magically were able to make this all happen, here's a rough sketch of things I expect to see over the next few years to get LaTeX back on its feet. Who knows, this might be their plan anyway. In any case, after I write my thesis I wouldn't mind helping out.

- With the next release of LaTeX 2_ε, the LaTeX 3 team releases a formal LaTeX 2_ε package that contains the designs of their LaTeX 3 syntax. This allows LaTeX 2_ε package writers to update their thinking and their packages and, importantly, to learn the new system. Wrinkles in the syntax can be ironed out with (hopefully) widespread use.
- At around about the same time, "someone" (a single person or small group better than a committee) writes a high-level specification of the LaTeX 3 document preparation interface. In short, a formal definition of every document element from chapter heading to footnote that could possibly be used within the large majority of documents written in LaTeX. Gather as much material from existing packages and classes with the intention of unifying all of the best ideas of the LaTeX 2_ε ecosystem into LaTeX 3. For example, built-in support for multi-page tables, multiple levels of footnotes, named referencing of document parts, and so on. This is just a design document, not the low-level code.
- Finally, the actual code is written. By now, we've got a syntax to write code in, and a specification of what needs doing, plus enough people that know the system who can help out. Port over as much as possible from LaTeX 2_ε, and LaTeX 2.5 is released, the interim unstable version of LaTeX that is backwards incompatible with LaTeX 2_ε

and that will converge eventually to LaTeX 3, which will remain fixed for another ten years.

- In 2030, repeat the process :).

Of course, talking is easier than doing. But the main theme here is "get people involved". Very few people are going to learn the LaTeX 3 syntax without something to gain from the process. As an academic exercise its appeal is limited, but if the syntax can be used to write LaTeX 2_ε packages then I think its popularity will be assured. (Coming from a novice package writer, the new syntax is a breath of fresh air.)

So back to your question: yes, I'm looking forward to sticking with LaTeX and I'm enthusiastic about its long term future.

DW: I'll close this interview by saying: Thank you for participating in our interview series; it has been good to hear the point of view of a relatively short term user of TeX. Also, best wishes for finishing your graduate work and your life and career after that. I hope we will be able to meet in person at some point.

Jonathan Kew

Jonathan Kew is best known in the TeX community as the developer of XeTeX.

[Interview completed 3 April 2007.]

Dave Walden, interviewer: Please tell me a bit about your personal history independent of TeX.

Jonathan Kew, interviewee: I had a fairly conventional upbringing, I suppose, living in the south of England (except for a year spent with relatives in Sweden, which I still remember as one of the best parts of my childhood). I was the middle of three boys, though whether that explains anything about how I turned out is debatable at best. Growing up, I was always the small, quiet kid, more likely to be found in my room with a book than out with a crowd. (Those who know me will realize that this hasn't changed too much over the years!) My interests tended towards the academic and scientific, with a touch of the practical thrown in; at various times I was fascinated by subjects like early Antarctic exploration, butterflies and moths, aviation, electronics and ham radio, mountain travel, and more.

A key event came when my typical teenage wanderings and wonderings led eventually to a commitment to the Christian faith. My family had always been clearly non-religious, so this was a significant decision, and not one I took lightly, knowing that it represented a break with my background. I think my father felt at the time that it was just another phase I would pass through, but as the years have turned into decades it has remained a defining part of my life, and provides a framework and direction into which all other activities fit.

Most of my adult life — the only career I have ever had, really ... has been spent working with SIL International, first in South Asia and more recently based in England. SIL is a Christian non-profit organization serving minority communities around the world with linguistic research, education, development, translation, and more, and has provided me with the ideal opportunity to combine my computing work with an interest in languages and writing systems. After starting out as a language surveyor, "roughing it" around Asia researching local languages, I soon found my real niche working on text processing and publishing systems for non-Western languages.

DW: Please sketch what a "language surveyor" does.

JK: As a language surveyor, I was involved in studying the languages and dialects of an area, and the patterns of language use among the communities there. For example, we collected word lists in different localities, to measure the percentage of shared vocabulary between communities; and tested comprehension of stories that we had recorded in other locations, to see how well people understood nearby dialects. Another aspect was studying bilingualism and multilingualism, to learn how national and regional languages were used in addition to the local mother tongue.

In the language survey I did in South Asia, I was always working together with local colleagues who were familiar with the area and fluent in the regional language. Each project involved both SIL personnel and local partners; we could not have carried out the work alone. While I learned enough of the regional language to get along in daily living situations, I was certainly not fluent enough to have worked effectively on my own.

DW: I know some churches (e.g., the Christian Science church whose publishing building is a block from my apartment in Boston) publish the Bible, daily devotional readings, the founder's books, etc., in many languages. But SIL is not a church, correct? Is the point that SIL's Christian mission is to help people with languages just as someone else's Christian mission is to help people in some other, not necessarily religious, area of need?

JK: It's tempting to just copy and paste some paragraphs from the SIL web site (`http://www.sil.org`), but I suppose that would be cheating!

Anyhow, you're right; SIL is not a church, though its members share a Christian motivation. We seek to serve minority language communities — regardless of faith or other factors — in a variety of language-related ways, as this is where our expertise lies. Linguistic and anthropological research contributes both to scientific knowledge in general and to the understanding and development of the particular communities where we work. It is a necessary basis for basic literacy and mother-tongue education, as well as supporting the transition into major-language education. This can help people interact on a more equal footing with their neighbors and with government and other agencies. SIL personnel, in partnership with local people, churches, and other agencies (both religious and secular) may be involved in almost any kind of development or educational work where linguistic expertise is important, from Bible translation to support an indigenous church to translation of basic health booklets or primary schoolbooks, or management of a community-wide literacy programme.

DW: Scouting around the SIL web site you mentioned, I find the following statement: "SIL members are volunteers who raise their own financial support." Should I assume this is also true in your case, and that you have to raise your own financial support and don't have another job?

JK: All my time serving with SIL has been on this basis, funded by contributions from several churches and a variety of individual friends and sponsors who are interested in supporting our work. I've worked full-time with SIL for over 20 years now, without any other job or means of support. And naturally the level of income received has varied, sometimes greatly, over the years, but there has at least been a roof overhead and food on the table throughout! I suppose I decided fairly early that it was more important to me to use the abilities I have in some way that could make a worthwhile contribution in the world, a significant difference in people's lives, than to concentrate on building a bank balance (or lavish lifestyle). And I think God honors that decision, through the faithful support of many individuals and churches. It's true that it takes a certain amount of time and energy — sometimes a substantial proportion — to find and maintain support in this way, which can be a frustration and distraction when there are other more "productive" things I'd like to be doing, but on the other hand I have been privileged to get to know some wonderful friends through the process.

DW: How did you first get involved with TeX?

JK: I first learned of TeX while at university in Cambridge. We didn't have TeX on the university mainframe, but I happened to find *The TeXbook* while browsing in the bookstore — this must have been in 1984, when it was quite new — and was fascinated by the system it described. It seemed so far ahead of the primitive text formatting software we had at the time. Mind you, even if we'd had TeX, it would have been difficult to get useful output on the line printers that were the main output devices of the day! There was a special Versatec printer that could do something like 200 dpi on special paper, I think, though as a lowly undergrad (not even in the computing department), I'm not sure if I would have had access to it.

Anyway, browsing *The TeXbook* in the store was the inspiration for the first "typesetting" software I wrote — a little program that took TeX-like input for equations and simple paragraphs of text, formatted them, and "drew" the resulting page on a drum plotter. An engineer friend and I used this successfully to produce some equation-rich pages to insert into his final-year thesis; I was quite proud of the results we achieved, with proper integrals, fractions, super- and subscripts, etc., considering that the normal output device for final copy was a daisy-wheel printer! This was not really TeX, of course, but it wouldn't have happened without my bookstore encounter with *The TeXbook*.

I think the first time I used TeX itself was in 1988, having managed to shoehorn Pat Monardo's Common TeX implementation into an old DOS machine, along with a LaserJet driver from Nelson Beebe's collection. By this time, I had spent a couple of years in South Asia working on text processing and printing solutions for several interesting scripts, and the potential of TeX and Metafont was clearly of interest. I'd been doing some Devanagari typesetting on home-built CP/M machines with 24-pin printers (we printed the body text in three passes, giving a 72-high glyph matrix, and then photographically reduced the output). So TeX and a 300 dpi laser printer was a great step forward, though the equipment I had was just barely adequate to run it. I spent many hours trying to coax Metafont to draw Urdu characters, and even printed at least one small book with them, though I must confess that it wasn't long before these were abandoned in favor of PostScript fonts.

DW: As a relative newcomer to TeX, I have not heard of "Pat Monardo's Common TeX implementation". Please tell me what this was or is and how it fits into the history of TeX engines.

JK: Common TeX was a version of the TeX program rewritten in C, primarily targeted at Unix systems, I think. As I understand the history, it was a hand translation of the Pascal/WEB program, done before the current Web2C system had been developed. Common TeX made it possible to get TeX running on machines that had a decent C compiler, but no reasonable Pascal system available.

I'm not sure whether Common TeX was 100% TRIP-test compatible, but for all practical purposes it was a standard TeX engine, it just avoided the need for a Pascal compiler and runtime system. I think as the whole Web2C system matured, the need for Common TeX eventually disappeared, as compilation via C became the most common implementation for all the TeX/MF family of programs.

DW: What sort of systems do you mean when you say you have worked "text processing and publishing systems for non-Western languages" for SIL? I see two papers by you listed on the Ethnologue.com (`http://www.ethnologue.com`) web site: "A computerized assistant for translators", 1992, and "Formatting interlinear text", 1990, with Stephen R.

McConnel. For how long has TeX been part of your work in this area or how did it begin to become a part of this work?

JK: Yes, I haven't generally written much for publication! (In more recent years, I've had papers published in the proceedings of a few Unicode and TUG conferences, but those are probably hard to find cited.) But I've worked on several projects over the years, including a text editing and data management environment for scripture translation; software for linguistic analysis and dialect adaptation; and of course text formatting/typesetting. In all cases, ensuring that the tools were usable with complex writing systems has been a key focus for me, partly because of my early experience in South Asia which brought me into contact with several interesting (Indic and Arabic-based) scripts and made me aware of the challenges involved.

My first use of TeX in this field must have been around 1988–89, I think, when I worked on a package for handling interlinearized texts (such as linguists love to work with). While studying and documenting languages, we often annotate the words of a text with multiple levels of information; for example, the division of the word into morphemes, various types of grammatical information, glosses in one or more other languages, and so on. The result is a stack of information, aligned below the original word; this can of course be handled very naturally in TeX as a `\vbox`. And the beauty of TeX, for publishing lengthy texts of this nature, is that it can turn a list of such stacked boxes into paragraphs and pages in just the same way as it does with normal words. Try doing that with a typical word processor!

Then, around the end of 1989, I began to look seriously at providing publishing solutions for minority languages using the Arabic script, and started some font work in Metafont. With the enhanced ligature capabilities and 8-bit support in TeX 3.0, I was able to get some useful results, though the contextual behavior of the script remained a challenge. Within a year or two, frustrated by the limitations of TeX's font and glyph handling, and looking for easier integration with standard text editing environments, I had begun to experiment with extended TeX engines that interfaced with external text rendering systems to handle the complexities of non-Latin scripts. Today's XeTeX, my main TeX project in recent years, has roots in that work back in the 1990s.

DW: Of course, other readers and I could look at your XeTeX web site (`http://scripts.sil.org/xetex`), but perhaps you can also tell us something about it here. For starters, how should I pronounce XeTeX — like Zee TeX? And why did you call it that?

JK: I don't have a strong opinion on the "correct" pronunciation, though personally I say *zee-TeX*. There was some discussion of this on the mailing list recently, and it was clear that the "natural" pronunciation depends on people's native language — which is fine with me.

The name was chosen to imply an eXtended version of ε-TeX, along with an association with Mac OS X (which was initially the only target platform). As one of the intended uses was for typesetting right-to-left scripts, a palindromic name seemed like fun; and the properly-typeset version is supposed to use the Unicode character U+018A LATIN CAPITAL LETTER REVERSED E for the first lowered "E", hinting at support of much more than the basic Western character set.

DW: Please sketch the technical approach you took to modifying or augmenting TeX to enable it to use fonts available on the operating system, as I saw you demonstrate at the PracTeX 2006 conference in New Jersey.

JK: The first point is that the `\font` command is augmented so that it asks the host operating system to find fonts (by their real names, not cryptic filenames) from whatever collection of fonts the user has installed. So all the same fonts should be usable for typesetting in XeTeX as in any standard GUI application, and known by the same names. There is no need for a TeX-specific font preparation or installation procedure any more.

When XeTeX finds a font in this way, what it finds is the actual font itself (whether PostScript, TrueType, or OpenType), not a TFM file; and therefore the paragraphing routine needs to measure text by referring to the real font, not by using the TeX-style character metrics. In addition, it needs to take account of the complexities of mapping characters to glyphs, particularly in cursive and non-Latin scripts. So rather than building paragraphs from lists of characters, each of which has fixed metrics, XeTeX builds paragraphs from "words", each of which is a whole run of consecutive characters in a given font. It can then call on a "layout engine" such as ATSUI (on Mac OS X only), ICU Layout (on any platform), or SIL's Graphite to carry out linguistically and typographically required transformations and effects, resulting in an array of glyphs and their positions that represent the word as laid out using the current font. The paragraph then consists of a list of such words (or chunks of text), interleaved with glue, penalties, etc.

There are further complications, of course; for example, hyphenation may require such "word nodes" to be taken apart and reassembled after finding possible break positions. But the fundamental idea is to collect runs of characters and hand them as complete units to a font rendering library that understands how to handle layout at the level of the individual glyphs.

DW: I assume you did this work on a Mac first because it was easier there. What made that so, and how have you now expanded things so XeTeX also works on Linux and Windows systems?

JK: It was easier for me, at least, partly because I was most familiar with the Mac OS X platform, particularly in the area of text, fonts, and internationalization. This familiarity, and even parts of the XeTeX code, dates back to work on earlier versions of Mac OS back in the mid-1990s; the first such "extended TeX" I implemented was based on Apple's WorldScript technology, which offered support for a number of non-Latin scripts, though with quite limited typographic features. This was followed by TeXGX, a reimplementation that used Apple's QuickDraw GX graphics system. This supported higher precision in text measurement and layout, and a more powerful implementation of complex script behaviors. Although TeXGX was never very widely used (to my knowledge), it did become known to at least a few people in the TeX community, and served me as a key tool for a number of years.

Sadly, QuickDraw GX never really succeeded in the marketplace, and Apple dropped it from later versions of the operating system. However, the advanced typographic features were reborn in ATSUI, the Unicode text layout library that is part of Mac OS X (actually, it was available on pre-OS X systems, though not widely adopted). With Apple's move to a Unix-based operating system, in conjunction with improved support for Unicode and international typography, it was natural to begin work on a successor to TeXGX that would work in this new environment; and so XeTeX was born.

When I began these experiments in integrating TeX as a page formatting system with existing libraries for font handling, international text, and glyph-level typography, the facilities available in the Mac operating system were significantly ahead of those on Windows — and Linux wasn't even in the picture as a desktop environment. I was aiming to leverage the available tools to provide maximum functionality for a minimum amount of effort, and so I used Apple's text and graphics technologies wherever possible.

Over the years, the picture has of course changed, and there are excellent libraries for international text layout on all the major platforms. And so once XƎTEX was functional and stable, I began to look at how it could be made cross-platform by replacing the Apple-proprietary components used with open-source alternatives. This meant supporting OpenType fonts through the ICU layout library, and replacing the original PDF output driver (based heavily on the Mac OS X graphics system) with an extended version of the existing dvipdfmx, among other changes. But as far as possible, I have tried to maintain the simplicity of use that I think made XƎTEX attractive to its early adopters when the first Mac-only version appeared.

DW: Do you believe other systems such as Dick Koch's TeXShop have hastened the popularity of XƎTEX, or do you think its intrinsic benefits would have led to its great popularity in any case?

JK: I think TeXShop has done a huge amount to make TEX (in general) on Mac OS X more accessible and attractive, and thus given a larger potential audience for any new development in this area. And perhaps because TeXShop made TEX accessible to less technically-inclined users, it also provided more fertile ground for XƎTEX, which allows such users to experiment with fonts that they would otherwise not even attempt to use.

DW: I suppose the reverse may also be true: XƎTEX's popularity has helped increase the number of TeXShop users.

JK: Without such front-ends (on any platform), the TEX user community would be significantly more limited, and would consist mainly of people willing and able to deal with arcane command lines, configuration files, and so forth. This might have meant that XƎTEX's approach to font access would have seemed less important to many. I suspect that its other major features — Unicode and complex-script support — would still have been highly attractive to some users, but perhaps to a much more limited, specialized community.

DW: Do you develop XƎTEX essentially alone, or do you have some sort of "open source" team helping you?

JK: It's been essentially a one-person (and part-time) project over the years, driven primarily by my own need for a powerful and flexible typesetting system with Unicode and non-Latin script support for the publishing jobs I'm asked to do. However, once the source repository was made public (a couple of years ago — I forget exactly), I have received valuable patches from several contributors, particularly in the area of CJK support. Suggestions for ongoing development are always welcome, and those accompanied by code are even more so!

In particular, I should mention Will Robertson's outstanding work on LATEX integration (primarily the fontspec package [discussed in his interview]), Ross Moore's work on the LATEX graphics and color drivers, Jin-Hwan Cho's help in extending the dvipdfmx driver, and Miyata Shigeru's contributions to improve vertical text and CJK support in both XƎTEX itself and the driver, and to provide support for PSTricks graphics. And with the integration of XƎTEX into the TEX Live sources, many people have helped find and solve portability and build issues on the wide variety of supported platforms.

DW: I don't know if you have read what Taco Hoekwater said in his interview about the differences between what he and others are working on and what you are doing with XƎTEX. Do you have anything to add about connections between the two projects?

JK: Not really. The pdfTEX/LuaTEX team is taking quite a different approach to some issues, and so it's unclear whether there will come a time when merging the projects makes sense. But I am of course happy to share ideas (and code), and hope that wherever possible we can provide features in ways that make it easy for macro writers and users to work with either system. If LuaTEX proves successful and popular, and develops to the point where it offers users all the same capabilities as XeTEX (even if the underlying implementation is quite different), I'll be delighted, and may no longer feel a need to continue working on XeTEX. But for the time being, at least, I think the two projects each need the freedom and flexibility to explore their own ideas, and users are of course free to work with whichever serves their needs best.

DW: Has XeTEX been extensively used to publish documents in SIL's domain? Or has the TEX community been more of an "early adopter" of XeTEX?

JK: SIL has never had a large TEX-using community; the vast majority of publishing work is done using commercial word processing and DTP systems. So my TEX projects, including XeTEX, have only had a few active users within SIL. We have found them invaluable for a number of challenging publications, but I wouldn't call it anything like "extensive" use. We're seeing an increase in interest these days, especially with the complex-script support XeTEX offers, but I've never expected it to displace products like Word, OpenOffice, InDesign, etc. on a majority of desktops.

When I released the first public version of XeTEX (for Mac OS X only), I was somewhat surprised at the level of interest and even excitement that it seemed to generate. I was very much aware that XeTEX's extensions mean that in certain cases, it is not 100% compatible with all existing TEX/LATEX/ConTEXt/etc. documents or macro packages, and for this reason I expected that it would be something of a specialist niche product, used by a few people who understood its approach and needed the Unicode and non-Latin features it provided. So it has been exciting to see it adopted with such enthusiasm by a range of people in the existing TEX community, and I'm very glad to have been able to provide something that many users seem to appreciate and enjoy. I hope my work can facilitate the production of beautiful books of all kinds, for the benefit of many communities worldwide.

DW: Thank you for taking the time to be interviewed. Your life story and its involvement with languages, fonts, and TEX is fascinating to me; you have my great admiration.

[Endnote: Since this interview was completed, Jonathan has embarked on a new project, TEXworks, aiming to create a cross-platform TEX environment with a similar design to TeXShop. Information about this is available at `http://tug.org/texworks`. He is no longer working with SIL, but currently works for the Mozilla Corporation and hopes to contribute to improved international text support and typography on the Web.]

David Fuchs

David Fuchs is renowned in the TeX community for his work with Donald Knuth in the earliest days of TeX.

[Interview completed 14 May 2007.]

Dave Walden, interviewer: How did you first come in contact with Donald Knuth and then get so deeply involved in TeX?

David Fuchs, interviewee: I came to Stanford as a Ph.D. student in 1978, in the Computer Science Department. Somehow, I got put in a group that was writing a Fortran compiler, which seemed rather retro to me even at the time. When I saw a bulletin-board posting that Prof. Knuth was looking for help on the TeX Project, I jumped at the chance; first, because of the thrill of working with someone famous, and second because I'd be working on software that might have hundreds, or, who knows, even thousands of users.

This was in the days of the old TeX ("TeX78") that was written in the Sail language. I worked on porting the code from the home-grown Waits operating system that Knuth used day-to-day, to the commercial TOPS-20 system that most DEC-20 mainframes used. The code was in five source files: TEXSYN, TEXSEM, TEXHYF, TEXPRE, and TEXOUT (if I remember correctly). TEXSYN handled the syntax of the language, while TEXSEM handled all the semantics. TEXHYF had a hard-coded English language hyphenation algorithm, and TEXPRE existed to populate the hash table with all the built-in control-sequence names. TEXOUT created files suitable for sending to our XGP printer. It was a special experimental printer that Xerox created based on one of their copier engines; only a few were ever made, and they were just about the only raster printers that existed at the time! It was about 200 dpi, though near the edges of the paper it was closer to 180.

Around 1980, we got a Versatec electrostatic printer with an 8-bit parallel interface. I had the job of getting TeX output onto it, since the XGP was getting old, and required almost the full time of a technician (who was also getting old) to keep it running. The XGP had a whole PDP-6 mainframe to control it, but I picked out a little Z80 microcomputer to handle the Versatec. Our mainframes only had serial RS-232 output, and you sure didn't want to be sending whole raster images over a 9600 baud line, so I had to program the Z80 to accept input that mixed character bitmaps to be cached in its small 64K memory along with commands as to where to place each character on the page. There wasn't enough room to build a complete bitmap of the page, and the printer itself simply accepted raster lines from the top of the page to the bottom, so getting it all to work efficiently was a bit of a trick. Also, if you didn't feed the printer the next raster line when it was ready, it would stop the motor that drove the paper, and since it was a wet-toner process (ugh), your output would get a big horizontal streak.

Prof. Knuth suggested that I write a new module like TEXOUT, to be called TEXVER, to produce output suitable for the new printer. I was astonished at what a bad idea that was; every time you wanted to be able to handle a new output device, you'd have to create a new version of TeX with the proper TEXOUT replacement; and users would have to run the right TeX that knew about their particular printer. It was quite a thrill to be able to tell the celebrated Donald Knuth that he was all wet, and that clearly the right way to go was to have TeX create its output in a device-independent format. I think he didn't like the idea of having to run another process after TeX just to get your output (if only because this meant reading and writing to disk twice as much data), but given the pros and cons, gave me the go-ahead. So, I designed the first version of the DVI output format. The goals were just to keep it small and concise and easy to interpret (remember, even our mainframes had a limit of about half a megabyte of core memory per process).

TeX was getting to have a bigger and bigger following, and there were already a number of departments that had installed clones of my Z80-and-electrostatic-printer scheme. Knuth and his students started work on the entirely new TeX (and Metafont), to be written in the (new) Web language on top of Pascal, and with all sorts of new features. I helped with various porting issues, but even more importantly, we had a brand new Alphatype CRS phototypesetter (with a claimed resolution of 5333 dpi) to interface to. Prof. Knuth had picked it out, based on the fact that the manufacturer was willing to divulge how it worked internally, and particularly how it encoded fonts. (In those days, each typesetter manufacturer had its own proprietary font scheme, not to mention its own proprietary typesetting software that sat on their own proprietary computer systems; those days are gone.) Knuth realized that the firmware in the integrated Intel 8008 system that ran the typesetter wouldn't be able to handle his Metafont-generated fonts, so he decided to re-write the entire firmware system for the device. Fortunately, there were cross-assemblers available for our mainframes, and the CRS would accept a new firmware "load" from a serial port.

Please realize that the code that Knuth was rewriting had to simultaneously accelerate, run, and decelerate the two stepper motors that controlled the horizontal and vertical position of the lens that was focusing the character images onto the paper, while simultaneously feeding character outline information to the two sets of two full-size S-100 bus special hardware cards that would extract vertical strokes of the character being imaged to flash onto the CRT in front of the lens (two sets because that would let you pipeline the next character while the current character was being imaged; two cards per set because with kerning, you might have two characters appearing in a single vertical swath). Plus, data would be coming in the serial port asynchronously, and all this was happening in real time. Somehow, he got the thing working with only a little hex debugger that you accessed from the 16-button front panel. And, as we learned the hard way, if you sent too much data up the serial connection too quickly, you'd crash the shared mainframe (since it only expected human typists sitting at computer terminals to be on the other end, so it had never been tested for robustness in this regard), making everyone around the CS department pretty angry.

I, of course, wrote the DVI-to-CRS software, which also required some tricky font caching (the algorithm for which is the basis of my only published paper, which was actually written by my co-author, guess who?). Those were some intense days of working together, getting it all to work. The CRS was in a cramped basement room, and I had to load and unload each sheet of photographic paper in the darkness, and feed it into the triple-bath developer. Any bug could be potentially in my code or Knuth's firmware, and as I mentioned, debugging wasn't easy. After a number of very long days, I came in one morning, and came into Knuth's office just as he was arriving and handing a stack of legal paper to his secretary. "Here's a paper I wrote, please type it in," he told her. I was floored. We'd been working night and day; did he write the paper in his sleep?

DW: When I look at the *TUGboat* list of authors (`http://tug.org/TUGboat/Contents/listauthor.html`), I see that your last "News from the TEX project" report was in 1986. Did you leave the project at that time?

DRF: Prof. Knuth chose to wind down the TEX project in 1986. The idea was that the code and features should be stable (indeed, one of the main features is meant to be that the code and features are stable), and also that he wanted to devote more time to his work on his books and such.

DW: Please tell me a bit about your personal history and life since those early days with Knuth and TEX.

DRF: While I was at Stanford, I'd watched as Andy Bechtolsheim started Sun Microsystems, and Len Bosack and Sandy Lerner started Cisco. (Actually, there are interesting TEX connections to both companies: Unless I mis-remember, Lynn Ruggles worked on creating the first Cisco logo with Metafont. And when Andy needed to create the first high-resolution printed-circuit-board masks for his first Sun workstation, in order to save a few thousand dollars that a commercial "tape-out" would cost him, he wrote a dvi output module to the ecad system he was using, and we actually typeset the artwork onto the Alphatype CRS!)

Anyway, I figured that the start-up business looked fun, and when I got a call from the newly-started Frame Technology, looking for a consultant to put math into their WYSIWYG document system, FrameMaker, one thing led to another, and I became their fifth employee (behind the four founders). Of course, the joke is that I never did get around to putting a math-mode into FrameMaker; I worked on PostScript output, and on Book functions (multiple "Chapter" documents making up a large book, with proper auto-numbering of pages, section/subsections, footnotes, cross-references, table of contents, and index generation).

After nine years, Frame was acquired by Adobe, where I was promoted to "Principal Scientist" in the "Advanced Technology Group", where they put all the old curmudgeons and prima donnas. But I yearned for the start-up life, so one year later, I joined a small Java company called Random Noise, that was eventually bought by Vignette just before the height of the dot-com boom. Actually, there's a funny story there. Random Noise had a very creative product that was just a bit ahead of its time (kind of like DreamWeaver from MacroMedia, but flakier because of early JVMs being way too buggy). But we didn't have actual paying customers, so eventually the day came when the boss told us all to go home. Just 36 hours later, I got a call, saying "Can you come in tomorrow and look busy?" So, we all showed up and continued development, while the deal to sell the technology got struck in the conference room that day.

After that, I got into some high-tech investing, which is fun but frequently frustrating.

DW: Do you still use TEX or one of the TEX-based systems today? (I notice from the TUG web site that you attended the 2004 Practical TEX conference.)

DRF: TEX has always had a special place in my heart. We made the world a better place for scientists and engineers. What other piece of software is still in active use, essentially the same as it was 25 years ago? Some years ago, I got a notion that, given its continued relevance, TEX deserved an internal make-over. The idea is to change the internals to be object oriented, but in a step-wise fashion that guarantees complete upward compatibility. This can open the door to improved enhance-ability while making it even more portable. Just as an example, making everything an object means that all the internal arrays (mem, fmem, trie, etc.) are gone, and so virtually all internal limits disappear (macro definition space, fonts, save stack size for nested macro calls, etc., even number of character widths in a font, number of characters in a font, ...; I think the only one I haven't addressed yet is the maximum of 256 of columns per table!) I'm pretty far along with this (and the painstaking process has even found a few TeX bugs that will surprise everyone), but it's been quite time-consuming, and I'm not making any promises yet.

DW: That's fascinating and brings additional questions to mind: Is the work you are describing at the conceptual and design level or have you written code for what you describe; and, if the latter, what programming language are you using, and are you still using some version of web/tangle-and-weave?

DRF: In order to preserve 100 percent compatibility with TeX, the scheme involves making evolutionary, small-step changes to Knuth's original TeX sources. This is accomplished by modifying Tangle (and Weave) to be able to essentially handle a large number of change files, each one of which moves the code a small, but testable, way along toward the ultimate goal. Each step gets checked against the Trip test, plus a few other large TeX and LaTeX documents. And, in the unfortunate event that a compatibility bug is found in, say, change number 100 while working on change 300, I can essentially "go back in time" and fix change 100, and then test again all the way through change 300 to make sure to fix any problems that may have cascaded. This way, I end up with code that I have a very high degree of confidence in, and which makes it relatively easy to fix any compatibility bugs that may be found, with minimal turmoil to any unaffected code. (Plus, it's relatively easy to accept a new `TeX.web` with any bug fixes, and run the clock forward over all my changes, to find the places that are affected. It's interesting to think how this scheme is similar to, but different than, a "source code control system".)

By now, I've made over 1700 of these "small steps". And, in fact, I lied, and there aren't 1700 different change files; rather there's one big change file that simply contains one set of changes after another. It's important to realize that the very fact that Tangle/ Weave didn't work this way to begin with is that we were dealing with computers that were very address-space limited at the time; there was no way to fit the entire sources to TeX in memory all at once. But now that's no longer the case; in fact, there are myriad design decisions in the TeX code base that were made in consideration of limitations that just no longer apply. Just as a small example: Each character in a font has indices into a table of widths/heights/depths, rather than just knowing its actual width/height/depth directly. Why? Just to save 8 bytes per character per font, that's why. Knuth was forced to make this trade-off to save space, even at the expense of slower operation (finding a character depth involves fetching a word, extracting a few bits of depth index, and then looking the depth up in a table), not to mention artificially limiting the number of character depths within a font to 16. I get to un-do that decision along the way. Toss in all the other such changes, and I've already got a code base with none of the original global arrays from Knuth's code; everything is an object (and all integer indexes have become object references). Voila! All limits are removed (and not simply by making the arrays grow). I hasten to add that all this is done with great sensitivity to speed and efficiency; all the backward-compatibility tests are careful to also keep an eye on the speed and memory footprint of the resulting system.

In order to ease the process along, it's been done in using an object-oriented extension to Pascal (there's a commercial compiler from Borland, as well as an open-source compiler from Free Pascal). However, I've been very careful to use only the most basic aspects of the enhanced language, with the goal of eventually being able to support an automatic translation into C# (easy) and Java (a bit harder) and perhaps even C++ (but I hate it so). But this part hasn't had any direct work done on it (other than keeping it in mind while doing all the changes).

DW: Are you replicating the current version of actual TEX, or are you also thinking about the extensions that have gone into ε-TEX, pdfTEX, etc.?

DRF: I decided to start by modifying plain, vanilla TEX. This is so I can ensure absolute compatibility. Also, because some of the extensions aren't necessary, given the way I removed various limits in TEX. That being said, it's certainly my goal to "catch up" with the missing features from these systems, as appropriate. In fact, that will be a perfect way to put to the test my claim that the "object oriented, simplified" code that I'm creating will in fact be easier to modify and extend.

DW: How do you see TEX in 2007 in the context of QuarkXPress, InDesign, XML, Unicode, the ease of accessing OpenType fonts from various OS apps versus TEX and its TFM files, the most recent math additions to Word, etc. — can TEX still play a significant role that makes it worthwhile to try to recode it to enable more "portability"?

DRF: Well, that's really the big question. Of course, I ask myself this every day. I looked at the new version of Microsoft Word, and found the math stuff to be a bit limited (not to mention that Word documents regularly change formatting from release to release, etc.) I don't expect TEX's niche market to shift to Word or Express or InDesign, but time will tell. In a funny parallel, there's still no replacement for FrameMaker, with its particular strengths for large, structured documents. For both TEX and FrameMaker, we've got users who think that "final, paginated form" is important, which may seem anachronistic to some, but note that Adobe makes billions of dollars a year on PDF, which would have been subsumed by HTML if not for its "just like paper" functionality.

DW: Thank you very much. I've loved hearing your unique perspective of the early history of TEX and what you have being doing since then.

Jin-Hwan Cho

Jin-Hwan Cho is the maintainer of the DVIPDFMx translator, and a leader in supporting and encouraging the use of TeX in Korea.

[Interview completed 21 May 2007.]

Dave Walden, interviewer: Please tell me a bit about yourself personally, independent of the TeX world.

Jin-Hwan Cho, interviewee: I was born in 1968. I am living in Seoul with my wife, an 8-year-old son, and a 5-year-old daughter. In 1999 I got a Ph.D. degree mathematics. After that I spent one year at Osaka City University in Japan in a post-doctoral position. After next spending four years as a research fellow at Korea Institute for Advanced Study, I have been teaching mathematics in the University of Suwon as a "Full-time Lecturer" since 2004.

DW: Before I move on to the question I usually ask next, I hope you won't mind if we talk briefly about your name, for those readers like me who are not familiar with Korean naming conventions. Which part of Jin-Hwan Cho is your "personal" name and which is your "family name"? Also, you sign your email ChoF; is this what I would call a nickname?

ChoF: "Jin-Hwan" is my "personal name" and "Cho" is my family name. In Korean, names usually consists of three Korean characters; one is for the family name and the other two are for the personal name. Because the personal name consists of two characters, some Koreans uses a space between them as "Jin Hwan" and some others use a hyphen as "Jin-Hwan" (my case). "ChoF" has been my nickname for more than 20 years. People often ask me the meaning of "ChoF". I always reply that it's top secret. But it is not really special because it is a combination of my name "Cho" and my Christian name "Francisco". 20 years ago people in the (Catholic) Church called me "Cho Francisco" but the name was too long so that they simply called me "ChoF".

DW: Thanks. Now for my usual next question — how did you first become involved with TeX?

ChoF: In 1987, my Calculus teaching assistant introduced PCTeX to me. His hobby was to make a Korean characters with Metafont. After that, until 1997, TeX was just a toy for me to make mathematics documents, mathematical papers, and thesis.

DW: You seem to be suggesting that your involvement with TeX changed in 1997. What happened then and thereafter with TeX?

ChoF: The web site called "ChoF's TeX Archive" started in 1997. The main goal of the site was: (1) to introduce the TeX system, especially with MiKTeX because almost all PCs in Korea were running MS Windows at that time; (2) to instruct users how to set up HLaTeX (`http://project.ktug.or.kr/hlatex/`), the most popular Korean LaTeX package written by Koaunghi Un; and (3) to provide an on-line place to discuss and share information in Korean.

At that time there were two famous web sites related to TeX in Korea. One was my web site and the other was run by Kangsoo Kim, now the director of the Korean TeX Users Group (http://www.ktug.or.kr/) and the current vice president of The Korean TeX Society (KTS). Based on experience of more than four years, Kim and I agreed in 2001 to combine the two sites into one on-line community, the Korean TeX Users Group.

Since then, I have spent quite a bit of time on TeX and related things. For example: the DVIPDFMx project (http://project.ktug.or.kr/dvipdfmx/) started, with Shunsaku Hirata, in 2002; two presentations were given at TUG 2003 and TUG 2005; etc.

Most recently, the off-line Korean TeX Society (http://kts.ktug.kr) community was founded, on January 27 of this year. I have a new job in KTS — creating a new TeX journal, the *Asian Journal of TeX* (http://ajt.ktug.kr/). The first issue is being printed and will be out during the week of May 21, 2007.

DW: Your answer bring several questions to my mind. First, I presume HLaTeX means Hangul LaTeX where Hangul is the Korean alphabet; is that correct? Is it a lot more complicated to use LaTeX with Hangul than with English?

ChoF: Right. Hangul is the native alphabet of the Korean language. Wikipedia describes Hangul as a phonemic alphabet organized into syllabic blocks, invented in the 15th century.

The main problem of CJK (Chinese, Japanese, Korean) languages in TeX and LaTeX is the huge number of characters. Theoretically, there is no limit for the number of Chinese characters and there are more than 1.8 billion characters for Korean. But, in our time, 11,172 Korean characters are used and they have already been included in Unicode.

As the TeX system has developed, it is not hard today to use those characters in LaTeX. For example, the CJK package developed by Werner Lemberg can typeset all CJK characters in a document. However, the CJK package lacks each country's own typesetting features. In Japan, pTeX is widely used because the engine supports Japanese typesetting features, and for the same reason the HLaTeX (http://project.ktug.or.kr/hlatex/) and Hangul-ucs (http://faq.ktug.or.kr/faq/Hangul-ucs) packages are used in Korea. It's a long story.

DW: What Korean fonts are typically used?

ChoF: Among CJK countries, Korea may be in the best position because we already have a set of free Korean fonts in Type 1 format, called the UHC fonts by Koaunghi Un (the author of HLaTeX). These fonts have been used with HLaTeX as well as Lemberg's CJK package. The translation from Type 1 to OpenType and TrueType format (called Unfonts) was done by Won-Kyu Park, and those fonts are the default Korean font for Hangul-ucs. Moreover, Unfonts are widely used in Linux and the famous multimedia software, mplayer, also uses the font to show Korean subtitles.

DW: Can you say a more few words on what DVIPDFMx is and why it is still important to be able to convert from DVI to PDF in these days of pdfTeX?

ChoF: Many non-CJK people have asked me the same question. As I remember, the first one was Hans Hagen. Korean TeX packages (and the CJK package too) are based on the subfont scheme dividing a set of huge characters into a set of fonts having 256 characters. In 2001, I implemented this scheme in both pdfTeX and in DVIPDFM (a program developed by Mark Wicks); my version of DVIPDFM was called dvipdfm-kor. At that time, I knew that there was also dvipdfm-jpn by Hirata in Japan which supported Japanese pTeX. It was natural to combine the two projects into one, so "dvipdfm-cjk" came out in March 2002. After messing up quite many parts of DVIPDFM, we changed the name to "DVIPDFMx" in October 2002. Because there had been no progress with DVIPDFM since the release of dvipdfm-0.13.2c in 2001, we also had many things to maintain and to improve relating to DVIPDFM (bug fixes, upgrades, new features) and that work is ongoing. Actually Hirata wrote a lot of code, especially for handling CID-keyed font technology and OpenType fonts. That is the most important part of DVIPDFMx; even pdfTEX does not handle those fonts.

Now return to your question. As I just said, subfont and CID-keyed font technology are the most important parts for typesetting CJK TEX documents. A recent version of pdfTEX supports subfonts as well. So, there is now no problem in using pdfTEX with CJK packages based on the subfont scheme. But still pdfTEX does not support pTEX. Because of that reason, DVIPDFMx is widely used in Japan. Another reason why some people still use DVIPDFMx rather than pdfTEX is on the size of the result. In the case of documents using many different fonts, the result of pdfTEX is ten times bigger than that of DVIPDFMx.

This past January, while I was writing a paper for *The PracTEX Journal* (`http://tug.org/pracjourn`), I thought about the simplicity of the DVI format. DVI is not good for use as a final format, but it is still good for an intermediate format to translate into another format. Imagine that you are trying to convert PDF file into another format, e.g., HTML or XML. There might be many things we can do with DVI format. I am still learning. Moreover, I think that the pdfTEX team will never drop the DVI format. In fact, pdfTEX is a really good engine for getting improved DVI output.

DW: Congratulations on the imminent publication of the first issue of the Asian Journal of TEX. What exactly is your role in this journal? According to Barbara Beeton's column in the last issue of *TUGboat*, your editorial board includes Prof. Haruhiko Okumura (Japan), Hàn Thế Thành (Vietnam), CV Radhakrishnan (India), and Werner Lemberg (Germany), as well as you; does this mean that other societies in addition to KTS are also involved, or is the journal a publication of KTS and merely has an international editorial board?

ChoF: Thank you so much. I'm (chief) editor of AJT. Now AJT has six associate editors, the four above and Hong Feng (China) and Kangsoo Kim (Korea).

It's time to explain how AJT came about. At first KTS tried to make a new TEX journal for Korean TEX users, and that work came to me. At that time, I noticed that there was no journal which accepts a paper written in languages other than English or European languages. So, my model for AJT was a TEX journal (somewhere between *TUGboat* and *The PracTEX Journal*) which accepts papers written in Asian languages as well as English. People in KTS agreed with my idea, and I got positive answers from the current editors of AJT.

AJT's goal is to be a journal of all TEX users groups in Asia. Because other TEX users groups in Asia are not active or do not have enough funds compared with TUG and the European LUGs, KTS took the responsibility for publishing the journal.

DW: Can you give us a hint at the table of contents of this first issue?

ChoF: The first issue contains seven articles written in Korean. It's a kind of proceedings of the conference for the 5th anniversary of KTUG, which was held in January with more than one hundred participants. The table of contents can be found soon (in the next week) from the AJT web site (`http://ajt.ktug.kr`).

DW: Are you also an officer of KTUG?

ChoF: No. There is only one officer in KTUG, the director.

DW: You say that KTUG is an on-line community and KTS is an off-line community. What do you mean by the distinction between on-line and off-line?

ChoF: The on-line community, KTUG, has no members. It's a kind of open place to discuss things related to TEX. There is only one director who maintains the web site. On the other hand, KTS has membership as TUG does. KTS will regularly send to its members printed copies of AJT and the KTUG collection CD (based on Akira Kakuto's W32TEX system).

DW: Is your work with TEX supported or encouraged in any way by your university, or is it a distraction from your academic work in math (as it has become for so many other mathematicians)?

ChoF: To date it gets neither support nor encouragement from my university. I am so busy since I do my own research (not related to TEX) to keep a position in the university. But I'm trying to show them that working with TEX is not a hobby but a kind of research. The paper published in LNCS became a good example.

We also founded KTS which was registered as a formal society by Korea Research Foundation (like another big societies, e.g., the Korean Math. Society). KTS is trying to collect research funds. We already have more than US$10,000 to host an international conference (Jan 25–26, 2008 at Gongju in Korea). I think that TEX and digital typography will be recognized as a new research field through the activity of KTS.

DW: What is your area of non-TEX research and, as a "full-time lecturer" what sorts of courses do you teach?

ChoF: Originally I studied Transformation groups in the area of Topology. Currently I am also working on Topological Dynamics in low-dimensional topology, and a mathematical approach to "phylogeny", a kind of bio-mathematics.

In this semester, I am teaching Calculus, Maple (mathematical software) and Topology for undergraduate students. Unfortunately, I haven't had any chance to teach TEX or LATEX to them.

DW: I can imagine that the field of phylogeny involves drawing diagrams as well as normal math typesetting. If so, do you make use of any TEX or LATEX graphics packages to help with that?

ChoF: The diagrams are not so complicated. I always use MetaFun by Hans Hagen.

DW: One of the concerns of many people in the TEX world is that TEX is relatively unknown in the larger worlds of typesetting and word processing compared with commercial programs such as Adobe's InDesign and Microsoft Word. How do you see the future of TEX when it comes to Asian languages?

ChoF: The situation is getting worse. I no longer say that the typesetting quality of TEX is better than other software (except for math typesetting). Since TEX was created for 8-bit languages, it does not have an advantage over alternative systems for the 16-bit or 32-bit Asian languages.

But I do not feel pessimistic about the future of TEX. In Korea, MS Word is not a dominant word processor. As far as I know, the market share of MS Word is less than 50 percent. Another word processor developed by a Korean company fits better for making Korean documents. This is a good model for TEX.

In my opinion, TEX must find its special place where it is better than other software. One of KTS's missions is to design a new TEX engine which supports Korean typesetting features better than other software. Using TEX as a base engine for automatic typesetting is a good example too.

DW: What configuration tools for TeX do you typically use (distribution, engine, format, editor, etc.)? Is there consensus in Korea about which set of tools are most appropriate for using TeX there, or does everyone have his or her own favorite as in the English-speaking world of TeX?

ChoF: In my case, I use MacTeX under Mac OS X. Because of DVIPDFMx, pdfTeX in DVI mode is my favorite engine. For editors, TeXShop and Vim are used.

In Korea, many people used Aleksander Simonic's WinEdt on MS Windows. In these days, people are moving from HLaTeX to Hangul-ucs because Hangul-ucs supports those 11,172 Korean characters included in Unicode. Unfortunately, the Delphi tool with which WinEdt was developed had some trouble in handling Unicode. So people are also moving to other editors which handle Unicode well.

Also, since 2005, KTUG and KTS have been developing our own TeX system based on Akira Kakuto's W32TeX (`http://fsci.fuk.kindai.ac.jp/kakuto/win32-ptex/`). The name is "KTUG Collection" and it is the only TeX system which KTUG and KTS support. The biggest problem is that there is no good editor which can be used without cost.

DW: You said that 11,172 Korean characters are included in Unicode. Is this sufficient?

ChoF: These 11,172 characters are for the modern Korean language; the default Korean fonts in MS-Windows and Mac OS X contain those 11,172 characters. In the case of typesetting the old Korean language, we need more characters.

There is another encoding for Korean characters which is not Unicode. The name is KSX 1001 or KSC 5601 (EUC). Some Korean fonts using this encoding contain just 2,350 characters.

DW: Thank you very much for participating in this interview. I previously knew nothing about Asian fonts and the use of TeX in your part of the world. Best wishes for the success of KTS and your new journal.

ChoF: Thank you so much for giving me this wonderful chance.

Nicola Talbot

Nicola Talbot is a LaTeX user, teacher, and package writer. [Interview completed 25 May 2007.]

Dave Walden, interviewer: Please tell me a bit about yourself personally, independent of the TeX world.

Nicola Talbot, interviewee: I'm third of six children. My father was British (he died in 1994), my mother is British, but was born in Brazil. Her father was a British ex-pat who lived in Brazil after his father (a merchant captain) was shipwrecked off the coast of South America, and her mother was a Belgian emigré, so I have family dotted about the world (Belgium, Brazil and even as far away as Fiji.) My mother's family moved back to England in 1963, but I've been able to visit some of the family who stayed behind, and some of them have come over to visit us.

I am married to Gavin Cawley (a lecturer at the University of East Anglia) and we have a seven-year-old son Cameron who has a mild form of autism. I studied mathematics at the University of Essex (where I met Gavin), and then went on to do a PhD in electronic systems engineering, which involved maths and computer simulations, no actual practical electronics. I then worked at the Institute of Food Research for what was then the Ministry of Agriculture Fisheries and Food and also for a European Union collaborative project, but I gave up full time work when Cameron was born.

DW: Please tell me how you first got involved with TeX.

NT: I've always liked writing novels in my spare time, and I switched from a typewriter to a word processor on an Acorn Electron in the late 1980s (I was well chuffed when I went from using a cassette to using an external floppy drive) which was fine for writing stories, but the technical reports I needed to write for my PhD required a lot of maths, and the word processor just wasn't up to it. Gavin was in the year above me, and he had started writing up his thesis using TechWriter (on an Acorn Archimedes) but it caused him so much hassle that he decided to look into LaTeX. He decided to buy Leslie Lamport's book, and installed ArmTeX. This was back in the early 1990s, so it was LaTeX 2.09, but I realised that it was exactly what I needed, so when I got my own Archimedes, I switched over to it. I was very glad that I did (not only from the typesetting point of view) as I accidentally deleted my PhD thesis, but because the source code was in an ASCII file, I was able to dump all the free disk space into a file, and I was able to restore it, including all the equations which I wouldn't have been able to do if it had been stored in a binary format. (Of course, the real moral of the story is to make backups!) I've used LaTeX ever since, both for research work and for creative writing.

DW: I had to look up "well chuffed" on an Internet-based dictionary of British slang. I gather it means "very pleased." (I also found a definition for "to chuff" but that seemed not to fit.)

You say you like writing novels in your spare time. When I look at your web site (`http://theoval.cmp.uea.ac.uk/~nlct/`) and think about your having a seven year old son to take care of, I think you must have an odd definition of "spare time". Are you still writing fiction, do you use LaTeX for it, and is any of it published or self-published (given what's possible these days with print-on-demand and Internet-base sales)?

NT: My spare time is usually after Cameron has gone to bed, so I don't write as much as I used to, but I still enjoy it when I can. I haven't had any of my novels published. I did actually try getting one published, but the publisher asked me to send it in Word format. Unfortunately I was in a bit of a flippant mood at the time: I refused point blank, and I'm afraid to say I mentioned something about not wanting to aid and abet capitalist hyenas!

I've thought about self-publishing. I've had a brief experiment with book binding. I typeset my grandfather's memoirs in LaTeX (I used the octavo class file together with psutils to make the signatures). I managed fine, until it came to actually fixing on the cover page. I put together a makeshift press, and after about four attempts I managed to produce one that looked vaguely straight, and I gave it to my Mum for Christmas a couple of years ago. I think it's the pride of her book collection, but next to her other books it stands out as a bit of an eyesore. I've been thinking about trying a print-on-demand company, but I've been a bit too busy lately.

DW: I see on your web site a page (`http://theoval.sys.uea.ac.uk/~nlct/latex/packages/index.html`) listing a dozen and a half or so packages you have developed. How did you get into package development, and how do you decide what packages you are going to develop?

NT: I think I started with the datetime package. I used it as an example in my LaTeX course. It was a fairly simple package back then, and I thought I may as well upload it to CTAN. The glossary package is another one that started life in a tutorial, but it seemed to take on a life of its own, and it reached the point where it was so full of fixes that I could no longer maintain it, which is why I've replaced it with the glossaries package.

A large number of the packages on my web site were written to help Gavin with his teaching. When he first started as a lecturer, he taught a maths course, so I wrote the probsoln package to help him with the assignments, but his teaching was changed shortly after I finished it, so it didn't get used much in the end. Likewise, I wrote all the UEA specific class files for him, and various class files that generate forms, because he didn't want to use the Word templates that were provided. The crkscrsh class file was to help one of his project students whose project involved using a palm top device to keep track of cricket scores, but I don't think it's used since then.

The two main packages that I wrote for my own benefit were the flowfram package, because I found writing posters such a pain, and the makedtx package/application. I can't remember why I wrote the csvtools package, but I found it very useful for mail merging when we moved, when I had to send a change of address letter to various utilities, banks and so forth.

DW: I also see on your web site another page (`http://theoval.sys.uea.ac.uk/~nlct/latex/apps/index.html`) listing applications code in Java, Perl, etc., that relate to LaTeX. In addition to being a mathematician (with a strong statistical inclination it appears from your list of publications) and writer, you also are a computer programmer. Do you see any common thread running through these activities?

NT: There's definitely a link between programming, LaTeX and mathematics. I think you need some understanding of maths to be a programmer, and LaTeX's excellent at typesetting maths, and in a way, LaTeX is a form of programming. As for writing, Lewis Carroll was both a mathematician and a writer. He wrote "Symbolic Logic" and "Game of Logic" as well as *Through the Looking Glass* and *Alice in Wonderland*, so perhaps there is a link between maths and writing, although I'm not quite sure what it is, my novels certainly aren't mathematical.

DW: How about deaf awareness and British sign language, which I see from your web site that you are certified in. Does the way you think as a mathematician or programmer help in any way in this other domain, or it is really a quite separate type of activity?

NT: I think it's a separate type of activity. The main reason I learnt to sign was because I had a profoundly deaf friend, but it's a useful skill, though I'm certainly not fluent in it.

DW: I also see from your web site that your staff development course on LaTeX course at the university has been canceled for lack of interest. Do you have an explanation for this, e.g., a general decline in interest in LaTeX, or everyone already knows it?

NT: I'm not sure really. I think that I might have scored a bit of an own goal when I put my tutorials (`http://theoval.sys.uea.ac.uk/~nlct/latex/index.html`) on my web site, as it was soon after that that the numbers began dwindling, but I actually found the course quite difficult as I always had a fairly diverse set of people attending. I would have a group ranging from computer scientists to linguists and secretaries. The computer scientists by and large caught on quickly, as they were used to the idea of writing source code and then having to compile it, but for those whose use of computers was limited to word processors and spreadsheets really struggled. It's very difficult to pitch a talk at the right level when you have such a wide range of abilities in the same class. The drop in numbers also coincided with our move from Norwich to a small village, so I probably would have stopped anyway because of the problems in getting there. When we were living in Norwich, I could catch the bus to the university after dropping Cameron off at school, but where we live now, it takes nearly an hour to get to the university by bus, and the last bus that will get me back in time to pick Cameron up leaves at half past one, which wouldn't give me much time to do anything!

DW: I suspect that TUG may have a bit of the same "own-goal" problem; because so much about TeX is freely available on-line these days (much of it supported by TUG), actual TUG membership for the purpose of getting its deliverables, *TUGboat* and the TeX software DVD/CDs, is not as useful as it once was.

You and I first became acquainted (by email) when you were drafting your one-page statement on "What Is TeX?" (`http://tug.org/pracjourn/2005-3/walden-whatis/talbot-r2.pdf`) for issue 2005-3 of *The PracTeX Journal*. Do you see what you said then being just as true today, or have you augmented or changed your view?

NT: I think that I ought to have clarified a bit better that plain TeX is also a format of TeX, but other than that I'd still say pretty much the same.

DW: You obviously have spent a lot of effort trying to make LaTeX more useful to yourself and others. How do you see the role of LaTeX in the world of word processing/typesetting and your use of it evolving in the future?

NT: I would like to see more publishers using LaTeX, especially if the work is likely to involve mathematics. Fortunately most of the scientific journals and conference proceedings publishers that I have submitted papers to are TeX aware, although it's very annoying when they supply a class file that doesn't conform to their own guidelines. I think that more people from outside the sciences are beginning to use it, which is good. I'd like to improve my Java application `JpgfDraw` (`http://theoval.cmp.uea.ac.uk/~nlct/`

jpgfdraw/index.html). I used it to create a newsletter for Cameron's school, and it turned out quite well. When he was younger, I used to write the newsletters for the parent and toddler group we went to, but back then I just used a standard one-column format. Many people seem to think that TeX simply can't be used for newsletters or brochures, but I think TeX is capable of producing pretty much any kind of document.

DW: What development configuration do you use for your TeX work?

NT: I use teTeX running on Linux with vim as my text editor. I've installed the vimspell plugin, so I can spell check as I type, that's the nearest I get to using a front end these days! I used to use MiKTeX and TeXnicCenter when I was teaching, but I've never been very keen on front ends. I did briefly play with plain TeX a few years ago, and I bought a copy of *The TeXbook*, which helped me gain a much better understanding of LaTeX, but now I mostly use pdfLaTeX.

DW: Does pdfLaTeX in its current form (plus all the LaTeX packages and classes) pretty much satisfy your needs, or are you longing for LaTeX 3, LuaTeX, or whatever, to become available?

NT: I think that pdfLaTeX in its current form pretty much satisfies my needs, especially when used in conjunction with hyperref and packages like ifthen, xkeyval, pgf/tikz and graphicx (actually, the list keeps expanding every time I think about it.) Offhand, I can't think of anything that I'd really like to be able to do, but can't.

DW: I see that UK-TUG (http://uk.tug.org/) has revived itself sufficiently that it is going to hold a 2007 AGM this coming October 22. Do you have a formal role in that revival? I saw that you gave a 124-slide workshop at last year's meeting on Writing a Thesis in LaTeX (http://uk.tug.org/2009/01/21/living-and-working-with-latex/)?

NT: No, I don't have a formal role in that revival (I only became a member of UK-TUG last year) but I'm glad that it is reviving, and I hope the UK-TUG membership continues to grow. I enjoyed last year's Living and Working with LaTeX Workshop, and it was good to see so many people attending. It was interesting meeting people from so many diverse backgrounds, and I think the informal sessions were a good way to find out about the type of things the participants were interested in knowing how to do in LaTeX. I don't know if UK-TUG had much feedback, but I hope that the participants enjoyed the day and found it useful. It certainly seemed very successful.

DW: I have one more query, that is sort of personal, but I hope you will address it anyway. You have a PhD; looking at your list of publications, you are obviously involved with a lot of research; and your courses and tutorials indicate that you enjoy teaching. Do you aspire to move more formally into the academic world once your son is older, or do you feel that your current mix of home life, connection to research and academia, and systems development work (e.g., with LaTeX) will satisfy you over the long run?

NT: I would like to move back more formally into the academic world (or, more precisely, get paid for doing the work that I do ;-) but I'm glad that I made the decision to stop full-time work when Cameron was born. I'm told that the first seven years of a child's life are the most influential years in terms of how they develop and cope with later life, and those years will never come back again. I also feel that it's even more important to give that extra support where the child has a problem like autism. (I once read somewhere that in cases of this type of mild autism, provided the child gets enough support in their early years, by the time they become an adult they will merely be viewed as eccentric — given that he says he wants to be a computer programmer, I think he'll fit right in!)

I have, however, been very conscious of how difficult it is to get back into research after a break, which is why I have always tried to keep up my research activities. Gavin and I work very well together — our skill sets are approximately orthogonal! (He can do bits I can't do, and I can do bits that he can't do.) Now that Cameron is at school for longer hours, I have more time for research work. Ideally I'd like to continue working from home, as it's reassuring to know that if the school do have any problems with him, I'm just round the corner. Also I see so many parents who spend their whole life in a mad rush: rushing to school, then rushing to work, back again to pick up the kids, it surprises me that they manage to get any work done at all!

DW: Thank you very much for participating in our interview series. It has been a great pleasure to learn a bit more about you and your activities, and I plan to spend more time scouting around your web site (`http://theoval.cmp.uea.ac.uk/~nlct/`) looking at all the resources you have posted there. I hope to meet you in person at some point; perhaps we will both be at TUG 2008 next summer in Cork.

Haruhiko Okumura

Haruhiko Okumura promotes and supports the use of TeX in Japan.

[Interview completed 4 June 2007.]

Dave Walden, interviewer: Please tell me a bit about yourself personally, independent of the TeX world.

Haruhiko Okumura, interviewee: My background was in particle physics and gravitation theory, but in those days I couldn't get a job at a university so I was teaching math at high schools. During that period I bought my first microcomputer, read Knuth's *The Art of Computer Programming*, and began studying algorithms. I got especially interested in data compression. I designed the algorithm behind the once-famous compression archiver LHA, assembly-coded by Haruyasu Yoshizaki. My basic idea, that combines sliding dictionary and entropy coding, is still used in zip and gzip.

DW: I was interested to read your history of such compression archivers on your web site (`http://oku.edu.mie-u.ac.jp/~okumura/compression/history.html`).

How did you first become involved with TeX?

HO: I wrote my first book, on statistical algorithms, in 1986 and my second book, on computer algorithms, in 1987. I used a Japanese word processor but I couldn't typeset math properly. I learned about Knuth's TeX but it was not designed for multibyte characters. Then a Japanese publisher made a version of TeX for Japanese, named pTeX. (There was another one named JTeX, but pTeX was superior.) I was quite excited and began writing books with it. I studied the traditional Japanese art of typesetting, worked with a professional printing expert to improve the TFM files for Japanese, and wrote style files. My third book on algorithms in C, typeset with pTeX, was selected as one of the best 100 computer books (including translations) ever published in Japan. But people began to look at me as a TeX guru, not as an algorithm master! I was asked to write many books on how to typeset beautiful books with pTeX.

DW: I see from your web site (`http://oku.edu.mie-u.ac.jp/~okumura/`) that you are now a professor of computer education in the education department of Mie University. I gather that you have moved completely away from physics and are now training new school teachers like you yourself once were. How did this transition come about, and what sorts of things do you teach now?

HO: In 1960's, as a child I was hooked on the Japanese anime series named Astro Boy (`http://en.wikipedia.org/wiki/Astroboy`), the story of a robot kid supposed to be created in 2003. When I bought my first microcomputer in late 1970's, I really thought that Astro Boy was coming soon. But the world did not change that fast. In 2003, at long last, we had a computer class in every Japanese high school. But it turned out that high-school computer teachers were quite unfamiliar with programming or the science underlying computing; many of them only teach how to use Windows and Microsoft Office. During 2003–2004 I was appointed to work part-time (confidentially) for the National Center for University Entrance Examination where I prepared SAT-like tests in computing. But since computing was optional for university admission, only a few hundred students chose the subject. All in all, I think our computer education is in trouble. I agree with Alan Kay who maintains that the present computer education only reflects pop culture, and with Edward Tufte who says PowerPoint is ruining science as well as education. I'm willing to dedicate my final ten years of professorship to improving the situation.

DW: Have you written other books in addition to those you mentioned on statistical algorithms, computer algorithms, and algorithms in C? I assume well-known volumes like Robert Sedgewick's *Algorithms in C* are translated into Japanese. Does your book on algorithms in C address the audience for a different audience or in a particularly Japanese way?

HO: My Algorithms in C book (and its Java version compiled later) is very limited in scope compared to Sedgewick's volumes. It is an alphabetical compilation of small but interesting algorithms, much like HACKMEM (I hadn't read this fine memorandum when I wrote my book). My newest book is a small textbook entitled "Computer Literacy" for college freshmen.

DW: The HACKMEM memo (`ftp://publications.ai.mit.edu/ai-publications/pdf/AIM-239.pdf`) is such a wonderful document. (I worked with Mike Beeler, who was a co-author of HACKMEM, for many years at Bolt Beranek and Newman, one of the places he worked after MIT. He was still doing recreational math when I worked with him. I think the last time I saw Mike in person was at Knuth's set of six lectures at MIT on "Things a Computer Scientist Rarely Talks About" (`http://www-cs-faculty.stanford.edu/~knuth/things.html`), based substantially on his earlier book *3:16 Bible Texts Illuminated* (`http://www-cs-faculty.stanford.edu/~knuth/316.html`). Of course, another of the HACKMEM authors, Bill Gosper, worked with Knuth for a while at Stanford in the mid-1970s.)

Please tell me something about the traditional art of Japanese typesetting, how that tradition may differ from the English typesetting traditions, and how improving the Japanese TFM files may also be different than the parallel work for Latin alphabet fonts.

HO: Japanese letters are basically square in shape. You can break lines almost anywhere. But non-letter marks (punctuation, parentheses, etc.) need not be square; you cannot break lines before the closing marks and after the starting marks. Also, juxtaposed marks need pair kerning. The detailed rules were compiled in Japan Industrial Standard JIS X 4051:1995, "Line composition rules for Japanese documents". Although the original configuration of pTEX didn't conform to these rules, pTEX was so versatile that if we rewrote the TFM files and set penalties and parameters properly, we could arrive at a fairly decent approximation to the traditional rules. (See `http://oku.edu.mie-u.ac.jp/~okumura/texfaq/japanese/ptex.html`.)

DW: Were the style files you mentioned developing related to use of the Japanese fonts or were they for other aspects of typesetting within the conventions for Japanese?

HO: My class files, jsarticle.cls (and friends), are equivalent to pTEX's jarticle.cls, which is in turn equivalent to article.cls, except for two exceptions: (1) jsarticle.cls discards pTEX's original font metrics and loads the improved TFM files; (2) it sets penalties and other parameters to better reflect traditional Japanese typesetting rules.

DW: When I trace the various links on your web site, I see a TeX Wiki, TeX questions and answers, a blog, and other ways you communicate with and support the use of TeX and other systems. I also do not see a Japanese TeX Users group when I look at the TUG web site.

HO: The Japanese TeX Users Group was discontinued long ago, because web sites, web forums (http://oku.edu.mie-u.ac.jp/~okumura/texfaq/qa/), and Wikis (http://oku.edu.mie-u.ac.jp/~okumura/texwiki/) turned out to be more appropriate for the impatient Japanese users. My site is getting so comprehensive that no one needs to buy my books!

DW: Have you written books in Japanese about TeX?

HO: Yes, I've written three or seven books, depending on how you count them. Two of them are out of date; four out of seven are the 1st through 4th editions of my LaTeX 2_ε book (I rewrite it every three years). One out of seven is actually written by my colleagues under my supervision.

DW: What set of tools do you use when working with TeX (operating system, TeX engine, TeX format, classes, editor, etc.)?

HO: I've used MS-DOS, BSD, SunOS, Solaris, Linux, Windows, and Mac. Now I use Linux for servers and batch jobs and Mac OS X for client-side computing. My favorite editor is Emacs with AUCTeX. I use pTeX (pLaTeX) and dvipdfmx to generate PDFs, because there's no pdfpTeX yet. Since pTeX for Unicode is now being developed and XeTeX is acquiring pTeX-like versatility, next year I'll be using either the new pTeX or XeTeX.

DW: You said earlier that a Japanese publisher created pTeX. Is pTeX a commercial product? If not, who is maintaining it now? Is it part of the TeX Live collection of software or does TeX in Japan exist sort of independently of that distribution which is jointly done by several TeX user groups?

HO: pTeX was created by ASCII Corporation (http://www.ascii.co.jp/), and is now distributed (ftp://ftp.ascii.co.jp/pub/TeX/ascii-ptex/) as a patch to teTeX 3.0. Its license is BSD-style. It is maintained by some engineers from the corporation with the help of a handful of outside volunteers. I wish it was incorporated in TeX Live, but I don't know how that can happen.

DW: Jin-Hwan Cho from Korea believes that TeX technologies are highly developed in Japan compared to Korea and China. Can you describe to what extent you believe this is true and why?

HO: I don't know much about Korean and Chinese TeX, but, yes, Japan has enjoyed 20 years of high TeXnology. We have had pTeX for 16-bit characters since 1987, and in 1990 Hisato Hamano wrote an article "Vertical typesetting in TeX" (http://tug.org//TUGboat/Articles/tb11-3/tb29hamano.pdf) in *TUGboat*.

DW: What sorts of projects is TeX used for in Japan beyond typesetting academic math? Is it widely used in the general publishing business, or are commercial systems like InDesign and QuarkXPress used by most Japanese publishers as is the case in the United States?

HO: TeX is used here for typesetting computer books as well as math and physics books. ASCII Corporation created a frontend to pTeX, called Editor's Work Bench (http://www2.ascii.co.jp/ascii/EWB/), mainly for the company's internal use. I hear it is much easier to use for non-techie editors. TEX is also used as a free substitute to PDFlib for Web-based systems. My university uses TEX to generate paper syllabi books from online syllabus system. But on the whole the trend is toward QuarkXPress and InDesign for publishers and Microsoft Word for authors. I don't think we can change the trend.

DW: You are listed as an editorial board member of the *Asian Journal of TEX*. Do you expect to participate heavily in that? Also, I am a little puzzled how a journal which apparently will have articles written in Korean, Japanese, and Chinese can work. I didn't think a reader of one of these languages can necessarily read another of them, or is the idea that readers of each language will find articles he or she can read in his or her native language?

HO: The CJK languages are so different from Latin ones that a journal dedicated to CJK typesetting is worth publishing. I'd like to participate in *AJT* as heavily as I can, but my time is quite limited.

DW: To what extent, if any, does your university encourage your involvement with TEX, and do you teach TEX to your students?

HO: I wish my university ever encouraged my involvement with TEX at all! I teach TEX, XHTML, CSS, C, Java, and all that my students should know, but almost all of them use Word to write essays and theses.

DW: Thank you for taking the time to participate in this interview and for educating me about some of the issues relating to TEX use in your country.

David Carlisle

David Carlisle is a member of the LaTeX team and deeply involved with issues of typesetting and displaying mathematics, including being an Invited Expert on the W3C Math Working Group.
[Interview completed 20 June 2007.]

Dave Walden, interviewer: Please tell me a bit about your personal history independent of TeX.

David Carlisle, interviewee: Born 1961 in Southwell, England, and grew up in Mansfield. At University I specialised in Mathematics at Manchester, both undergraduate and postgraduate, finishing up with a PhD in Pure Mathematics in 1985 (typeset on an IBM Golfball typewriter with large brackets drawn in by my wife, who has a steadier hand ...). There then followed a two year post doctoral position at Cambridge before returning to Manchester in 1987. I worked as a researcher in Manchester in several projects in either Computer Science or Mathematics, until 1997. In 1998 I moved to NAG, a mathematical software company in Oxford, to work initially on OpenMath and MathML, but now more generally on their XML systems. Outside of NAG I'm an editor of the MathML specification, and quite active in the community around the XSLT XML transformation language.

I now live in Souldern, a very small village in Oxfordshire, with Joanna, my wife (who uses TeX more than I do), and Matthew who's 3 and a half and quite computer literate but not, as far as I know, a TeX user.

DW: What does your wife use TeX for?

DC: Prior to having Matthew, Joanna taught mathematics (age range 11–16 mainly) so worksheets of various sorts got typeset with TeX, but even now, letters and stuff, and the occasional poster for some village events gets typeset in TeX I believe.

DW: Does NAG develop the same sorts of products as our local Boston area company MathWorks (e.g., MATLAB)? And why/how is XML important to math software products?

DC: Probably this isn't the place for a comparative review of commercial software, but in general MATLAB offers an interactive environment in which to solve problems of various sorts. NAG's main products are lower level libraries of mathematical functions which are often embedded into other products rather than used directly by the end user. However, for those who don't want to program directly in C or Fortran, we do offer interfaces to the libraries from problem solving environments, including Maple and MATLAB.

DW: When and how did you first get involved with TeX?

DC: September 1987, when I returned from Cambridge I took up a position at the Computer Science Department in Manchester which had (at the time) one of the largest

Sun networks in Europe. So right from the start I had the benefit of the graphical "Sunview" environment and the `dvitool` previewer which was far ahead of its time (and one of the best dvi viewers I ever used). Actually it's not quite true that I had that environment from the start; when I first got there my machine was still on order, and so I was at a bit of a loose end. I asked some of the other post docs what I should do to orient myself to life in the CS department, and one of them gave me *The TEXbook* to read. I remember I read it right through to the end, before I ever got chance to try out TEX.

The Computer Science department had by then quite a lot of experienced TEX (almost all LATEX) users, so it was a good environment in which to lean TEX, Also I maintained close contacts with colleagues in the Mathematics department who were just starting out with installing personal computers and so I also spent some time helping them get TEX set up. It was while using TEX on these early (512K) PCs that I first started looking at the internals of the LATEX system, developing some locally modified versions that had a slightly more usable startup time. A direct descendant of those efforts can still be found on CTAN as `mylatex.ltx`. Another unusual aspect of the initial environment in which I learnt LATEX was that right from the start I had access to scalable fonts. Most people of that era associated TEX with Computer (or Almost) Modern fonts in bitmap form, but Mario Wolczko had modified LATEX 2.09's `lfonts` file to use scalable fonts so I had (as I recall) `latex` (CM), `pslatex` (Times), `pslatex-n` (New Century), and `pslatex-b` (Bookman). We had good on-screen PostScript preview, with Harlequin scriptworks, and later, Ghostscript.

DW: You are well known for your involvement with the LATEX team. How did you move from learning TEX/LATEX at the university in Manchester to becoming part of the LATEX 2_ε core development team, and what is your role on that team?

DC: I'd posted a few stylesheets to (pre-CTAN) TEX archives and had answered a few (or a lot) of questions on the `comp.text.tex` (I think initially `comp.text`) newsgroup, so I suppose I got noticed somewhere. I did email Frank quite early on to ask if he minded if I distributed my `narray` style (which consisted largely of a complete copy of his array style). He said he didn't mind but that it would probably be better to instead distribute `narray` in a form such that it input (rather than copied) `array.sty`. So that's what I did. In the end of course we abandoned `narray` and merged the two back together (although anyone looking at the internal array package documentation can still see the join). I joined the LATEX 3 team by way of a trick! Frank and Chris mailed me one day out of the blue with the offer of a free trip to Hamburg for the weekend. Checking with Google suggests that would have been 1992. It was the DANTE meeting that launched the NTS project. (They kindly held the last session in English as non-German speakers were present.) The LATEX 3 project then had a meeting over the following two days. I think Frank, Rainer, Chris and Johannes, plus Phil Taylor (who was, I assume, mainly there for NTS) also sat in. Shortly afterwards I obtained a copy of the LATEX 3 kernel as it was at the time, and generally got involved in the development of LATEX 2_ε and its subsequent maintenance. In the end it seems I found that the mechanics of producing mathematics papers was taking more of my time and interest than actually producing the mathematics, and these days I work full time on (mainly mathematical) document markup and production, rather than being a research mathematician.

I'm not as active as I was in the LATEX maintenance, though I'm still on the core team and get all team emails and any messages sent to the LATEX bug system, but I have less TEX-related time than I used to have, with changing jobs and family circumstances.

DW: From your biography page on the NAG web site (`http://www.nag.co.uk/about/dcarlisle.asp`), I see that you are much more broadly involved in math typesetting and display (MathML2 Recommendation, co-chair of the World Wide Web Consortium Math Interest Group, editor of a draft update to the ISO entities for characters, an editor of the OpenMath Standard, and a member of the OpenMath Society), much more widely than just in TeX. How do you see TeX playing in the math typesetting and display world as the world continues to evolve?

DC: Yes, actually I should update that page. The W3C re-chartered the Math activity to work on MathML3, the first draft of which was published earlier this year. I stepped down as co-chair of the group, but will again act as co-editor. As for the future, that's always hard to predict. TeX has far more competing products these days, most notably the office suites (Microsoft, OpenOffice.org, etc). Personally I've never felt comfortable authoring in a WYSIWYG environment but I am apparently in a minority with that view. In stark contrast to the situation when I started to use TeX, people who prefer that kind of environment can gain pretty good mathematical typesetting. For example, the math layout rules in Office 2007's math layout are explicitly modelled after the TeX layout rules as documented in Appendix G of *The TeXbook*. (See `http://blogs.msdn.com/murrays/archive/2006/09/13/752206.aspx` where it says, "*The TeXbook* is a user manual that includes a detailed specification for mathematical typography. We have used many of its choices and methodology in creating our solutions, which are appropriately enhanced with the use of OpenType tables and some additional constructs.") This means that even in TeX's core constituency of the academic working in the mathematical sciences, TeX does not have the totally dominant position that it had as an authoring system. On the other hand the rise of XML (including XML output from office suites and database systems) but also DocBook, XHTML, and any number of more specific XML languages means that there is a greater than ever need for a high quality batch oriented typesetting system. (The PDF version of the MathML spec is typeset by pdfLaTeX for example.)

TeX would make an ideal basis for such a system; however, the main problems (when using traditional TeX) relate to Unicode input, and TeX-specific font output encodings. It's not that it's impossible to work around these issues, but managing the mappings between an external Unicode world and an internal 8 (or 7) bit TeX is a black art that always limits TeX acceptance in larger projects. For various reasons Omega never seemed to gain the momentum to take over as the main TeX engine and I'm glad to see XeTeX (which I must admit I haven't had chance to use yet) is gaining real acceptance, being part of the TeX Live distribution, etc. A major reason for using TeX is its portability, so (as was clearly seen with ε-TeX) people are reluctant to use experimental versions of things if they have to be downloaded/installed as there is no guarantee that the person receiving the document will have the appropriate software version. However once a system is installed by default on most TeX systems (even if most TeX users are not using it) then it becomes possible to fairly quickly "move" the community. If LaTeX font packages start working (or working more effectively) if running on a Unicode-based TeX system (whether that be XeTeX or Omega or something else yet to be produced), then the system will rapidly gain acceptance even if a large part of the existing community is English speaking mathematicians who don't immediately see any real benefit from moving to Unicode (just as they didn't really have immediate gain from the disruption of TeX 3 moving to 8 bit).

DW: You mentioned (and your author bio in *The LaTeX Companion, Second Edition*, also mentions) that you are involved with the XSLT language. What is that and what is your involvement with it?

DC: XSLT is a language for transforming an XML document to something else (another XML document, or HTML, or text, normally). It is probably one of the most widely installed programming languages ever, as most systems have several XSLT engines installed. (Mozilla/Firefox, Internet Explorer, Opera, and Safari each include an XSLT engine, as does the Gnome desktop in Linux, and the Java and .NET frameworks each have XSLT as standard as well.) So many people have an XSLT engine to hand even if they are unaware of it. It recently acquired a new related language, XQuery, which is more targeted at database usage. I have avoided being on the standardisation committees for XSLT, but I'm one of the more active members of the main community forum (`xsl-list`) and probably my activity on `xsl-list` accounts for the reason that I am a rather infrequent poster to `comp.text.tex` these days—I can only handle one high volume list!

DW: XƎTEX (increasingly in widespread use) and LuaTEX (moving into the beta demo phase) seem to be creating a good bit of buzz in the TEX world these days, and ConTEXt seems to be increasingly used, perhaps at the expense of LATEX. How do you feel about activities such as these and the continuing role of LATEX as the TEX world moves forward?

DC: See above, on XƎTEX. I think that a Unicode-aware TEX-like system that can use system installed fonts is an absolute essential for TEX going forward. I'm happy to see that XƎTEX seems to be working towards this. LuaTEX I know less about. There have been several attempts in the past to integrate TEX with scripting languages, Perl, Python, etc. Unlike with Unicode and font support where one can say that more or less any progress is a good thing, the success of a language merger is almost all to do with the fine details, so I can't really comment until I've seen it. As for the growth of ConTEXt at the expense of LATEX that's inevitable as essentially there is nowhere else for ConTEXt users to come from other than people who are, or would be, LATEX users. I think, though, that LATEX's more open package-oriented approach will always mean that it's more popular than ConTEXt, which as I understand it has a far more "monolithic" approach to system design, where the core has far more features but it's harder to add to that core. But ConTEXt's core is of course newer than LATEX and has benefited from that experience, and Hans has made a very nice (and extensively documented) system. There has never been any sense of rivalry between the ConTEXt and LATEX teams and we had several joint meetings as well as meeting at several more general TEX conferences around the time that LATEX 2_ε and ConTEXt were being initially developed.

DW: I believe you developed a system called `xmltex`. Why did that project get started, how does it work, and what is its status?

DC: Most of `xmltex` got written in a couple of "weird weekends" so it was never really a long term project, although Sebastian Rahtz stress tested it while using it for his PassiveTEX system that typesets XSL-FO XML, as well as TEI XML and a few other formats. A long time earlier I'd written a small package that tried to typeset HTML (`typehtml` is still on CTAN). That was mainly concerned with typesetting the math component of the ill fated HTML 3.0 draft specification. When Sebastian told me he had been using it as a basis for some experiments in typesetting XML, I was sure that something better could be done; much of `typehtml` is complicated by the need to infer missing markup and "tag soup" that is HTML. The stricter requirements of XML parsing are supposed to make it easier to write robust parsers. I ended up writing a fairly full XML and XML Namespace parser, with some non-conforming behaviour forced by TEX's normalisation of white space (some of which can not be controlled by TEX macros) and its inability to effectively deal with UTF-16 encoding. `xmltex` does however have table driven encoding support that in principle allows any 8-bit encoding to be used, as well as the full Unicode UTF-8 encoding. Dealing with these Unicode encodings with a classic 8-bit TEX accounts for almost all the complexity of `xmltex`, harder really than parsing XML syntax.

How does it work? Basically you change round the default catcodes so that the XML control characters (< and & mainly) are "active" and defined to macros which look ahead and parse the XML element and attribute syntax. People seem surprised that this is possible, but actually it's easier (modulo character encoding issues) to parse the highly regular XML syntax than something like a LaTeX tabular column specification, which also has to be parsed character by character by the TeX macro layer. However, the fact that it is possible doesn't necessarily mean that it's a good idea. Parsing XML with TeX isn't necessarily that fast and more importantly it's quite hard to give sensible errors or recover in a graceful way from any mistakes in the input. An alternative strategy that I'd really recommend these days is to use a real XML parser to parse the XML; this can then handle error reporting, and normalising any encodings used. XSLT or similar technology can then be used to generate a TeX document in more standard TeX syntax and in ASCII format, which is easier to process with TeX. That said, `xmltex` does seem to be used in some places still and has had very few bug reports so, within its limitations, it does seem to work well enough. I recently had a request from someone asking if he could take a more active maintenance role in `xmltex`. I have no objection, so (depending if this person decides that he wants to take it on) I may be handing over `xmltex` in the near future.

DW: Please tell me about your motivation for becoming a blogger (`http://dpcarlisle.blogspot.com`).

DC: I've often been active in public forums (`c.t.t`, `xsl-list`, ...) but in a blog one is less constrained by the mailing list process. One reason for not blogging earlier (apart from lack of time) was a feeling that I ought to do as some other well known XML bloggers have done, and design my own XML-based blogging engine. That would be possible, but at some point you realise that there are some projects for which you'll never have free time. Also, and perhaps more importantly, I think one of the main jobs of the Math Working Group is to tell people how to put mathematical documents on the web, and in particular to make it as easy as possible for people to do that. If the answer to having a mathematical blog is to design your own blog engine, and use a highly customised web server, then effectively you are telling people that it can't be done. So I thought I'd try just using an off-the-shelf blogging engine and see how I get on. Google's blogger service is perhaps the archetypal free blog. It's early days yet, I've only made 13 posts, and at times I find the blogger interface infuriating; it appears to be impossible to get MathML into comments for example, and its editing interface has a habit of "helpfully" inserting `<BR>` tags at random places thus making invalid MathML (or even XHTML) that is being submitted, but it works and they seem to be actively working on it (I just joined after blogger had made a big upgrade to which they have now switched all existing bloggers). So far it's a more or less technical XML-oriented blog; I haven't tried the more discursive style with photographs, family incidents, etc that one finds in some other blogs. Nor have I mentioned TeX yet! As I say, it's early days, I'm not sure yet where the blog is going, if anywhere, we'll see....

DW: Thank you very much for participating in our interview series. If your involvement with W3C ever brings you to its headquarters in Cambridge, Massachusetts, at some point, please let me know so we can meet in person.

Dick Koch

Dick Koch is the creator and lead developer of TeXShop, a renowned front end for TeX on Mac OS X. [Interview completed 12 July 2007.]

Dave Walden, interviewer: Please tell me a bit about your personal history independent of TeX.

Dick Koch, interviewee: I grew up in Haven, Kansas, population 1000. The land there is so flat that you can see all the way to the grain elevator in the next town. I got a scholarship to Harvard because the admission folks thought that Kansas is esoteric, sort of like Kazakhstan. One or two of us might liven up the place. When I left for college, my dad arranged for the Sante Fe train to stop next to a wheat field; we waited in the darkness at midnight with only lights from distant farms visible miles away, until the train appeared and I left Kansas behind.

My first Harvard adviser was in the building housing the original Mark 1 computer, still there in 1957. Harvard said it was the first real computer. After getting a PhD in mathematics from Princeton, I worked at the University of Pennsylvania across the street from the Moore School of Engineering, where the Eniac was made. Penn said it was the first real computer.

I've been teaching mathematics at the University of Oregon since 1966 in the oldest building on campus, Deady Hall. The citizens of Eugene guaranteed that it would last 1000 years when they gave it to the state. It will.

I play harpsichord on an instrument built as a kit, and your readers are very lucky that they will never have to listen.

DW: When and how did you first get involved with TeX?

DK: At Harvard in 1957, I went to a couple of free lectures on programming before deciding to attend a lecture by Robert Frost instead. But I saved the programming handout packet and filed it away. Years later I rediscovered the packet, which explained how to read a paper tape on a Univac by writing assembly code.

No more computing for me until 1978 when I got a Radio Shack TRS-80 and was hooked. In 1984 I got one of the first Macs. But it couldn't be programmed, and two months of MacPaint is enough. Still, I pulled it out of the closet when visitors arrived and explained that it represented the future of computing. In the years after 1986 I learned to program the Mac, even working during a nine month sabbatical at Tektronix as one of three Mac folks in their printer division.

A colleague, Ken Ross, was secretary of the MAA and got a personal demonstration of TeX in Donald Knuth's office shortly after the program was introduced. Knuth told him that a high quality laser printer would cost $100,000, but an adequate printer for drafts might be had for $50,000. Ross reported back to us that we could ignore TeX.

In 1989 I got a NeXT machine. By that time I was old enough to deserve a toy, and it was a NeXT rather than a Ferrari. The idea was to demonstrate it to my friends whose envy would be unbounded. But in practice I never had a successful demo. Mac owners said "it's just like a Mac and why did they put the scroll bars on the left?" Unix people opened a gigantic Terminal window on the screen, typed a few lines, and complained that it didn't have the latest version of curses.

So I gave up on demos. But gradually I discovered that Unix and a GUI make a powerful combination, and that NeXT provided an understated but wonderful working environment.

In the years when it was marketed for academics, the NeXT came with a free TeX including a previewer named TeXview by Tomas Rokicki himself. After a few weeks, I was a TeX fanatic. The NeXT didn't have much software, but for a mathematician it was wonderful. Mathematica and TeX — who could ask for more?

Although I still worked on Macs, my mathematical work was done on the NeXT from 1990 on, and I celebrated wildly on December 20, 1996 when Apple bought NeXT. This meant a free TeX on the Mac. The command line programs would port since "it's just Unix", and Rokicki's source code was available. But then Apple dropped display PostScript and it looked like rough sledding ahead for TeX on OS X.

DW: I'm not sure what you mean when you say "dropped display PostScript." Please say another word about that.

DK: NeXT machines used Display PostScript to draw to the screen. This brought many wonderful consequences: rather than a discrete drawing palette $Z \times Z$, the screen looked like $R \times R$ to a programmer, and its symmetry group was the full affine group rather than just rotations and reflections by multiples of 90 degrees. Adobe Type 1 fonts were used for text on the screen, and any drawing or text could be rotated arbitrarily on the screen.

Another advantage was that the same PostScript language drew to the screen and the printer, so anomalies when printing vanished. NeXT's printer was quite inexpensive because it didn't need PostScript — the computer rasterized images for it.

At the first developer conference after Apple bought NeXT, the company revealed plans to base Mac OS X on NeXTStep. In particular, the Mac would use Display PostScript as an imaging model, and adopt NeXT's object oriented programming system that was based on Objective C and a class library later named Cocoa,

But Apple had a difficult time convincing programmers to adopt this model. All of the major developers like Microsoft and Adobe were noncommittal. So a year later at the next developer conference, Apple's plans changed considerably. Instead of Cocoa, the company announced and pushed the Carbon programming model, which was essentially the old Mac OS 9 programming system modified in small ways to support Unix and its multitasking environment. Although they didn't make a big deal of it, Apple dropped Display PostScript in favor of a new graphic environment to be developed based on PDF. These major changes postponed the introduction of Mac OS X by a year or more.

The switch from Cocoa to Carbon was particularly significant. I wrote several NeXT programs, so I knew that Cocoa was a jewel. In contrast, Apple's system 9 had become more and more baroque and Carbon didn't look much better. About this time I got a chance to go to a developer conference. Great masses of programmers attended Carbon sections, but the Cocoa sessions, sparsely attended, were run by former NeXT engineers who seemed to be hanging on by the skin of their teeth.

I believe the success of TeXShop is partly due to my one programming advantage: I knew from the beginning that Cocoa would be the future of the Mac. It took many years for the majority of Mac programmers to come to this conclusion.

Let me come back to that new graphic system, now called Quartz. At the time, the announcement of this system was a great disappointment because it meant that Apple would not use Display PostScript. But it gradually became clear to me that Quartz was as powerful as Display PostScript, and its introduction meant that PDF would be fundamental for Mac OS X, easy to create, and trivial to display.

DW: You said "it looked like rough sledding ahead for TEX on OS X," but you are well known for TeXShop (`http://www.uoregon.edu/~koch/texshop/texshop.html`), so obviously you either decided to take things into your own hands or somehow got roped into taking things into your own hands. Please tell us about how that came about.

DK: I have spent a lot of time on NeXT and Cocoa because it is intimately connected to the history of TeXShop.

By the early 1990's I had come to depend on four NeXT programs: TEX, Mathematica, Mail, and a Web browser. Although I didn't mention it earlier, I was writing a certain amount of Macintosh software and used a Mac regularly for graphics and other tasks.

The sale to Apple meant that these two worlds could come together. I was so excited by the prospect that I switched to Mac OS X while it was still in deep beta mode, two or three years before the actual release. I only needed Mail, which was part of OS X, a Web browser, but Omniweb soon appeared on OS X, Mathematica, but Wolfram was one of the few developers committed to OS X, Cocoa, but that existed even if it wasn't promoted, and TEX. In short, I'd be in heaven as soon as TEX made it to the beta OS X.

After only a couple of months on OS X beta, I discovered a TEX distribution for it. This was pre-Gerben Wierda, and I have forgotten the details. Perhaps it went something like this: someone ported TEX to the PowerPC version of NeXTStep, producing a NeXT install package; I tried to use this package on OS X but it wouldn't open in Apple's installer; then I discovered that the package could be opened as a directory containing a pax file. I had never heard of pax files, but man pages told me that they were sort of like tar files, so I used a Unix command and surprisingly got a working TEX distribution. Something like that!

The trouble with this working TEX is that it produced DVI files and I had no DVI previewer. So no cigar. But then, quite by accident, I discovered that one of the command line programs installed was pdfTEX, and pdfTEX output pdf files rather than DVI files. This was the single most important discovery of my entire TEX adventure because PDF is the native graphic format on OS X. So instantly I could preview TEX files produced by the TEX distribution. The inventor of pdfTEX, Hàn Thế Thành, became my hero. To be sure, it was a shock to realize that the current version of his software was 0.14! But gradually I realized that version 0.14 worked fine.

For a while, I edited files with Apple's Edit, typeset from the command line, and previewed using Apple's Preview. It was awkward, but it sort of worked, and showed that an adequate TEX must be just around the corner (modulo a serious glitch I'll explain in a moment).

So by a miracle I had TEX and only needed a front end. In the next years as I worked on TeXShop, Gerben Wierda appeared and produced an honest TEX distribution designed specifically for OS X. At the time I didn't know how important Gerben would become, but it was certainly a relief to have the real thing.

At first I believed that a TEX front end would appear soon after his work. I kept asking my Apple representative, who assured me that Apple understood the importance of TEX. But nothing seemed to materialize.

Then I had a chance in 2000 to go to WWDC, the Apple developer conference. I was still teaching at the University, but my assignment was Discrete Mathematics, a required course for computer science majors, so that seemed to justify the trip (!!). Sitting in the sparsely attended sessions on Cocoa, I began to realize that it might not be difficult to do a TeX front end myself.

After I was back from the conference and school ended, I began experimenting. For a front end, I'd need an editing window, a preview window, and a typesetting command which connected the two. A third party editor could be used, but I couldn't figure out how to get that third party editor to call TeX and typeset. On the other hand, making an edit window is trivial with Cocoa, and adding a typesetting button to my own program was easy. So TeXShop got an edit window because I was lazy.

To call TeX from my Cocoa program, I needed an appropriate Cocoa command. About a half hour's work of thumbing through the Cocoa documentation led to the `NSTask` class, which makes it trivial to call Unix programs from within a Cocoa program. An hour later I was typesetting.

Finally I needed to display the result. Everything depended on Cocoa's facilities to display PDF files. Could Cocoa open a PDF and tell me the number of pages? Yes. Could it be instructed to display page 15? Yes. Indeed, a little reading showed that all of the necessary commands were present in the three or four pages describing classes to display PDF. After that, finishing the first version of TeXShop came quickly.

A short time later, I released the program under the GNU free software license. I don't know the date of the first release, but my guess is that it was in the summer of 2000, when the essentially free "public beta" of OS X was available, but before the first official release version.

However, there was one "minor" problem: Apple's PDF display routines could not interpret fonts embedded in a pdf file. They only worked if the font was one of the standard OS X fonts installed by default. Thus a TeX document typeset fine with TeXShop, with only the following mild restrictions:

1. main text must be Times Roman
2. no mathematical symbols allowed

As a stopgap, I added an alternative preview mode to TeXShop. Rather than using Cocoa to display the output PDF, it could call Ghostscript to rasterize this PDF file to a bitmap and then display the bitmap. This worked, but the result was much slower and much fuzzier than direct Cocoa display of the PDF. Slowly, a few users on the network began typesetting with TeXShop in that "fuzzy mode".

In March of 2001, Apple released the first official version of OS X. I now know that this release was called "Cheetah", although I began learning cat names quite a lot later. To the annoyance of developers, there was no prerelease version to test until a couple of weeks before the official release. I recall my excitement when I realized that Cheetah could display embedded fonts — suddenly TeXShop worked. There was just time before the official Cheetah release to rip out that alternative preview mode.

DW: I see from your university web site (`http://cc.uoregon.edu/cnews/summer2002/koch.html`) that Apple gave you an award for TeXShop. Do you think TeXShop (and perhaps XeTeX) are increasing the popularity of the Mac for TeX use, particularly among mathematicians?

DK: No.

Sometime between 1990 and 1995, TeX captured the mathematical world completely. It was a revolution. Before that revolution, mathematicians wrote in longhand and departments had a platoon of mathematical typists; after the revolution the typists were gone and virtually all mathematicians used TEX. I watched that revolution at the University of Oregon. At first our new hires all used TEX, sometimes on the Mac and sometimes on Linux machines. Soon the older faculty switched. At about the same time, graduate students switched to TEX for everything from quizzes to conference talks.

The last people to switch were older faculty. Often they made the change when they began a book project. But even here the revolution was complete. I helped some of these faculty buy a new machine and answered questions about "cutting and pasting" for weeks. I thought to myself "if even the fundamentals of computing cause this much trouble, it will be hopeless to get this guy to learn TEX." But after a few days explaining TeXShop or another program, I found that mathematicians take to TEX like ducks to water. It speaks their language. I got lots of computer support questions, but essentially never about TEX.

My first TUG meetings were a great surprise — listening to talks about "does TEX have a future?" I gradually learned that switching to TEX in other fields is controversial, and dealing with academic journals can be difficult. All of these problems seem foreign to a mathematician.

I am proud that TeXShop (and TEX and many other related programs) are free; this makes it easier to introduce mathematical undergraduates to TEX. At Oregon, we have a small center for undergraduates; students writing honors theses tend to pick up TEX from older undergraduate peers. The standard question "how do I get TEX on my own machine?" has easy answers on Windows, Linux, and the Mac.

Over the years I've had interesting interactions with users outside mathematics. Many developments, certainly including XeTEX and ConTEXt, make TEX attractive to these users. From my vantage point, the TEX world is very dynamic and active.

DW: You have had many collaborators; they are listed in TeXShop's "About Panel" and elsewhere. Please tell me about these collaborations.

DK: TeXShop is provided with source code, so users proficient in Cocoa can easily add features. Over the years, many of these features were sent back to me and integrated into the program. This includes many of the "power user" features because I am not such a user myself. By power user features I mean things like auto completion, command completion, macros, and AppleScript support.

This collaboration was done very informally; I'm sure it has been frustrating for some contributors. The main attribute contributors need is persistence, because I often ignore email when I'm working on something else and "no answer" doesn't mean "I don't want it." Let me tell a story to illustrate that point.

Geoffroy Lenglin was a master's degree student in Aeronautical Engineering at MIT. He sent a "LATEX Panel" which lists mathematical symbols; clicking on a symbol inserted the corresponding TEX code in the source file. I thought the panel was important as soon as I saw it and sent Lenglin some encouraging words. But I was teaching at the time, so nothing happened. Common courtesy would require sending an explanation of the delay, but no such message was sent. Maybe six months later, spring break arrived and I got around to integrating Lenglin's code into the program. When I wrote Lenglin asking if I could list his name in the contributor list, he wrote back "thank goodness you wrote; I finished my degree and am leaving for a job in France, and this email address will be active for four more days."

I will not list numerous other such cases out of embarrassment. If some of your readers contributed something and got no response, they should write now. I will specifically mention another two or three participants in this informal collaboration.

Nicolas Ojeda Bar was a high school student in Argentina who sent code to preserve source code tab indents. When TeXShop won an Apple Design Award, I converted the computer equipment into money and distributed funds to the contributors. Bar got a small amount, and asked for an Amazon gift account due to Argentina's financial crises at the time. I was delighted to learn that he bought theoretical mathematics books!

Mitsuhiro Shishikura is an important theoretical mathematician in Japan. His collaboration is a model for the type of interaction I prefer. Shishikura revised the PDF display code to permit continuous scrolling through pages, side-by-side display, and many other features. He added a magnifying glass, which I wanted desperately. When the Tiger operating system from Apple appeared, much of Shishikura's code could be replaced by code from Apple's PDFKit framework, but that framework was virtually isomorphic to Shishikura's approach, a great compliment to him. The vital magnifying glass code still comes from Shishikura.

When Shishikura made his modifications, he sent a revised code base so I could immediately experiment with his modifications. The modifications were carefully set off with comments, and I could pick and choose what to use and what to avoid. Shishikura sent a detailed document listing exactly what he had changed and why. This made it very easy to add his modifications with certainty that I understood what he had done. Thanks, Mitsuhiro.

It is easy to work with collaborators when they make one addition, possibly in several different files, and clearly explain the change. A few programmers work globally, making many changes at once and even changing the program interface in dramatic ways.... In these cases I have to either accept or reject the entire change because it isn't possible to pick and choose. I've found it impossible to deal with that approach. Some of these proposed changes were probably excellent, but I couldn't digest them. If I adopted the change, I'd no longer understand the code.

It isn't my goal to be fair here by listing colleagues in order of importance. But I must list one recent worker, Max Horn, who has had to suffer through long email silences just like everyone else. Horn rewrote large sections of TeXShop, cleaning up the code dramatically, and improving the speed of the program in several important ways. But miraculously, I still understand his code; and making changes is as easy as it ever was. Horn managed to preserve all of the important method calls and procedures. It is sort of mysterious that he could revise so much and still make me happy. The current version of TeXShop uses Horn's revisions.

DW: I looked you up in the Mathematical Genealogy Project (`http://genealogy.math.ndsu.nodak.edu`) database and see that you are descended only a few generations from David Hilbert! This brought a question to mind. Do you think the availability of high quality mathematical typesetting has significantly changed mathematics or how it is done? Would someone like Bernoulli have been able to write more papers if he had TEX available to him, or was he better off without it?

DK: My previous comments apply here. I don't think that Bernoulli would have written more, and to use the extreme case, I don't think Euler would have written more. But I think they would have have seen TEX as a completely natural tool.

DW: There is a lot of talk these days about the new version of Word having better math typesetting capabilities. Do you think TEX will still continue to hold its own (minor) position in the mathematical-document preparation market.

DK: My department has one Word user, and the rest of us use TEX. So I'm afraid the question doesn't interest me.

Incidentally, nobody in my department promotes TEX. This would be considered unseemly. They just use it, on various operating systems, and get on with their mathematical lives.

DW: To what extent, if any, is there coordination of the TeXShop effort with the XeTeX effort?

DK: I think Jonathan's work is very, very exciting. But so far there has been just a little coordination. I added the "engine" architecture and the ability to set a file's encoding using a line at the top of the source code when I saw the harder instructions Jonathan provided. Later I added a template for XeLaTeX to encourage its use, and Jonathan criticized my initial attempt and provided a reasonable template.

I should add that Jonathan went to WWDC this year and I saw him in several sessions. He is always bubbling with ideas, and some of these ideas will make it into TeXShop. So in the future .... The trouble is that I can absorb about one idea a day and Jonathan can provide two or three an hour.

DW: Does your TeX work get support, or at least encouragement, from your university? You obviously have done lots of development related to TeX; how do you fit that in with your academic responsibilities and ambitions?

DK: The department has been great. For a number of years I was head undergraduate adviser and spent a lot of time working with undergraduates, so my TeX work may have seemed an extension of this sort of "academic service work". I understand the thrust of your question, which can be a real problem for younger faculty, but it hasn't been a problem for me.

DW: I have one last question. You have mentioned Mathematica several times, but I'm not sure what it does. How is Mathematica used in combination with TeX by a mathematician?

DK: Mathematica is a symbolic mathematics program, able to perform algebraic manipulations, integrate symbolically, solve differential equations, and graph in two and three dimensions. It is one of a small number of such programs; others include Maple and Macsyma.

I often use Mathematica to create TeX illustrations. But it really is a complementary tool: TeX for writing mathematics, Mathematica for symbolic calculations, and the blackboard for serious work!

DW: Thank you very much for participating in this interview. Even though I am not an OS X user myself, I can tell by the buzz in the air that there is a lot of excitement among TeX users about TeX and OS X and that your contributions are very much part of that excitement.

Oleg Katsitadze

Oleg Katsitadze maintains Eplain (`http://svn.tug.org/eplain`) and is a contributor to Texinfo (`http://www.gnu.org/software/texinfo`).
[Interview completed 4 August 2007.]

Dave Walden, interviewer: Please tell me a bit about your personal history independent of TEX.

Oleg Katsitadze, interviewee: I grew up in Dushanbe, Tajikistan, where I completed two years of Systems Engineering in a polytechnic school. This was the closest to computer science they offered, and by that time programming had already been my passion for quite a while.

This was a time of political and economical instability in Tajikistan following the collapse of the Soviet Union, and I had to drop out in 1998 when my family decided to move. After we moved to Simferopol, Ukraine, I had to work for several years to help support my family. It was only in 2002 that I enrolled as a computer science major, and this year (2007) I finally got my MS.

Oh, and I almost forgot to mention one of the best experiences of my life — while in high school, I spent the 1994–95 school year in the US as an exchange student. I lived in LaPorte and Michigan City, both in Indiana.

DW: How did your being an exchange student to the United States come about?

OK: This program was part of the Freedom Support Act (FSA) of the US Congress, and that was its second year in Tajikistan. Although it was called an "exchange program", there was no exchange, it was one-sided. Selection was merit-based — students had to take a series of English language exams based on TOEFL, and those deemed best got a chance to live in the US for one year, with a monthly scholarship and travel expenses paid by the US government.

DW: Your English is so good and so Americanized; did you spend more time in the United States later? And might you visit the US again at some point? I'd love to meet you in person.

OK: No, I've never been to the US after that program, but I really liked it there — economically, of course, but also culturally. Strangely, I felt more at home there than I do here. Although this is getting increasingly difficult, I'm anxious to live and work in the US. It'll be my pleasure to meet you, if I ever succeed in getting to the US.

DW: I presume you already knew a good bit of English before doing your exchange year in the United States. Was the study of English a standard part of the school curriculum in Tajikistan? I assume you also had to study Russian and the Tajik (?) language; did you also have to learn Ukrainian when you got to Ukraine?

OK: Yes, I studied English for seven years as a standard part of the curriculum. This is standard practice — high-school students have to take a foreign language, usually with a choice between English and German, sometimes also French. Of course, I was studying

English a good deal on my own, mostly just reading books — otherwise I'd never have passed the exam.

Russian was mandatory in all high schools in the Soviet Union. In most regions a local language (Tajik for me) was also mandatory, but with fewer hours allocated and a much lower standard of teaching. Even though I officially took, I think, three or four years of Tajik, at the end I knew next to no Tajik. (Tajik is a dialect of Persian, by the way.)

I also had to take the mandatory three semesters, one hour every two weeks, of Ukrainian at the university in Simferopol, but of course, that was not enough to acquire a working knowledge of a language. Besides, the Crimea region where I live is historically Russian-speaking, so I didn't get to practice Ukrainian in real life (and I don't watch television). I can understand Ukrainian quite well, but this is mostly because Russian and Ukrainian are very similar.

DW: Can you say something about what it was like to live through the collapse of the Soviet Union, how your family chose Ukraine to go to, was there physical danger in the move, etc.?

OK: Well, I must say this was the experience of a lifetime for my family. By the end, we had surely seen some action.

As soon as Tajikistan became independent, a civil war broke out, with several clans fighting to gain control over the country. This resulted in shortages of food, gas and electricity, and of course, lower and in some cases no incomes for people. I remember standing in queues for 4–5 hours to buy bread, sometimes at night, and using candles for lighting. We had to sell off some of our old clothes and utensils to buy food.

Of course, being a teenager, it didn't seem so bad — it was fun watching tracer bullets at night zipping over our roof, and skipping school for weeks on end because of the military action in the city (this was the best part :). Once my brother, who's two years younger than me, was let by the soldiers inside a tank which was guarding a television station nearby; I was so sorry I wasn't with him. Our neighbor had a fragment of an artillery shell stuck in his roof — cool! Another time, an adventurous woman from our neighborhood decided to go check out the situation, and when she was about 500 yards away from home, a skirmish started, so she had to crawl all the way back home, being a plump woman. Seemed funny at the time. Good thing she didn't get hurt.

After having so much fun my family decided to emigrate to Georgia, my dad's native country (*not* the state of Georgia in the US), but were unsuccessful, and so we had to travel back to Tajikistan. We were lucky we didn't (couldn't) sell our apartment in Tajikistan before we left, so we had a place to come back to. On the way back we found ourselves landed on the Caspian shore with no money and the Karakum Desert to cross. Fortunately, we were traveling together with an old woman who said she was happy to pay our fare if we took care of all arrangements for her, like finding a hotel room, buying train tickets, etc. If not for that woman, I'd probably be herding dromedaries in Turkmenistan now.

After the civil war had more-or-less subsided and we could sell our apartment for something more than the cost of traveling out of Tajikistan, we decided to move to Crimea. The choice was mostly arbitrary — we didn't have any relatives or friends there, and hadn't even once been there before — but we'd heard that apartments were cheaper there than, say, in Russia, while universities still taught in Russian. So this is how I ended up in Simferopol.

As for the physical danger in traveling — the return on our first trip (from Georgia) was rather risky, because we had to go by train across Central Asia and the times were really crazy — thousands of people moving back and forth, overcrowded trains, troops all around. If we disappeared, no one would notice or care. But the trip to Ukraine was much less exciting because we took an airplane to Moscow and skipped the dangerous part of the trip.

DW: I'm curious about how programming first became your passion — how and at what age did you come upon programming in Tajikistan?

OK: The first time I saw a computer was at the age of ten, I think, at the place where my mother used to work, at the computer center of the Ministry of Communications of Tajikistan (she was an economist, not a programmer). One of her co-workers, a programmer, let me play Digger (`http://en.wikipedia.org/wiki/Digger_(computer_game)`) on one of the PCs they had, and I was instantly and completely hooked.

Later, my dad gave in to the incessant pestering and purchased "Partner", a Russian-made 8-bit microcomputer. It was an Intel i8080 clone with 32Kb RAM and no graphics card. At that time I mostly played games, but also did a little BASIC programming, learning from some book or manual, I don't remember now what it was exactly.

Some time later my dad bought "Poisk", a Ukrainian-made i8088 clone, mainly for typing and printing some documents for his job. For me it was a huge improvement — it had a CGA card, good for games :).

When I was about 14, our school introduced a new course, Informatics and Computers. This immediately became my favorite course, I couldn't get enough of it — we only had it once a week. I took every extracurricular programming course the school offered. This is when I really started learning programming, and I spent most of my free time in front of Poisk.

DW: When and how did you first get involved with TeX?

OK: This was in 2002, I think. At the time I was switching from MS Windows to GNU/Linux and I had to find a way to create and print simple documents, to replace MS Word. I remember trying OpenOffice (or was it StarOffice then?), but after it crashed on me twice within 30 seconds of starting up, I gave up, and now I'm glad I did. (Not that OO is bad — it's just different.)

I'd heard that TeX was the typesetting engine used by the GNU Project for its documentation, so I decided to give it a try. For about a year it was nothing much — mostly exercises from *The TeXbook*, and an occasional one- or two-page document.

But then I enrolled at the university and had an opportunity to try TeX at something bigger. There was severe shortage of textbooks at the library, and new books were hard to find and too expensive for most students. So I decided to typeset an old textbook on differential equations that was used in the course I was then taking.

I was soon overwhelmed with the amount of work required to develop the macros for cross-references, table of contents, etc., so I started looking for a macro package. I might have used LaTeX, but one of the purposes of this exercise was to learn TeX, and I felt LaTeX, although much friendlier for the task, would happily help me ignore too many low-level details. So I came across Eplain (`http://svn.tug.org/eplain`), and it looked just like what I needed.

It took me over a year to typeset a 300-page book (A5), but one thing is for sure — I learned TeX quite well, and differential equations beyond the course requirements :).

DW: What language was the book typeset in? More generally, have you been using TeX for the various different languages you know?

OK: It was in Russian. Besides Russian and English, I used TeX for Ukrainian. Ukrainian, like Russian, uses the Cyrillic alphabet, with four additional letters compared to Russian.

DW: Was the book published?

OK: Oh, no, I didn't do it for publishing. I just put it up on the Web so that anybody could download it, together with the sources in case someone would want to improve it/make corrections. It's still there, by the way, at `http://geolsoft.freeshell.org/elsgolts.diff.ur.var.is`.

DW: Today you maintain Eplain and I know you help or have helped Karl Berry in a couple of other areas. How did those activities come about?

OK: One of the goals for the differential equations textbook I mentioned was to make it an ebook with hyperlinked cross-references. The choice of the PDF output format was easy, of course, but unlike LaTeX, Eplain had no support or provisions for hyperlinks. I was hoping I could write a macro package to be loaded after Eplain, which would add the hypertext capabilities to Eplain macros. This turned out to be unrealistic — on many occasions I had to copy the original macros from Eplain just to add a couple of my own lines in the middle, so if such an Eplain macro was changed later, my modified macro would fail or break some other Eplain macros.

Hence I suggested to Karl that I add the hypertext support directly to Eplain, and he was very enthusiastic about this (and provided invaluable assistance, by the way). Naturally, I had to delve deep into Eplain source code to do what I wanted, so I became familiar with it.

Then one day Karl asked me if I'd want to take over Eplain maintenance, and it seemed like fun to me, so I agreed.

Occasionally, when Karl was overloaded with the many things he does, he asked me to deal with some bug reports for the `texinfo.tex` macro package from the Texinfo documentation system (`http://www.gnu.org/software/texinfo`). Then, during summer holidays of 2006 I had some free time, so I asked Karl what he'd suggest for a summer project. He said that `texinfo.tex` badly needed support for different input and font encodings, so I went on with this project. A by-product was a more flexible font management system; the current one focuses on Computer Modern fonts and does not accumulate font face changes. By the end of the summer this was mostly complete as a set of standalone macros, not yet integrated with `texinfo.tex`. Unfortunately, since then I've had very little time to work on `texinfo.tex`, and the project is still underway.

DW: Should I infer that now that you have graduated, you have a job that takes precedence?

OK: Yes, I have a job now which takes almost all of my time. It is a programming job — writing a sprite-based game for video game machines. I'm not part of any free software projects other than Texinfo and Eplain, unfortunately — simply no time for that.

DW: Is this for a Ukrainian-based game company, or is the game company somewhere else in the world and hires Ukrainian programmers as part of "globalization"?

OK: This is a very recent local start-up (this is their first game) and the game is for the local market. But globalization did reach Simferopol — there are several locally owned companies which take orders from Western companies and hire local programmers to do the job. Because wages here are much lower, software development costs drop tens of times. This is a booming industry right now in Simferopol. The companies usually try to get graduates or last-year students from universities, but they will hire *anybody*; they even provide training if needed.

DW: Do you foresee continuing to be involved with TeX; and, if so, will you strictly stick to Eplain, or might you drift into LaTeX, ConTeXt, LuaTeX, etc., at some point?

OK: Of course, as much as the time permits, I'll stay involved with TeX. I still have some unfinished business with Eplain and Texinfo :). As for LaTeX, ConTeXt, etc., they are all very interesting projects, but I don't see where I'm going to find the time to participate, not in the foreseeable future anyway. I hope they stay around until I do find the time :).

DW: Thank you for participating in our interview series. Your story is fascinating, and your diving in to maintain one of the key TeX systems is laudable.

[Endnote: at the end of 2007, Oleg immigrated to the USA and is very happy to now be living in Portland, Oregon, and working for a division of HP.]

Jim Hefferon

Jim Hefferon is one of the key maintainers of CTAN and a member of the TUG board.
[Interview completed 13 August 2007.]

Dave Walden, interviewer: Please tell me a bit about your personal history independent of TEX.

Jim Hefferon, interviewee: I'm in the Math Department at Saint Michael's College, in the vicinity of Burlington, Vermont. I'm married and have two sons. In my free time I like to jog and to do ham radio.

DW: That's an interesting combination of hobbies — first run and then sit? What kind(s) of ham radio do you do?

JH: I do both voice and Morse code, although I like the code better. I am trying to bring my words-per-minute up to where I can compete in contests.

For me running is a meditation. Usually when I leave for a run I have a lot of brain chatter but when I come back it is gone. Many times I have had a math problem, or a coding problem, or a writing problem, and gone for a run. When I come back then I have the perspective to understand the problem.

DW: What sorts of math do you teach at Saint Michael's?

JH: St. Mike's is a liberal arts school, with about 2000 undergraduates and no graduate program in Math. I often teach service courses such as elementary statistics in addition to major's courses such as Abstract Algebra.

DW: Please tell me about how you first became involved with TEX?

JH: I wrote my PhD thesis using a commercial product. They sent me an ad promising that some aspect of their new version would be " ... as good as TEX." So when I wrote my *Linear Algebra* (available at `http://joshua.smcvt.edu/linearalgebra`) I thought to try it in TEX.

DW: What was your PhD topic?

JH: My thesis was in the Theory of Computation (Recursion Theory). It is a fun topic to think about, although I don't have as much time to think about it today as I would like. Once a year I get to teach a course on the topic for the CS majors. I'm considering using the experience from teaching that course to write a book for it, but we'll see.

DW: How did that first try with TEX—writing a math book—go?

JH: My first experience with TEX was illuminating. I had a visiting job at Union College. Their computer people were very kind and agreed to help me get the files that I needed—it seems incredible now but at that time no one had ever ftp-ed. But we got the materials from `labrea` and installed.

Then I had to make output. I had only Lamport's book. I decided to try a letter. But everything that I tried gave me the same error message, something like "I'm stumped. Ask your local guru." I often reflect on that experience: the author's assumption that there was anyone around that I could ask told me that he lived in a world very much different than I do.

That is, it was illuminating for me to encounter the culture in which TEX lives, with of course all its assumptions of shared experiences and ideas. It is a culture that I admire, but it is very different from the general culture. For instance, people at St. Mike's typically don't know what an "editor" is, including the CS students (they use integrated graphical interfaces for coding).

DW: Did you move to St. Michael's from Union College or were there other stops along the way?

JH: I worked for a while for a defense contractor, but I have been here since 1990.

DW: You say that people at St. Michael's typically don't use a traditional editor? Does that mean they also don't use TEX, or is TEX also used via an integrated development environment?

JH: The Math faculty use TEX, and another person or two. But the use is declining, that I can see. I don't think students would encounter it at all.

DW: You yourself have gotten pretty deeply involved in the TEX world, for example, involved in CTAN maintenance and a member of the TUG board. How did that come about?

JH: When I used TEX for my book, I found that I admired the design choices and that I admired the people who were working to keep the software available and alive. At that time things in computing looked dark. Most people had Windows 3.11, which was astoundingly bad, and sometimes I worried that what I enjoyed about computing—elegance and power—could go away.

But one day I read a post by Tim Murphy (I think) saying that this "Linux" thing was great for running TEX and people should try it. I downloaded it—Slackware with a pre-1.0 kernel version packaged on seventy-five floppies—and got it to run. It was indeed great: suddenly I could accomplish things. So I wanted to give back. St. Michael's was kind enough to let me offer a CTAN mirror, which means they gave me an Internet address and agreed to support the traffic (it isn't much but they didn't know that).

Then I helped Karl Berry out with some web stuff for the North American core CTAN site and he asked me if I would take on running that site. St. Michael's again graciously agreed to handle the traffic. The other core maintainers, Rainer Schöpf and Robin Fairbairns, have also helped me a great deal.

I'm happy also to be able to do what I can on the TUG board, although in truth mostly Karl does the work.

DW: I see from your web site (`http://joshua.smcvt.edu/math/hefferon.html`) that your Linear Algebra book is available for download for as is your monograph on Number

Theory. Were either of these ever available from a regular publisher and, if not, what was your motivation for writing them and making them available for free?

JH: I've sometimes talked to publishers about the Linear Algebra book, and being able to distribute it that way would be great. But it has also been great to get emails from people in far-away places who say that the fact that it is freely available has made it available to them. (Let me note that Number Theory's main author is W. Edwin Clark; my version is just a revision that I made working with him.)

DW: I'm seeing a few books these days that are available commercially from real publishers as well via free downloads. Two books from Lawrence Lessig come to mind: *Free Culture* (`http://www.free-culture.cc/freecontent/`) and *Code version 2.0* (`http://codev2.cc/`). Of course, the latter, a revision of his earlier *Code* book, was developed via a wiki with help from many people; also, of course, he is a zealot for the Creative Commons Licenses (`http://creativecommons.org/license/`), etc. I suppose the average college level math book does not have such a wide potential audience that the publisher would be willing to simultaneously allow free downloads.

JH: Googling "free math book" gives some very good choices. Also, an open book has advantages. I offer the LaTeX source so people do translations to other languages a line at a time, keeping the math (so far, I know of Portuguese, Italian, and Chinese). Another person made a wiki out of the source.

DW: How about any book you write on Theory of Computation — will that be produced and available the same way?

JH: I don't know. It is really just an idea at this point. For content I'm thinking about talking more than is usual about the ideas underlying the course (in the course as I run it now, I try to get students thinking about ideas by requiring them to read *Gödel, Escher, Bach* by Hofstadter), to start with Turing machines instead of Finite State machines, and to do the constructions by coding in Scheme. I haven't thought at all about how I would offer it. We'll see if it ever gets done.

DW: Please tell me more about CTAN, its mirrors, its coordination among the administrators involved, and its on-going and potential development.

JH: The Comprehensive TeX Archive Network is the Internet repository of materials for TeX and friends. There are three core sites where things are added or deleted, and now about a hundred and fifty sites that mirror those materials and in turn make them available to their visitors.

The core sites are: `dante.ctan.org` run by Rainer in Germany, `cam.ctan.org` run by Robin in Great Britain, and `tug.ctan.org` run by me in the US. We work together closely, perhaps twenty to thirty emails a week.

For each of us, people upload materials and we install it. That means checking the package authorship and license, checking that the file tree looks right (it has a README file and documentation, for instance), updating the package description database, some other details, and finally installing the material to the file tree. The installation script causes the other two core sites to quickly retrieve the new package, and then the other mirrors usually grab it within a day.

My big project for some time has been to automate more of the process. Perhaps ninety percent of the cases go the same way and it seems possible to build a system that a person could manage by pushing buttons in a web interface instead of by typing command-line commands.

There are two problems with this. The first is that when I started I knew nothing about the technologies and so the learning period has been long. The second is that having ninety percent of the cases go the same way is like having a watch that is right ninety percent of the time — you mostly worry about the other ten percent!

Nonetheless, I'm under the delusion that we will soon have up a beta system. I hope that it makes the work easier to accomplish; that's the test.

DW: How do you see TEX's prospects more generally?

JH: It is up to us; it depends on the energy that we develop around the technology. People are getting more sophisticated about computers and we have the chance to show them the better way. Also, a source of excitement for TEX now is that there are so many developments: modern TEXs don't have the arbitrary restrictions of the original programs, we can now produce a beautiful web-friendly PDF with ease, we are seeing solutions to the font issues that frustrate even reasonably skilled users, and people are developing for the future with projects such as LuaTEX.

But a development burst isn't sufficient. If, say, a Physics graduate student is assigned to make a lab manual, do they think of LATEX? Certainly if they tried LATEX and found that setting up the desired font was too hard then they'd go on to something else, so the new stuff is crucial. But having that person think first of TEX requires more; we have to help average potential users to see all the great things.

As I've talked about above, personally I am interested in the challenges faced by people who feel isolated and I'd like to help them see how TEX can solve some of their problems. For instance, on CTAN I have been taking some steps to help novices navigate the holdings. Another example is that I've written articles for *TUGboat* and *The PracTEX Journal* that are aimed at the level above novice, because I'd like to help develop some "local gurus".

DW: I've read some of what you've written, and they seem very useful to me, e.g.,

- "LATEX documentation pointers" (http://mirror.ctan.org/info/latex-doc-ptr)
- "Getting something out of LATEX" (http://mirror.ctan.org/info/first-latex-doc)
- "LATEX resources" (http://tug.org/TUGboat/Articles/tb28-1/tb88heff.pdf)
- "Minutes in less than hours: Using LATEX resources" (http://tug.org/TUGboat/Articles/tb26-3/tb84heff.pdf)
- "CTAN for starters" (http://tug.org/TUGboat/Articles/tb25-2/tb81heff.pdf)
- "Why TEX?" (http://tug.org/TUGboat/Articles/tb22-1-2/tb70heff.pdf)

I also know from watching the video of your presentation at TUG 07 (http://www.river-valley.tv/conferences/tex/tug2007/) and the related article (http://tug.org/TUGboat/Articles/tb29-1/tb91heff.pdf) that you put a tremendous amount of effort into CTAN for the benefit of us all.

Thank you for participating in this interview.

Rainer Schöpf

Rainer Schöpf was a co-founder of the $\LaTeX\,2_\varepsilon$ and CTAN projects, and is still a key maintainer of CTAN. [Interview completed 27 August 2007.]

Dave Walden, interviewer: Please tell me a bit about your personal history independent of TEX.

Rainer Schöpf, interviewee: I grew up in a town not far away from the city of Mainz, and consequently I went to university there, studying physics. When I started my studies I couldn't think of doing anything else, although I didn't have a very clear idea of what I would do later. My specialty was elementary particle physics; I did a PhD thesis in string theory — a very hot topic in the mid-eighties.

During my thesis I spent a lot of time on playing with computers, one topic in particular being computer algebra. REDUCE was what some theoretical physicists used, so I became involved with the people developing it. I spent a year at the University of Heidelberg, but realized early that this wasn't what I wanted to do. This was in spring 1990 — half a year after the Berlin wall came down. I combined a trip to the reunified city with a visit to the Konrad-Zuse-Zentrum für Informationstechnik Berlin — and soon had a new job doing computer algebra and combined symbolic-numeric methods.

Unfortunately, this was only a temporary position, until 1994. I found another job, again in Mainz at the university computing centre, supporting the Unix systems. At that time, Linux was still a rather new system, lacking many of the features that the more mature commercial Unices offered. There were a lot of them: if I remember correctly we supported nine or ten different computer architectures. 64-bit systems were new; a lot of software didn't work very well in 64-bit mode. For example, I spent a few days trying to find out why Ghostscript wouldn't run on the DEC Alpha with OSF/1. Of course, it always came down to tacit assumptions on the programmer's side: casting pointers to ints and back, assuming that pointers are 32-bits long, assumptions about signedness, and so on.

The six years I worked there were an exciting time, because many old assumptions about how computers are used changed: they brought the rise of Windows and Linux as real operating systems, more or less pushing everything else out of the mainstream; the coming of the World Wide Web, and SPAM. At the same time, many good ideas and systems were abandoned (too many to list).

In 2000, I joined the newly founded biotech company ProteoSys, where I still work, doing systems support and developing specialized software.

DW: When and how did you first get involved with TEX?

RS: Around 1983 or 84, I'm not sure. My first contact was an article in the DFG-Nachrichten, the printed newsletter of the Deutsche Forschungsgesellschaft (German Research Foundation). I was intrigued by the report of that group in Bonn. Some time later, I came to know Roderich Schupp, a student from the math department. He had somehow managed to get hold of TEX and get it running on the Multics university computer system. However, there was no output device suitable for TEX, so he wrote a DVI interpreter in PL/1 that drove the hardcopy device for the HP graphics terminals. Can you imagine printing 300 dpi output on such a 50 dpi device? It was loud, it was slow, and it produced sheets with only part of a page. I typed my diploma theses with a typewriter.

Over time, the situation improved. The physics institute acquired their own new VAX/VMS computer system with two DEC LN03 laser printers. Now we could produce DEK's "masterpieces of the typesetting art".

During that time I met "this other guy from the math department who supported TEX there", Frank Mittelbach. He often came over to our institute, it was in the next building, and we physicists had larger workrooms (ours had been intended as a lab), and always a cup of tea ready.

DW: Did you eventually begin to use TEX as well as support it?

RS: Oh yes. This came with TEX for the Atari ST series of computers. I bought my first Atari 1040 ST in 1985, together with other students. When I could first get my hands on a Pascal compiler I tried to compile TEX on it, but didn't succeed. Others did: there was the group of people around Joachim Schrod in Darmstadt, and two guys from the Nuremberg area (Stefan Lindner and Lutz Birkhahn) who eventually produced the free TEX and Metafont implementation for Atari, including DVI drivers for dot matrix printers. Then we could finally run TEX and print the output. A lot of the early work was done on the Atari (including part of the AMS-LATEX development in 1989/1990).

DW: Is there any use of TEX in the biotech world — do you support it, among other things, at ProteoSys?

RS: There are applications in the biotech world. One example is the `texshade` package for typesetting peptide and nucleotide alignments. However, I'm afraid we do not really use TEX at ProteoSys, the main reason being interoperability. There are de facto standards for documents being exchanged between collaborators, and TEX isn't one of them.

DW: You are well known for taking over LATEX maintenance from Leslie Lamport and then developing LATEX 2_ε, for developing the New Font Selection Scheme, and for your contributions to AMS-LATEX, among other things. In the *TUGboat* author list I see the following papers, all but the first of which were jointly written with Frank Mittelbach:

- Drawing histogram bars inside the LATEX picture–environment (issue 10:1, April 1989)
- A new font selection scheme for TEX macro packages — the basic macros (issue 10:2, July 1989)
- Towards LATEX 2.10 (issue 10:3, November 1989)
- With LATEX into the nineties (issue 10:4, December 1989)
- The new font family selection — User interface to standard LATEX (issue 11:1, April 1990; reprinted with corrections in 11:2, June 1990)
- A new implementation of the LATEX `verbatim` and `verbatim*` environments (issue 11:2, June 1990)
- Towards LATEX 3.0 (issue 12:1, March 1991)

How did your deepening involvement with LATEX development come about, and what was your motivation for spending your time this way? Apparently you were pretty intensely involved for about a two-year period from 1989–1991; had this intense work actually started well before 1989?

RS: The dates on the *TUGboat* articles are misleading; *TUGboat* had a fair backlog then. NFSS, the New Font Selection Scheme, was conceived and first implemented well before 1989, possibly even in 1987—although I find it difficult to attach an exact date. The histogram bar package is even older.

RS: Frank Mittelbach and I shared an interest in TEX and LATEX early on. At first, LATEX didn't fit in the small computers' memory. But when that changed, it was obvious to us that LATEX would be the way to go for the typical user. At the same time, we became aware of its shortcomings: its fixed set of fonts, its lack of complex mathematical typesetting, its US-centrism in layout. The problem was not that you couldn't change these things, but that this created mutually incompatible variants.

I think it was in 1986 that we could finally send and receive emails via the university mainframe computer. I do not recall when we sent the first email to Leslie Lamport, or when we received his first reply. Eventually, the connection became better; we reported and corrected a number of bugs, discussed improvements and changes. We discovered some TEX bugs as well.

Out of this grew a number of extensions, like NFSS or Frank's `multicol` environment for balanced multicolumn typesetting. We knew how we wanted LATEX to evolve, but Leslie would not develop it further. When Frank won the 1989 Knuth scholarship, he went to Stanford for the 1989 TUG conference and met Leslie and DEK in person. Leslie agreed that we would continue LATEX development; the plan for LATEX 3 was hatched. It was not only us two: Chris Rowley was there from the beginning; others joined us later. So we became what is now called the LATEX Project.

AMS-LATEX was done in winter 1989/1990. The AMS wanted to use the extra math fonts and math typesetting capabilities of AMSTEX in LATEX. We convinced them that everything should adhere to LATEX syntax, and implemented the first version. However, one big problem remained: AMS-LATEX, as well as other extensions, was different and slightly incompatible, required separate format files and separate commands for running. In 1994, LATEX 2_ε solved this, by incorporating all the changes and improvements we wanted back in 1989. [*See endnote. -Ed.*]

DW: How did you and Frank work together?

RS: That's difficult to describe. It just sort of happened. Sitting together nearly every day and tossing ideas about was very important. Only after I had left Mainz (when we worked on AMS-LATEX) did we divide the work. Even then we needed the regular meetings. Fortunately, Heidelberg isn't far away from Mainz. It became more difficult when I moved to Berlin a year later. We talked a lot on the phone, but couldn't meet as much as before. Fortunately, email had become an easy way of communication.

DW: How, if at all, did NTS (`http://nts.tug.org`) relate to all of the above?

RS: In 1989, Don Knuth made the last change to TEX and Metafont. It was obvious to many people that this could not be the end. Even DEK himself lists a number of possible improvements which would not be implemented. Stability is good, but stagnation isn't.

The NTS group wanted to build on TEX, using its stability to progress. I soon realized that I couldn't put in the necessary effort and effectively dropped out of the project. I think we were too naive: we underestimated the amount of work and overestimated our influence. Creating PDF instead of DVI, or 16-bit input and fonts with more than

256 characters are much more important than some changes in the macro language. Graphics inclusion is no longer the problem it was 15 years ago. At the same time, other (commercial) programs have improved a lot.

DW: Today I think that perhaps your main involvement with TEX is with CTAN. The interviews of Jim Hefferon and Robin Fairbairns speak somewhat to that. How did you come to be involved, and what keeps you involved?

RS: I'm still with the LATEX Project, although I do a lot less now. What keeps me involved with CTAN ... that's a good question. There seems to be no one else....

In the early nineties, I helped with maintaining the German TEX software repository, at that time an ftp server at the University of Stuttgart. Naturally, I was involved in discussions with the other repository people. So, I became one of the maintainers when CTAN started, and never managed to run away :-)

As far as TEX goes, CTAN takes up most of my time, that's for certain. It would be nice to delegate the routine work and spend more time on improvements. But volunteers do not grow on trees, and even the routine tasks have a pretty steep learning curve.

It is perhaps interesting to note how CTAN reflects the change in TEX usage. Nowadays, the bulk of downloads (80 percent) are MacTEX, MiKTEX, and TEX Live. When a major new version comes out we have to be careful to not exceed our bandwidth limits.

I do take a certain pride in the fact that CTAN predates CPAN for Perl. CPAN is definitely better organized, has more software, more mirror sites, better interfaces, and so on. But we were there first! :-)

DW: You have been deeply involved in at least two major advances in the TEX world—the development of LATEX 2_ε/AMS-LATEX and the development of CTAN. Do you see yourself again contributing in as major a way as you did previously, or has the center of initiative passed on to a new generation of TEX developers? More generally, do you in fact see TEX as remaining viable going forward?

RS: Without doubt, there is a new generation of developers, maybe even two generations. My interests have changed; I'm content that others have taken up the work. CTAN alone is enough to keep me busy.

TEX as such is stable and frozen, so there will not be much progress with TEX itself. It gives us a basis for typesetting our documents and for further development. Of course, there are a lot of add-ons that we didn't imagine 20 years ago. Think of the wonderful things Hans Hagen does in ConTEXt, or look at PSTricks! Still, I believe that there is room and need for change. Occasionally, I'm surprised by someone stating that TEX has everything we need. That wasn't even true in the eighties, when computers where much smaller and slower than they are now. And let's not forget that other programs—competitors—have improved over time. TEX is no longer ten or fifteen years ahead. Ease of use has become more important, even more for some than quality of typesetting.

Fortunately, there are a lot of projects going forward. Whether these developments can keep TEX alive in the long run remains to be seen.

DW: Thank you for participating in this interview. I have heard your name since I first heard of LATEX and it has been a pleasure to get acquainted with you, if only by email. I hope that if your work for a biotech company ever brings you to the Boston area (lots of biotech effort is going on here), we will be able to meet in person.

[Endnote: Complementary additions to Rainer's sketch of his history with LATEX are on pp. 1–6 of the second edition of *The LATEX Companion* and in Rainer's foreword to George Grätzer's 4th edition of his LATEX book, *More Math Into LATEX*. For the latter, see pp. xxi–xxiii at `http://mirror.ctan.org/info/Math_into_LaTeX-4/Short_Course.pdf`.]

Cheryl Ponchin and Susan DeMeritt

Cheryl Ponchin (left photo) and Susan DeMeritt (right) are both members of the TUG Board of Directors (Sue is secretary of the board), give workshops on LaTeX, and use TeX daily in their technical typing work.

[Interview completed 27 August 2007.]

Dave Walden, interviewer: Susan, please tell me a bit about your personal history independent of TeX.

Susan DeMeritt, interviewee: I grew up in Lawrenceville, NJ (just outside of Princeton). I graduated from Lawrence High School in 1979. I went to Mercer County Community College and Trenton State College. In 1983, when I was 21 I joined the U.S. Navy, where I met my husband, Blair. We were both stationed on Treasure Island, San Francisco. We married in 1984 and our daughter, Katherine, was born in 1985. In July 1986, we transferred with the Navy to Japan. I was stationed at the U.S. Navy Fuel Depot in Tsurumi (near Yokohama). My husband was on the USS Reeves out of Yokosuka. In 1987, I got out of the Navy when our son, Mark, was born. In 1989, my father, who worked at IDA CCR Princeton (where Cheryl works) told me that a similar facility would be opening in San Diego, California. In 1989 my husband received orders to the USS O'Brien out of San Diego. In July 1989 we returned to the United States. I interviewed for the position of Technical Typist at IDA CCR La Jolla. I started in August 1989 and I am still here today. My family and I have lived in San Diego ever since.

DW: And Cheryl, please tell me a bit about your personal history independent of TeX.

Cheryl Ponchin, interviewee: I also grew up in Lawrenceville, New Jersey. I graduated from Lawrence High School in 1978 and also graduated with an Associates degree in Secretarial Science from Mercer County Community College in 1980. I got married in 1982. My husband, Paul and I have two children, Rachel (23) and Matthew (21). My daughter is attending nursing school and my son is at West Virginia University studying business. I also work for IDA CCR, but in New Jersey.

Sue DeMeritt and I actually grew up around the corner from each other. I knew who Sue was, however, I was one year ahead of her in school and we didn't really hang out together. She started working at another IDA site in La Jolla, California. Sue had come to Princeton for me to show her how to use TeX. We instantly became best of friends. It's funny what a small world we live in.

DW: Will each of you please tell me how you first became involved with TeX.

SD: I first became involved with TeX in 1989 when I started working at CCR La Jolla in August of 1989. In October, as Cheryl just mentioned, I was sent to CCR Princeton to learn TeX from her. As she also mentioned, we were acquainted already — we grew up in the same neighborhood and went to all of the same schools. Once Cheryl started teaching me, we soon became fast friends. She is one of my closest friends.

CP: I started working for the Institute for Defense Analyses in Princeton, New Jersey in 1984. I was using a Lanier word processor to typeset math papers. In 1987 we started using TeX. When I first started I just wanted my Lanier back. It seemed so much easier at the time. TeX seemed frustrating when first using it. It didn't take long when I realized the capabilities and really started to enjoy it. I have since trained many people at CCR. As she said, in 1989 Sue came to Princeton, and I was to show her how to use TEX. We instantly became best of friends. I, along with Sue, have taught many workshops for TUG as well as doing workshops on my own at area colleges (i.e., Rutgers and Princeton).

DW: Cheryl, at that time did you regularly teach new employees to use TEX, or was Sue a first?

CP: I taught one person at IDA CCR in Princeton before Sue and several people after Sue.

DW: Did you have or were you developing a theory of or syllabus for teaching TEX?

CP: I did not actually have a syllabus. Since I had not been using TEX all that long, I just started teaching by putting together a simple document. After that was accomplished we started adding different things that TEX could do.

DW: Sue, how did you feel about TEX as you learned it?

SD: When I first learned TEX, I was very overwhelmed. I was given a hard copy paper that needed to go into TEX. With Cheryl's guidance, I was able to complete the paper. I have been learning ever since.

DW: Did you then teach new TEX users at your office rather than them continuing to go to New Jersey for instruction from Cheryl?

SD: I was hired as the TEX person at our facility. I was the only one who went back to Princeton to train with Cheryl. I continually help others here at CCR La Jolla with their LATEX problems.

DW: Cheryl, you mentioned that in addition to the TUG workshops, you have also taught non-TUG workshops in your region? Did the latter start before or after the TUG workshops?

CP: The non-TUG workshops started after doing the TUG workshops. People that attended the workshop for TUG suggested that I do a similar workshop for the employees that were not able to attend the TUG workshop.

DW: Are the other people that you teach or help other technical typists or the people actually doing doing the technical work or both?

CP: Outside of my main job I have taught support staff people who are typing for someone else as well as students who will be using it for their own work. At my main job, I have taught support staff people and also help the technical staff with their LATEX problems to complete their work.

SD: The majority of the people I help are mathematicians writing papers. Some of them are just learning TEX for the first time and others have used it much more but are having problems getting things to work.

In the classes that Cheryl and I teach, there is a variety of people, i.e., mathematicians, people working for publishers, and people from other scientific companies.

DW: Does TEX dominate your technical typing or are there other typesetting and word processing programs you use?

CP: LATEX dominates my main job. However, I do a lot of HTML work and create shell scripting programs for the tasks that I need that help ease the final steps of our LATEX papers. Besides using LATEX picture and other graphic TEX programs we use FrameMaker to create some graphics and convert them to postscript. We strictly use LaTeX 2ε now. Any papers we get in other forms need to be converted to LaTeX 2ε.

SD: When I say TeX, I mean LaTeX 2ε. TeX definitely is the majority of my job. Some people may turn in papers in other forms, i.e., plain TeX, ASCII plain text, FrameMaker, or hand written. But they are all converted into LaTeX 2ε.

TeX is my word processing program of choice — not only for math papers, but for writing letters, creating projects for other people, etc.

DW: Most people in the world eschew TeX and its command based approach in favor of visually oriented typesetting or word processing systems such as InDesign, Word, etc. What makes TeX preferable to those for you?

CP: Word and other visually oriented typesetting or word processing systems are good for many things, such as, letters, labels, envelopes, mail merges, etc. However, mathematics is not one of their best qualities. I have already done one presentation and I am doing another in October for Princeton University to show why (La)TeX is better for mathematics. I briefly explain how and why Don Knuth started TeX. Then I proceed to explain and show the difficulties in Word versus the ease in LaTeX. Since most college students do some form of programming I explain how it is just another form of code.

SD: Visually oriented systems such as Word are fine for WYSIWYG systems. But when it comes to mathematics, there is so much more control for the user using TeX. I have worked on papers that need much more specific spacing in the mathematics than any systems like Word, FrameMaker, etc., can provide.

DW: Cheryl, how did you come to join TUG and give workshops for TUG, did you do the workshops together from the beginning, how many or for what events have you given them, and how has the content developed over time?

CP: I became a member of TUG because of Sue. She also initiated doing the workshops. Sue also encouraged me to be on the board, which was a good thing. From the beginning we have been a team doing the workshops. The content has changed with the new features that LaTeX has to offer over TeX. Our classes basically haven't changed too much because it is more of a beginners workshop and there are usually new people. I believe some people attend the workshops more than once for a refresher because they might not need all the features all the time.

DW: Does CCR support these workshop activities in any way, or do you give them on your own time?

CP: CCR supports the workshops for me as long as they are in conjunction with a conference. Our company is also a TUG institutional member. If I do any outside workshops other than TUG, it is on my own.

SD: CCR La Jolla supports my workshop activities. They like that I am on the Board of Directors (as Secretary). They support all of my travel for TUG events.

DW: Sue, Cheryl's earlier answer indicates you became a member of TUG before she did. What led you to join TUG and how did your participation in TUG evolve?

SD: When I was first hired here at CCR La Jolla, my boss suggested that I join TUG. I was not that active until I started going to the conferences. I enjoy being involved in that sort of planning. I got to know various board members and I decided I wanted to be on the board because I thought I could be of some help. There was an open slot which I was happy to fill.

After being on the board for a few months, I realized that Cheryl would be a great addition. So I spoke to her about it and she was willing to do it.

Cheryl and I started implementing workshops because it seemed that all of the TEX conferences were technical and not at all user friendly. There were a lot of people out there who wanted to share how they were using TEX. The first workshop, TEX Northeast, was in New York City; it was a great success and well attended.

DW: Cheryl, will you please tell me a little more about the format and content of the workshops you give with Sue or alone? And how many TUG workshops have you done to date?

CP: Sue and I have done five together and I have done one on my own for TUG. We have a sample document with the basic information you would need to do a math paper. It shows how to do sections, subsections, etc., as well as doing theorems, lemmas and so on. We show how to do tables, figures, table of contents. We also show how to do different types of equations, labeling and referencing, and adding graphics. There is a sample on the TUG web site for the workshops: `http://tug.org/practicaltex2006/workshop.html`.

DW: Please tell me any thoughts either of you has for how someone who can't take your workshop or learn TEX personally from one of you should go about learning TEX in the most efficient manner?

CP: I would suggest going to the TUG web site. Click on the link LATEX. This will bring you to a page that says: *LaTeX—A Document Preparation System*. This gives very helpful information on getting started. I would then get a book. There are many good books; one good one is *Math into LATEX: An Introduction to LATEX and AMS-LATEX* and another is *A Guide to LATEX* by Kopka and Daly.

DW: More generally, since you often teach more-or-less beginning users of TEX, are there common stumbling blocks you see?

CP: The biggest problem we have is when the computers don't work properly. As for the TEX, if we have TEX Live loaded things are o.k. for a beginners' workshop. We use the basic math and fonts packages.

DW: Thank you both for taking the time to participate in this interview. It has been a great pleasure for me to learn about you and your involvement with TEX.

Ross Moore

Ross Moore is a long-time TUG board member and TeX contributor, especially in the areas of mathematics and Unicode support.

[Interview completed 12 December 2007.]

Dave Walden, interviewer: Please tell me a bit about your personal history independent of TeX.

Ross Moore, interviewee: I'm an academic mathematician, lecturing at Macquarie University in Sydney, Australia. My undergraduate studies were at the University of Melbourne followed by a few years of postgraduate work at the University of Oxford, before returning to Australia. There were several years spent in Canberra before moving to Sydney, where I've lived now for more than 20 years. Much of that time was spent with Penny (now deceased), both as a bridge partner and partner in life. Although we had no children together, there are four girls from her previous marriage, and now five grand-children. The 2007 year was a very busy one for me. For five months I was on sabbatical in Switzerland, working at ETH Zürich helping to prepare for the largest-ever meeting of (applied) mathematical scientists. My partner Robyn accompanied me. We travelled a lot, including a quick trip back to Australia when my mother died, and during this time we decided to get married. The knot was tied at the end of September, after we had been back in Sydney for a couple of months.

DW: Congratulations to you and Robyn.

RM: Most of my research work, since leaving Oxford in 1981, has concerned developing software techniques that should be of use to mathematicians; e.g., helping to present their work in the best possible ways, using electronic software tools. Much, but not all, of this has been TeX-related. Also, programming languages such as PostScript, Mathematica and Perl have been, and remain, very important to my work.

DW: Looking at your web site (`http://www.maths.mq.edu.au/~ross/`), I detect that you are holding back some personal information, for example, about the Bush Band and what kind of music it plays.

RM: I was not part of the band. Mostly they played folk music. In Australia this tends to be derived from Irish, English and Scottish folk tunes, perhaps with lyrics reworded to describe a local historical event.

DW: Having a university math faculty position that allows you to do research on software to help do math rather than doing research in math itself sounds a little unusual. The last several math professors I interviewed said they got little encouragement and no support for their TeX activities. The Macquarie University web site (`http://www.mq.edu.au/`) calls it "The Innovative University". Is the university non-traditional in some way? Should

I presume that you do have to do some traditional math teaching and research as well as your software work? And what is the set of software tools to help mathematicians you have worked on?

RM: The "Innovative" title refers more to research and development, with quite strong links to commercial companies located close to the campus, than to teaching practices. Certainly we do traditional teaching of mathematics, though I prefer to use computer software in my teaching, rather than writing down everything on a blackboard, whiteboard or onto overhead-projector slides.

As for my software efforts, this is not so much writing completely new software tools, but more about realising the ability of existing tools to become much more useful in areas where previously they had not been sufficiently-well applied. This includes writing macro packages for TeX, programming directly in PostScript, and coding in general-purpose software applications such as Mathematica and Maple. And then there is LaTeX2HTML, written in Perl, and coding in PHP for the production of web-pages containing mathematical content.

I have been lucky in finding professors, both at my university and elsewhere, who have recognised the value of this kind of work and have provided support, including travel. In return I have helped them produce "camera-ready" copy for four books published in hard-cover, mostly Proceedings-like volumes, and one monograph in soft-cover. Each of these projects has involved developing some special TeX techniques that were not hitherto available. It has also led to my involvement in the organisation of large conferences, including the one in Zürich, where I develop the web site for collecting and processing abstracts both for online access and for printing in the Program and/or Abstract Book(s).

As a specific example, the original version of Xy-pic showed great promise to be useful for commutative diagrams and such-like. Category theory is a particular strong point in my Department, and their work requires more than just the straight-line kind of diagram that was supported to some extent by existing macro packages. So I added support and drawing methods for spline curves, which then extend to methods for specifying knots, braids and 2-cells, as well as general curved paths and arrows. Also I added color and driver-specific output support for different TeX engines. In particular, the PostScript back-end which I developed, greatly improves the quality of output that can be produced by Xy-pic, and allows for some graphic effects that are not obtainable in any other way. A direct result of this is that Xy-pic has become a vital part in publishing research work in category theory world-wide, not just at my university.

DW: How did you first get involved with TeX?

RM: Aaah, that goes back to the early 1980s. I'd been dabbling in symbolic manipulation packages to do mathematical calculations. Back then it was REDUCE, Macsyma and muPad (where now we have Mathematica, Maple, and MatLab). I needed a way to present the machine-generated results and a colleague showed me the LaTeX manual. I got an account on some VAX machines, which could be used to run the mathematics and also typeset it. There was a visitor, from Germany I think, using the same laboratory who used plain TeX rather than LaTeX. This prompted me to read *The TeXbook*, and find out how to get around all those annoying aspects of LaTeX layout that were so hard to change. Thus I became a TeX programmer, rather than just a (La)TeX user.

After a while Macintoshes started appearing at the university. This changed the computing paradigm to a WYSIWYG kind of interface, for word-processing. I experimented with these for awhile, and (dare I say it) rather liked the abilities of the earliest versions of Microsoft Word on the Mac, at least when compared to MacWrite. But then they bloated the interface and kept changing how to do things. This turned me right off of it. By now there was a decent TeX application, which soon became Textures. It cost a bit of money, but was fun to use. OzTeX also came onto the scene, and was more like the interface that I'd been using under VAX/VMS and Unix. I started to understand the issues concerning different drivers and printer resolutions.

It wasn't until LaTeX was rewritten in the 1990s, with much improved support for packages and document classes, that I began to embrace this instead of continuing to use Plain TeX. I needed a package for general commutative diagrams that could be used with LaTeX. AMSTeX and LAMSTeX were candidates, but not sufficiently flexible. Then I discovered XYpic, and helped Kris Rose extend it to be much more useful for mathematics. The first Proceedings volume that I edited used both LaTeX and Xy-pic (note the name change); this appeared in 1995.

This is about the time that the World-wide Web was born, and the first HTML recommendations. But that's the start of another story.

DW: And your part of that story is....

RM: ... extending the mathematics support within LaTeX2HTML. This conversion software, written in Perl, was originally developed at the Computer-Based Learning Unit of the Education Department at Leeds University, primarily by Nikos Drakos. This was when web-browsers were not yet very sophisticated. Support for mathematics was minimal, based upon simply creating a (LaTeX-generated) image. This could not work properly with regard to equation-numbering, cross-references, or hyperlinking to sub-parts of a set of displayed equations, and such-like, and had difficulties getting displays properly sized and aligned. So I set about developing different levels of mathematics support, based upon the structure of the layouts used within different environments. There are now options that allow mathematics coding to be fully parsed down to the level of individual characters and symbols, or to lesser levels at which images can be generated and aligned. The resulting HTML coding can refer to mathematical symbols in any of various different ways, according to what a browser can show; named entities, parametrised entities, UTF-8 strings, or as images.

The way that indexes and bibliographies were handled by LaTeX2HTML also needed an overhaul, as well as extending the parsing of tabular material by doing more detailed processing of the column-specifier argument. In order to be able to align images in a web-browser, there is delicate TeX programming in the preamble of the LaTeX job that is used to automatically generate the images.

Also, I did some work to support old TeX-based pre-processor methods for typesetting Indic languages. This results in LaTeX-generated images, such as with the earliest ways to handle mathematics. As Unicode has become more widespread, these methods will become obsolete; nevertheless, they continue to work with legacy compuscripts.

DW: Will Robertson mentioned in his interview that you are doing some development work related to XeTeX. Please tell me about that and other TeX development work you are doing (or have done), in addition to just using TeX.

RM: The first part of this work was to provide backward-compatibility with existing LaTeX documents, written to use packages that are now quite redundant for processing by XeTeX; for example, the `inputenc` and `fontenc` packages. XeTeX requires Unicode-compatible input (ASCII, UTF-8 or UTF-16), whereas support for different languages in LaTeX has been to refer to characters in special fonts, each having its own customised encoding. We are all familiar with using macros such as `\'`, `\"`, `\^`, etc. for putting accents over letters, and

`\textcopyright`, `\textsterling`, `\textdegree`, etc. for other characters.

To work with XeTeX, all such macros needed to be redefined to produce references to Unicode code-points. I wrote a new LaTeX package, now called `xunicode`, that encodes the correct Unicode codepoint for all the symbol-producing macros that occur within the standard font packages in a usual LaTeX distribution. Along with Will's `fontspec` package for accessing OpenType fonts, the `xunicode` package is recommended to be loaded whenever processing LaTeX source that has not been prepared entirely in UTF-8 or UTF-16. It actually does a bit more than this, since it was written to be fully compatible with LaTeX's NFSS font-selection scheme. This means that, by simply changing the value of `\fontencoding`, a document can use the older LaTeX method of accessing legacy fonts, as well as the new (XeTeX-only) direct method.

More recently, Will, Chris Rowley and myself have been working on developing full XeTeX support for mathematics using Unicode-encoded fonts; in particular, the new STIX fonts, and other fonts that include mathematical symbols at the proper Unicode code-points.

DW: How do the various tools you are working on as part of your research (Mathematica, TeX, etc.) fit together?

RM: This is a good opportunity to talk about labelling graphic images. Software such as Mathematica is great for producing graphs of mathematical functions and scientific data. However, typically the labelling features of such programs are rather poor, using just ASCII strings to label axes and tick-marks. Typically the graphs need touching-up in a sophisticated graphic editing tool such as Adobe's Illustrator software. But if you want properly typeset mathematics in labels, even this is not enough.

One approach is to pre-typeset labels using TeX or LaTeX, then include these using Illustrator. Because of the non-standard encodings of the fonts that TeX has traditionally used for mathematics, this method may not always work. Also, changes with different versions of Illustrator has meant that graphics files produced this way have stopped working properly with later updated software.

A good solution to this problem is to keep the graphics and labels separated; that is, import the graphic into a TeX document as an image, then overlay the image with the desired labels, which then have the mathematics correctly typeset. This has the added advantage of keeping the style and fonts used in the labels consistent with what appears within the surrounding text content of the document. LaTeX's "picture" environment is one way to achieve this, using a coordinate system that needs to be set up for the environment containing the image. Another way is to use the `xyimport` extension, which I wrote for use with Xy-pic diagrams, which then gives a natural way to use the full drawing capabilities of Xy-pic to annotate graphics with symbols, lines, paths and arrows as well as typeset labels.

Taking this a step further, the `warmreader` package implements the idea of having symbolic labels to indicate places of interest within an imported graphic. (This is like using LaTeX's `\label` command to attach a name to a location within a document.) For this to work, there needs to be a kind of auxiliary file that contains information about the size of the image and coordinates for the named points of interest, called "marked points". Wendy McKay had a real need for this kind of labelling technique for a collection of images that had been originally created years earlier, using the then-current versions of Adobe Illustrator. So we enlisted the help of a programmer at Adobe Systems Inc., Thomas Ruark, who wrote a "Marked Objects" plug-in tool that gave a point-&-click interface for selecting places of interest and recording their coordinates and a symbolic name within a file, using the appropriate data-format.

DW: Your math department page (`http://www.math.mq.edu.au/staff/ross.html`) tells me that part of your post graduate work in the UK included a PhD from Oxford. The math genealogy web site (`http://genealogy.math.ndsu.nodak.edu/html/id.phtml?id=14166`) lists a Ross Moore whose advisor was Roger Penrose

RM: Yes, it is. I wasn't aware of this entry until you mentioned it. Probably someone at Oxford or Cambridge has submitted a list of Roger Penrose's students. My entry should now have been updated with a bit more information.

DW: The typesetting world has largely moved to InDesign, QuarkXPress, etc., the word processing world has largely move to Word, and the (claims for) typesetting capabilities of these other systems keep getting better. Will there be reasons for mathematicians to continue using TEX into the indefinite future?

RM: Yes, indeed. Apart from the results being aesthetically more pleasing, the "language" that TEX uses to record a mathematical expression is just so much easier than with any of these other tools. This is particularly true for displayed equations, matrices and tables; not to mention commutative diagrams, expressed with Xy-pic say.

Agreed, these other systems are getting better; in particular Unicode and the new STIX fonts will help close the gap even further, by moving a lot of the layout aspects of mathematics presentation into the fonts themselves. This will mean that mathematics will be represented using strings of UTF-8 or UTF-16 characters, rather than as ASCII strings as in traditional TEX (or LATEX) source. But this requires appropriate, easy to use, tools to construct such character strings, or generate them from something else (such as TEX coding). These tools do not yet exist, or those which do are not close to having widespread use within the mathematics community.

For example, systems such as LyX and Scientific Workplace use LATEX as the underlying typesetting engine and as the export format for publishing and interchange with colleagues who may be using other tools. MathML has not yet attained general acceptance within the mathematics community; it is used by some publishers, but the best typesetting of it requires conversion back into TEX or LATEX anyway.

DW: You have been a member of the TUG board for a number of years. Please tell me how that came about.

RM: Back in 1997, at the annual TUG meeting in San Francisco — the first that I had attended — Kris Rose and I were asked to sit in as "observers" at the Board meeting. There were several vacancies becoming available on the Board, and I was naïve in not realising that we were in effect volunteering to fill these. I've been there ever since, which has been quite fun and has allowed me to do some things that otherwise wouldn't have happened.

DW: What is your personal or general view of the work done by individuals such as Kew, Koch, Hagen, et al., to keep TEX development moving?

RM: I jumped in quite early with Jonathan Kew's work on XETEX, which I see as having the potential to become the platform that will most likely support use of the STIX fonts for mathematics. Either this, or it will evolve by merging with pdfTEX (or LuaTEX) to create a bigger, better, more flexible system employing the "best of all worlds".

The Macintosh computer has always been very popular with mathematicians. (I first used one at work in 1985, and got my own in 1986.) The change to a Unix-based operating system, Mac OS X, meant that existing software for TEX would become obsolete. This included the Textures application, which had been very popular in parts of the mathematics community; because of some "ease-of-use" features that it had, which were not available in other TeX applications. Gerben Wierda and Richard Koch were already doing the work that unleashed all the power of a Unix-based TeX system, but with a "Mac-like" human interface. With more than a little urging by Wendy McKay, other people joined-in and their work has became the MacTeX project, which is now the free Macintosh variant distributed with TeX Live.

As for Hans Hagen, he just does so much that it is impossible to keep up with all his work. Some TUG members may remember TUG 2001 (`http://tug.org/tug2001/bulletin/preprints/`) in Delaware; where I gave three talks, and Hans gave four. I'll not repeat that performance, but Hans does so frequently.

DW: Your math department page also says you are webmaster for a couple of math societies, you mentioned the first conference proceedings you did with TeX, and you recently told me you are involved with another conference proceedings. You obviously do a lot of pro-bono work; what is your motivation for that? Also, what improvement to the world of TeX would help you do such work easier?

RM: Software for data presentation and publishing is moving ahead rapidly, quite irrespective of the special needs of mathematics. This is perfectly natural; but it can be leaving the average mathematician far behind, using older tools which may become incompatible with the newer developments and techniques. It takes someone with sufficient mathematical expertise and training to be motivated enough to even test new combinations of software techniques applied to mathematical content.

The main motivation is about seeing needs arising, or an opportunity developing, where I have appropriate experience, knowledge and ability to make a useful contribution. Whilst this kind of work is not really scientific research *in* mathematics, it certainly involves a kind of social research *for* science and mathematics. My work can, and does, lead to techniques and time-saving improvements to the way other researchers conduct, record and publish the results of their own research work. Greater recognition of this aspect, by research-funding agencies, would make my university life easier, by improving chances for promotion and research grants.

DW: Thank you very much for taking the time to participate in this interview series. It has been a pleasure for me to learn a bit about your life and work.

Peter Gordon

Peter Gordon is the editor at Addison Wesley for Donald Knuth's books and the company's TeX and LaTeX books.

[Interview completed 8 January 2008.]

Dave Walden, interviewer: Please tell me a bit about your personal history independent of TeX.

Peter Gordon, interviewee: Before settling into an editorial position at Addison-Wesley, where I've been for nearly 30 years, I had begun (just barely) a career in philosophy and enjoyed (rather extensively) a world of travel. I today live a distributed life between New York City, Tokyo, and New Hampshire, all with Sachiko, my wife of many years.

DW: I first heard your name as "the editor of Knuth's books" (e.g., in Barbara Beeton's introduction to your remarks reprinted in *TUGboat* 7:2 (1999), "Introducing Donald Knuth and *Computers and Typesetting*" (pp. 93–95). When and how did you first become involved with Donald Knuth and his books?

PG: I first became involved with Don in the early 1980's, just in time to help celebrate (in a limited, hexadecimally numbered, leather-bound edition) the first book composed with TeX, *The Art of Computer Programming, Volume 2: Seminumerical Algorithms, Second Edition.* I have been his editor ever since.

Knuth's books have been the bedrock of our computer science list, still selling well after all these years.

DW: I am interested in some of the details of how deeply you work with Knuth. Do you edit all of his books?

PG: I am the editor responsible, since the early 1980's, for all of Don's AW books, which includes all the TeX-related books he's published with us.

DW: Do you have an involvement in the translation and publication of Knuth's books into other languages?

PG: I have no direct involvement with the translation of his books into other languages (translations being handled through our foreign rights department), although I am sometimes consulted when decisions need to be made.

DW: Do you have direct dealings with Duane Bibby or does Knuth arrange that himself?

PG: Don generally works directly with Duane Bibby, although we have sometimes engaged him ourselves (e.g., to work on covers).

DW: When editing Knuth's books, do you have early and frequently involvement or only late and infrequent involvement, and involvement of what sort?

PG: When asked in another interview how I work with Don as his editor, I answered only half facetiously: I try to stay out of his way. I can advise him around the edges, but those edges are very slim. The same is true of our production staff's interactions with him. We see the end-product of Don's work, not the TEX markup.

DW: I think I read that article — in *Technology Review* in 1999. In that article you are referred to as Knuth's "publishing partner at AW" — what does "publishing partner" mean?

PG: Publishing Partner is my title at AW; there probably are many people within the company who also would like to know what the term means.

DW: I believe I remember you being acknowledged in one of the *LATEX Companion* books. Are there other people at AW also editing TEX-related books and books or do you do them all?

PG: I am the editor for them all.

DW: Please tell me about AW's relationship to TEX more generally — the market for TEX books, the typesetting of books in TEX, etc.?

PG: TEX and LATEX books probably serve as broad a cross-section of Pearson Education's markets as any others. Whereas most of the books published in my division address primarily the needs of programming and software development professionals, TEX/LATEX books are useful to people in virtually every scientific and technical discipline, and they are so throughout the world (one reader we heard from was a urologist in Kenya). TEX/LATEX is also the system of choice for many of our authors who prefer to do their own typesetting (which is fine with us, as long as they know what they're doing and don't spend more time typesetting than writing). That said, most of our authors these days deliver their manuscripts in Word files, and TEX/LATEX is rarely used by our professional compositors to produce final pages.

DW: I believe the METAFONT trademark resides with AW. How did that come about and what responsibilities does it entail?

PG: It was a matter of convenience, inasmuch as we were about to publish *The METAFONTbook*. We are a caretaker of the name; that's all.

DW: Before we end this interview, are there any particularly memorable moments relating to Knuth and his books you'd like to share?

PG: There have been many memorable personal moments. What pops into my mind with regard to books, though, is standing with Don and his wife, Jill, in their garden, examining the board Jill had constructed to chart the publication schedule of at least two dozen Volume 4 fascicles. It was a great graphical representation of just how large a task Don had undertaken. I'm not sure the board still exists, and I can't recall what the projected completion date was (and probably don't want to ask), but the fascicles keep coming. Before too long, we'll have enough for the first full-sized Volume 4 hardcover.

DW: Thank you very much for your participation in this interview. I greatly appreciate your contributions to the world of TEX.

Jon Breitenbucher

Jon Breitenbucher is interested in the use of TeX in educational situations and is a member of the TUG board.

[Interview completed 22 June 2008.]

Dave Walden, interviewer: Please tell me a bit about your personal history independent of TeX.

Jon Breitenbucher, interviewee: I am originally from a small town in Holmes County, Ohio. I attended The College of Wooster, a small, residential, liberal arts college in Wooster, Ohio, for my undergraduate degree. From Wooster I went on to The Ohio State University to study Analysis. I ended up studying Special Functions and did my thesis with Stephen Milne on extending one of Ramanujan's Third Order Mock Theta Functions. I left Ohio State to return to a teaching position at The College of Wooster and eventually ended up in a split position. I now teach one class a semester and the rest of my time is spent as an Instructional Technology Specialist.

While I was at Wooster as an undergrad, I met my wife. We were married right after graduation and still haven't had a real honeymoon. Shortly before graduating from Ohio State we had our first and only child. We've settled in a small town a little north of Wooster and are very happy. We spend our time entertaining our Lhasapoo and playing games. My wife and I are into the World of Warcraft and our daughter is into Webkinz.

DW: I guess I am not in touch with the World of Warcraft and Webkinz. What are these?

JB: The World of Warcraft (`http://www.worldofwarcraft.com/index.xml`) is a Massively Multi-player Online Role Playing Game (MMORPG); others include City of Heroes (loosely based on comicbook heroes) and Everquest (a fantasy based MMORPG). WoW is based on Blizzard Entertainments Warcraft real-time strategy games and set in the same universe. The universe draws heavily from the worlds created by Tolkien and Gygax. Currently there are over nine million subscribers worldwide. And as this implies it is a monthly subscription to play and all your character information is stored on central servers maintained by Blizzard. Your computer only has the image data and other elements that would require high bandwidth to transmit in real-time. I am on the Thorium Brotherhood server if you ever feel the desire to try it out. My character name is Cauchy.

Webkinz (`http://www.webkinz.com/us_en/`) are stuffed animals which come with a computer code that allows you to enter the digital Webkinz world online and redeem a digital representation of your animal. In this world you can buy things for your animal such as a house, furniture, clothes, food, etc. Of course you need money to do that and you make money by playing games. Some of the games are not educational per se such as Tetris, but a number of them are very educational. Children really learn how to manage money and whatever skills the games are teaching. It is rather a neat thing.

DW: When and how did you first get involved with TEX?

JB: I'll start a little before I got into LATEX. All seniors at The College of Wooster are required to complete a Senior Independent Study Project. This project can and often does produce original results for students in research fields and the result for all students is a thesis of between 75 to 200 pages. I was a senior just around the time that Microsoft Word 4 or 5 was available for the Macintosh and had to write my thesis with that software. Even then I was preparing to use LATEX but didn't know it.

I broke the parts of my thesis up into separate documents, figured out how to get Word to generate a Table of Contents, Table of Figures, Table of Tables, Table of Symbols, Index, how to number equations, and how to format mathematics without the use of equation editor. I also figured out how to get Word to print the documents in order and paginate things correctly with the proper numbering style for the different sections and how to make use of styles. In the end I had one of the most professional looking theses that the Math department had ever seen. I thought it was immensely fun and didn't care that it took me three times as long to type up my thesis.

That Fall I was in an analysis class with Paul Nevai and I'll never forget his comment when handing back our first homework assignment, "Don't any of you know how to properly write mathematics in TEX?" He said this in his mild Hungarian accent and just could not believe that we had given him hand-written homework solutions. He offered to use some of his grant money to pay part of the cost for each of us to get a copy of Michael Spivak's *The Joy of TEX*, 2nd ed. He took names and told us each to bring him ten dollars. A few weeks later about ten of us got our copies and started figuring out what this AMSTEX was all about. We also learned that Paul had thought the books only cost $20 and had ended up actually paying $20 per student since the book cost $30. I still have my copy sitting on the shelf in my office.

It wasn't long after that that I had the Borders near my apartment order a copy of *The TEXbook*. With those two books I began to create templates for my homework assignments and fell in love with the beautiful mathematics TEX produced. A few years later I discovered LATEX when I started writing my thesis. I couldn't believe that it made it so easy to do the things I had done with Word for my Independent Study thesis. Numbering, pagination, generation of various tables, indices, styling, and entry of mathematics was so much easier than what I had done with Word. It was at this time that I started to fiddle with class development since I needed to tweak the Ohio State thesis class to match the university guidelines after the original class author had graduated.

When I returned to Wooster I was horrified at the visual quality of the theses being produced by the Math majors and took it upon myself to develop a thesis class for Wooster. I started by trying to alter the Ohio State class and the first few versions of the Wooster class were based on it, but I eventually threw it out and started with a more generic class and did some heavy modifying to arrive at the current version. Each year I ask the students what abilities they need the class to support and try to make sure that it can. During this entire time I have been offering sessions to students on how to use LATEX and have started requiring my own students to type up their homework. I don't require them to use TEX but it is strongly encouraged.

DW: Please say a little bit more about your work developing a new class. What class did you start with, what other classes (if any) do you use in it, and did the result have to go through any sort of university or department approval process?

JB: Ultimately I ended up altering the book class. I have provided options to print only the abstract, to include a copyright notice with a Wooster image, to color the links black for printing, to have an index, to use the listings, floatflt, verbatim, lettrine, and alltt packages, a modified fncychap package, and an option to have a colophon. The class also auto-detects if the document is using XeTeX or TeX and loads the packages that are not optional with the appropriate options. The required packages in the class are ifpdf, ifxetex, textpos, amsthm, amsmath, amssymb, setspace, eso-pic, ifthen, natbib, float, caption, subfigure, hyperref, and fancyhdr. In the case of XeTeX we also load fontspec, xunicode and xltxtra. In the case of pdfTeX we load graphicx and microtype. That's a lot of packages but they have been added to meet particular needs identified by students.

The final look of the document was approved by the Secretary of the College and the Director of Public Information because it used official College images. There was no real approval for the general format of the document. I based the format on my dissertation requirements at Ohio State. You can see an example at `http://woolatex.wooster.edu/pdf/latex/IS_guide.pdf` for which I think used XeLaTeX.

DW: I remember from meeting you at Prac[]TeX in New Jersey that you are very interested in helping students use TeX (and this interview, so far, confirms that interest). What are some of the useful TeX-educational resources you've used with your students, and what's missing?

JB: I have used *The Not So Short Introduction to LaTeX 2ε* and a few others; they are listed on the wiki I maintain for my LaTeX work at Wooster (`http://woolatex.wooster.edu/latexwiki/Guides`). Images, tables, and matrices are the things I get the most questions about at Wooster. I still haven't figured out how to do a matrix where the rows and columns are labeled with the labels outside the brackets of the matrix. Maybe that's just me though.

DW: I am sorry to say that I had not heard of The College of Wooster before I heard you mention it at the meeting in NJ. Is it a fairly typical liberal arts college, or does it have an unusual approach that drew you to it in the first place and back later?

JB: Wooster is known for its Independent Study program. Many institutions have Senior capstone projects for honors student or which students can elect to do, but at Wooster our curriculum centers around Independent Study which every senior does. Wooster starts from day one to prepare its students to undertake their year-long independent study project that will result in a written thesis at the end of their Senior year. I found that to be exciting when I was looking at colleges as a student and I really wanted to return to have the opportunity to mentor students as they did their projects. The official College page has a better write up than I could possibly provide: `http://admissions.wooster.edu/each/original.php`.

DW: What led you to be willing and interested in serving as a member of the TUG Board?

JB: I don't have a lot of money to donate to help further the development of LaTeX, XeTeX, ConTeXt, and friends or the mission of TUG, but I do have time. Thus I thought if I could get involved with TUG and donate my time to help with whatever I was qualified to do I'd be doing my part. I've benefited greatly from the work of TUG and all the developers that make TeX and friends possible and want to make sure others are able to benefit in the future.

DW: As I understand it, most of your time at Wooster is spent doing instructional technology work, and your web site (`http://jbreitenbuch.wooster.edu/~jonb/`) and blog (`http://jbreitenbuch.blogs.wooster.edu/`) certainly mention many technologies. Can you briefly summarize the sorts of instructional technologies you are working with? Also can you speculate on whether any of these might be of practical use for an organization like TUG in helping its members with aspects of learning and using TEX?

JB: I work with mostly Web based technologies such as blogs and wikis. I also oversee our Moodle installation (course management software) and am involved with video projects involving iMovie, Garageband, Audacity, and similar technologies. I am in the process of identifying faculty members to work with in the development of an information literacy project involving del.icio.us and on-line research sources. I am also in the process of finding projects that might lend themselves to Second Life or similar virtual environments. I think TUG could make wider use of a wiki (and may already be doing so). A wiki would provide a place where the community could develop living documentation. A blog for active development projects would provide a nice place for users to be informed about progress and comment on the direction of the projects. It would also allow the developers and users to communicate in a more public venue than mailing lists to which a number of users might not be subscribed.

DW: Thank you for taking the time to participate in this interview. Your descriptions of how Wooster functions make me want to return to college.

Arthur Ogawa

Arthur Ogawa is a long time member of the TUG board and well-known package developer.

[Interview completed 14 July 2008.]

Dave Walden, interviewer: Please tell me a bit about your personal history independent of TeX.

Arthur Ogawa, interviewee: I am a high-energy particle experimental physicist (Ph.D., UC Berkeley, 1978), now in my second career as a computer consultant in the field of electronic publishing.

I was born in Milwaukee, Wisconsin, in 1948, did my undergraduate work at the University of Wisconsin, Madison, and California Institute of Technology, Pasadena (BS, 1970).

I live with my wife Marian Goldeen and children Grace (20) and Evan (18) in Three Rivers, California, an unincorporated village in the foothills of the Sierra Nevada, at the entrance to Sequoia National Park.

I am active in my local community, working on local food sources, among other things. I ride my bikes (mountain and road) in the best bicycling area in the world.

DW: When and how did you first get involved with TeX?

AO: I had been working as a post-doc at the Stanford Linear Accelerator Center (SLAC) and had had experience with earlier computer-based systems for the creation of technical documents. Some time about 1980, I heard about a new system authored by my old math professor, who was then working on the Stanford University campus.

I had taken a course in algebra from Donald Knuth when I was a sophomore at Caltech, and I was now eager to try out TeX82, version 0.9999, which I found running under VMS on a Digital Equipment VAX 11/780. I ran a sample document through, and printed it out on the local printer, a Canon LBP-10: I was hooked!

Notwithstanding the remarkably obscure error message I encountered when I made one small (invalid) change to the source file on my second run. This was a humbling experience, indeed.

I obtained the manual (by going to the Computer Science office down on the Stanford campus), studied it thoroughly, and I was off and running. I became one of the ten institutional *TUGboat* subscribers at SLAC, got to know the other TeX users well, and started writing my own macro package — still available on CTAN, it is called Psizzl (`http://mirror.ctan.org/macros/psizzl`).

Over time I was asked to help people use TeX on their own documents, and I became familiar with the experience of deciphering `\tracingall` output at 3am.

About 1985 or so, I helped Dr. Anthony Siegman and his TeX-based typesetter, Laura Friedman, complete his book on Lasers (University Science Books, see `http://www.tug.org/TUGboat/Articles/tb08-1/tb17complete.pdf`, page 8). It was my first venture into TeX consultancy. I eventually purchased a Macintosh Plus (1MB RAM, fitted out with a 20MB disc drive) and ran FTL Systems' MacTeX.

By 1987, I had formed my modest firm, TeX Consultants, in Palo Alto, California. After a call from Lynne A. Price (who herself had served on the TUG Board), I began working for Hewlett-Packard (HP) at their corporate offices. Their SGML-based publishing system HPtag was much like the XML-based publishing systems of today, in use by, for example, the American Physical Society. In the case of HPtag, documents were first coded in SGML, validated, and then translated into TeX for typesetting by the macro package I wrote. HP product manuals of all kinds were produced using HPtag.

By this means I supported myself and my growing family. I worked for any number of corporate clients, including Apple Computer, the NASA Ames Research Center, and others. I also typeset books for publishers, producing films suitable for use in offset printing.

I began collaborating with William E. Baxter, another TeX-based typesetter and programmer. He had attended UC Berkeley math department at the same time as my wife; upon graduation, he went into the business as SuperScript (`superscript.com`).

I was a pioneer of working in color printing with TeX. At the 1989 TUG conference at Stanford University, I demonstrated how I was using TeX to create color separations (through the vehicle of PostScript). I even showed how TeX could accommodate the need for trapping, something that few people in the audience understood or appreciated. Afterwards, Don Knuth asked me for my opinion on how well TeX worked with color.

With 20/20 hindsight, I now wish I had responded differently than I did: I believed at the time that color could be handled adequately by putting `\special` commands into the DVI output. Unfortunately, I was wrong. It became clear shortly thereafter that the color of the ink is in all ways like the font of the glyph: TeX should keep track of both attributes on the same footing: those familiar with TeX's internals know that each glyph "remembers" its font, and the color of the glyph's ink should be handled in the same way. (Rules should remember their ink color as well.)

The upshot of my conversation with Knuth was that he made major changes to TeX in 1989 (when TeX version 3.0 came into being) without addressing the issue of color. The problem remains with us today. For an example of the problem, create a document with a colored footnote that breaks over a page.

After working with many publishers and corporate clients in the Bay Area, the advent of the Internet enabled me to perform all my work out of my home office, and we relocated from the Bay Area to Three Rivers in 1993.

DW: Please describe what you are currently doing in the world of TeX.

AO: I am presently developing macro packages for the American Physical Society and the American Institute of Physics.

The APS authoring package REVTeX 4 was released in 2001; the release of REVTeX 4.1 is under development now (spring 2008) and will incorporate a module that covers the journals of the AIP.

DW: You wrote an article in *TUGboat* issue 22:3 (September 2001) about version 4.0 of REVTeX.

AO: REVTeX 4 is a LaTeX 2_ε document class, a complete rewrite of REVTeX 3, itself a

LaTeX 2.09 style dating back to the late 1980s.

Work on REVTeX 4 was started by David Carlisle; I took over his pilot project. I added powerful low-level machinery based on the work of William Baxter (the `ltxutil` and `ltxgrid` packages), enabling two-column typesetting and other features. REVTeX 4 uses the `natbib` package of Patrick W. Daly, and its BIBTeX styles are generated using Daly's `custom-bib` package, both of which were extended for the sake of REVTeX 4. This work was done by David Carlisle, Patrick Daly and me, under contract to the APS with Mark Doyle as the contract officer. Dr. Baxter has graciously allowed his inventions to be used gratis.

The `ltxutil` package provides OOP capabilities along with more primitive things, notably an algebra that eliminates the explicit use of `\if` and `\fi` (making the code easier to debug).

The `ltxgrid` package completely redoes LaTeX's output routine and float placement algorithm, allowing among other things the placement of both single-column and full-page-width floats in the same multicolumn document.

REVTeX 4 tries hard to achieve compatibility among the many LaTeX supported packages; it even has code that allows David Carlisle's `longtable` package to work properly in a multicolumn layout, something that you cannot accomplish with LaTeX's own `multicol` package.

DW: When I look up REVTeX (`http://authors.aps.org/revtex4/`), it appears to be a fairly major package.

AO: REVTeX is a fourth-generation macro package. Earlier work I did entailed a nearly complete rewrite of LaTeX 2.09, predating LaTeX 2_ε. William Baxter and I worked cooperatively on that package, using it to create commercial typesetting systems. The NASA Ames Research Center's NASATeX is based on that work.

DW: Issue 15:3 (September 1994) of *TUGboat* shows that you gave a presentation on "Object-oriented programming, descriptive markup, and TeX".

AO: I gave that talk at the Santa Barbara TUG meeting (1994); William Baxter gave a companion talk describing his OOP extensions to TeX. TeX macros implementing OOP and the new output routine are now part of the `ltxutil` and `ltxgrid` packages.

DW: Issue 20:3 of *TUGboat* (September 1999) shows you participated in a panel on the Future of LaTeX and gave a talk on doing database publishing involving Java and using TeX as the typesetting back end.

AO: The Vancouver TUG meeting featured the "Future of LaTeX" panel, which I chaired. On the panel were the movers and shakers of LaTeX 2_ε and LaTeX 3. I challenged them by pointing out that they had taken on the task of bringing out a successor to Leslie Lamport's LaTeX, but despite the passage of 10 years, they had failed. Afterwards, friends told me "that was really bad." I thought it was exciting. We are now coming up to the 20-year anniversary of Team LaTeX's inheritance of the LaTeX development responsibilities. Perhaps we should have another such panel discussion.

Database publishing has always been a keen interest of mine. The talk I gave at that conference had to do with a system I created for Patrick Chan, the author of the Java Almanac. Dr. Chan would aim a Java program at Sun Microsystems' internal documentation for Java, turn the crank, and out would pop his book.

TeX's markup language is a terrible one for the author — if he is not a computer. On the other hand, a computer program can talk to TeX just fine, thank you. Don Knuth anticipated this use of TeX at the outset. It's a wonder that people are still coding TeX documents by hand at this late date.

DW: Earlier in this interview you mentioned a SGML-based publishing system (`HPtag`). So clearly you have spent some time thinking about how TeX fits into the world of typesetting and publishing and computing more generally. Please tell me your current thinking about TeX and its current and future utility.

AO: TeX has two severe drawbacks: its front end, pertaining to document creation, and its interface to the macro writer, the programming interface.

As early adopter Dr. Anthony Siegman understood, descriptive markup should be the only TeX commands to be used in the document instance. Leslie Lamport also understood this well, as his remarks at the Santa Barbara TUG meeting made clear. But, as Theodor Holm Nelson explains in ("Embedded Markup Considered Harmful" (`http://www.xml.com/pub/a/w3j/s3.nelson.html`), it does not go without saying that embedded markup is itself correct. So, TeX should really have a front end, such as is supplied by Scientific Word (`http://www.mackichan.com/`). Note that in the case of that software, the internal representation of the document is a collection of objects, and the LaTeX form is used only for document storage and exchange. Other representations are therefore possible. Meanwhile, the document maintainer (the "author") does not have to concern herself with markup at all.

The programming interface is how we macro writers create an abstract formatting engine. For example, this is what I do when I create a LaTeX document class. However, dealing with the macabre TeX programming language is not the right way to get the job done. A cleaner interface is provided by, e.g., FrameMaker or QuarkXPress, where your interface is a panel with sliders, menus, and other modern UI tools. In fact, PCTeX is now offering such a system, and Scientific Word had one back in the early 1990s.

At the same time, progress has left TeX's markup paradigm behind. With the advent of Unicode, it is no longer necessary to use control sequence names for many glyphs, like `\alpha`. Unicode itself evolved alongside of TeX, and it is really too bad that TeX was not Unicode-aware in the first place.

People are pretty strongly wedded to the idea of TeX remaining compatible with its original behavior. At the same time, alterations to TeX (with a compatibility switch) have greatly changed its functionality. I think the time has long since arrived when we should rethink some of the original design decisions that went into TeX almost 30 years ago.

The first relates to color; I discussed this issue earlier.

Another aspect has to do with the math infix operators (like `\over`). The infix operators are what cause the four math styles (`\displaystyle`, `\textstyle`, `\scriptstyle`, and `\scriptscriptstyle`) to be handled in such an awkward way. When a math list is being compiled, you do not know for sure which style you are in — all because of the existence of the infix operators. If these are done away with, the macro writer has much more effective control. And there is no compelling need for infix math operators: it was simply a decision, and it was one with (um) strong consequences for TeX.

Consider what happens when you enter the output routine: some items in the Main Vertical List are discarded, never to be recovered. Information should not be discarded; an effective alternative would be to present the items in `\box255`, but marked as discarded for the purposes of that tour of the output routine. If the output routine throws the contents of `\box255` back onto the MVL, the items marked discarded would reappear. The decision to discard items in this way is the source of enduring grief for those writing an output routine, as I did.

An annoying limitation of TeX is that there is a single class of `\mark` objects. An enhanced version of TeX with, say, 255 `\marks`, such as William Baxter's SuperTeX, enables one to take care of the output in an elegant way.

Yet another problem in TeX has to do with the algorithm that breaks paragraphs into lines: when that algorithm fails, it throws all the `\badness` into a single line. This means that upon failure, the output is very ugly. A better outcome would involve a softer landing.

Finally, the font data is static rather than dynamic: once read, it cannot be superseded or discarded. This misfeature stems from the notion that a font's data would be read in once and for all at the beginning of a job. Who would ever want to do otherwise?

Let us put these matters into perspective. TeX, in its day, had been considered a relatively large program, yet its executable (that is, not counting any storage) is a mere one-eighth of a megabyte of machine-language code (this is the case for older computers with compact instruction encoding; 64-bit computers may differ). Modern computers are many orders of magnitude speedier than the DEC System 10 that TeX82 originally ran on. Even in storage, Small TeX is no longer "large": it could fit on the *stack* of a modern personal computer.

Many of the design decisions of TeX were compelled by the limited storage and speed of 1980-era computers. Such limitations now perhaps apply to, say, running TeX on an iPhone—but certainly do not apply to running TeX on a Mac Pro, where one could conceivably call TeX as a function with all of its storage in a stack frame. Indeed, multiple instances of TeX could run simultaneously, each with its own storage.

If TeX were to be redone today, one could retain all of its good features while jettisoning its bad decisions, making it into a much better engine than before. At the same time, it would still have a compatibility switch that would make it pass the trip test.

Under the hood, it might use garbage collection and other modern programming paradigms. It might be integrated into the runtime library of your operating system, putting TeX's calculations at the service of any program running on your computer. It might take advantage of the multiple cores present in your computer. The possibilities are enormous, once you get your mind free of the mental blinders.

DW: The comprehensive list of officers and board members of TUG at `http://tug.org/board.html` shows that you have been a board member since 1997, were secretary for four years, and vice president for two years after that. Karl Berry also tells me that you and your wife "came through" for TUG by operating the TUG office in 1997. How did you come to be involved in TUG governance, why do you continue to participate, what was the situation that led to you providing the TUG office function (for those of us not familiar with TUG history), and what did you learn for yourself or TUG from the experience?

AO: In late 1986, I called the TUG office to renew my membership and had a conversation with Patricia Monohon, then the Executive Director. Patricia, cashing in on the considerable goodwill in our relationship, asked me if I would be willing to assist her in organizing the TUG 1997 conference to be held at the University of San Francisco.

Glossing over a great deal of *tsuris*, in the months between then and July 1997,

- I decided to run for TUG President, then changed my mind and ran for the Board,
- was appointed to the board early by then TUG president Michel Goossens,
- agreed to supervise Marian Goldeen (my wife) in temporarily running the TUG office when Patricia completed her term of employment as TUG Executive Director in about May of 1997,
- took responsibility for the TUG 1997 conference in San Francisco,
- handed over the TUG office at the end of that conference to the newly installed TUG President Mimi Jett,
- agreed to work as TUG Secretary.

I continued to serve on the TUG Executive Committee, first as Secretary and later as Vice-President, until 2003.

I saw my role on the Board as responding to a need for transparency and responsibility to the TUG membership. We also had to figure out a new business model where we could afford to have an employee. This was at a time when *TUGboat* was chronically late in getting out, and TUG members were wondering what benefit they were receiving in exchange for their dues. As it happened, TUG decided to distribute the TeX Live software as a benefit of membership, which did much to bolster our fortunes.

My service to TUG reflects my sense that, as a self-employed person who benefitted from the existence of the TeX software and the large base of users of TeX, I had an obligation to do what I could to see to the health of TUG, the organization whose purpose was to benefit users of TeX.

Now that we have Robin Laakso as Executive Director and Karl Berry as TUG President, I think we are much better off than at any time since I began serving on the Board.

DW: Thank you, Arthur, for participating in this interview. I have greatly enjoyed hearing what you had to say.

Hàn Thế Thành

Hàn Thế Thành is the creator of and still maintains pdfTEX. [Interview completed 24 July 2008.]

Dave Walden, interviewer: Please tell me a bit about your personal history independent of TEX.

Hàn Thế Thành, interviewee: I was born in Vietnam in 1972 and lived there until 1990, when I got a chance to go study in the Czech Republic (at that time still named Czechoslovakia). I studied at the Masaryk University in Brno from 1991 to 2001 and got a Master's degree and later PhD degree in Computer Science. Then I went back to Vietnam and worked at the University of Pedagogy in Ho Chi Minh City (also known as Saigon). Since 2006 I have been living with my wife in Bielefeld, Germany, where my wife is studying.

DW: What was your job at the University of Pedagogy?

HTT: I was teaching introductory programming and working as a network administrator.

DW: Please tell me when and how you first got involved with TEX.

HTT: During the first years at the university, I heard from time to time from my schoolmates that TEX is an amazing typesetting system, very powerful also but very difficult to use. But I didn't use TEX myself at all until I had to choose the subject for my Master's thesis in the fourth year. There were a number of subjects to choose among, and I picked one that sounded like "Automated typesetting systems" or something similar. The idea of my supervisor was for me to rewrite TEX using a high-level language. Later it became clear that rewriting TEX in a high-level language was a too difficult task for a student like me, so my thesis supervisor changed my topic to "TEX typesetting system and the Portable Document Format". The intention was more or less what pdfTEX does today: to change TEX so that it can produce pdf directly. So, I first had to learn about TEX — to get really involved with TEX. Before that I only heard about TEX but never used it. That was in 1994.

DW: One can argue that a key reason TEX remains so vibrant today is the existence of pdfTEX. From what you just said it sounds like you sort of stumbled into creating pdfTEX which everyone uses today — that your thesis supervisor pushed you in this direction more than that you had an initial deep desire to work in this area. Is that correct?

HTT: Yes, pdfTEX started more or less like that: my supervisor, Professor Jiří Zlatuška, used to be a very active TEX user and developer. Jiří is also a fan of logical programming. So his original intention was for me to rewrite TEX using a declarative language like Prolog and use that for further development. I had little (if any) clue what all this meant. I picked the subject I did simply because: (1) I liked logical programming; (2) from what

I had heard about TeX, the subject sounded interesting; and (3) I didn't find a more interesting subject to choose from the available topics.

After a few months of playing with rewriting TeX, it was clear to me and also to Jiří that rewriting TeX in Prolog was too difficult for me. Suddenly one day Jiří called me to his office, gave me the printed PDF specification version 1.0, and said that I might try to change TeX to produce PDF output directly (later I learnt that Jiří got that idea from some discussion with Phil Taylor and Knuth at Stanford University). I was keen about the idea and the original plan also seemed unrealistic; so we changed our plan. I started to read the PDF specification and to learn how to hack TeX with the Knuthian web system, Web2c, Kpathsea and friends. After a few months I made a "Hello, world!" PDF from TeX, and it was rather an exciting moment for us. But I didn't expect pdfTeX to be as widely used as it is today (I think Jiří didn't expect that either, but I might be wrong here).

I learnt TeX "the hard way": I started with reading *The TeXbook* since that's what Jiří gave me in the beginning. Then I started using plain TeX since I had heard that LaTeX was not as good as plain if you wanted to learn the details of TeX, to control every part of typesetting, and so on. So I used plain TeX to typeset a periodical, thesis work of my friends, and other occasional materials. But later I started using LaTeX, since doing everything in plain is rather painful. So I use LaTeX mostly, and use plain TeX only for a few very specific applications that would be better done in plain TeX.

Learning the PDF format was not very hard, since the specification of PDF version 1.0 was a very thin book (I would have given up immediately if I got, for example, version 1.3 or later). But learning web change files, Web2C and friends was rather hard for me: too many steps were involved, and when something goes wrong, it is not easy to find out where the mistake is.

Jiří wanted me to follow the literate programming paradigm and have everything done via the change file mechanism. However later it became more and more difficult to maintain things this way, so I decided to move certain things to C. The main criteria in deciding what to keep in Pascal WEB or and what to do in C is this: if it is backend-related, it should be in C; otherwise it should be in WEB. Jiří was not happy with my decision, but more or less accepted it (or at least let me do it).

DW: Did you finish an operating version of pdfTeX as your Master's thesis, or did you somehow finish your thesis and then keep working until an operational version of pdfTeX was available?

HTT: I cannot recall when pdfTeX became really "functional for use", since the development was gradual with contributions by many people in various areas. When I finished my Master's thesis, the state of pdfTeX was about as stated in Petr Sojka's article: support for embedded Type1 fonts, virtual fonts, hyperlinks, LZW compression (later LZW compression was replaced by zip compression). There was no image inclusion yet!

DW: Are you referring to the article entitled "The Joy of tex2pdf—Acrobatics with an Alternative to DVI Format" by Sojka, Jiří, and you, in *TUGboat* 17:3 (1996)?

HTT: Yes.

DW: How did the greater TeX world become aware of your pdfTeX system and come to include it in all the TeX distributions?

HTT: I got connected to other people in the TeX world for the first time when Jiří corresponded with Sebastian Rahtz about pdfTeX (at that time still 'tex2pdf'). Sebastian was interested and started playing with pdfTeX, supporting it in various ways: he set up the pdfTEX mailing list, compiled and tested it on other platforms, introduced it to other users, etc. Sebastian gave a vital push to pdfTEX development in those early days.

Later pdfTEX was seen by Knuth during his visit to Masaryk University and it received positive comments by Knuth, which was very encouraging for us (me and Jiří). The first article about pdfTEX was the one I just mentioned, by Petr Sojka. The pdfTEX mailing list was an extremely useful place to discuss pdfTEX development in the beginning. And one day Hans Hagen showed up on that list and started experimenting with pdfTEX, reporting problems, discussing new ideas and features, etc., which was another great impact on pdfTEX. The fact that such well known and active members of the TEX community (Sebastian, Hans, etc.) liked pdfTEX was the key to pdfTEX becoming more "known". Then it got included in teTEX by Thomas Esser. Once something is in teTEX, usually it will be accepted consequently by other TEX systems.

DW: Please clarify for me the distinction, if any, between pdfTEX and the microtypographic extensions to TEX described in your PhD thesis that was reproduced in a special issue of *TUGboat* (volume 21, number 4), "Microtypographic extensions to the TEX typesetting system".

HTT: The goal of my Master's thesis was to make PDF output directly from TEX. When I started my PhD study (also under Jiří), we only knew I would do something related to typesetting, but we did not know exactly what. During the first year or so of my PhD studies, I was still developing pdfTEX and also looking for an idea for the PhD thesis. I came up with a few, then Jiří told me to stick with the micro-typographic extensions, which was again a very wise decision in my opinion.

DW: Please clarify for me the timing of your Master's studies and your PhD studies. You said you were at Masaryk University from 1991 to 2001. When did your Master's degree finish and your PhD studies begin?

HTT: I finished my Master's studies in summer 1996. A few months afterward I started my PhD studies.

DW: Please elaborate a bit more on your approach to learning about micro-typography, to making the necessary extensions to pdfTEX, and the research component necessary for a successful PhD thesis.

HTT: I don't feel very qualified to talk about how to do a successful PhD thesis, since I was struggling with mine to get it done at all.

DW: Sorry; I didn't mean to remind you of a stressful time. Mainly I am interested in how you learned what you needed to know about micro-typography?

HTT: I cannot recall exactly how I learned about micro-typography — it was a gradual process, as for most people, I suppose. I started by reading some books and articles, and then I searched for more relevant resources. The most useful resources I can remember were the paper by Hermann Zapf "About microtypography and the hz-program" and the brochure about the hz-program by URW, the German type foundry. I also experimented a lot with Adobe InDesign, which claims to have some modules from the hz-program integrated. It's interesting to see that some ideas of the hz-program were inspired by TEX itself originally.

DW: I know that pdfTEX was quite operational by the time you finished your PhD thesis. Did you keep developing pdfTEX after you returned to Vietnam?

HTT: When I returned to Vietnam, in the beginning I had a long break in pdfTEX development due to difficulty with network access and various things. Then occasionally I found time to make small extensions to pdfTEX, but it was no longer active development as before. Of course other people have been contributing to pdfTEX, too. The most significant contributions to pdfTEX in the recent years were done by a very quiet person named Hartmut Henkel. His patches greatly improved pdfTEX in many aspects: speed, stability, cleaner code, better functionality, etc.

DW: More recently you seem to have gotten more involved in developing pdfTEX again.

HTT: Yes, I have been more involved with pdfTEX since I moved to Germany with my wife. In Germany I work at home as a consultant for River Valley Technologies — Kaveh and Radhakrishnan's company. I support network administration, automating some editing tasks, and also pdfTEX deployment.

DW: I gather that pdfTEX development works in some fashion as an "open source" development effort. And you told me in a message last week that you had to take a few days away from our interview because Karl Berry wanted you to fix something about pdfTEX immediately for the upcoming TEX Live release. Please tell me about the on-going organization and coordination of pdfTEX development.

HTT: pdfTEX development has evolved over time, and presently works more or less like this. There is a project page for pdfTEX hosted at `sarovar.org` where people submit bug reports, feature requests or patches. There is also a mailing list for people interested in pdfTEX development. And there is a core team (Hans Hagen, Taco Hoekwater, Hartmut Henkel, Martin Schröder and me) where we discuss the decisions made on pdfTEX.

DW: I understand that you have spent (a lot of) effort adding Vietnamese support to a number of fonts. How did you get involved with this and how did you go about it?

HTT: As I was learning TEX, I was interested in using it for Vietnamese too. At that time there was a package called `vcmr` by Werner Lemberg, which already provides quite good support for typesetting Vietnamese. However, I was not happy with the shapes of Vietnamese letters, so I decided to add Vietnamese letters to the CM fonts by myself. It was only a hobby activity, and I didn't have any artistic background. I learnt mostly by looking at existing fonts and reading materials that I could find, as well as from comments I received from experienced people. I added the Vietnamese letters to CM fonts using Metafont. To convert those fonts to Type1 format, I used a combination of several tools: Metafog, FMP (by Y&Y), `a2ac`, and some of my own Perl scripts. To add Vietnamese letters to existing Type 1 fonts, I used more or less the same route, although I drew the accents using FontLab.

There are more people involved in `vntex`: Werner Lemberg and Vladimir Volovich for LATEX support, and Reinhard Kotucha for testing/maintaining the package and making everything neatly conform to TDS and providing what is required by TEX Live and CTAN such as having a `README` file, copyright notices, etc. There is no active development on `vntex` anymore, since `vntex` has quite a large number of fonts already. There is even a Vietnamese translation of the math font survey for TEX by Stephen Hartke, which means that most of the text fonts mentioned in the survey have a Vietnamese version, too.

DW: Thank you, Thành, for taking the time to participate in this interview. It has been an honor for me to communicate with someone who has had such a major impact on the continuing use of TEX.

[Endnote: In reviewing this interview, Thành noted these important co-developers of pdfTEX: Pavel Janik added tiff support (later removed); Heiko Oberdiek added color stack support; Jiri Osoba added jpeg support; Ricardo Sanchez Carmenes added encryption support (later removed); Robert Schlicht made a LaTeX package for micro-typographic features; Martin Schroder maintained pdfTeX for many years; and finally, of course pdfTeX is just an extension of TeX, and would not exist if Donald Knuth had not written TeX itself. He offers his sincere apologies if anyone else who should be given credit was missed!]

Tomas Rokicki

Tom Rokicki created dvips and TeX's original Pascal to C converter.

[Interview completed 15 August 2008.]

Dave Walden, interviewer: Please tell me a bit about your personal history independent of TeX.

Tomas Rokicki, interviewee: I live in Palo Alto with my wife Sue and our yellow Labrador Andy. I moved out to California from Texas to attend Stanford, and liked it so much I've felt no inclination to move away. My favorite pastime is still programming, whether it's cellular automata (Golly), solving Rubik's cube, or programming the Propeller microcontroller. When I'm not programming, I'm usually training for my next marathon.

DW: I was reading about some of those activities at `http://tomas.rokicki.com`, gathering background information for this interview.

TR: I grew up as just another math/science geek. Grammar school near Chicago during the 70s was Radio Shack 150-in-1 kits, disassembling radios and electrical appliances, and studying an electronic engineering textbook my parents purchased for me. High school in Texas was slide-rule competition, microcomputer programming, and chess.

I was fortunate to be accepted into Texas A&M University, but even more fortunate to meet Professor Norman Naugle there. Professor Naugle helped me find jobs that complemented my classwork, and always had a challenging program that needed writing.

DW: Your web site also mentions that you recently had cochlear implant surgery.

TR: My deafness is in remission: The cochlear implant is working *amazingly* well. If you saw me in person it would probably be the first thing you notice about me. I have some words on `http://radbits.blogspot.com/` about it. This is just a *touch* personal, but my life has been so greatly impacted by this amazing miracle that I'm really glad to mention it.

DW: When and how did you first come in contact with TeX?

TR: In my junior year at Texas A&M, Professor Naugle introduced me to TeX; he was trying to get it running on campus in various departments. In particular, he needed a way to print from TeX to the newfangled QMS laser printers. These laser printers were huge, about the size of a corner mailbox, printed at an incredible 300 dpi, and were controlled by a proprietary language. The first TeX code I wrote was a driver for those beasts.

Another task was to get TeX running on the Unix minicomputers that were in use at that time. Since the Unix Pascal compiler was not up to the task of compiling TeX, I wrote a script using lex and yacc to compile the TeX code to C.

Professor Naugle and I flew out to Stanford for one of the early TeX User Group meetings (I believe this was in 1984), and it was here that I met so many of the famous

TeX people, including Don Knuth himself, Barbara Beeton, David Fuchs, and so many others. Once I saw the campus and the people and got a taste of the excitement in the computer science department at the time, I knew that was where I wanted to go for graduate school.

Between graduation from Texas A&M and my first semester at Stanford, during the summer of 1985, I had the unique opportunity to work on the TeX project. David Fuchs generously allowed me to stay with him for a while until I could secure lodging on campus. That summer, and the next few years at Stanford, were some of the greatest times of my life.

DW: Was your method of compiling TeX into C related to how TeX is currently compiled using Web2c?

TR: Sure; it's the same code. The current Web2c project is derived from that code I wrote back in the mid 80's. Many people have extended it over the years, such as the Kpathsearch integration, and better portability, and much, much more.

DW: What part of the TeX project did you work on that summer before graduate school at Stanford?

TR: The primary work was the design and implementation of the PK tools. At that time, disk space was relatively precious, especially on the microcomputers of the time. The PK format stored the same information as GF files, but in approximately half the disk space. So I wrote `gftopk`, `pktogf`, `pktype`, and a few other utilities.

DW: You said your years at Stanford were great times. Tell me something about what you did during those years and that made them great times.

TR: Well, ... the "Programming and Problem Solving Seminar" course was spectacular fun, both the one I took, and the one I later was a teaching assistant for—fairly open-ended problems solved (or just worked on) by groups of first-year doctoral candidates.

Learning to play go from Daniel Weise, and playing my classmates in Margaret Jacks Hall.

Knuth's Concrete Mathematics course was a blast.

Programming the Amiga, and leading a student club centered around that machine for a few years. I had a blast programming that machine.

Just being a graduate student at Stanford back then, and learning really neat things from my classmates and the classes, was just amazing.

DW: Please tell me about when and how you came to develop `dvips`.

TR: I developed `dvips` on the Amiga, based on `dvisw`, a QMS SmartWriter driver I had written earlier. The SmartWriter driver was extremely limited because that laser printer had only about 64KB or so of memory, so there wasn't much room for downloaded fonts. Even the PostScript printers available then had limited memory, however, so managing that memory and making sure a document that used a lot of characters from a lot of fonts did not run out of memory when printing was a challenge.

In any case, converting `dvisw` to drive PostScript was not all that difficult; most of the code remained the same. I wanted to generate fairly concise PostScript (disk space being somewhat precious; I did not have a hard disk, and floppies only stored 800K each) so there was some effort there.

Getting the output fully correct turned out to be a real challenge; there were bugs in the PostScript interpreters at the time that needed to be worked around. Over the years, as PostScript showed up on different devices, many changes had to be made to support all the different interpreters and their differing characteristics.

One early example is maintaining an even baseline. For downloaded type 3 fonts, the vertical displacement of a character bounding box from the baseline is specified along with the glyph data. For some interpreters, there was a discontinuity at 0; characters with a negative vertical displacement would show up one pixel offset from their desired position. Thus an 'e', which might live entirely on or above the baseline at a particular resolution, would be placed correctly, but a 'g', with its descender going below the baseline, would be rendered one pixel too high. This made characters in a line jump up and down on the baseline in a very ragged manner—but only by a single pixel. At 300 dpi it was fairly noticeable, but at any resolution it was wrong. So `dvips` had to pull some PostScript tricks to make sure these lines rendered correctly both on interpreters with this problem, and on interpreters that did not have this problem.

Another example is rules. `dvips` had been running along well for a long time when NeXT came out with their computer and its printer. For whatever reason, rendering rules on the NeXT was just incredibly slow. Rules were rendered by `dvips` using the "imagemask" operator in order to guarantee precise placement and size, and the NeXT version of PostScript just did not like the imagemask calls that `dvips` generated.

It should be noted that Don Knuth himself performed the conversion of `dvips` to support the virtual font format, and along the way he made some significant improvements to `dvips`. I believe at least one note from him to me remains in the source.

DW: I don't yet have a solid fix on the timing of your original `dvips` work. Was it originally for PostScript level 1 in 1984 or for some other version of PostScript?

TR: I'm not quite sure on the timing myself, but I'm pretty sure I made it work during 1985 or 1986. It was indeed for PostScript level 1; the first version was developed against an original LaserWriter.

DW: Have you continued to maintain `dvips` over the years, or has that been passed on to others in the TEX community?

TR: Frankly, Karl Berry has done the great majority of the work, and for that I am very grateful. I have not been following the TEX community for some time.

The authorship of `dvips` is a lot of people at this point. The original program was entirely my own of course, but Don Knuth made a dramatic cleanup when he modified it to support virtual fonts. The Type 1 support was added by Sergey Lesenko, although at this point we use code from pdfTEX instead. Major contributions have been made by many people; here's a partial list (in alphabetical order, hopefully to prevent hurt feelings), although I'm still a bit nervous about all the great contributors that I am forgetting:

> Karl Berry, Peter Breitenlohner, Mark Doyle, Jim Hafner, Yannis Haralambous, David M. Jones, Akira Kakuto, Don Knuth, Sergey Lesenko, Dave Love, John Plaice, Fabrice Popineau, Sebastian Rahtz, and Ulrik Vieth.

DW: We can certainly add names to our interview's web site if more contributors come to mind later.

TR: In any case, I certainly intend to support `dvips` to the best of my ability and to encourage people to contact me with questions or issues, but most recent issues have about things I really don't know much about, so other people end up doing most of the work.

DW: How do *you* pronounce `dvips`?

TR: I used to always pronounce `dvips` as `d-v-i-p-s`, but a friend of mine always pronounced `d-vips` (in one syllable), and I have sort of adopted that pronunciation.

DW: Please sketch your work life after graduate school, e.g., I've heard your name mentioned in connection with NeXT. Also, is Radical Eye Software a real company?

TR: The only thing I did for NeXT was NeXTTEX, which was as close to a clone of AmigaTEX as I could make it. I did both AmigaTEX and NeXTTEX while I was in grad school.

AmigaTEX did have the previewer and TEX connected through inter-process communication, so you could immediately preview pages even while TEX was still running, and it would immediately refresh the current page when it got to it. (Remember, back then, systems were slow, especially when running from floppies.) In addition, TEX stayed resident and after processing, it was immediately ready for the next job. Over the years additional enhancements were added, like integrated bitmap and PostScript graphics in the previewer. All that work was done under the Radical Eye Software name.

The Radical Eye Software name actually goes back to programs I wrote while still at Texas A&M University; I generally copyrighted anything I wrote with that name, whether it was free software, contracted work, or commercial software.

After grad school I worked for HP Labs for a very pleasurable number of years, with some fun colleagues. I stayed at HP until 1999, when I started Instantis with a few friends, where I still work.

DW: Thank you very much, Tom. It has been exciting to talk with you. Yours was one of the first names I heard when I started using TEX about 10 years ago, and discovered that I needed to use `dvips` every few minutes.

TR: Thanks! I have benefited from TEX in so many ways, personally and professionally, and I am just so grateful to have been part of the early days and have the chance to make my small contributions.

Yuri Robbers

Yuri Robbers is a TeX user and is a production editor for *The PracTeX Journal* as well as maintaining the journal's web site.

[Interview completed 24 August 2008.]

Dave Walden, interviewer: Please tell me a bit about your personal history independent of TeX.

Yuri Robbers, interviewee: Some people compare me to a cat, but one living all nine lives at the same time. I also have the proverbial curiosity of a cat. This already started when I was very young. I couldn't get enough of having stories read to me, and as soon as I could read I became a voracious reader, and an equally voracious experimenter. I always wanted to find out more about my surroundings. Whether it was reading about space travel — I've wanted to be an astronaut since I knew they existed — or blowing up all the fuses in the house, I was eager to find out more.

My love for books didn't stop at reading them. I also wrote from an early age, and have been cutting and folding little booklets, and as soon as I had a computer capable of running primitive DTP software (a Commodore 64) I experimented with DTP, font design, et cetera. The fact that my father worked as a professional typographer (then at Brill Academic Publishers), at first still setting lead type in hundreds of languages, may have had something to do with my love for letters and the printed word.

Growing up, I devoured everything that would sit still long enough to read. Literature, the sciences, mythology and ancient religions, art, computers, history, etc. I've always aimed at being an *uomo universale*, an ideal that I'm sure one can't really accomplish any more in this day and age, but that has never stopped me from trying.

It was difficult for me to decide what to read in university. Eventually I chose biology, and I have never regretted it. Although, admittedly, I have always taken extra courses in subjects ranging from mathematics to celtic languages. My research has taken me to three continents, the first time out of Europe being my fieldwork in Indonesia, studying orang-utan social behaviour in the wild.

After living in quite a few countries spread over three continents, I am now back in Leiderdorp, the little village in the Netherlands where I was born back in 1973. During this period I have gotten myself a masters degree in ethology, the study of animal behaviour, and I have been working on a discontinued PhD project in mathematical biology. I now work as a teacher of various subjects in a secondary school (the grammar school I graduated from), while still doing research at Leiden University, this time pursuing a PhD in behavioural ecology. In addition I still read and write loads, enjoy walking, especially in forests, study subjects ranging from folklore and mythology to typesetting, science and literature, meet with friends, play games and visit museums and concerts.

My first published book dates from 2005, and is a scientific work on vertebrate social behaviour, titled *Agonic and Hedonic Styles of Social Behaviour* and co-authored with my friend Koen Kortmulder, who was one of my teachers in University. We are now working on another book.

DW: When and how did you first get involved with TEX?

YR: I've been working with DTP programs and word processors since I found out they existed, which was in the early eighties, near the end of primary school. I've never been quite happy with them though. I did what I could to make documents I created on the computer look as nice as I possibly could.

In 1992 I went to university, and in the first two years dabbled with *roff, and later Basser Lout. The assignments I had to hand in were, however, group assignments, so I did those in WordPerfect in order to remain compatible with my fellow students. After my fieldwork in Indonesia in 1995, a fellow student introduced me to Linux and with our Linux distribution came a TEX distribution. I was hooked. Both to Linux and TEX. I started working in LATEX. Everything I had to write by myself, I typeset in LATEX. Some of my fellow students were impressed and started using it too. Ever since 1995 I have used, installed and maintained TEX systems on many types of computer, including Linux, VMS, IRIX, Commodore Amiga, Windows, Mac OS 8, 9 and X, etc.

DW: In some of our exchanges of email about my typesetting, you have also given me advice on using TEX systems beyond LATEX.

YR: I've used LATEX, plain TEX and ConTEXt for work as well as for pleasure. Just hacking around in *TEX for its own sake was — and is — pure pleasure. I would not claim to be an expert, but I have a fairly extended experience. I've written all sorts of macros and fixed all sorts of problems for myself as well as for friends and colleagues. I even — my five seconds of fame — solved a minor bug in AMS-LATEX at one point. I've played with the base systems as well as with many add-on packages and experimented with fonts, with styles, and with graphics.

In 1997 I co-authored a rather large introductory mathematics reader for the university. Unfortunately I was required to do this in MS Word for the Mac. I was not very happy: I was too used to the ease and beauty of TEX and LATEX. A similar step "back" in my experience was the publication of that first book of mine on vertebrate social behaviour. It was typeset by a third party using InDesign, and I was not too impressed with it. Especially not with the fact that we had to generate the index by hand, and had to regenerate it by hand when the publisher made some changes to the layout that changed the majority of our page breaks in unpredictable ways. Also the few polytonic greek words required in the book had to be typeset in LATEX by me, and submitted as graphics files. Neither was I too impressed with the format the publisher imposed on us: 1 1/2 linespacing, for example, may be fine for manuscripts, but in an actual published book it is a bit too much for my tastes.

I wouldn't dare to claim that *TEX is ideal for everyone, but it is definitely the system I prefer using. It offers me ease of use and beauty, and I have gotten so used to it — and its little idiosyncrasies — that I do not often run into problems anymore.

DW: You and I first met (on-line) in regard to publication of *The PracTEX Journal.*

YR: I've always intended to contribute to TEX. As I've said above, that started out by helping friends and colleagues. I've also answered the occasional question on TEX mailing lists, and filed that one bug fix I've mentioned. In 2006 I decided to offer helping out with TPJ. My offer was accepted, and ever since I have worked as a production editor. I deal with authors, edit papers, and run the scripts that keep the web site going. I've also written some papers, acted as Nelly (the typographical agony aunt) regularly, and managed to contribute one tiny script to the web site, one that eases generation of the whole issue PDF.

Since I've joined the TPJ production team, I've also been invited to join the *TUGboat* production team, although I must admit I've not had the time to contribute much to *TUGboat* yet. I still owe them at least two papers as well. Through TPJ and *TUGboat* I've had the opportunity to work with some wonderful people, most of whom are far more knowledgeable when it comes to *TEX than myself.

DW: You co-wrote an article for TPJ on creating book covers using PSTricks (`http://tug.org/pracjourn/2007-1/robbers/`). Have you been involved in the actual publication of books to a significant extent?

YR: I have done some typesetting (a few novels, a book of collected stories and a bunch of small booklets with short stories) for an independent publisher (Saga Whyte Press).

I used LATEX and Peter Wilson's Memoir for these projects, and I've used the Minion Pro fonts — which I bought for this purpose — along with Achim Blumensath's Minion Pro support for TEX. For these books and short stories I've also created the covers. I have not done the actual artwork, but I did implement everything in LATEX and PSTricks, and provided feedback to the artist, Annemarie Skjold, my co-author for the paper you have mentioned.

At university I was one of the editors, and for several years the editor-in-chief of a magazine for biologists. When I became an editor, this magazine was typeset in WordPerfect, and nowadays it is typeset in MS Word, but in between it has been typeset (mostly by me) in LATEX and a class file that I wrote, using `report.cls` as a basis, for this purpose.

After graduating, I was the Secretary of the Dutch Society for Theoretical Biology for five years. All correspondence and booklets, conference programs etc., issued by this society were made in LATEX. My predecessor had left me a huge collection of macros and programs, including a complete mail merge system he and other people wrote. During my five years I have adapted and expanded these macros, and created quite a few new ones. During this time I have also created a BIBTEX style file for the new bibliographical format of the *Journal for Theoretical Biology* called `jtbnew.bst` (it supersedes `jtb.bst`), which matches the old bibliographical format. I've used Patrick Daly's magnificent `makebst` script to create the basis, and then tweaked the result by hand. This project did, therefore, not require a great amount of programming skill — mostly a good eye for detail, a willingness to spend a lot of time on niggly-naggly conventions and problems, and a basic understanding of the `.bst` format.

I am currently working on a two-volume book on the behaviour of Asiatic Barbs, again co-authored with Koen Kortmulder and on a PhD thesis. For the PhD thesis I am using LATEX and Memoir. Regarding the book, it depends on the publisher: if our publisher will do the typesetting in-house, the decision will of course not be mine, but if they leave the typesetting to the authors, I will do it myself using some form of *TEX — most likely LATEX or AMS-LATEX with Memoir again.

DW: Was your interest in typesetting only spurred by your father's work, or did you also learn some craft from him?

YR: He taught me a lot of the visual aspects of typesetting and of fonts. He showed me many examples of good and bad typesetting, and explained about the errors made in many pieces of typeset material. I also have him comment on the things I make, and use his criticism to improve my own work.

After I graduated from secondary school my father arranged a summer job for me in the printer's company where he worked at that time. I got to do four weeks of full-time work as his apprentice in the macro-typography department. We would get the typeset pages from micro-typography (where I also got to learn a thing or two), and we would lay out the originals for the printing presses, usually 16 pages per sheet of paper. We would also place any additional material such as illustrations, photographic material, backgrounds, etc. We would then photographically transfer everything to large sheets of film. These would be checked for errors, both typographic and photographic, and if everything looked fine transfer the image from film onto large metal sheets which would go onto the press.

DW: Tell me about your interactive fiction activities.

YR: When I was still a child, my uncle introduced me to Interactive Fiction, or as it was called back then, text adventures: computer games where one reads a bit of a story, types commands to be executed by the main character, and then receives the feedback, etc., until the story ends. One plays, as it were, the main character in a novel, solving puzzles and trying to bring the story to a happy end. At first these games were rather primitive, with simple verb-noun commands all that one could type. Nevertheless: I was hooked. Later I discovered games with far better parsers (the parser being the bit of the program that translates whatever the player types into something the program can work with) such as those by Magnetic Scrolls, Level 9 and especially Infocom.

I not only played these games, but I created a few simple ones as well. At first I used BASIC, but later I've used other computer languages as well. At some point I discovered Graham Nelson's language Inform, which is an Object Oriented programming language for Interactive Fiction. He also provided a parser which mimics the Infocom parser. Actually the last (or as I hope latest) game from the Infocom people was written in Inform.

I started exploring Inform and created a Dutch version of Graham's parser for it. The quintessential test of such translations is a translation of the original Adventure by Will Crowther, which I've also provided.

I wrote some small games of my own, and also used the parser to create educational software which is used in the school where I work. Also I have helped some students create such software using my Dutch parser and some additional modules I wrote for these educational programs.

DW: Some of your specific connections to Interactive Fiction are particularly fun for me to hear about. I knew a couple of the key Infocom guys when Infocom was an independent company (back in the decade starting in about 1977), and Will Crowther was my programming mentor.

Thank you, Yuri, for taking the time to participate in this interview. I've greatly enjoyed learning more about your background and activities beyond what we have talked about in our interactions over TPJ.

Amy Hendrickson

Amy Hendrickson has made her living for over twenty years as a TeX/LaTeX macro writer for publishing companies and academic societies; she also does book production and teaches LaTeX.

[Interview completed 14 September 2008.]

Dave Walden, interviewer: Please tell me a bit about your personal history independent of TeX.

Amy Hendrickson, interviewee: I have an undergrad degree in music composition from the University of Wisconsin, Madison, and a master's degree in music composition from the New England Conservatory. After graduating from NEC, I took a job as an office assistant at MIT in the VLSI office, partly because I liked MIT and partly because I hoped to pick up a computer skill that would support me since my chosen profession, writing contemporary classical music, seemed very unlikely to do so.

DW: When and how did you first come in contact with TeX?

AH: TeX was the computer skill I developed during my time at MIT — a fortuitous choice which has had the effect of not only employing me over the succeeding years, but which has put me in touch with a very interesting and pleasant clientele, scientific authors and publishers.

Within a year I left the MIT job and set off on my new career using and teaching TeX and later LaTeX. This was in the early 1980's. I initially worked for MIT professors, typesetting their books, then learned enough about macro writing that I was able to write macro packages for many publishing companies and academic associations. I imagine this seems an unusual development, since I don't have formal computer science education, but perhaps my engineer father lent a genetic predisposition to my doing technical work, while my creative impulse found some outlet in coming up with solutions for knotty macro writing problems. I still find it enjoyable to come up with novel solutions, most recently using TeX to parse the output of Acrobat forms to be used for automated report generation, or to choose the input for database publishing.

I go into this background in a little more detail at `http://www.texnology.com/who.htm` and `http://www.texnology.com/innov.htm`.

DW: You talk about "using TeX to parse the output of Acrobat forms". How does that work?

AH: PDF forms produce a text file, `*.fdf`.

This file may be parsed by inputting the `*.fdf` file into a prepared `.tex` file which calls a parsing style file which I've written. When LaTeX is run on this file, new definitions are written to another file, called `*.inf`. These new definitions are formed by interpreting the information in the `.fdf` file, and are sent out using `\write` and `\csname ... \endcsname`.

Since we supplied the original form, and are looking for answers to specific questions that were asked in this PDF form, we can build a `.tex` file that expects and uses these newly defined commands, by inputting the new `*.inf` file at the top of a prepared `.tex` template file.

Then, when LaTeX is run on the template file it will expand the new LaTeX definitions to produce results that reflect the responses to the original PDF form.

This new document can be used in any number of ways, including automated report generation, where a specific data set is represented in text and even with customized graphics. The possibilities for using LaTeX/PostScript in this way for data visualization seem almost unlimited. Particularly in the area of bioinformatics, I could imagine that there might be many useful applications.

The new document could also be used to build a customized report by including specific parts of an existing database of text or graphic information, the PDF form in this case serving the purpose of choosing the specific bits that are wanted for a particular report, out of the much greater set of existing text/graphic files.

If there was a good reason to start with an HTML form, rather than a PDF form, a similar set of steps could be followed, with the same flexibility of possible applications.

DW: You write macro packages, you teach LaTeX, you do book production, among other things. Do you do all of these functions and all of this work yourself, or do you have other people to whom you sometimes subcontract part of the work?

AH: I subcontract very infrequently. I rather enjoy doing book production myself, although not more than 10 books a year. The authors are often enjoyable and the topics interesting even if my level of understanding is hindered by my lack of a real science/math background. Occasionally I will work in partnership with one or more people, but I don't usually subcontract.

DW: What do you see as the continuing prospects for TeX et al. in the face of the continuing evolution of programs in the commercial world, e.g., InDesign, PDFs, new standards for how fonts are specified, etc.?

AH: I see the growth area in LaTeX being web-based automated production of custom PDF, in response to either PDF forms or HTML forms, and using databases of some sort. The programmability of LaTeX combined with the possibility of including PostScript code seems unique to me, and the value-added features that can be included in a PDF file that starts with a TeX file leaves much room for exploration.

Beyond these areas, there is the mostly unrealized potential for LaTeX to be used in truly aesthetic book production. This is not due to any shortcoming in the capabilities of LaTeX combined with PostScript, but only due to the fact that it is usually thought of as a "techie" tool.

DW: What software tools do you use?

AH: I use a simple Emacs-type editor, usually with the dvipsone package developed by Berthold Horn and distributed by the now defunct Y&Y company. I usually work on a PC, though I own a Mac. (Heresy I expect for Mac enthusiasts!)

DW: Please tell me a bit more about yourself.

AH: I have spent a good part of the last seven years doing very active political organizing, as part of the antiwar movement. Part of this work has been organizing peace concerts held at MIT and Harvard, a MLK concert at Mass Art, and recently a benefit concert for the Children of Gaza. I have also helped organize demonstrations locally in the Boston area, and helped get people to New York City or Washington, DC, for national demonstrations.

And I've hosted innumerable speakers, shown films, and met lots of concerned and humane people that are terribly saddened by our government's actions.

One of my most satisfying efforts was organizing an international demonstration before the onset of the Iraq invasion, hoping to stop the war before it started. This involved finding collaborative organizations to co-sign an invitation email and sending the email out to overseas organizations whose contact info I found on the web, inviting people to demonstrate with us in the USA in October of 2002. Organizations like Greenpeace and Global Exchange and more, also used their international email lists to contact people world wide. On the given day people in 17 cities demonstrated in front of their local American Consulates, including Nepal, many places in Europe, Japan, and other countries at the same time as we were demonstrating in NYC. It was thrilling, and leads me to think that people-to-people international antiwar communication and cooperation may have some potential to stop wars in the future. We've only begun to explore the wonders of the Internet and Web as organizing tools, but it is obvious that we are in a new paradigm now that people can communicate directly over national borders unmediated by their governments.

As for music, I do hope to resume composing some time in the future — meanwhile I have become a grandmother of two lovely grandchildren who are growing up in Dublin, Ireland, with their American father, my son, and Irish mother, my daughter-in-law.

DW: Do you ever use TEX as part of those activities?

AH: Not specifically. I've written many hundreds of flyers, which I started producing in TEX, but soon learned that Word, flawed though it is, seems a faster protyping and production tool for a one or two page flyer. I did use TEX for making lawn signs for a candidate for the Senate whose campaign I was involved in, and I used it also for producing some newspaper ads.

My TEX work and political work are perhaps related, in that the TEX community with its international reach and its democratic nature surely shares the same global outlook, as does the science world in general, that nationalism is only a impediment to pure truth seeking and exploring the nature of reality, and where the ideal products are useful to all people everywhere.

I'd like to add that I also am most grateful to Donald Knuth for building the solid and open-ended programming language that I've worked with on a daily basis for the last twenty plus years. His kind spirit set the tone and example for the generous TEX users who have shared thousands of their `.sty` files, fonts, and ideas, in a worldwide collaborative effort, allowing all of us to be part of a welcoming, humane, and international community.

DW: Thank you for participating in this interview. Since we both live in the Boston area, perhaps we will meet in person at some point.

AH: I'd like that! Thanks for the interview, Dave.

Bogusław Jackowski and Janusz Marian Nowacki

Bogusław Jackowski (left photo) and Janusz Marian Nowacki (right) have made and continue to make many important contributions in the world of TeX fonts.

[Interview completed 27 September 2008.]

Dave Walden, interviewer: Will each of you please tell me a bit about your personal history and life.

Bogusław Jackowski, interviewee: I came to this world in the middle of the previous century, in 1950, in Gdańsk (Danzig). My school years I spent in another city, but I always dreamt about coming back to Gdańsk which I have considered extraordinary. The city is picturesquely placed between the Baltic Sea and the band of postglacial hills covered with beautiful forests. So, for studies I came back to Gdańsk. I studied chemistry at the Gdańsk University of Technology, but I didn't feel like a chemist whatsoever. Having finished studies (1972), I switched immediately to the realm of computers: I started to work as a programmer in a computing center at the Gdańsk University, and next as a teaching assistant in the Department of Mathematics in a newly established Division of Computer Science.

Oh, the giant machines of those days, placed in specially conditioned large halls, paper tapes, drum memories, teletypes, line printers, consoles resembling typewriter machines.... No screens, no color/laser printers, no pen drives, no CDs, unbelievable!

Still, the work with students was exciting: there was no magic in the computer — each behavior was explicable. It was unforgettable experience to see how hard it was for students to accept that wrong results imply unavoidably an error in their programs: "I checked thoroughly, there is no mistake in my program; it must have been the computer's slip." And next long, laborious line by line checking of the printout and eventually — eureka! — "aaaa, it is this little semicolon, responsible for completely screwed up results!" Nowadays, I'd never try to convince newbies that the computer is infallible.

Incidentally, neat program listings was my first experience with "computer typesetting".

Janusz Marian Nowacki, interviewee: I was born in 1951. I live in Grudziądz, in the northern part of Poland. I studied journalism at the Warsaw University and worked as a journalist. Hence my interest in typesetting and typefaces — I was familiar with the printing technology of that time.

In 1981, martial law was introduced in Poland by the Communist government (in order to clamp down on the independent "Solidarity" movement) which in my case resulted in unemployment and loss of prospects for further development. I started a private enterprise — photo services. Next, I began to produce stamps, manufactured then with lead types.

DW: What kind of stamps are you talking about, Janusz — postage stamps or some other kind?

JMN: Sorry for being imprecise. I meant rubber stamps (now, actually, polymer stamps or flash stamps).

DW: Please tell me, each of you, how you first came in contact with TEX.

BJ: During my work at the Gdańsk University I encountered *The Art of Computer Programming* by Donald E. Knuth (there was no Polish translation). I was delighted with the theoretical part of the book, although I have never been convinced that it was a good idea to provide programs in MIX and only in MIX for all algorithms.

Anyway, we tried to use as much as possible from Prof. Knuth's marvelous book, although not only that. We "harassed" our students also with the ideas of Edsger W. Dijkstra, Niklaus Wirth, Tony Hoare, et al.

In the middle of the seventies there was a rumor that Prof. Knuth had suspended his work on *The Art of Computer Programming* and begun to work on a new typesetting system, $\tau\epsilon\chi$). In the meantime, however, I changed my job. My new task, in the Polish Academy of Sciences (PAS), was numerical programming of hydrodynamical processes. Theoretical computer science was no longer needed. I was about to forget Prof. Knuth's achievements....

Fortunately, in such institutions like PAS, there was an obligation of writing annual reports. Of course, reports contained math formulas and the most common method was using a typewriter machine and manually adding formulas with a pen. One nice day the situation improved: a program named ChiWriter was issued. Then I remembered about $\tau\epsilon\chi$.... I wrote one or two reports using ChiWriter (it was a nightmare in comparison with the traditional "technology"), but pretty soon we had TEX in our institute which resulted soon afterwards in my abandoning the work in PAS and beginning a private enterprise—a small typesetting firm. I work today in the fourth incarnation of that enterprise.

JMN: In 1992, I learnt that rubber stamps could also be produced using computers. However, I was 40 years old, I did not possess a computer and had no idea how to use such a computer. Roughly, I understood that so-called typesetting-dedicated software was needed. At the early nineties, only two programs were practically available: commercial Ventura Publisher and free TEX. Obviously, I decided to get the hang of the latter. If I knew then that TEX is actually a programming language....

I bought a computer with a printer. Jacko—whom I met by chance—provided a polonised version of TEX, called LEX, which he prepared with Marek Ryćko. I came back home, connected cables, switched the computer on and ... I was not able to do anything more. I did not know that there existed such things as operating system, command lines, etc. To make matters worse, I didn't speak English.

But I am a dogged person. With a very-small-steps method, I finally made my first stamp using the computer. The situation was rather difficult, as there was nobody in Grudziądz (about one hundred thousand inhabitants) to contact for help. I guess that there were several PCs in the city then. But all in all, I was successful; the money for the computer was not spent in vain.

DW: Please tell me, each of you, how you first got involved with fonts?

JMN: Having TEX run on my PC, I realised that the collection of fonts coming with TEX was insufficient for practical applications other than typesetting *The Art of Computer Programming*. There were only Computer Modern fonts and their polonised version, the PL fonts. That was all. About PostScript (with its collections of fonts and possibility of scaling) I knew nothing. Imagine now, that you were expected to make a stamp for "Grudziądzkie Zakłady Przemysłu Gumowego" (literally: Grudziądz Rubber Industry Plants) where the font should have the size 12 points and the width of the stamp was 5 cm, and so should be the width of the text.... Among my lead types, there was a typeface

REX (similar to supercondensed Helvetica), that I previously had used for this then very important customer. Therefore, I prepared a bitmap (PK) REX-like font containing only necessary glyphs and nothing else, in particular, no kerns. One can say that the work was trivial if not trifling, but I managed to retain the customer.

Still, I missed other genuine Polish typefaces that used to be commonly available in lead type. The achievements of Polish typographers are worth noting — there exist quite a lot of really interesting designs. I had a pleasure to be acquainted with one of the most respected artists, Zygfryd Gardzielewski from Toruń (Thorn), the designer of Antykwa Toruńska. I liked the font very much but a version usable with TEX did not exist which was annoying for me. Therefore, I started experiments with the electronic replica of Antykwa Toruńska (in 1996). Finally, I contrived to produce a Type 1 font using a bunch of varied tools. If I knew then what nasty beasts are fonts....

BJ: If your native language is not a diacriticless English, you have no other choice once you started to fiddle around with TEX — you have to get involved with fonts.

Being very enthusiastic about TEX, my friend Marek Ryćko and I worked on polonisation of TEX since 1987. Part of the polonisation was, of course, preparing a Polish-oriented version of Computer Modern fonts (the PL fonts). After a few interim stages, we released a stable version of Polish plain TEX, called MEX (at the end of 1991). The letter "M" stood for the Polish encoding, Mazovia (the word is the Latin name of the region in Poland where our capital is located), popular then in Poland. Remember that there were no coding pages containing Polish diacritical letters; CP-852 came only with MS DOS 5.0 (September 1991). Actually, there are "veteran" customers of my firm for whom I still typeset in Mazovia.

Working a lot with fonts, I slowly became aware that bitmap fonts were becoming extinct. The world around used primarily outline fonts (PostScript Type 1 fonts, TrueType fonts), keeping bitmap fonts (of relatively low quality) only for screen applications. From this point of view, I feel now, after a quarter of a century, that making METAFONT heavily bitmap-oriented was a misconception.

So, I started to think about preparing an outline version of the PL fonts. I thought, and Janusz just worked. All of sudden, in 1997 at the Polish TEX Users Meeting in Bachotek (BachoTEX), he announced the outline version of the PL fonts. He based his work on the AMS Computer Modern fonts in the PostScript Type 1 format, which had very good quality and were newly released as freeware (in March the same year).

When the outline version of Polish TEX fonts had been published, I hoped that I could retire from font works.... However, I underestimated Janusz. He came up with the idea of us preparing an engine for generating outline fonts, employing either METAFONT or METAPOST. The idea was so exciting that I agreed. Later, Piotr Strzelczyk joined us. The result of our collaboration was MetaType1 which we still use today for our font projects.

So, the warning of Prof. Knuth — "Type design can be hazardous to your other interests. Once you get hooked, you will develop intense feelings about letterforms; the medium will intrude on the messages that you read. And you will perpetually be thinking of improvements to the fonts that you see everywhere" — turned out to be prophetic.

DW: Janusz said that you two "met by chance", but there must be more to the story than that for you to have created such a long-lasting collaboration.

JMN: Well, I had a lot of questions, Jacko was sufficiently patient to answer them.... The distance between Gdańsk and Grudziądz is about 100 km, not too far, so we could meet when the problems were too difficult to solve them using the telephone. Very important were our annual TeX users meetings in Bachotek (organised continuously since 1993); the main organisers were from the very beginning Jurek (Jerzy, George) Ludwichowski and Jola (Jolanta) Szelatyńska. We could spend there a few days discussing, solving problems and just talking.

The outlined version of the PL fonts (consistent with the bitmap, i.e., PK, version released with MeX) was prepared by me. I managed to polonise the CM fonts publicly released by AMS within two months and to announce the result at the Bachotek meeting. Later, in collaboration with Jacko, the outlined PL fonts were improved.

DW: I'm also confused about how many firms we are talking about (Jacko mentioned a "fourth incarnation"); are you in business together today or in separate businesses?

BJ: Janusz and I run separate firms. My firm BOP, established in 1993, is being run only by me and Piotr Pianowski, although he and I collaborate with Janusz (occasionally) and with Piotr Strzelczyk (more regularly). My earlier attempts to establish a private enterprise failed, mainly due to my lack of experience in business.

DW: Let me be sure I now have this straight. Janusz's firm makes rubber stamps, and Jacko's firm does typesetting; and you both originally worked with fonts to have available what was necessary for application in your stamp and typesetting work — correct?

JMN: Yes.

DW: However, you have continued to work with font development in a major way, perhaps beyond what is needed for your businesses. Why is that?

JMN: When I started to work with a computer, everything installed there was from abroad, namely from the USA. But I wanted to use genuine Polish typefaces, such as Antykwa Półtawskiego, Antykwa Toruńska, Kurier, Cyklop, etc. This was my primary motivation. Of course, the best situation is when the work you are doing to achieve your business goal is also your hobby — that was my case.

BJ: Beside the motivations mentioned by Janusz, I'd add another one (I'm pretty sure that Janusz shares my opinion): we got a lot from many people who contributed to the TeX system. We got it for free. We felt obliged to reciprocate with what we could reciprocate. Fonts was the area in which we were most advanced, for the reasons mentioned earlier.

DW: Is there any specific division of work between the two of you, and Piotr?

BJ: Roughly, Janusz manipulates with Bézier curves, I manipulate with METAPOST macros. Piotr collaborates with us at the level of concept; sometimes we write macros together, and we ask him always for help while debugging (METAPOST code or resulting fonts).

DW: Can I assume all this work is done on the computer, or is some of it done with actual paper, brushes, and ink?

BJ: We have no education in drawing art, the more so in typography. Thus, we would not dare to attempt to design glyphs using "paper, brushes, and ink". Moreover, there are a lot of well-designed fonts around, drawn by skilled artists, awaiting digitization — enough to fill our time to the end of our days.

DW: How do you interact in doing this work — in person, on the phone, email, Skype? I imagine it is hard to talk about character designs without actually seeing them.

JMN: We contact each other in all possible ways. But it is a personal meeting that is most important in this kind of work. Especially, informal meetings turn out to be very stimulating and fruitful.

DW: How did you meet Jerzy Ludwichowski and other TEX people, and how did they influence your work in the TEX world?

BJ: Most of the TEX people with whom I'm still in touch I met at the founding meeting of our TEX users group, GUST, in 1992. In particular, I met there Jola Szelatyńska and Jurek Ludwichowski. With some people, however, I was acquainted earlier. For example, Marek Ryćko, with whom I worked on MEX, used to be my student.

No doubt, our most important relationships developed during our annual BachoTEX meetings. I was there from the very beginning. Janusz appeared already at the second meeting. It is difficult to tell *now* how particular people influenced us — everybody in his or her personal way. But even people who appeared once or twice at BachoTEX might have influenced us with their questions, problems, ideas, etc. Also, one can not overestimate our contacts with many colleagues from abroad, which originated from BachoTEX and other TEX users meetings.

DW: Turning to the actual designs, will you please briefly describe your major works and how each came about.

JMN: Our first major common work was tuning the outline PL fonts. It was a prelude, in a way, to the Latin Modern and TEX Gyre projects, the most complex ones we are carrying out. Another common work of ours, which urgently awaits its finishing, is Antykwa Półtawskiego, the first parametric font programmed in MetaType1. In fact, we developed MetaType1 to make Antykwa Półtawskiego.

In the meantime, I worked on other fonts. My first replica was Antykwa Toruńska. Its initial version was prepared without MetaType1, but as soon as that programming tool was available, I immediately switched to it. Using MetaType1, I prepared Kurier, designed by Małgorzata (Margaret) Budyta, Iwona (a variant of Kurier by me) and Cyklop, of unknown design.

(Examples of some of the fonts described in this interview are included at the end of the interview.)

DW: You've written a number of articles about technical aspects of the fonts, for example, the list at `http://tug.org/TUGboat/Contents/listauthor.html#Jackowski,Boguslaw` which includes Jacko's joint publications as well as solo papers, and `http://tug.org/TUGboat/Articles/tb29-1/tb91nowacki-cyklop.pdf` which is by Janusz alone. However, perhaps you can also tell us about some of most frustrating and some of the most rewarding incidents during your efforts involving these fonts.

JMN: The lack of the precise specification of the fonts we are expected to provide, i.e., fonts in the OpenType format, claimed nowadays to be the worldwide standard, is perhaps the most frustrating aspect of our work (compare, for example, existing documentation (?) of the OpenType format with Prof. Knuth's documentation of the TFM or PK files). But this cannot be called a passing incident — it is a permanent state.

BJ: Another frustrating, if not annoying, aspect is a worldwide licensing madness. We have to spent our time struggling with license problems, an area in which we are completely ignorant, because licenses became an obligatory part of software packages. At the same time, we are aware that the GPL, being recently in fashion, is hardly suitable for such font projects like TEX Gyre. Moreover, we have to answer arrogant letters from commercial firms because we happened to use in an unfortunate context a registered font name, etc. How can intelligent people seriously consider such things? The incredible heritage of mankind awaits for every newborn man, in particular, speech, art, technology, and science. Such a man grows making use of *all* mankind's achievements, but then invents serendipitously a new dot or a comma and demands a long-lasting protection of "creator's" rights....

A nice story was told by Hermann Zapf during the European TEX Users Meeting in Pont-à-Mousson, 2005. One of the first persons who brought a lawsuit (incidentally, in the USA) for an unauthorised usage of his typeface design, was Frederic W. Goudy. After Goudy's long explanations of what is the font design, the trial was practically concluded by the judge's question: "Mr. Goudy, are you the inventor of the alphabet?"

Well, about the dark sides of life one can talk ad infinitum (smile).

JMN: Most rewarding and stimulating is being aware of the fact that a lot of people use our work and not infrequently express their gratitude and are interested in further developments. Of course such things as receiving awards is always a pleasure—I received twice the so-called "Gustav prize" from our GUST organisation. Both Jacko and I are honorary members of GUST. All this is encouraging as it means that our efforts have been acknowledged by the TEX society.

BJ: Janusz hit the bull's eye. But to drift a little bit from a too serious tone, I'd like to mention an incident which was at the same time highly frustrating and rewarding. It was also during the European TEX Users Meeting in Pont-à-Mousson. I wanted to explain in my talk, in the presence of Prof. Knuth, a long-standing bug in kerning in Computer Modern fonts, unremovable for obvious reasons. It was one of my arguments against the idea of preserving 100% compatibility between the Latin Modern and Computer Modern fonts (whatever 100% compatibility might mean here). Imagine my jitters when, after my explanations, Prof. Knuth stood up, said "but" and ... sat back down. And can you imagine my relief afterwards.

DW: Thank you very much, both of you, for participating in this interview. I am sure I am not alone in appreciating, as an everyday user of the fruits of your effort, how much you have contributed to the TEX world. Examples of your fonts follow, for readers' pleasure.

Family **Latin Modern Roman** — Based on Computer Modern, 72 fonts; nearly 800 glyphs per text font

OHamburgefonsz

ąæàáâãäåăắặằẳẵấậầẩẫȁạǽảāą́ǻ

Family **Antykwa Poltawskiego** (Półtawskiego) — regular, bold, normal and italic; more than 1000 glyphs per font

OHuńgąrfóńśż

Family **Antykwa Torunska** (Toruńska) — light, regular, medium, bold, normal and italic; circa 1300 glyphs per font

ÓHůňǵąŗföñsź

Family **Kurier** — light, regular, medium, bold, heavy, normal and italic; nearly 1500 glyphs per font

ÓHůňģąŗföñsź

Family **Iwona** — light, regular, medium, bold, heavy, normal and italic; nearly 1500 glyphs per font

ÓHůňģąŗföñsź

Family **Cyklop** — normal and italic; circa 900 glyphs per font

ÓHůňģąŗföñsź

Family **TeX Gyre Adventor** — regular, bold, normal and italic; circa 1000 glyphs per font

ÓHůňģąŗföñsź

Family **TeX Gyre Bonum** — regular, bold, normal and italic; circa 1000 glyphs per font

ÓHůňģąŗföñsź

Family **TeX Gyre Cursor** — regular, bold, normal and italic; circa 1000 glyphs per font

ÓHůňģąŗföñsź

Family **TeX Gyre Heros** — regular, bold, normal and italic plus condensed variants; circa 1000 glyphs per font

ÓHůňģąŗföñsź

Family **TeX Gyre Pagella** — regular, bold, normal and italic; circa 1000 glyphs per font

ÓHůňģąŗföñsź

Family **TeX Gyre Schola** — regular, bold, normal and italic; circa 1000 glyphs per font

ÓHůňģąŗföñsź

Family **TeX Gyre Termes** — regular, bold, normal and italic; circa 1000 glyphs per font

ÓHůňģąŗföñsź

Family **TeX Gyre Chorus** — italic; circa 800 glyphs

ÓHůňģąŗföñsź

Jonathan Fine

Jonathan Fine is a long time participant in the TeX community. He is current chair of the UK TeX Users Group and is employed supporting TeX at the Open University.

[Interview completed 14 December 2008.]

Dave Walden, interviewer: Please tell me a bit about yourself.

Jonathan Fine, interviewee: At school I was good at mathematics, which pleased my father, and I studied mathematics and philosophy at university. I then wrote a PhD in pure mathematics. I wrote it by hand, and the technical typists then typed it up, using the IBM golf-ball typewriter. Special symbols were obtained by changing the golf-ball print-head. This was the standard way of doing things then. In the prior generation, maths PhDs were typed in the usual way, with space into which the formulas were handwritten.

DW: I'm curious — what was the title of your thesis?

JF: The title is not important. I proved some results on the resolution and completion of algebraic varieties. In other words, it was in algebraic geometry. Since then I've done some work using the connection between toric algebraic varieties and convex polytopes. I've also done some work on the Vassiliev-Kontsevich knot invariants. But I've not published much, and so didn't have a research career.

I've taught mathematics in some colleges in the USA, spent time doing research (but with few results or publications to date), spent time consulting, and worked writing software in both commerce and publishing.

Since 2003 I've been working as a TeX expert at The Open University, which is the UK's leading provider of distance learning. My main work there is to maintain and develop the TeX system that is used for producing course materials for the maths courses and upper-level physics courses. Lately, partly with external funding, I've been doing a lot with mathematics on web pages, and TeX as a web service.

I enjoy spending time with family, which often means traveling. For example, this summer I went to Greece, for the first time, for my nephew Joel's wedding. His mother-in-law is Greek, and he's making progress with the language. He and his wife live in Brussels.

Apart from the wedding and meeting my family, one of the high points (and in a sense literally) was taking the train from Athens to Thessaloniki. This journey went through the mountains in the north, and at one point Mount Olympus was on the left and the sea on the right. I also got a great deal out of visiting one of the roots of our culture. There seemed to be a real awakening of the human spirit and society at that time.

Over the past 10 years or so I've benefited greatly from the teachings of Vietnamese Zen master Thich Nhat Hanh and the monks and nuns at the monastery Plum Village that he established in France. I find the practice rewarding, but also at times difficult, particularly when caught up in the stresses and tensions of software development and support. I do wish I could communicate better.

DW: When and how did you first get involved with TEX?

JF: In 1985 I was working in Boston in the USA ...

DW: I've lived in Boston for 45 years; I hope you liked our city.

JF: One of my favourite places in Boston was the Museum of Fine Arts. I also liked the Arnold Arboretum in Jamaica Plain. And there were many interesting places to eat. But this is all a long time ago now, and I've not been back for many years.

DW: Excuse my interruption. You were saying ...

JF: There was an interesting event at the Computer Museum in Boston. It was Donald Knuth giving a talk for a "coming out" party for TEX and the publication of his series of books *Computers and Typesetting*, the first volume of which was *The TEXbook*. It was rather a miserable winter evening, cold and raining, and much to my regret I decided to stay at home. So my first encounter was a near miss.

The following year I was writing a paper, with help from an expert, using the Unix troff system, and a colleague gave a talk on the new mathematics typesetting that the American Mathematical Society were adopting, and he showed us how he encoded the University letterhead (which used only text) using this new system, called TEX. I was impressed, but continued to use troff to finish the paper.

The year after that, 1987, I was at the Indiana University, and their mathematics journal was produced using TEX. I got to know the technical editor for this journal, and she introduced me to TEX. Indiana University also had a scheme where staff could buy TEX for PCs at a discount. So I got a TEX distribution on many 360k disks, to run on the new PC I bought especially to run TEX. As I recall, mostly it was ArborText software.

The PC, by the way, was a 10 MHz 80286 with a 40 MB hard disk and 1 MB of memory. Pretty soon, I bought another 1 MB of memory and the excellent DesqView multitasking platform for running MS-DOS programs. I also bought a 300 dpi HP LaserJet II. At that time, TEX was a demanding program, and I need both the storage (mostly for bitmap fonts) and the processing power.

DW: But now you have a job as a TEX expert. Did you actually use TEX in ever more sophisticated ways over the years, or did you just get hooked on TEX or typesetting as a sort of complex hobby as some TEX experts seem to have done?

JF: I did get hooked by TEX, because of the excellence of its output, the absence of bugs, and its unique ability to typeset mathematics. And like many others, I spent many hours learning the TEX macro language.

For some time I did try to do more sophisticated ways of making TEX do things, by writing complicated macros such as Active TEX. I still have to maintain and write complex macros as part of my work, but I'd like to move over more to something like the PostScript model.

I'll explain what I mean. Drawing programs that generate PostScript output rely on a static header file that wraps the PostScript primitives into something a bit more usable, and a program that manages data structures and fonts and the like, and which emits intermediate level PostScript (as defined by the header). The admirable dvips PostScript driver for TEX's DVI files does exactly this. One could write dvips almost entirely in PostScript if one wanted to, but that would not be sensible.

No-one writes a drawing program in PostScript, although it could be done. We know that PostScript is not the right language for that sort of task. But TEX experts try to write complex output routines using TEX macros, and then argue that because it's so hard to do this, we should develop and use a TEX extension instead.

I think the best way to use TEX (or some extension) is as a module that extends some well-established scripting language. There are two major challenges here. First, interfacing the high-level language with the typesetting engine, and second, running typesetting engine as a daemon.

By the way, in one of his interviews Don Knuth said that it was his intention with TEX to write "just a typesetting language", and that many macro language features were added only as a result of pressure from users.

I've solved the second problem already, as part of the MathTran project (http://www.mathtran.org/), which makes TEX available as a high-performance web service.

DW: After I joined TUG, my first memory of hearing of you had to do with Active TEX. Please tell me about the motivation and history of that.

JF: There are two sides to Active TEX, namely a programming language and a means of user input. At that time, like everyone else in the TEX community, I thought that the way to make TEX do new things was to write TEX macros. The idea of using a modern scripting language, such as Perl, Python, Ruby or Lua, was not widespread. In fact, Perl and Python only reached maturity in 1994 and 2000 or so respectively.

TEX is a wonderful typesetting program, but its macro language is not suitable for writing complicated programs. Active TEX makes TEX easier to program, but few people were interested in using it, and over time I lost interest myself.

Here's an example of Active TEX. Most languages have named parameters to functions. Well TEX doesn't have functions, but it does have macros. But its macros don't have named parameters. With Active TEX you could write

```
def mymacro #width #text {
  hbox "to" width { text }
}
```

and the effect would be the same as

```
\def\mymacro #1#2{\hbox to#1{#2}}%
```

which is not nearly so easy to write or to read.

On the input side, TEX macro packages from Knuth onwards (and this includes both LATEX and ConTEXt) use changes of what are known as category codes to allow verbatim (or unescaped) input. As a result, you can't use \verb in LATEX arguments. For example

```
\section{The \verb|\iffalse| command}
```

will bomb out, even though \verb works in ordinary paragraph text.

Today, many people use wiki languages. One could write a wiki-language parser using Active TEX, but I wouldn't recommend that now. I'd use a modern scripting language (Python is my favourite) to translate the input into fairly low-level TEX commands.

In case you want to know how it works, Active TEX makes all characters active, and it gives you tools for giving each character the meaning you want.

DW: I next heard about your involvement with the UK TEX Users Group (http://uk.tug.org). Please tell me about your history with that.

JF: I've been around for a long time. I joined both TUG and UK-TUG in 1990 or so. I've served on the Committee of UK-TUG for several years, and in 2006 I was elected chair. I've just been re-elected, to serve to 2010. At our last AGM we adopted a new constitution, which will help us a lot.

In 1995 I was the main organiser of a very successful UK-TUG meeting in London on "TEX, SGML and PDF". (This was before the invention of XML.) It was a sell-out, with about

120 delegates. Unfortunately, the UK-TUG committee did not build on the momentum created.

Today, UK-TUG is rather weaker than it was then. We're managing to keep things ticking over, and to organise a meeting once a year. I'd like to have more time for this, but my main focus is on software development.

I would like, next year, to provide some new online resources for TeX documentation and training.

DW: You mentioned your MathTran project earlier. I have seen the video of your presentation of your MathTran project from the last TUG annual conference. Will you please say a few more words about it, its purpose, and its implementation.

JF: MathTran makes TeX available as a high-performance web service. You send it a url, with TeX-encoded mathematics in the query string, and you get back the typeset formula as a bitmap graphic. This allows you to include graphics in your web-page without having to install TeX.

Google Charts provides a similar web service, except it returns a pie chart or a graph or whatever.

It takes TeX perhaps 0.25 seconds to initialize, and next to no time at all to typeset a small formula. MathTran runs TeX as a daemon, to remove the start-up time from the loop. It does something similar for dvipng. As a result, typesetting and rendering to a bitmap takes about 10 milliseconds.

But before we can safely run TeX as a daemon, we have to secure it against unwelcome input. For example, a user might send TeX the string `\gdef\alpha{\beta}` in an attempt to cause confusion later, possible for other users. MathTran uses a variant secure plain of Knuth's plain TeX format, in which commands such as `\gdef` are not accessible to the user. In fact, in secure plain, `\gdef` is an undefined command, and the primitive command `\gdef` is instead stored as `_gdef`. Because of category codes, the ordinary user cannot access `_gdef`.

Put more simply, with secure plain the user can access only appropriate commands, and the others are inaccessible.

MathTran is an open source project, coded in Python and hosted on SourceForge. JISC (a UK higher education funding body) and the Open University provided funding.

DW: Please tell me a bit more about the role of TeX and your role in supporting it at the Open University (and while you're at it, what sort of university the Open University is).

JF: As I mentioned already, the Open University is the UK's leading provider of distance learning. It was founded in 1969, and gave many people an opportunity they would not otherwise have to take higher education. Many of our students are people who for personal or social reasons were not able to go to college after school. When it started much of the course material was broadcast in the early hours by the BBC, and so the OU became known as the university of the air.

Nowadays, the Internet is widely used to distribute OU learning materials. I'm the TeX expert in LTS (Learning and Teaching Solutions), which is the publishing division of the OU. Initially my work was entirely with print, but now I'm very much involved with web-pages and on-line activities.

Getting mathematical content to work well on web pages is one of our major challenges, and allowing students to author mathematics in forum posts and so forth is another. I'm in the middle of a two year research project on this area, which built on MathTran.

DW: Finally, what challenges and opportunities do you see for TeX and its communities of users and developers?

JF: Everyone has their own answer to this, based on what's important to them, and on their own experience and problems. For example, getting math on the web is a major problem for me, whereas for others Unicode text and internationalization are more important.

It's very easy to see one's own problem as being more important than those of others, and I'm very concerned that this focus can be causing division and conflict in our community, and is holding us back. Here's an example. Generating PDF is important to many users, but so are applications based on the original DVI format. I'm in favor of generating PDF and I'm also in favor of generating DVI. But it's so easy for this difference to become a cause of conflict.

The core of TeX, namely TeX the program, Metafont and the Computer Modern fonts, was authored by one very skilled, highly motivated and well supported developer, namely Don Knuth. I don't think we've seen any similar contribution to TeX, either by an individual or a team, since then.

We have seen many valuable incremental contributions, such as the emergence of LaTeX 2_ε, PostScript and PDF support, cross-platform builds for TeX, improved packaging and distribution, the CTAN archive, ConTeXt, international fonts and hyphenation (and apologies for the many omissions in this list).

But TeX was completed in 1992, and frozen by Don Knuth in 1999. Much has happened since then. Computers have become more powerful, the Internet is much more pervasive, Unicode has emerged, and there are powerful and widely-adopted scripting languages (such as Perl, Python and Ruby). In addition, XML has become a standard and there are many lightweight (or wiki) markup languages.

I think our biggest challenge is moving forward, as a growing community of both users and developers, with an extension of TeX (which must of course be given some other name) that responds sensibly to these new challenges and opportunities.

It will be really important, of course, to avoid dividing or otherwise damaging the community, and to avoid what is known as creeping featuritis. Scholarly users of TeX really admire its stability across both time and space.

My main emphasis, which I think comes out in the interview, is:

1. Not replacing TeX the program unless we have to
2. Running TeX as a daemon
3. Running TeX as a web service
4. Improving the programming interface to TeX

I was at the 2008 TUG Conference, and wished that the level of technical communication and debate was higher. I felt, for example, that LaTeX 3 and LuaTeX/ConTeXt were ignoring each other. Both projects share problems and a platform, but I'm not aware of significant ongoing discussion or sharing of code involving both these projects. Similarly, XeTeX use an extended DVI format (called xdv), while so far as I know LuaTeX ignores it, and has nothing similar.

It's easy years on to look back on the past as a golden age, but I feel that 25 or so years ago there was an excitement and confidence and energy in the TeX community, similar for example to the more recent emergence of GNU/Linux as a free operating system. I don't see enough of this energy present today, and I think this lack is one of our major challenges.

The hope for the future, as always, must be in the skills and abilities and motivation of the younger generation. Older members of the community, such as myself, have a responsibility to share our experience with them.

The sort of thing I'd like to see happen soon is for TeX, or if necessary a minor extension of TeX, to be incorporated into platforms such as Firefox as a mathematics rendering engine. This could be done in the next two years, given fairly modest resources and sufficient enthusiasm. Such a development would make an enormous change to the use and perception of TeX and related software.

DW: Thank you very much for taking the time to participate in this interview and for sharing your story and views with me. I can keep up with your activities by reading your blog (`http://jonathanfine.wordpress.com`).

Yannis Haralambous

Yannis Haralambous is well known for his Omega system and his study of non-Latin fonts.

[Interview completed 6 January 2009.]

Dave Walden, interviewer: Please tell me a bit about your personal history.

Yannis Haralambous, interviewee: I was born in Athens, Greece, in 1962. My father was one of the first Greeks to obtain a Ph.D. in Geology in the fifties, in Bonn (Germany), and that is where he met my mother. Whether scientific or literary, the house was full of books, in many languages. Already as a teenager I got fascinated by the Fraktur script trying to read an old Brockhaus. One of my hobbies at the time was already related to typography and history: I was collecting stamps with errors (you have to detect and explain the error). My first book, at the age of sixteen, was a catalogue of Greek postal stationeries. I always wanted to be a mathematician, and as I went to a French school (the "Lycée léonin") it was only natural for me to go abroad for studying. So at the age of 17 I left Greece to study mathematics in Lille, France. I graduated in Pure Mathematics in 1985, and in 1990 did my thesis in the field of Algebraic Topology.

DW: Please tell me how you first became involved with TeX.

YH: In 1987, the Math department of Lille University decided to buy two Mac Plus machines to run a piece of software called *Textures*. A few days later my Ph.D. advisor handed me a copy of *The TeXbook*. I loved it so much that I read it overnight (what I liked the most was the drawing of the computer drinking coffee). It was that event as well as my encounter with Klaus Thull, in 1988, that completely changed my life and made me switch from Mathematics to Computer Science.

DW: Yet you still did your thesis in pure math rather than in computer science. Was your decision to change fields in 1988, yet the actual change happened after you finished your degree in math?

YH: No, I took the decision to change fields after my thesis (and after the TUG meeting in Cork), when I realized that working on TeX was far more exciting. I still taught math for another year, but spent all my free time on studying oriental scripts to model and create them in TeX and Metafont.

DW: Why did your advisor think you should read *The TeXbook*?

YH: To be able to write my publications and ultimately my thesis in TeX. At that time there was no LaTeX yet (or let's say: LaTeX wasn't very convincing) and one would still write math in plain TeX.

DW: Who is Klaus Thull and what was your encounter with him about?

YH: Oh god! You don't know Klaus Thull? He's a great figure of early TeX in Germany. He was the first to write a public domain Metafont for MS-DOS, and for that reason he is an honorary DANTE member, for life. He worked on fractals and on Sanskrit and on many other interesting fields. Unfortunately I lost his trace many years ago. You should absolutely interview him.

My first email correspondences over the Atlantic were with Silvio Levy, Barbara Beeton and Dikran Karagueuzian. When I went to my first TUG meeting (in Cork, 1990), two months after my thesis, I had already developed my Gothic fonts and my first Arabic system, and I was discovering a wide and wonderful new world.

DW: Did you use Metafont or another system to develop those fonts?

YH: Metafont is a fabulous system for making fonts. Instead of drawing contours one would rather use pen strokes with their dynamics, their tension, etc. And since I worked mostly on historical fonts for various oriental writing systems, using a pen was only natural. Not to mention that metaness is a great thing when you have various font sizes for titles, text, footnotes, critical apparati, marginal notes, etc.

DW: My impression is that work with fonts is not typically central to careers in either mathematics or computer science. I see your work history on your web site (`http://omega.enstb.org/yannis/`). Please tell me a little about these positions and how your work with TeX and fonts fits in.

YH: My research is on digital typography, electronic documents and the preservation of the cultural heritage of the book in the digital era. When I left University I started my own business (Atelier Fluxus Virus), together with my better half, Tereza, who is an artist and a font designer. It was hard but we were able to maintain two parallel activities: typesetting for various publishers all around the world; and doing research, organizing conferences, keeping up with the developments in this field. Finally I accepted a position as Computer Science professor at Télécom Bretagne, a very nice place where I can teach and do research.

DW: Please tell me about the Omega project and how John Plaice fit into that effort.

YH: In the early nineties all the typesetting systems I developed (Arabic, Hebrew, Syriac, Sinhala, Khmer, Mongolian, and more), were based on pre-processors written in C. A pre-processor will read a TeX file with a special syntax, will process stuff properly tagged and leave the rest unchanged. This is cumbersome and adds yet another complexity level to typesetting. John was still in Canada at that time (in 1993?). He wrote me an email asking whether I would be interested in a new TeX where these things would happen inside the engine. He had a lot of experience writing compilers so he naturally thought of a special Lex-like language for describing what my pre-processors were doing, which would be compiled and run at high speed inside this new TeX. I was enthusiastic and a few days later he was in Lille. We spent days and nights discussing and analyzing the various issues involved in typesetting all writing systems of the world, and one of that nights (between 3 and 5 am) we decided to call the new system Omega. It would be based on Unicode (which was just released) and have its own fonts. And so it did.

DW: My understanding is that John Plaice eventually split off from the Omega project. And from the *TUGboat* archives I see you are now working on something called Omega$_2$ with Gábor Bella. I also think I remember seeing that Aleph was somehow related to Omega and its functionality is being subsumed by LuaTEX. Please help me understand what you are working on now and how it relates to those other systems or, for instance, to XeTEX.

YH: When John left the Omega project I continued working on it as an experimental platform. My student Gábor Bella did his Ph.D. on a new atomic unit of text, called *texteme*, to solve the problems of the artificial character/glyph duality introduced by Unicode. He partially implemented textemes into Omega, and this is what we called Omega$_2$.

Aleph is the typical example of what can happen in the world of free software: a group of people took the code of Omega, added some minor functionalities to it (the extra features of ε-TEX, except for bidirectional typesetting, which was already handled by Omega in a different way), and gave it an entirely new name. They did fix some bugs and Aleph is indeed more stable for production than Omega, but does this deserve a new name?

LuaTEX is a great project and I am very glad that the main features of Omega survived in it (although Taco claims he will not be supporting Omega Translations Processes in the long run). A Byzantine music project I'm working on will be entirely based on LuaTEX.

XeTEX is a nice compromise for those who trust their operating system to do part of the typesetting process. What I always liked with TEX is its independence from the surrounding operating system: one is able to fix his/her own rules and re-invent the wheel, if necessary. Not so with XeTEX, which relies on the operating system to do part of the job. Of course, if the end user simply wants a stable and friendly tool to get his/her documents typeset, he/she will find that in XeTEX. But all the adventure of breaking the rules and "boldly go beyond" is lost.

Most of my current projects are not related to building typesetting engines. Whenever typesetting is involved, I use LuaTEX.

DW: Do you see yourself producing a production level engine, or do you see yourself more as doing experiments and prototyping that others may pick up for production engines?

YH: When Omega started we were rather heading for the first goal, but in the last years we switched to the second one.

DW: You directed me to your web site for the polytonic system for Greek (`http://www.polytoniko.gr/index.php?newlang=en`), which says it must remain neutral but as a lay reader it seems to me that you personally favor the system. What was your motivation for this involvement and what do you hope to accomplish?

YH: It is my conviction that the monotonic reform of 1982 has been a monumental mistake of the Greek government, and that it is our moral duty to return to the polytonic system, in order to save the Greek language. The arguments of monotonic linguists are based on the assumption that written language exists *only* to represent oral language, and since accents and breathings have no effect on the latter, they are useless. This assumption is clearly wrong, since, as we all know, written text carries information different than oral — but nevertheless very important. This information is lost when the language is written monotonically.

You misunderstood what I meant by "neutrality". This Web page is clearly not neutral on the issue of accents and breathings. But it has to be remain *politically* neutral;

indeed, among the people requesting the return of the polytonic system there are—unfortunately—some who belong to rather obscure groups (pagans, nationalists, and others). Their presence can give false impressions to people who are discovering our initiative and our arguments.

What I hope to accomplish is to persuade people that they have been fooled by unscrupulous politicians and linguists, and that their cultural heritage has being stolen from them, under their noses. Many people realize at last that the "simplification" of this reform breaks the historical continuity of the language. Please visit our Web site to learn more about this very important issue.

DW: Is Atelier Fluxus Virus continuing business? If so, what is the connection between your research projects and your business?

YH: Yes, of course. Tereza has taken over Atelier Fluxus Virus, with clients in France, the US and Greece. There is practically no connection between my research projects and the business, at least for the moment.

DW: More generally, your research and other involvements cover a broad area. To what extent do you see TeX being relevant (and how) to these domains in the future?

YH: I can't imagine myself starting a project which involves document production without using TeX. It is my conviction that an electronic document should be optimally presented, including on the text level. Building typesetting engines other than TeX would be re-inventing the wheel, and I think that Don has invented a very nice wheel for us. Of course, when we speak of the "TeX invention", we refer to many things which are not all equally important. I think that the most fundamental aspect of TeX is the node model: to consider a text as chain of characters, penalties, glue and other types of nodes. This model reflects the rationale of traditional typography and is much more powerful than the character/glyph model of the Web. Of course, it can become even more powerful if we consider additional properties of nodes or new node types. This text model, together with the algorithms used in TeX, is, IMHO, the heart of TeX, and this deserves to survive.

A typical example of a research project involving TeX is an ongoing project with the Voltaire Museum of Geneva on building a computer-driven Monotype machine. TeX is producing a DVI file using special fonts and then we post-process the result to adapt it to the mechanical constraints of the Monotype machine.

DW: I have thought before about buying a copy of your book on Fonts and Encodings (the English edition), and now have a copy in hand—very impressive. Please tell me about your effort to publish that book.

YH: I have been dealing with encodings and with font formats ever since the late eighties. At some time I realized that I had gathered a lot of contacts and documentation and that this subject was not treated in any published book. Everybody knows what PANOSE is, but it is very hard to find its specification. There is a description of TrueType hints on the Microsoft Web site, but it is rather obscure and can certainly not be used as a primer. So I proposed to Xavier Cazin, a good friend working at the French division of O'Reilly, to write a book on these issues. He immediately encouraged me and we agreed on the basis of a 600 page book. As it is often the case, while working on the book I discovered more and more subjects, and we ended up with a bit more than a thousand pages (most of it typeset in 9 points!). It was a very intense experience and I am very proud of it. The book is dedicated to my father, who passed away while I was writing it.

As Xavier explained to me, when O'Reilly US is interested in a book published by some branch outside the US, they will ask a US author to write on the same topic. In my case and for the first time, they decided to translate the book. I was very lucky since I found the ideal translator: Scott Horne is a native English speaker with an outstanding talent for learning an uncountable number of languages. He is a computer scientist, a TEX user and a musician. And a perfectionist in everything he does. He did a first translation of the book and as I was reading it I rewrote many parts which needed to be updated, so that the English version was up-to-date when it came out (in the fall of 2007). Not only did he find and correct all the errors of the original edition, but he even translated jokes and *jeux-de-mots* so that I got very positive critics saying "The result is a book that seems to have been written by a human not a droid" (Rick Jelliffe) and "Thus this book becomes the first technical reference text we're aware that actually contains a running gag" (Designorati).

Currently (early 2009), the book is being translated into Russian. My knowledge of this language is probably not sufficient to interact with the translator in the same way I did with Scott. But I will rewrite parts of the book which need to be updated (latest versions of FontLab and FontForge, font management in LuaTEX, photofonts, etc.).

DW: In one of our email exchanges, you mentioned "third-world" writing systems. Please tell me more about this.

YH: Computing has been invented and developed in the West. The way we deal with text is not compatible with oriental writing systems. For example, Chinese ideograms are either encoded using Unicode code points (which means that adding new characters is lengthy and can certainly not be spontaneous) or by using higher-level markup like CDL (which needs special software and uses dozens, if not hundreds, of bytes for a single character): neither approach is optimal. Another example: the Arabic writing system is fluid; typography (both hot lead and electronic) segments Arabic into individual glyphs, but this segmentation is absurd: in Arabic calligraphy letters are naturally connected, when drawing one letter you already think and prepare yourself for the next one. Arabic produced by the method invented by Gutenberg (segmenting and re-assembling) is bound to be artificial, unnatural, degenerate. For these and many other reasons, it is quite difficult to adapt computers to oriental writing systems, unless of course one makes many compromises and gets doubtful results.

What I call "third world" writing systems are those which have suffered so much from technical compromises that it is too late (or very hard) to return to their authentic form, that is, the form they had before the computer. Unfortunately it happens quite often that the complexity of a script is inversely proportional to the size of its market; that is the case of Mongolian, Khmer, etc. Although both Microsoft and the Unicode consortium have spent a lot of time and effort on this kind of scripts, they will always remain bounded to technical insufficiencies. TEX has always been an open alternative to legacy systems, and this openness is a source of hope for a better future for these scripts. But for this to happen, TEX-based systems must remain independent of OS resources such as Uniscribe or Pango; this is the case for LuaTEX but not necessarily for XeTEX.

As for your last question, knowledge of a language and of its script are orthogonal. To be competent in a script you need to know its history and evolution, the esthetics surrounding it, its relation with other scripts, the differences between handwritten, calligraphic, and printed, etc. None of these is trivial, and one must be constantly in contact with written material to get the "touch" of a script. A lot of harm has been done to many writing systems by incompetent font designers....

DW: Thank you, Yannis, for taking the time to do this interesting and (for me) educational interview.

David MacKay

David MacKay is a scientist at Cambridge University and an enthusiastic user of LaTeX.
[Interview completed 10 February 2009.]

Dave Walden, interviewer: I already know something of your background, since you and I met in person two or three times in the 1990s; and, in the years since, I've periodically reviewed your web site (`http://www.inference.phy.cam.ac.uk/mackay`), including your personal (`http://www.inference.phy.cam.ac.uk/mackay/bio`) and scientific (`http://www.inference.phy.cam.ac.uk/mackay/bio2.html#scibio`) bios. Nonetheless, for readers of this interview, please speak about your personal history.

David MacKay, interviewee: I studied Natural Sciences at Cambridge University (1985–1988), specializing in Physics; then did a PhD at Caltech in Computation and Neural Systems. I've always enjoyed working in a wide range of sciences, and computing, engineering, and mathematics too. At Caltech I considered working in experimental neuroscience but decided that theoretical work was more my thing. I did a PhD on applying Bayesian probability theory to neural networks, so as to make them work better.

Back in Cambridge I took advantage of my postdoctoral research fellowship to pursue some new research interests: via my interest in approximate inference methods, I stumbled into coding theory, developing sparse-graph codes for communication systems. Radford Neal and I managed to reinvent low-density parity-check codes (first invented in 1962 by Bob Gallager, but forgotten by the coding community for 30 years), and the codes that I developed have influenced some new standards for satellite broadcast and for hard drives. What the coding theory community realised at the end of the 90s was that most of Shannon's communication problems are best solved by codes based on relatively simple sparse random graphs — rather than the elaborate algebraic coding theory of the previous 30 years. These sparse-graph codes are decoded using simple local message-passing algorithms. I happened to be writing a textbook on information theory and machine learning (*Information Theory, Inference, and Learning Algorithms*, Cambridge 2003) while this revolution in coding theory happened, so this book managed to become (among other things) the first textbook on modern coding theory. I like to make and exploit connections between diverse topics, and this textbook also features a chapter on evolution, natural selection, and sex.

Another interest that developed during my postdoc was the idea of making a new communication system by taking arithmetic coding (the state of the art in text compression) and turning it on its head to define an information-theoretically-optimal gesture-to-text system. I wrote a first prototype of Dasher, which is what we call the software based on this principle, and recruited a PhD student to develop the idea. Dasher is now distributed as free software and is part of the GNOME desktop.

After three and a bit years of postdoc I was lucky enough to get a faculty position in the Physics department in Cambridge, teaching Physics, and continuing my research in information theory, approximate inference methods, and computational neuroscience. Over a period of four years, I did several months of voluntary teaching in Africa. Then I decided there was a need for a numerate, factual, unemotional book about energy, to guide constructive conversations on energy policy. During the last three years I have devoted more and more of my time to energy matters, especially the public understanding of 2+2.

DW: In fact I downloaded Dasher from its web site (`http://www.inference.phy.cam.ac.uk/dasher/`) and tried it while preparing for this interview, and I have been reading your writings on energy.

But let's come back to your 2+2 and other work later, and first ask a TeX question. When and how did you first encounter TeX or LaTeX and begin to learn to use it?

DM: My second summer job, as a student (1987), was at a Ministry of Defence establishment, working in a pattern-recognition/machine-learning group. The group had a cluster of Sun workstations running Unix on which I ran neural networks as background jobs. During my ten-week placement I picked up LaTeX, which was the recommended way of writing reports in the group. I wrote two reports — one on my research project, and a second reviewing the field of neural networks, which was having a loud rebirth at the time. (I'd attended the first International Conference on Neural Nets earlier that summer.) A year later when I arrived at Caltech, Suns and LaTeX were standard there too.

DW: I believe you have written two big books (the abovementioned *Information Theory, Inference, and Learning Algorithms* (`http://www.inference.phy.cam.ac.uk/mackay/itila/`) and *Sustainable Energy — without the hot air* (`http://www.withouthotair.com/`)), and presumably many papers, using LaTeX. Please tell me about the TeX distribution, editor, and other tools you use for this work, and how your approach has developed over time.

DM: Initially on Sun workstations I was using the Suntools text editor, and perhaps I wrote my PhD thesis in that; but for ages (probably since 1992) I have been using Emacs. I think I picked up BibTeX to automate my bbls about 1992 too. I stubbornly used LaTeX 2.09 as long as I could, because if things are not broke I don't want to fix them. So I was still using LaTeX 2.09 while writing the first book on Information Theory. It probably would have been good to switch, because (doing my own document design) there were a lot of things that probably would have been easier in LaTeX 2_ε. Eventually, towards the end of writing that book (which took me eight years) I did switch to LaTeX 2_ε.

I used xfig and gnuplot to make PostScript figures (to include in the LaTeX documents) for a long time, but always found the results a bit disappointing — especially those of xfig. A friend introduced me to MetaPost in about 2002, and I have become quite keen on MetaPost as a replacement for xfig. I started using MetaPost in the first book. MetaPost is a product of the TeX world, so (a) you can get things to look perfectly matched with the TeX text; and (b) you have to learn a bit of classic TeX to be happy using MetaPost.

I still use gnuplot for most graphs, but I am thinking of migrating graphs to MetaPost eventually. I love the appearance of MetaPost output, but working with MetaPost is always a bit cumbersome, and the error messages are often worse than useless. During the first book I used a nice Emacs mode called reftex to automatically traverse the hundreds of TeX files that made up my book.

At some point a system upgrade broke my reftex mode, however, so I haven't been using it in the second book. I just open all the TeX files manually with Emacs, and switch buffers by hand instead of by reftex-magic.

While writing my own document designs for my books, I have rewritten the definitions of many of the objects in LaTeX (parts, chapters, sections, figures), but I don't really know what I am doing. I'm sure it would be a good idea to read *The TeXbook* properly some time. Some LaTeX packages that I always use are booktabs (to make LaTeX tables look great instead of crappy); and colordvi (to get colourful text). I currently use natbib to handle my in-text citations.

I don't use LaTeX only for my papers, for my two books, and for examining and teaching. I also use LaTeX in presentations, but in a rather non-standard way. I don't like the standard LaTeX presentation style — I only tried using it once or twice. It's a bit too slow and cumbersome to use and the results tend to be dull and stereotyped. (I especially loath those fake three-dimensional blue m+m bullet points.) I've become addicted to a little known super-lightweight presentation tool called magicpoint. Magicpoint has the lightest imaginable slide-writing syntax, and it's very easy to include colourful LaTeX in it, using a simple script to filter LaTeX source embedded in the magicpoint file (`http://itila.blogspot.com/2008/08/how-to-use-latex2epssh-to-make.html`). So, when I'm out giving talks, the main way in which I am using LaTeX is for little one-liners to make nice-looking simple presentations.

DW: The LaTeX part of your web site (`http://www.inference.phy.cam.ac.uk/mackay/SourceTeX.html`), has a six-page introduction to LaTeX called "Please write your report using LaTeX", stating "LaTeX is the typesetting program to use in scientific publishing." In your view, is suggesting LaTeX simply part of teaching students how to get along in the scientific community, or is there more to it than that? Also, is there explicit support for learning and using TeX in your college or within the whole university, or is each department or research group more or less on its own?

DM: The last time I looked at alternative ways of writing reports, I felt there was no alternative. I've occasionally been forced to use Microsoft Word, and have hated every moment. I think the logical structure of LaTeX is good for scientists, emphasizing content and leaving the details of document design to Leslie Lamport. If people want a WYSIWYG environment, they can always use a clever LaTeX front-end such as LyX.

One of the main reasons I recommend LaTeX is I often meet grad students who are groaning about the pain of dealing with their bibliographies. A user of LaTeX/BibTeX who has a sensible makefile never has any such pain. The bibliography just happens, and is perfectly formatted in whatever house style is desired.

I'm not saying there are no alternatives out there, of course. But I think I would recommend all students to use LaTeX for its bibliography-handling alone.

For mathematical students I think LaTeX is absolutely mandatory. In LaTeX you can easily make math expressions look professional. It's very rare that people manage to make good-looking math without LaTeX. (Though of course I know it is possible.)

DW: Do you participate in or draw on the resources of the worldwide TeX community?

DM: Yes, I've often used CTAN when I was adjusting my book design and trying to use extra features of LaTeX. I've sometimes emailed other members of the open source TeX community to ask for their insights, and I think I may have once or twice contributed patches.

DW: As a major user of LaTeX but self-professed as not being an expert, no doubt there are things about LaTeX that frustrate you.

DM: Yes. Because LaTeX is beautifully content-oriented, and doesn't give you control over layout on the page, there is inevitable frustration when you are actually trying to lay stuff out on the page :-).

The way that LaTeX places floats (figures and tables) and handles page breaks in text is what I'm talking about. Friends have given me some helpful hacks which seem to help, sometimes. For example:

```
{% begin troublesomepage hack
% this should be *before* the start of troublesome page
\renewcommand{\floatpagefraction}{0.8}
...
% troublesome page
...
}% end troublesome page hack
```

but when these problems arise, it feels a lot like herding cats. Or playing a marble/maze/holes game.

DW: I'm in the same boat with you — major-user-non-expert. When it's time to prepare the final manuscript, I find myself making a good bit of use of the position option in figure and table environments, some use of `\enlargethispage` plus or minus one or two lines, and occasional use of changes to the `\floatpagefraction`, etc., commands. Maybe a reader of this interview will have suggestions for dealing with this issue more automatically.

DM: Another minor defect of basic LaTeX 2.09 and LaTeX 2_ε is the way that it is willing to let marginpar objects overhang the bottom of the page. I make heavy use of marginpar for marginal figures, and it's a shame to have to manually check all of them.

DW: Both your books have the entire book available as a PDF for free download in addition to being available in paper copies. The first book was published by Cambridge University Press, and the publisher of the second book is listed (at `Amazon.co.uk`) as UIT. Please tell me what your thinking is about making these books available to the world, and what were the publishers' points of view.

DM: I am enthusiastic about open-source and the fact that, in the digital age, information can be copied almost for free. I think it makes sense to exploit this virtue of electronics.

UIT is a traditional but relatively small publisher, who was willing to go along with the "free online" approach. Cambridge University Press are also now happy with "free online", but when I initially suggested the idea to them, they were not so keen. My view on free-online books is that the *only* way for written materials to have a significant impact is for them to be available for free online. If work is not available free, people will simply move on and read something else that is free.

I think that giving away a book for free online is also a good way to enhance sales of the paper book, as long as the book is a good book. If people download my information theory textbook and print it out without paying, I am delighted. They have chosen to spend their own printing resources on creating a piece of advertising for the book! Publishers spend lots of money trying to get advertising onto peoples' desks, and most of that advertising just turns into junk mail that goes straight in the bin. What a waste! If Fred prints out my textbook in order to read it, maybe ten of his friends will see the printout, and maybe two of them will end up buying the textbook on paper. Last time I checked, the information theory text had sold 10,000 copies, so I don't think that CUP is disappointed. I think they view it as a success.

I believe that *Sustainable Energy — without the hot air* has a good chance of commercial success too, not "in spite of being free online", but "because of being free online".

One benefit of the open free-online attitude is that the author can put half-written materials on the web before publication, and benefit from bug-fixes from early readers. Both my books have certainly benefitted in this way.

I am passionately enthusiastic about open source software. I depend on it. Everything I have done for the last 15 years has been done using open source software. It's not a perfect system — two examples of imperfections with open source:

1. I worry that the open source community will keep on creating more and more new apps (some of which may be flashy but flakey replacements for existing high-quality old apps) and will not have enough enthusiasts to look after the old apps.

2. My group's software, Dasher, which is free software mainly intended for people with disabilities, is probably not reaching its target community very effectively because that community is served by middlemen salesmen with glossy catalogs and commissions to earn; free software doesn't fit into the glossy catalog system so it doesn't get promoted.

My group is a partner in a new open source research project led by Sun. The project is called AEGIS and the aim is to develop a new open source programming framework such that all apps developed in that framework will have excellent accessibility support, i.e., support for users with any disabilities).

DW: Do you do your own book design, as well as typesetting, or do your publishers help you with the design?

DM: When I was signing up with CUP (in about 1996) I suggested to them that they should give me a book design. They showed me some options, but I didn't like them, so I decided to make my own book design, and just ask CUP's "experts" for TEX help when I was trying to make particular features work. In the end I asked their expert for help once, and the expert was useless and gave incorrect advice. So I did it all myself, with a little bit of feedback from friends (especially Sanjoy Mahajan (`http://mit.edu/sanjoy/www/`)); a little bit of advice from a typographer, and with the help of (a) Tufte's books and (b) Robert Bringhurst's *Elements of Typographic Style*; and of course by poring over other textbooks for design ideas.

DW: Returning to your interest in energy and your mention of 2+2, will you say a bit more about what your interests and intentions are with this work. Or is this more of a hobby — or does it somehow fit within your academic situation?

DM: There is a problem of wishful thinking today. People seem to believe, when it comes to energy, that $2+2=100$. But the correct answer is that $2+2=4$. People are anti-fossil fuel, anti-tidal barrage, anti-wind farm, and anti-nuclear. Yet they want the lights to come on. They seem to think that a few renewable facilities the size of a figleaf could power a modern lifestyle. In Britain, total energy consumption is 125 kWh per day per person. (In the USA, it's 250 kWh per day per person.) In Britain, renewables provide about 1 kWh per day per person, or perhaps 2, depending how you do the thermodynamics. Of that, wind power contributes less than 0.2 kWh per day per person. If we had a really big increase in wind power (against public opposition), it might deliver 4 kWh per day per person.

Hardly anyone is talking about energy plans that add up!

I wrote the book to try to help the public have an intelligent numerate and constructive conversation about energy (instead of the normal Punch and Judy show of anti-wind and anti-nuclear).

This activity is an amateur interest for me, but it has become a near-full-time activity, and it is an activity that my department supports warmly. Energy is a popular topic with students, and I'm engaging with academics (in economics, engineering, and business) who work on energy policy.

I haven't figured out exactly where I am going next with this full-time hobby. I wrote the book to try to get all the numbers down in one place, so that now I can talk to people. The task for the next couple of months is to figure out whom I should talk to. I'm not sure whether I should focus on public education, or on talking to civil servants. We need a plan that adds up. It's not going to be easy (especially not in a high density country like Britain) — but it is possible.

DW: Since learning about your book, I have been recommending it to everyone I know who is interested in thinking about the energy situation based on some factual numbers rather than an a priori political or moral position, and it surely doesn't hurt that it has a completely professional and authoritative feel while being available on-line for free.

Perhaps we can close with another personal question. You write and think about the energy problem. However, it seems you also try to live a green life to some extent. Your web site mentions that part of the reason for returning to Cambridge after Caltech was getting back to a bicycle rather than car society; your web site also mentions your involvement in something called Cast Iron aimed at replacing a bus system with a train; and I loved your analysis of the efficient way to boil hot water (`http://www.inference.phy.cam.ac.uk/sustainable/hotwater/`). Can you say a few philosophical words about what you see as the right mix of just trying to get along in life (make a living, stay warm in the winter, etc.), spending time trying to understand the realities of the situation, living green at a individual level, and trying to improve the world more generally.

DM: When I give talks about energy, people quite often ask me what car I drive, how much I fly, and so forth; it goes down well with these people if my response indicates that I'm trying to live a green lifestyle. And indeed I don't drive cars any more — I just ride bikes and trains and buses.

But the truth is, when you honestly quantify everything, it's incredibly difficult to get close to sustainable targets, in particular to the greenhouse gas emission targets for 2050 recommended by climate scientists. So while I enjoy playing the game of reducing my energy consumption at home (in the winter, because my home is now usually below 55 F, I've cut my natural-gas consumption by 60 percent), I honestly view these personal privations as curious science experiments rather than effective actions. Even my 60-percent-reduced domestic gas consumption still contributes 2 tons per year of CO_2! (And the recommended target for 2050 is 1 ton per capita per year.)

So for me the bottom line is pretty clear: the only way to live a useful green life is to influence governments' policies. Through policies, we can transform the way everything works. There will still be consumer choice; but through good legislation we can ensure that the consumer can have any colour, as long as it's green. If it seems like I have to get on an aeroplane occasionally to try to influence government policies, I'm going to do so. Maybe I'll see you in Boston this year!

DW: Thank you, David, for taking the time to participate in this interview. I do hope we meet again in person at some point. I recommend to readers of this interview that they spend some time scouting around your web site; there's a lot of interesting stuff there.

Arthur Reutenauer

Arthur Reutenauer is the president of Groupe francophone des utilisateurs de TeX (GUTenberg) and is active in other aspects of TeX use and development.

[Interview completed 3 March 2009.]

Dave Walden, interviewer: Please tell me a bit about your personal history independent of TeX.

Arthur Reutenauer, interviewee: I'm the eldest of six children (and a seventh one is on the way). We have different sets of parents, but to simplify, let's just say that the first five of us have the same mother, and that we all grew up together in Southern France. The youngest child is my half-brother from my father's side, who has been living in Montréal for over 20 years. The seventh one will be a girl, also from my father. I should probably also mention that I have been born in Paris. We moved to the French Riviera when I was five, and, at that time, 2½children.

Although it might not be obvious at first, my family is actually deeply rooted in Alsace, the part of France bordering Germany on the Rhine, that has had such an unfortunate fate in history. Apart from my father in Canada and my mother on the Riviera, the vast majority of my relatives live there, in different parts of the region. Some also live in Germany, where one of my grandmothers comes from (initially in Torgau in Saxony, on the Elbe River). Thinking back about it, I think that having my origins in this very special region, and the fact that I never lived in it, had a deep influence on my development.

DW: In what way?

AR: Through my German grandmother (my father's mother), I was introduced to an alternate history I would never have learned at school. I learned the dark side of it, which somehow she took as natural, though in a non-fatalistic way. The most gruesome anecdote that happened in my family's history was when, ten days after the end of the war in Europe, her father was killed by a party of Red Army soldiers looting in the city (we were in the part of Germany that the Soviet Union took over; in fact, Torgau is supposed to be the city where the U.S. and Soviet armies joined, even if they actually joined somewhere in the outskirts). That's where my family's "little" history encountered the "great" history.

But back to my own past: the place where I grew up was a small village in Provence and we had a nice house with a few dozen olive trees, which my parents learnt how to take care of (my mother also grew up in the countryside in Alsace). But they were by far no agriculturers: all "three of them" (mother, father and stepfather) were math teachers, so I was kind of predestined :-). In fact, while we don't have the concept of suburb in France like you have in North America, this was probably the closest thing to a suburb: a small neighbourhood next to the big cities on the coast, and we had access to rather fancy schools.

I went to some of them: first, four years in a mixed primary-secondary school where we had intensive music education (I took piano, cello, and singing lessons). We got to travel a lot, including on a few tours abroad. The farthest I went thanks to that school was Opole in southern Poland, when I was 10. Then five years at a school with intensive language courses, where I had the great opportunity to learn a couple of different languages: first, obviously German because of my family's origins, then English, Arabic, and finally Chinese. The latter started as a joke with my mother: at the beginning of high school, the school administration wished to encourage the study of "rare" languages by paying the fees of the reputed distance-learning organization. If I remember correctly, the interested students had the choice between Ancient Greek, Portuguese and Mandarin Chinese. Now, for some reason, at that time I wanted to learn Ancient Greek for a long time, but on that evening, my mother and I decided that I would give a try to Chinese instead, as a sort of bet. This would probably have been my last chance of learning dead languages, but I definitely chose for the living ones.

That was probably all for the best, since, thanks to my parents, we got to travel a lot. They took us all over Europe, and to America (where one of my mother's big brothers lived for a long time, in Boston). We crossed the U.S. from east to west, twice. During a trip to Scandinavia, we even pushed as far as Saint-Petersburg (not the city in Florida ;-) — we went there on our second American trip). I was 12 then and was fascinated by what I saw during the few days we spent there. My stepfather, who had been learning Russian, taught me the Cyrillic alphabet and I tried to read the signs on the street. But some things seemed really odd to me. I just couldn't make heads or tails out of it, and I couldn't pin down what it was. Only many years later did I realize that I had been witnessing, with my Westerner child's eyes, what Russia looked like a few months after the breakup of the USSR.

DW: This is all fascinating. What a special, and educational, childhood. How did your formal education continue?

AR: When it comes to higher education in France, it really seems like you have only one golden path for scientific studies, which is the dreaded "classes préparatoires" (let's use preparatory schools as a translation). It's that kind of crazy place where you have to study like an animal in order to take competitive exams which give you access to a row of very reputed schools. The pressure is often intense. But I was really brilliant at math, I just loved it; and I was confident enough that I would do well.

I went to Paris — since, obviously, the most reputed places were in Paris. I took the exams two years in a row, and succeeded the second time. It gave me access to all the schools I wanted, and I chose the "École normale supérieure", a school destined to train students to work in research and higher education (although when it was founded, during the French Revolution, it was meant for secondary education). At that time I was really into math, and started liking physics. So, it was the deal: I was going to be a researcher in math. Or maybe physics. Or. . . .

There were a couple of indecisive years, but in some way I had earned them. They really got me further than anything I could have imagined. You see, one of the unusual things at the École normale, like at a few other schools where you can go in by taking the exam after the classes préparatoires, is that you're actually paid for making your studies. It's not a bursary, you're really paid as a training civil servant during four years. I was of course to take advantage of that.

I started to go on a series of trips. To Italy. To China, with my family. To Italy, again. To China, again, through Russia on the Trans-Siberian railway. And over Mongolia on the way, since a bunch of corrupt Russian officers threw me, again with dozens of other foreigners, out of the train; but, together with a handful of other young people, we found our way out. It was 2002, and the pretext for me to go to China was that the International Congress of Mathematicians took place in Peking that year. I say "pretext" because, obviously, I would have found other pretexts otherwise.

At that point, the school administration decided that my results weren't that satisfactory, and cut me off the funds for one year. I had to take a couple of exams again, which I soon went through with, and by the end of the first semester I was ready to be on the road again. To China, obviously! Through Russia again, and this time I could stay on the train until the destination I had chosen. I made a round trip to Japan where one of my cousins celebrated her marriage, and came back to China, where I stayed three months. This was the moment of the SARS outbreak and, though a bit frightened at first, I decided to stay and to take advantage of my long holiday as soon as I could. After a few weeks I started to travel a lot around the country, and I could, in particular, see the Great Dam on the Yang-Tse river two weeks after they had completed the first part of the work, and flooded the area (the water went up to 135 meters above the reference level, if I remember correctly). The final phase of the construction should be completed this year, 2009. After my visa expired in China I went to Australia, which was the summer destination of my family this year. We went on a huge tour around the continent down under, and on the way back I made a stopover, to my great joy, in Taiwan (but I didn't get to see much more than the insides of the international airport).

That big trip lasted a bit over six months, and I could resume my studies (and my funding) happily after that. I graduated in 2005 with the "agrégation" in mathematics, another competitive exam that allow the successful candidates to teach at secondary school.

I did that for one year. It wasn't such a positive experience, and I wouldn't like to get into details about it. Let's just say that I wasn't enough prepared for what teaching a class of teenagers would be, and I didn't succeed very well. After the first year, I decided to take a break to think about my career path a bit more.

DW: And what happened?

AR: I had a couple of rough years where I had no job and no clear direction where to go. At one point I resumed my studies, in Brest and in CS this time, in the hope to start a Ph.D., but this led nowhere either. Very recently I have been offered a position at a startup in Paris, whose founder is a mathematician who wanted to develop a product based on algorithms he discovered for organizing databases. He was looking for a mathematician with a working knowledge of programming to work with him, and I had a contact with him through a colleague of my father. I thus came, by complete chance, to come back to my beloved natal town and to work in a great and inspiring environment. Since we have no office yet, I work at my boss' home, and often at my home, too; my boss is happy with that.

One of the other coincidences is that the algorithms on which our product relies make heavy use of radix trees, that is ... tries, like in TEX's hyphenation patterns!

DW: How and when did you first get introduced to TEX?

AR: I was introduced to TEX by my stepfather during my first year in classe préparatoire, in the spring of 1998. As I mentioned, those were years of intense studies, and we hardly had time to do all the assignments that we were given, but on top of that we were supposed to make a bit of "research work" about a not-so-original subject. There was some general theme ("approximation", I think), and my father suggested to me continued fractions, which I really enjoyed. Thus, I set to write a report about it, and started learning LATEX. I was immediately fascinated with what the output looked like and spent hours polishing it—which in retrospect was rather vain, as I had almost no knowledge at all; the only book I had was Lamport's, and my stepfather assisted me with some instructions. I remember my mother sounding really desperate that on top of all what I had to do, I stayed up half the night going over and over my DVI file, and—to tell the truth—I'd rather not see the source now! Of course it's long gone (I had several backups, but all of them must have gone down the drain). Thanks to my father, I still have a printed copy of the final report, that I, somewhat narcissistically, dated to my 18th birthday, at the end of that spring.

DW: Please tell me a bit about your use of TEX in the years since then.

AR: My first uses of TEX were, of course, related to my math studies. At the École normale, the first-year students in math were actually required to write one of their reports in LATEX, which suited me well, since I was already familiar with it. I also remember helping my father to type the text of one of his lessons during that period. A few years later, as a math teacher, I wrote all my assignments with XETEX and the Baskerville font for text (math was in Computer Modern). This gave me some reputation among my students who were apparently used to the all-Times appearance of Word documents.

At one point, I discovered a whole new use of TEX: a fellow students who was acting as a sort of system administrator showed me how to typeset Chinese! I was amazed at the beginning, because I had no idea it was possible. This introduced to the world of character sets and encoding, and also to font handling in TEX. I used Werner Lemberg's CJK package, and at that time the fonts that were available with it were bitmap fonts in a special format, hbf, derived from X11's bdf format where the metrics were compressed: since Chinese characters have fixed width, you can save a lot of space by including the metric information only once. There was a small utility for converting hbf to PK that was called by mktexpk for each subfont; hence the first runs were usually very long and intimidating. This was quite an abrupt introduction to font issues in TEX! I was very happy when I learned, a few years later, that pdfTEX could embed TrueType fonts directly.

My most serious use of TEX was probably when I was responsible for typesetting our school's yearbook. We had a tradition of having people tell about their interests, and type in their favourite quotes, in any language they wanted. And since the École normale is a place where you find people with specialized knowledge of many different fields, you were bound to see quotes in many different languages: folk from humanities liked to quote a sentence or two in Ancient Greek, scientific geeks would put a line in Quenya, etc. The yearbook had already been set in LATEX for years, and I switched it to Omega that year. The year after me, it was switched to Aleph, and I understand they use XETEX now. To be completely honest, I have to say that the team-management experience wasn't so good for me, and I never delivered the yearbook to the printer; someone had to take over for me. But I really learned a lot on the technical level.

DW: I see from the *TUGboat* author list that you have written two papers that relate to the use of TEX for different languages.

1. A brief history of TEX, volume II (Vol. 29, No. 1, 2008)
2. Putting the Cork back in the bottle—Improving Unicode support in TEX (Vol. 29, No. 3, 2008)

What motivated your interest in that aspect of TEX?

AR: The first article, especially, was inspired by my experience with typesetting many different languages with TEX. It was also the subject of my first big talk at a TEX conference, at EuroBachoTEX in 2007. It was also, of course, related to my interest for history, but I soon realized that I saw it from a particular angle, which made my paper very different from Phil Taylor's "first volume" with the same title, ten years before mine (I came up with the title independently and contacted Phil Taylor, who of course "allowed" me to use the title for my own talk).

The second paper is a bit different: it described the work I did with Mojca Miklavec on the hyphenation patterns in TeX Live, in the spring of 2008. We knew that something needed to be done, because all of them were in some 8-bit font encoding, and XeTeX can't work with that, it expects UTF-8. When it was included in TeX Live 2007, Jonathan Kew came up with a neat hack where the patterns were automatically converted to UTF-8 when they were loaded by XeTeX (in contrast to Knuth's TeX, pdfTeX, etc.) This worked, but it was much less than satisfactory: you would really like for the patterns to be in UTF-8, and convert them to the appropriate 8-bit encoding if needed, for compatibility. Even more so, actually, as LuaTeX was coming up in TeX Live 2008, and it also expects UTF-8 input by default. So we did that — I have to say it was all Mojca's ideas and inspiration that started it — and Karl gave us his blessing. It was all very quick, and in retrospect somewhat crazy, but now I'm all the more convinced that it needed to be done: the "old" patterns use some tricks, which for some languages date back to TeX 2, before 1989! There were other weird things; read the paper for the detail.

DW: Where and how did you meet Mojca?

AR: We met at the first ConTeXt conference in Epen, The Netherlands, in March 2007, and every few months since then. Actually, I already saw her the year before at the BachoTeX conference, but she claims she doesn't remember me from that time! We started a lot of projects together, some of which we actually completed in time ... well, at least one of them, the hyph-utf8 package I document in my second *TUGboat* paper. She has incredible energy and is extremely committed to everything she does. It may be a bit overwhelming at times! But it's always great. The ConTeXt community should be really thankful for everything she achieved.

DW: I believe you have been involved in contributing code to ConTeXt and LuaTeX. Please tell me about that and, more generally, how you got involved in TeX development as well as use.

AR: I can hardly say I contributed code, but I've been following their development for a couple of years. I became interested in LuaTeX in 2006; I remembered being particularly excited during the TUG conference in Marrakesh, when it became clear that LuaTeX was going to be more than simply Lua + TeX and was on the verge of becoming the next generation's TeX. My interest for ConTeXt started at the same period.

I did contribute a few bugfixes for LuaTeX; I believe I am the first person who compiled it on Mac OS and on Solaris, just like I had been the first one to compile XeTeX on Solaris earlier. I like doing experiments with LuaTeX and I hope to get the LaTeX developers to provide better support for it; in fact, the relative lack of reaction of the LaTeX's community to LuaTeX eventually drove me away from LaTeX, and I now prefer to use ConTeXt.

DW: You participated in the Summer of Code last year and you have agreed to serve as an administrator this year if TUG's application is accepted, about which we should know in a few weeks. [Editor's note: Google rejected TUG's application.] First, will you please briefly summarize what the Summer of Code is.

AR: It is a program by Google aiming at attracting students of computer science and other fields to the free software/open source community, started in 2005. It works in a rather simple way: Google first selects organizations creating open source programs ("mentoring organizations"), which are invited to suggest project ideas to students, together with mentoring developer(s) for each project. The students then apply for concrete projects based on these ideas, and the organizations select the ones with the most merit, which are awarded a grant of $4500 for completing their project during the summer. The mentoring organizations also get $500 for each successful project.

Last year, three students participated in GSoC with TUG (I was one of them), and when I asked Karl if he was ready to renew the experience in 2009, he told me that he would be fine with pursuing it, as long as I could take care of the bulk of the administrator's job.

DW: Please tell me how you became involved in the Summer of Code, what participating and being an administrator entails, and what you see as the purpose and value of this activity, especially to the TEX community.

AR: Again, I have no shame in saying that it was all Mojca's idea in the beginning, and that I merely helped her to implement it. She didn't have a precise idea in the beginning, but she felt that there would be benefits to the TEX community in participating in it, and this prompted me to ask Karl about it, shortly before the program started in March.

I believe the main benefit is to make TEX development a bit better known in the general open source community and to communicate with other projects. It is a long process but it can be most fruitful on the long term, and Google provides us with a really great infrastructure there: you just go to the GSoC sites and look for a project that may be of interest to the TEX community (there were over a thousand last year!). It also creates connections inside the community; as far as I am concerned, GSoC is really the reason I came into close contact with Karl.

In comparison, I think the actual projects the students work on are less important, even if that may sound a bit provocative: the important part is bringing the people together with a little incentive, and discussing your goals. Hence, the actual projects (and the $5000 ...) are of course essential because nothing would happen without them, but they would be useless if you don't prepare for them beforehand (and try and draw some conclusion from them afterwards). This is what I intend to do for this year, and I surely hope Google will continue with this program in the future.

DW: You are the president of Groupe francophone des utilisateurs de TEX. Please tell me how your involvement in GUTenberg started, how you came to be president, and something about the activities of GUTenberg.

AR: I became a member of GUTenberg in 2002, when I was made "TEX admin" of the student-run workstations at the École normale. I remember buying some TEX fetish items at that time, like the fluffy TEX lion the German publisher Lehmann's made (I later gave it to the son of a Dutch TEXie). From the outside, the group seemed quite inactive at that time, and I have to say it hasn't changed much since then. I became member of the board in 2007, and president right after (the president is elected by the board according to our bylaws). We suffer under the same general problems as TUG and the other user groups, I guess, but we also had specific internal problems.

Anyway, I have great hopes for the future. Thanks to TEX conferences, I realized how active the international TEX community still was, and even if it's not comparable to, say, your average GNU/Linux/free software/open source convention, it still attracts enthusiastic new users, and there are a lot of projects. I already met many French people who seemed really motivated, and I think we will be able to start things over.

One of the most enjoyable feeling that I get from the conferences is that we're building a tight group that is truly international; my first impression was that here in Europe, there were three LUGs leading the march: NTG (Netherlands), DANTE (Germany) and GUST

(Poland). The "leaders", so to say, know each other very well and communicate a lot, which is a great asset to the general community. And of course, this helps interaction with TUG, where Karl is always attentive to what happens here. Many recent projects would have never existed without this tight relationship (I'm thinking of Latin Modern, TeX Gyre, LuaTeX, mplib ... to name but a few that I've witnessed over the past years).

DW: Although you mentioned that your new job involved a data structure such as TeX uses, I got the impression that TeX isn't actually part of the job. Do you foresee still being able to be involved (and interested) in the world of TeX?

AR: Indeed, I do not use TeX at all as part of my job. We're doing databases, and right now I'm polishing an SQL parser, and tearing my hair about all the incompatibilities between the major database engines and the ISO standard (which no one implements and, being basically a two-person company, we're not anywhere near implementing it either). But I'm still fortunate enough to use beamer to make presentations with my boss!

I don't think I will lose interest in TeX any time soon; it is one of my greatest joys, and, since a few years, most of the trips I've made were because of TeX conferences. It's thus a great way to combine two of my major hobbies! I also won't forget that my interest in TeX was the force that drove me to my current career: I simply learnt programming thanks to TeX. My first modest contribution to a program was a patch for font-related utilities for Omega, in C, which I had been learning from the K&R book, and from thorough reading of files in the TeX Live source tree. I could go on, but I have probably been praising TeX a bit too much already.

DW: Thank you for participating in this interview.

AR: Thank *you* for your endeavour, and for your patience during this interview.

Raph Levien

Raph Levien is a programmer with a special interest in graphics applied to type. He is also a typeface designer. He holds several patents and is a past maintainer of Ghostscript.

[Interview completed 16 May 2009.]

[Background of this interview: TUG, through the TeX development fund (`http://tug.org/tc/devfund`), supported Raph Levien's font work to a small extent. When it came time to document his work, Raph suggested an interview instead of a formal paper, which we were glad to oblige. Dave Crossland (`http://understandinglimited.com`), another type designer and colleague of Raph, shared in the conversation.]

Karl Berry, interviewer: Please tell us a bit about your personal history independent of typesetting and fonts.

Raph Levien, interviewee: I was born in Enkhuizen, the Netherlands, and moved to Virginia when I was three, so I don't really speak Dutch or anything but I do find myself with a liking for herring. I was something of a gifted child and, after a few somewhat disastrous years in public school, did a combination of homeschooling and taking classes at nearby colleges, mostly Virginia Tech and mostly math and physics. After a few years of trying to sell software on my own (with my dad helping on the business side), I decided that I really wanted to go to grad school, so I moved to Berkeley for that. I'm just now finishing my PhD (hopefully by the time this interview is published), and the topic is interactive curve design — motivated by my desire to have better tools to design fonts.

Between working at Google on spam prevention, finishing my thesis, and parenting two boys, I don't have a whole lot of time for hobbies but I do like photography.

KB: Did you get a bachelor's degree along the way? It would be quite unusual if you received a Ph.D. with no undergraduate degree

RL: Indeed, I took a bunch of undergraduate classes when I was younger but never actually got a degree. Berkeley has a great tradition of people with nontraditional backgrounds, and of taking some risks.

KB: I know you from the world of typography and fonts. How and when did you first get introduced to typesetting and font design?

RL: Among other things, my father made a number of books (he's especially well known for his miniature editions) and was very interested in fonts and typography. One of my earliest memories of books is an old Phil's Fonts catalog (an old New York phototypesetting vendor who I think mostly served the advertising market), which had a big letter on each page. So I sometimes say I learned the alphabet that way — A is for Aachen, B is for Baskerville, C is for Caslon.

In the mid-'80s, I wrote a batch typesetting system called Byso Print. It was in some ways fairly ambitious — among other things, it had autokerning based on the shapes of the individual glyphs. In other ways (especially compared to TEX) it was fairly crude. It did scaling of fonts by starting from a 256-pixel per em bitmap and scaling that. So, you can imagine, it looked pretty rough at large sizes. It also piggybacked on top of WordPerfect to do the hyphenation and justification.

My first serious attempt at a scalable font was a techno design called Zaltbommel (for a sample of this, and a bit more of my early history, see `http://typophile.com/node/54857`).

Ever since really diving into TEX, I've been fascinated and impressed with how advanced it was for its day. It's a shame its usability problems kept it from ever going mainstream, but it's good to see that it's carved out a solid niche for itself, and that there's still interesting development. Metafont in particular was way ahead of its time. I've only come to appreciate how good its interpolating spline algorithm is after going deep into the theory behind them for my own thesis. A good way of understanding it is as an approximation to the Euler spiral spline, basically as close as you can get to that using a cubic Bezier as the primitive segment. I think if it had been easier to use, it might have become popular. As it is, you have to be a hardcore computer scientist to understand Metafont programs — I'm even a little intimidated by them.

Metafont's use of cubic Beziers is very efficient, but I figured we have orders of magnitude more CPU power than then. What would the absolute *best* curve look like, if you had unlimited computing power? It turns out to be a trickier problem than I first thought, but I've come a long way to answering it in my thesis. Some of the optimization-based approaches, like Henry Moreton's Minimum Energy Curve and Minimum Variation Curve, took many seconds to solve a curve, but I've figured out some numerical techniques (strongly influenced by what John Hobby did for the curves in Metafont and MetaPost) that get you to interactive speeds without any problem. And, of course, the fact that you're drawing letters on the screen instead of writing a program makes the design process easier too.

I did a lot of tracing existing metal fonts using my curves. That was a good way to put my curves through their paces, but before long I started itching to do my own original design. I saw there was a niche to do a better monospaced font than what was already out there in the free world, and went for it.

Dave Crossland, interviewer: Metafont was one of the first graphic-program languages, and the way it is used has not changed much since the 1970s when it was invented. The success of Logo with children suggests that such languages need not be so intimidating, and perhaps different approaches to the way Metafont programs are written could help. Recently this set of languages has become an active area, with Processing, DrawBot, NodeBox, ShoeBot and others; perhaps the most advanced is Field, with its tight integration of a text editor to the graphic output of the code in that editor. There's a good video of this at `http://vimeo.com/3034647`. Do you have any suggestions for the way that Metafont could be made less intimidating?

RL: I'm not sure Metafont itself has much more life in it, sadly. While it was amazing technology for the time, its output can't be easily converted to standard font formats. That's pretty much a dealbreaker. (I know of various efforts, including rasterizing at high resolution and converting that to vectors, but that's not really acceptable for professional font design).

I think you could easily do Metafont-like things though, and the tools you listed are extremely promising. I think one of the most important things is to make it interactive rather than batch mode. In the '70s, batch mode made sense, but these days, if there's a coordinate, you really need to be able to click on the point and drag it.

I think one of the most exciting developments today is JavaScript in the browser, using either SVG or Canvas to do the drawing. Just in the past year or so, you have really good, fast JavaScript implementations, and a solid 2D rendering engine beneath. A couple years ago, it would be nearly impossible to get interactive performance. Today, by developing for the Open Web platform, you can make tools accessible to a lot of people, and having JavaScript right there means you could combine programmability with interactive graphics in interesting ways. I think John Resig's `processing.js` is a huge step in that direction.

KB: I'm intrigued by your passing mention of autokerning. Is autokerning implemented in any program today? I have never come across it. I've tried to write programs along those lines from time to time, for kerning and interletter spacing in general, but never succeeded.

RL: Yes, there are a few interesting autokerning systems out there. The first one that was really any good was the Kernus system by the Ikarus people. I think a version of that shipped with PageMaker 5 in the early '90s. Adobe then shipped a more refined version in InDesign, which is used by lots of people.

One of the more interesting things going on now in that space is iKern, by Igino Marino. I don't know too much about how the algorithm works, but I have tried it out on my Century Catalogue. The results are quite good, even better than InDesign in my opinion. Last I checked, he's not interested in releasing the tool itself as open source, but there are free font designers who are interested in using it. The quality of spacing is one of the huge determiners of quality between an amateurish font and a truly excellent one.

DC: Marino is apparently not interested in releasing it at all — he operates it as 'software as a postal service' where you email him a font and he emails it back with better spacing.

RL: Yeah. I hope that works out for him, but it pretty much limits the scope for his ideas to have broad impact.

KB: I'd like to hear a little more about these new curves. In reading your blog (`http://www.advogato.org/person/raph/diary.html`), I see that they're called Euler spirals or Cornu spirals. Can you say a bit about the difference a designer would see working with these spirals instead of Beziers? And would it make a visible difference to the ultimate reader?

RL: Well, Euler got there a hundred and thirty years before Cornu, so I think he deserves the credit for it. Actually, James Bernoulli first wrote down the equation for the curve in 1694, so it goes a long way back, but he didn't actually plot it and it's not clear he had a clear picture what it looked like. Since then it's been rediscovered any number of times in a number of different applications and, each time, given a new name. Fresnel found that their equations were useful for solving diffraction problems, so they're also known as the Fresnel integrals. Cornu figured out you could plot those and read the answer to the diffraction problem off the plot, so the curve got his name. It was also rediscovered a few times by railway engineers looking to make smooth transitions between straight sections of rail and curves, so the train doesn't suddenly lurch from side to side. In that domain, it's now most commonly called the clothoid.

And, in fact, I don't just use the Euler spirals, I use a mixture of curves (my package is called spiro, which is kind of an abbreviation for polynomial spirals). Most of Inconsolata (the monospaced font mentioned above) is drawn using G4-continuous splines, which are a very close approximation to the Minimum Variation Curve of Henry Moreton. I now think that's overkill, and G2-continuous splines (the Euler spiral ones) are plenty, and could be done with fewer points.

DC: Øyvind Kolås (`http://pippin.gimp.org`) mentioned to me that he came to the same conclusion — using G2 points as default and G4 points where extra smoothness is desired. And for me, FontForge allows one to switch quickly between Spiros and Beziers (although the conversion is not yet optimised); I find myself using Beziers by default, and then using Spiro splines when drawing curves that are tricky to keep smooth with Beziers, like S-bend curves — ones that double back on themselves — the vertical stroke of a '7', or the tail of a two-story 'g'.

RL: Interesting. I haven't actually tried working that way myself, and one of the things I worry about is making the interface too complex, but having more choices certainly fits into the free software aesthetic.

I've lately redone the optimized conversion to Beziers to be quite a bit faster (it used to take over a minute for most glyphs, now 15 seconds or so, and that's in Python). Maybe if that were recoded in C, it would be fast enough you could flip back and forth inside the drawing program and it would be fast enough not to interrupt the flow.

You can draw any curve you like using either Beziers or splines like I'm using. But I'm absolutely convinced that the tool you use has a profound effect on the shapes you draw. Almost all "contemporary" looking fonts you see produced these days have shapes that are very characteristic of Bezier curves. And, if you look at their outlines, you'll see that most often one quadrant of, say, an 'o' is drawn with a single cubic Bezier. So that gives you a palette. A reasonably rich one, but ultimately there are only two parameters describing a cubic Bezier that traverses exactly one quadrant of arc. You can go past it, but it takes more work, and it's easier to get lumpy results.

The curves you get using Spiro are a different palette. I think they're more classical, more like a French curve (and, in fact, I believe the Euler spiral is at least used as inspiration for French curves). So I think ultimately Inconsolata is a different font than it would have been had I drawn it using Beziers.

DC: Your Spiro package includes GTK and GTK2 prototype GUI programs for drawing with these splines, and since the release in 2007 they have been integrated into FontForge and Inkscape. Do you have any suggestions about what the free software community can do to make Spiro more popular?

RL: Part of the problem is that the Spiro integration has been on development branches, and it's fairly painful for most people to build from scratch, getting all the libraries, and so on. When you can just 'apt-get install' your apps that have Spiro turned on by default, I think lots more people will use those curves.

The other thing that I think might make a big difference is to build a good vector drawing editor for the Open Web platform. I have a prototype of Spiro for that too, but unfortunately it's too unfinished to actually draw in, and I don't have much time to work on it now. It would make a great project for someone who wanted to do something awesome in that platform, and get lots of users.

KB: Let's turn to that monospaced font you've designed that we mentioned above, named Inconsolata. Please tell us where the name came from, and about your design ideas for the font.

RL: My original idea for the name was "Unconsoled", which was intended to be both descriptive and self-deprecating as is common for free software projects (keep in mind that one of the projects I worked on was The Gimp). One idea for the font is that I was going to optimize it entirely for very high resolution rendering, and make no concessions to adapting it to a low-res pixel grid, which is of course the space that most monospaced fonts need to work in. I was very inspired by Consolas, a beautifully executed design, but I felt I could do some things better for the print domain, free to do some subtly angled strokes that just don't work when you're fitting to a grid. Ironically, most people use it as a terminal font anyway. On Mac OS X and (to a lesser extent) Linux, the rendering is pretty good, but on Windows it's fuzzy and users aren't as happy.

Hrant Papazian came up with the name "Inconsolata", which is more or less the Italian translation. I thought it sounded classier, so I went with it.

I wanted it to be a classical sans, clean like the Franklin Gothic series. I wanted to make the spacing as smooth as possible, so even though it is of course monospaced, it doesn't necessarily *look* like it is. That's one of the highest bits of praise I got—somebody saying that it had the color on the page of a proportionally spaced font. There are also quite a few glyphs with subtle curves in them, like the lowercase 't v w'. Some people don't like those, but I think they make text look warmer.

Since I was designing for very high resolution, I also wanted to play with an idea I got while looking at gothic fonts in Japan—the microserif, or very small spur. My idea was that it would make the font look a little sharper and crisper, and visually more interesting. In very small sizes, it's hardly visible at all (and of course not at all on the screen), but it's still cool knowing they're there.

KB: What's the current status of Inconsolata (I see it's available from `http://www.levien.com/type/myfonts/inconsolata.html`), and the Century Catalogue project you also mentioned, and any others you might have in the offing (post-thesis presumably)?

RL: Inconsolata is pretty close to what I'd consider done. It's shipping in a bunch of Linux distros, and there are quite a few people using it. There are a few more tweaks I want to do before calling it completely done, mostly responding to feedback I've gotten from users. In fact, a lot of that feedback has been in the form of people releasing their own versions with changes, which really feels to me like the free software spirit at work.

I did a lot of work tracing existing metal fonts, including Century Catalogue, to wrap my mind around the way the old masters worked (scans of these, mostly from the amazing American Type Founders catalogs, are available at my web page, and the raw high-res scans are on `tug.org`). Now, I think I've gained more confidence in doing my own designs. My latest work-in-progress is Cecco, for which I now have a complete lowercase and uppercase alphabet. It's intended to be a good working text font, and I'm pleased with the way it's turning out. With the amount of free time I have now, it'll take a while to finish, but that is one of the nice things about fonts—working slowly and steadily eventually gets the job done.

KB: I'm glad you consider Inconsolata at least pretty close to be being done, since we're using it for the typewriter material in this book.

Fonts in general have had a torturous legal history, going back to Goudy at least (as

I've heard it). Please say a few words about why you chose to release Inconsolata under the SIL Open Font License.

RL: It's very important to me that Inconsolata (and other fonts in the same vein) be useful for use in free software. I looked at the available licenses, and found problems with a lot of them. A lot of the licenses people use are for software, and aren't really appropriate for fonts. In particular, it's important to grant the right to embed the font into documents, and software licenses tend not to be clear about that — for GPL-licensed fonts, there's usually an explicit embedding exception. I also considered Creative Commons licenses (which are fairly popular among visual artists), but those may not be compatible with purist free software distributions.

To me, the exact legal terms are only part of the reason to choose a license. They're also important to signal intention and, to some extent, membership in a community. The OFL community tends to produce high quality fonts, like Victor Gaultney's Gentium and the excellent work of the Greek Font Society. I felt that choosing the OFL communicated my intent to do fonts better than most of the stuff that's out there for zero cost, but at the same time actually be useful for free software.

KB: Going along with font legalities, I noticed that you hold several patents, while licensing them for use in GPL'd software but not otherwise. Have you found that holding the patents is worth the bother of getting them, and what are your general thoughts on patenting of software and algorithms?

RL: Well, I'm very fortunate in this regard, because I have actually gotten some good revenues from licensing my patents over the years, both some early work I did on security (I was in fact eleven when I filed for my first patent) and more recently on halftone screening work. The screening work is used in the free Gutenprint inkjet drivers, and also commercially by several well-known companies. I think my strategy of using the free software release to bring more publicity to the work was a good one, and it would be great if the same thing happened with the curve work.

But the business of patent licensing is very hit or miss. Some of my better ideas never got licensed at all, and the ones that did were largely out of luck. The way the game is rigged, the best strategy for making money from patents is to be a patent troll, but that's never what I wanted to do — I just wanted to be able to create new technology and find a way to make some money.

Generally, I think the world would be better off if software and algorithms weren't patentable. The actual incentive to individual inventors — the main motivation you see cited — isn't very strong, and the potential for abuse is huge. It's also expensive and time consuming to get patents, so mostly you see big companies doing it. In general, I wouldn't recommend bothering.

KB: I also noticed you are or were one of the maintainers of Ghostscript, a crucial package in the free software world. How did that come about?

RL: I was one of the maintainers until a couple years ago, when I went over to Google — I unfortunately don't work on it any more. At the time I started on Ghostscript, around 2000, I was doing various 2d graphics projects in free software, including libart and the Gnome canvas, and Artifex was looking for people to work on projects for Ghostscript, both for release as free software and for their commercial licensing business, which continues to grow at a healthy clip. I started out with implementing PDF 1.4 transparency, and, after that worked out pretty well, joined Artifex as a full time employee. Ghostscript is, as you point out, a core component of the graphics and printing infrastructure in free software, and I'm still very friendly with them and wish them the best.

KB: I'll close with a general question. As we all see every day, there are seemingly an infinitude of fonts already in existence (many for centuries), some of insurmountable beauty, others of insurmountable ugliness. You've talked about the technical reasons you had for creating Inconsolata, but it seems to me that very few new fonts have such a background.

Why do you think fonts are still being created in such incredible proliferation? What is it that makes them such an attractive goal?

RL: Good question. Mostly, designing fonts is very satisfying creative work, I guess for certain people anyway. I enjoy drawing but can't do it very well, and I find that with fonts I can continually refine and improve the curves until it looks like what I wanted.

Also, fonts (especially good ones) tend to last a pretty long time, while most software gets thrown away quickly. It's especially satisfying to me to create something which might be more durable.

KB: Thank you very much for participating in this interview, and all your excellent work.

RL: My pleasure!

Endnote: Raph provided several figures showing the Inconsolata development process. He writes:

> The left-hand image shows the prototype GTK software I used for drawing all the Inconsolata glyphs — extremely minimal, but I found the clean and beautiful antialiased rendering really helped me focus on the shapes of the letters. The right-hand image is the result of converting that to optimized Beziers:

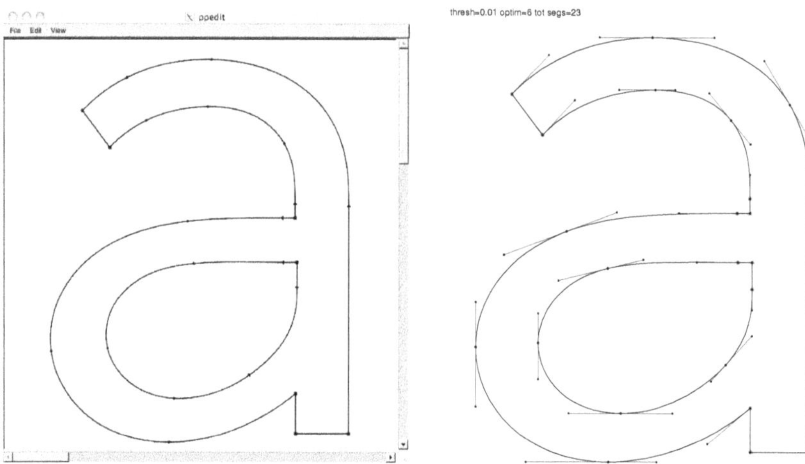

(continued)

Here are the Spiro sources for most of the lowercase:

Last, this is a screenshot of FontForge (`http://fontforge.sf.net`), which I used to put all the shapes together into a font, and produce Type 1 and OpenType font files.

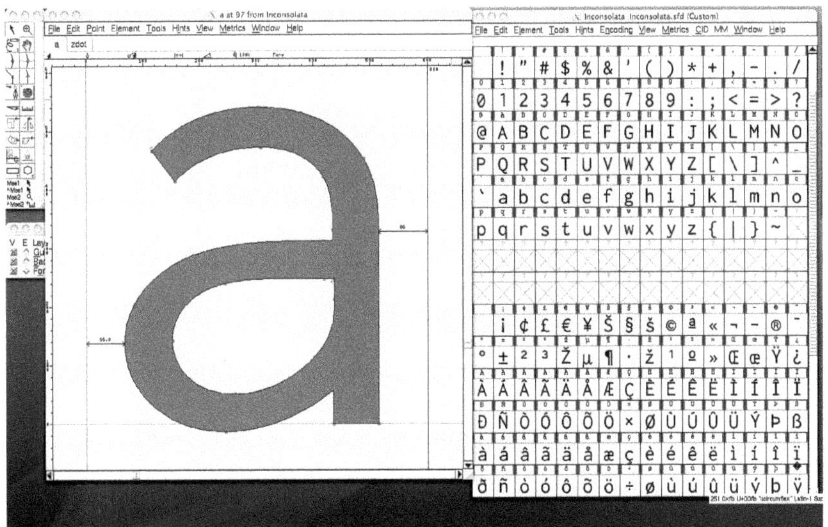

Sebastian Rahtz

For 15 years, Sebastian Rahtz was involved in an amazing variety of TeX and TUG activities.
[Interview completed 12 March 2009.]

Dave Walden, interviewer: Please tell me a bit about yourself.

Sebastian Rahtz, interviewee: I suppose the main emphasis in my life has been on the past. My father is an archaeologist, I studied Classics and Modern Greek at Oxford in the 1970s, I did an MA in archaeology, and I worked for some time as an archaeologist. Even when I drifted into computing (because it was easier to get a job), I specialized in the humanities and archaeology. It's hard to escape. Even now, my favourite place in the world is the Protestant Cemetery in Rome.

I live in Oxford now, with my partner and two teenage girls, who are even more beautiful and intelligent than those from Lake Wobegon. I make my living as Information Manager at the university Computing Services.

DW: When and how did you first get involved with TeX?

SR: I was a lecturer in humanities computing at the University of Southampton in the early 80s. I had become quite involved in typesetting working at Oxford, using a Monotype Lasercomp, for example for *The Lexicon of Greek Personal Names* (typesetting Greek nicely). So I was ripe for conversion when Professor David Barron showed me the first TeX for PCs (on 5 1/4 inch floppies). I was completely gobsmacked; then we got our first Unix TeX on tape from Pierre MacKay, and I did not recover from the spell for the next 15 years or so (I still haven't recovered from the Unix spell). Almost all the work I did from 1985 or so onwards until 2000 revolved around TeX.

DW: Please tell me about those "TeX years" — the deeper involvement with TeX and the series of projects and activities you got into and how.

SR: Really quite a lot of what I did in the "TeX years" was about the community. So I started by copying Sun TeX tapes for people, then I joined in the work around the UK TeX archive, from there I went on to work on CTAN in its early days (I believe I created the first instantiation late one night at Aston University), and from there it was an obvious step to the TeX Live CD, which I edited for the first 7 or 8 versions. I also worked for the user groups (TUG and UK-TUG) a lot in conference organisation, newsletter editing and so on (my highest post was as Secretary of TUG). Coupled with teaching TeX, supporting it (Michel Goossens employed me for some fruitful years at CERN), and publishing articles and books, it all comes back to helping the community rather than doing anything very deep. My efforts on the side as macro writer are relatively small, although my hyperref package lives to this day (now in the safe hands of Heiko Oberdiek).

How did I fit all this into real life? Some of it I did when I was at Southampton, then I had a few years as self-employed consultant (which was when I worked with Michel at CERN), before spending five years in production at Elsevier Science where I was paid to work on TeX-related things full-time.

I am quite proud of writing two of the LaTeX Companion volumes with Michel and Frank, assisting Hàn Thế Thành promote pdfTeX, helping launch TUGIndia, starting CTAN with Rainer and George Greenwade, and starting TeX Live. At the TeX meeting in Oxford in 2000, I was presented with a specially-drawn Bibby cartoon showing some of these things. That was about the culmination of my TeX career....

There were low points, usually around personality conflicts in the user groups which used to cause me immense grief. I am amazed that Karl and others have been able to carry on for so long — they have more equable tempers than me.

Like almost all TeX people, I would cite Don Knuth as the great unifying force, inspiration, and reason for using TeX. I don't understand almost anything he does, of course, but I was gratified to find we have a shared interest in road signs.

DW: I think I first saw your name in connection with NFSS. Where does that fit into your sketch of the TeX years?

SR: Ah, that is because of PostScript. I loved PS as soon as I saw it, and I still think it is a really great bit of design. We had a first model Apple LaserWriter, and of course we wanted to use its fonts, not the mangy Computer Modern (sorry, but I never did like that font). So I got stuck into AFM to TFM font metric conversion and tinkering with DVI ...PS software early on. When Mittelbach and Schöpf released NFSS, I was an early and very happy adopter. My setup for a lot of common typefaces got canonicalized as PSNFSS which I worked hard on for years; Walter Schmidt took it over, luckily. There was also the weird and wonderful fontinst package from Alan Jeffrey (Ulrik Vieth took that over, and now it lives with Lars Hellström) which underlies the LaTeX packages. Good stuff there, most of what I knew about it went into the *LaTeX Graphics Companion*.

DW: Also please tell me a bit more about TeX Live, particularly the teTeX/TeX Live relationship — and more generally about how you founded TeX Live and when you left it. I ask partly because this was so important to the viability of TUG during the late 1900s and early 2000s.

SR: It's hard to remember now that distribution of TeX was a big deal in the days before universal broadband, and that 650 megabytes was really an awful lot. It was obvious that a CD with all the TeX goodies on would make people happy. The Dutch 4AllTeX folks did it first, but their CD was pure Windows, and I wanted a Linux equivalent. Using Esser's teTeX was really a simple choice — it was all working, well-engineered, and Thomas was nice and helpful. All I did was expand on it, adding hundreds more packages and lots of Unix binaries. It was always a collaborative effort, getting friends to compile binaries for obscure systems — a lot we did at CERN and at Florida (thanks to Mimi Burbank). Getting a single source tree and one giant compilation script was a challenge!

The first CD was ready for TUG in Russia in 1996(?), I think. It even had the first version of pdfTeX on. Burning the first master took practically all one long night in the empty Elsevier offices. Then it turned into a regular production, Michel and I wrote a better manual, and a lot of the work became monitoring CTAN and keeping the source texmf tree up to date. That occupied my time for years — it became an instinct to grab an update from CTAN and bang it through the sausage machine every day. Many people helped out, of course, especially during the yearly compilathons. I remember especially Fabrice Popineau and his sufferings with Windows. Some people tried to "help" by releasing updates of their packages an hour or two before the deadline....

A lot came out of TEX Live, I believe. It focussed people's minds into packaging properly, automated procedures, common documentation, etc. It was symbiotic with CTAN, of course, and both of them stimulated the massive job of overhauling all packages to make sure they had proper open source licences—some people (not me especially!) have done great work there. Making TEX interoperate properly with the open source world was an important achievement.

I had to stop 100 percent daily work on TEX Live when I started my present job, it was too too time-consuming. I stopped reading the mail list properly in about 2006, and don't look much now at all. A pity, but it is not a job for someone on the sidelines. I pride myself on having passed on most of my TEX projects and *not* hung on to them in a dog-in-a-manger way.

DW: From your earlier answer, it sounds like you began to lose some of your interest in TEX about 2000 and an interest in XML (is this right?) began to build. I presume this change was driven at least partially by other things you saw happening in the world. Please tell me about this change and your subsequent activities.

SR: I was employed by Elsevier to work on conversions between TEX and SGML, so I started to hang out at SGML conferences. I also, like everyone else, was bowled over by the web. When the great Jon Bosak revealed the first draft of XML at one of the SGML meetings, it just seemed so *right* that I knew this was the future. It was not that TEX-the-engine was wrong, just TEX-as-input-language.

DW: TEX-as-input-language.... ?

SR: I mean that writing documents using backslashes and braces is just not on any more. I don't mind writing style files like that, but for an input document I want a syntax I can validate...

DW: Now I understand. Please go on.

SR: When I had a chance to leave Elsevier in 1999 and join computing support at Oxford, I was specifically asked to work on bringing documentation into a common format using XML, and I threw myself into it with a will. At the same time, I suddenly appreciated how brilliant the fledgling XSL was, and Lou Burnard reintroduced me to the Text Encoding Initiative (of which I had been vaguely aware during the 1990s). Those two new toys excited me so much that I had no energy left for TEX; sadly, but there are only so many hours in a day. I did put a lot of effort into automated typesetting of XML using TEX; my weird PassiveTeX package, named as a dig at Jonathan Fine, had some traction as an XSL-FO engine, but I could not ever make it 100 percent reliable.

It's all about the web, really. The web is so omnipresent, so omnipotent, so exciting. I just don't care enough about fine typesetting any more, because I don't produce printed matter much. Remember I am not a mathematician, so I don't share the obsession with beautiful formulae. I do use TEX a lot in the background, converting XML to LATEX using XSL, and processing it using pdfLATEX or XELATEX, but I don't tweak the result much. Philip Taylor would spit on my work these days! (but then he always did).

In many ways my life these days in the world of the TEI is like my old days in the TEX world—lots of community work. I teach, write guide material, do distributions, develop infrastructure, work for the user group, etc. No change there.

DW: Please tell me a little more about the Text Encoding Initiative and the OSS Watch and what you do with those. In particular, Karl Berry tells me you have a job as "open source software watcher" for Oxford; watching rather than doing doesn't exactly fit with my impression of your activity over the years.

SR: OSS Watch is a national advisory service on Open Source in higher education, based here at OUCS where I work. I led the bid which secured funding, was its director for 4 years, but I stood down in 2007 due to work pressure. Yes, I was and am an open source bigot! It was good to evangelize and explain for a few years. Last year I started a new project from the same funding to look at geolocation services and information delivery on mobile phones, called Erewhon — now *that* occupies my every waking moment!

The Text Encoding Initiative produces guidelines for people encoding digital texts. It's a hugely well-documented XML schema, in a way. I use it to write our web pages, but most people want it for encoding Hamlet, medieval manuscripts, dictionaries, stuff like that. My speciality is the metalanguage we use to define XML schemas.... But I also spend a lot of time on the politics and business of the Consortium which runs the TEI, just like I used to for TEX.

DW: I see lots of travel photos at `http://www.flickr.com/photos/srahtz/` (there's even a link at the end of `http://tug.org/interest.html` where it notes that you originally created that web page), and you said we have to get this interview done before you go to Taiwan. Is travel a sort of hobby for you, or are you still looking at archeology sites (or road signs), or.... ?

SR: I do travel a lot, mostly for work. Taiwan is to teach a TEI course, no road signs or archaeology I am afraid! We do travel a fair bit as family — a few years ago we spent two months in East Timor where my partner was teaching. That was really a big adventure :-). I am afraid my carbon footprint is a bit unhealthy.

Yes, I like taking photographs, though I am not very good. I love my camera. Though I love my DAB radio even more.

DW: Thank you, Sebastian, for taking the time to participate in this interview. As a late arrival at TUG, it is gratifying for me to communicate with you, someone whose fingerprints are all over the TUG and TEX world.

SR: Thanks, I like the idea of those fingerprints. Good for future archaeologists.

www.ingramcontent.com/pod-product-compliance
Ingram Content Group UK Ltd.
Pitfield, Milton Keynes, MK11 3LW, UK
UKHW051130260726
13967UKWH00010B/2967

9 780982 462607